The End Game

The End Game

The Final Chapter in Britain's Great Game in Afghanistan

SUSAN LOUGHHEAD

AMBERLEY

First published 2016

Amberley Publishing
The Hill, Stroud
Gloucestershire, GL5 4EP

www.amberley-books.com

British Library Cataloguing in Publication Data.
A catalogue record for this book is available from the British Library.

ISBN 978 1 4456 5993 0 (hardback)
ISBN 978 1 4456 5994 7 (ebook)

Typesetting and Origination by Amberley Publishing.
Printed in the UK.

Contents

Acknowledgements

A number of people have played a really significant role in helping me to get this book off the ground and see it through to the end. First and foremost, my gratitude goes to Hazel Hastings, the daughter of the British Ambassador in Kabul, Sir Giles Squire. I tracked her down in the first couple of months of my research in 2013 and she immediately invited me to her home to discuss her family history and share her extensive photograph collection from Kabul. At the beginning, she helped provide life and colour to the people I had been reading about in the archives. Thenceforth, I had a picture in my head of the cast of characters who were beginning to absorb my inner world, and direct contact with someone who had actually lived at the British legation in the mid-1940s and met some of the people I would go on to write about. Since then, Hazel and I have been on this journey together and met many times at her son Robert's house in London. She has read and reviewed chapters as they emerged hot 'off the press', helped me decipher her father's handwriting in his journal, and introduced me to her younger sister Gillian, who spent six years of her childhood in Kabul.

In 2013, two other people helped set me on this path too: His Excellency Hedayat Amin Arsala and Sir Richard Barrington. I had worked with HE Arsala while he was a minister in President Karzai's government. Since then, he has been unfailingly supportive of my research. He appreciated that the focus was on British policy and perceptions, and has kindly supplemented my partial knowledge of the Afghan scene with his personal recollections of many of the Afghans who feature in this book. His father worked for Ali Mohammed Khan, the Foreign Minister, and he remembers the king's three uncles, Hashim, Mahmud and Shah Wali Khan visiting his home many times when he was a child. All three played a pivotal role in the Afghan government during this period. HE Arsala also became friends with Afghan entrepreneur and minister Abdul Majid

Zabuli in later life in Washington. The other person who was incredibly helpful that year was Sir Richard Barrington, who had been a junior diplomat in Kabul in the early 1960s, and then covered Afghanistan in his role as British High Commissioner in Pakistan in the early 1990s. He not only pointed me in the direction of key books, but also introduced me to a PhD student at Loughborough University, Maximillian Drephal, who by sheer coincidence was studying the British legation in Kabul from 1921 to 1947. Max has been unfailingly helpful throughout.

A number of other people have been incredibly supportive on my journey too. First and foremost, huge thanks are due to Ann Freckleton and her husband John Tacon. They lived in Afghanistan for many years, including during the Taliban and Mujahedin periods and through the events of 9/11, introduced me to Sir Richard, and told me about the condition of the former British embassy in the 1990s. In her capacity as head of the UK's aid programme in Afghanistan, Ann explored whether a joint diplomatic and aid office could be set up in the embassy's hospital compound after 9/11. Ann and two other good friends, Charlotte Heath and Louise Walker, have also read and commented on chapters as I have gone along, helping to ground some of the points in local realities and think through what writing style worked best. Partly through their advice, I moved away from telling my grandfather's story – the starting point – towards a more political piece about British–Afghan relations because that was the compelling narrative emerging from the archives.

Others have kindly shared photographs and reminiscences. Katherine Himsworth's 1970s booklet on the embassy is invaluable, while her friend from Kabul days, Annemarie Wilson, has shared some photographs that fill gaps in my pictures of the compound. Jon Moss joined my first visit to the former embassy in 2010 at the start of my journey, and has since provided helpful insights on the impact of an extensive irrigation and power generation scheme along the Helmand River Valley, which began in the late 1940s, on local social relations to this day. His colleague from Lashkar Gah, Mark Harvey, worked on rehabilitating the irrigation ditches and roads between 2008 and 2010. His photographs provide a sense of the Helmand Scheme's scale and complexity, and its continued relevance to the economy of the region. Louise Walker and Jackie French have also contributed photographs from visits to the British cemetery and former British embassy when my camera started to play up. I have also included some photographs from 1969, which are part of a collection of more than 300 pictures taken by a member of the embassy and now in circulation among the international and Afghan community in Kabul. Their contribution to pictorial records of Afghanistan before it was broken apart by a series of conflicts since 1979 is invaluable. I wish to add my gratitude to this anonymous family for sharing their treasure trove.

At the eleventh hour before publication, I have also been fortunate to meet Colonel Prendergast's son, Major (retired) John Lancaster, who lived in Kabul as a child, and son-in-law, Hugh Priestley. Both welcomed me into their homes, shared stories and photographs and showed enthusiasm for this enterprise, just what I needed to see it through to the final hurdle. John Prendergast added more local colour – an affair between my grandfather's colleague in the Military Attaché's office and a nanny. He also remembers playing Monopoly with my grandfather, my first tangible connection to anyone who knew him there.

Beyond these individuals, I am profoundly grateful to The Historical Association and Amberley Publishing for launching a history writing prize last year and selecting my manuscript for publication. Without this, the book may have never have seen the light of day. I hope the final product meets their expectations. Since winning the prize, Aaron Meek and Alex Bennett, my editors, have been consistently helpful, encouraging and supportive in spite of the numerous questions I have bombarded them with. I have really appreciated this support to a first-time author. Amberley Publishing and I would particularly like to thank Hugh Alexander at the National Archives in Kew for helping me to secure permission to use copyright material. To my knowledge, none of the photographs taken by an international mission to record events at Moghulgai in June 1949, and thus avert the escalation of tension between Afghanistan and Pakistan, have ever been published before.

My final thanks go to three people without whom this would not have been possible. The first is to Alison Kennedy, who helped format and proofread the whole text at a time when the demands of my job made it difficult to meet the publishers' deadline. The second goes to my brother, Tim, who has drawn the maps and digitised the photographs. Without this technical help, I would have been lost. My final thanks are reserved for my mother, Pat. This has not been an easy journey for her. When my grandfather returned to Manchester in 1950, she barely knew him and they had a mixed relationship from that day forth. Throughout, however, she has shared family reminiscences and been unfailingly supportive, especially – and not surprisingly – when the story shifted towards a wider historical narrative.

Susan Loughhead
London, May 2016

List of Illustrations

Maps

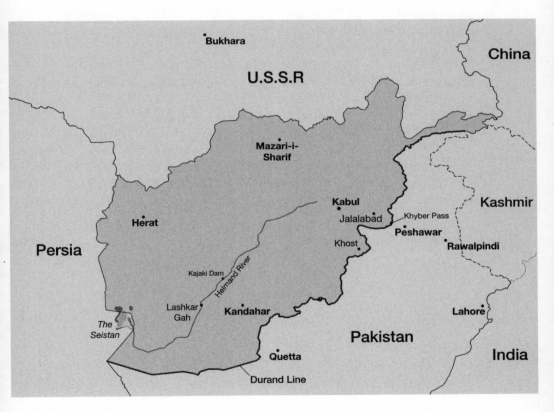

Afghanistan, 1947.

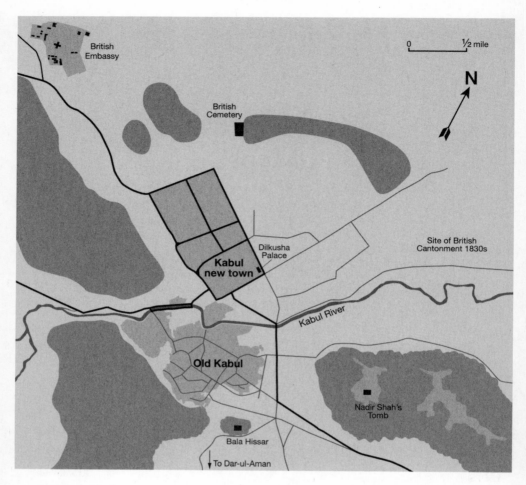

Kabul, 1947.

Main Personalities

British Legation and Embassy, Kabul, 1947–51

Sir Giles Squire (1894–1959) Minister in Kabul from 1943 to 1948, Ambassador 1948–9. After Kabul, he tried to find voluntary work in Britain, and then settled in Rhodesia (now Zimbabwe). He spent his last few years involved with the Central African Federation of semi-independent British colonies.

Sir John Gardener (1897–1985) Full name Albert John, but was always known as John. Began his career in the 1920s in the Consular Service in the Levant. Head of Establishment and Organisation Department, Foreign Office, 1946–9; Ambassador to Afghanistan 1949–51; and Ambassador to Syria 1953–6.

Lt-Colonel Alexander Stalker Lancaster (1892–1967) Military Attaché in Kabul from 1935 to 1948, with a one-year break in 1938–9, returning to Kabul when war broke out. He retired from the Army a year later and died in Jersey.

Lt-Colonel John Hume Prendergast (1910–2008) Indian Army officer who became Military Attaché in Kabul 1948–50 on temporary promotion to Colonel. Retired 1960 and became a travel writer.

Patrick Keen Worked at the legation in Kabul in the 1930s, and returned as Second Secretary, Kabul, 1948–9.

Derek Martin Hurry Riches (1912–97) First Secretary, Chancery. Was later knighted and became Ambassador to Libya 1959–61, and to the Congo 1961.

Dr Ronnie D. Macrae Indian Medical Service Officer. Ran the Embassy hospital until late 1948 when he left for a doctor's practice in Canada.

Squadron Leader Jonnie Lee-Evans Member of the Royal Air Force training mission who flew with Keen and the other members of the international community to Moghulgai.

Raymond William Murray Brooks (1929–93) Clerk in the Military Attaché's office, 1948.

Sam Simms (1908–89) Clerk in the Military Attaché's office, 1948–50. Left the Army in 1951 and returned to Manchester.

British High Commission, Delhi, India
Lt-General Sir Archibald E. Nye (1895–1967) High Commissioner to India, 1948–52.

British High Commission, Karachi, Pakistan
Sir Lawrence Grafftey-Smith (1892–1989) High Commissioner to Pakistan, 1947–51.

North-West Frontier Province
William Mitchell Carse (1899–1987) Deputy High Commissioner, Peshawar, Pakistan, 1948–51.

Sir George Cunningham (1888–1964) Counsellor at the British legation in Kabul 1925–6; Governor of North-West Frontier Province 1937–46, and again for a few months after independence in autumn 1947.

Sir Ambrose Dundas (1899–1973) Former India Service officer who replaced Cunningham as Governor of North-West Frontier Province, 1948–9, and was then replaced by the first Pakistani Governor.

British Government, 1947–51
Clement Attlee (1883–1967) Prime Minister, 1945–51.

Ernest Bevin (1881–1951) Foreign Secretary, 1945–51.

Main Personalities

Herbert Morrison (1888–1965) Foreign Secretary, 1951.

Phillip Noel-Baker (1889–1992) Secretary of State, Commonwealth Relations Office, 1947–50.

Albert Alexander (1885–1965) Minister of Defence, 1946–50.

Foreign Office Staff

Sir Orme Sargent (1884–1962) Permanent Under-Secretary at the Foreign Office 1946–9.

Sir Robert Heatlie Scott (1905–82) Head of South-East Asia Department 1949–50; Under-Secretary for Asian affairs 1950 onwards. Permanent Under-Secretary at the Ministry of Defence 1961–3.

Sir Harold Caccia (1905–90) Under-Secretary responsible for the Foreign Office's overseas establishments in the 1940s. Permanent Under-Secretary, 1961–5.

Richard Clarence Blackham Desk Office for Tibet, French and Portuguese India 1949–50, South East Asia Department.

William Bernard John Ledwidge (1915–98) Desk Officer for India, Pakistan and Afghanistan, South-East Asia Department.

Peter Murray Desk Officer for Burma, Ceylon, Nepal and Tibet, 1949.

Afghan Kings and Members of the Royal Family

Ahmed Shah Durrani (c. 1722–72) Credited with founding the modern state of Afghanistan and established the Durrani empire reaching west into Persia, north to the Oxus River, east into Kashmir, and south to the Arabian Sea.

Shah Shuja (1786–1842) Seized power in Kabul in 1803, but removed after conflicts within the ruling family. Installed as a puppet Amir by the East India Company in 1839, but then assassinated by his godson at the end of the First Anglo-Afghan War in 1842.

Dost Mohammed (1792–1863) Took the Kabul throne in 1826. Forced into exile by the British. Once the British retreated from Kabul in 1842, they allowed him to recover his throne.

Wazir Akbar Khan (1816–47) A son of Dost Mohammed who played a prominent role in the First Anglo-Afghan War. Killed the British envoy, Sir William Macnaghten, and paved the way for the ill-fated British retreat from Kabul. Probably poisoned in 1847.

Amir Abdur Rahman (c. 1844–1901) Recognised as Amir during the Second Anglo-Afghan War, and agreed to receive British subsidies in exchange for ceding control of foreign policy. Negotiated the Durand Line in 1893. Built government systems and suppressed tribal opposition to his rule.

Amir Habibullah (1872–1919) Crowned after a smooth transition of power from father, Abdur Rahman, to son, an unusual occurrence in Afghan history. Introduced educational systems and began to open up Afghanistan to the world. Assassinated.

Amir Amanullah (1892–1960) Son of Habibullah, and may have been implicated in his murder. Began reforms to modernise the country but fled in early 1929 in the midst of a popular uprising. Abdicated and died in exile in Italy.

Nadir Shah (1883–1933) Former general in the Afghan army who led the troops in the Third Anglo-Afghan War in 1919. Claimed the throne in 1929 and instituted a number of economic and constitutional reforms. Assassinated.

Zahir Shah (1914–2007) Son of Nadir Shah, became King in 1933. Actively led the government from 1963 with a reformist agenda until he was deposed in a coup led by his cousin, Daud, in 1973. Returned to Afghanistan from exile in 2002.

Afghan Government 1945–53
Sardar Mohammed Hashim Khan (c. 1886–1953) Brother of Nadir Shah; Prime Minister, 1929–46.

Sardar Shah Mahmud Khan (c. 1894–1959) Brother of Nadir Shah; Prime Minister 1946–53.

Sardar Shah Wali Khan (c. 1885–1976) Brother of Nadir Shah. Minister in London 1930–31; Minister in Paris for most of the time between 1931 and 1946; Ambassador to Pakistan 1948–9; Ambassador in London, 1950–52.

Sardar Mohammed Daud Khan (c. 1909–78) General commanding Kabul Army Corps to 1946; Minister of War, 1946–8; Ambassador in Paris, 1948;

Minister of Defence with responsibility for Interior and Tribes cluster of Ministries, 1949–53. Prime Minister, 1953–63; President 1973–8. Assassinated.

Sardar Mohammed Naim Khan (c. 1911–78) Minister in London, 1945–8; Ambassador to Washington, 1948–50; Minister for Public Works, 1949; Foreign Minister, 1953–63. Assassinated with his brother, Daud, in 1978.

Ali Mohammed Khan (c. 1891–1977) Began as a teacher and inspector of schools. Afghan Minister in London, then Foreign Minister, 1938–53; Acting Prime Minister, 1951; Deputy Prime Minister, 1953–63; Minister of Court, 1963–73.

Abdul Majid Zabuli (c. 1896–1998) Founded the Afghan National Bank in 1932; Minister of Trade in 1938 and then Minister for National Economy 1939–49. Retained advisory role under President Daud in 1950s.

Sardar Faiz Mohammad Zakria (c. 1892–1979) Foreign Minister 1929–38; Ambassador to Turkey 1938–48; Ambassador in London 1949–50; Minister of Education, 1950; and Ambassador to Saudi Arabia, 1955; Ambassador in London 1960–61.

Dr Najibullah Torwayana Otherwise known as Dr Hajibullah Khan in the 1940s (c. 1905–65). Director General of Ministry of Foreign Affairs 1946, Special Envoy to Pakistan 1947–8; Acting Minister for Education 1948–9; United Kingdom 1952–4; Ambassador to India; Ambassador to the United States 1956–8. Published a history of Afghanistan.

Other Significant Afghan Figures, 1947–53

Mahmud Tarzi (1865–1933) The intellectual force behind the Young Afghan movement and Amir Ammanulah, and a key influence for the democrats in the 1940s.

Dr Abdul Rahman Mahmudi (c. 1909–1962) A Hazara and one of the first graduates from the Faculty of Medicine at Kabul University. Elected to the Liberal Parliament 1949 and founded a political party in 1950. Spent ten years in prison once Daud came to power. Released in 1962 because he had contracted tuberculosis and died a few months later.

Ghulam Muhammed Farhad (c. 1901–1984) Studied in Germany; Director of the General Electric Company 1939–66; elected Mayor of Kabul 1948–54. A noted Pashtun nationalist, who formed a political party in the 1960s, became a political prisoner in 1979–80, then freed in a general amnesty.

Mir Ghulam Mohammed Ghobar (*c.* 1898–1978) Political prisoner 1933–5 and political exile 1935–42. Prominent historian, poet and journalist who entered the Liberal Parliament in 1949; formed the *Watan* party and newspaper; imprisoned again 1952–6. His book on Afghan history was banned by the government. He eventually moved to Germany.

Mohammed Amin Jan Half-brother of Amir Amanullah, who mobilised tribesmen to enter Afghan territory in 1949, culminating in the Moghulgai incident in June.

Pakistan Government
Mohammed Ali Jinnah (1876–1948) Governor General of Pakistan.

Liaquat Ali Khan (1895–1951) Prime Minister of Pakistan. Assassinated.

Sir Zafarullah Khan (1893–1985) Served in the International Court of International Justice, becoming President 1970–73; Pakistan Permanent Representative to the UN 1961–4.

General Iskander Mirza (1899–1969) Secretary of Defence 1947–54; Governor-General then President 1955–58; imposed Martial Law 1958, and forced to resign soon after. Exiled in the UK.

Mohammed Ikramullah (1903–63) Foreign Secretary at the Ministry of Foreign Affairs 1947–51 and 1959–61. Ambassador to Canada, France, Portugal and the United Kingdom.

Abdur Rab Nishtar (1899–1958) Minister of Communications 1947–9; Governor of Punjab 1949. Leader of the Muslim League late 1950s.

Major General Sir Walter Joseph Cawthorn (1896–1970) Deputy Chief of Staff of the Pakistan army 1948–51. Established the intelligence service, the Inter-Services Intelligence Directorate, in 1948.

Pakistan Embassy, Kabul
Ismail Ibrahim Chundrigar (1898–1960) First Ambassador to Afghanistan 1948–50; Governor of North-West Frontier Province 1950–51; briefly Prime Minister in 1957.

North-West Frontier Province

Abdul Gaffar Khan (1890–1988) Leader of Frontier Congress and Pakistan's Pashtunistan movement. Spent some time in self-imposed exile in Afghanistan.

Dr Sahib Khan (1882–1958) Leader of Frontier Congress and Pashtunistan movement, Chief Minister of the NWFP, and Chief Minister of West Pakistan 1955–57. Assassinated.

Indian Government

Jawaharlal Nehru (1889–1964) First Prime Minister of India, 1947–64.

Sir Girija Shankar Bajpai (1899–1954) Foreign Minister and Secretary General, Ministry of External Affairs 1947–52; Governor of Bombay State 1952–4.

V. K. Krishna Menon (1896–1974) High Commissioner in London 1947–52; Ambassador to the UN 1952–62; Defence Minister 1957–62.

Indian Embassy, Kabul

Wing Commander Rup Chand (c. 1882–1958) First Indian Ambassador in Kabul 1948–52.

Girdhari Lal Puri Former Deputy Speaker in the Legislative Assembly in NWFP, and member of embassy staff from 1948. Published a book on Abdul Ghaffar Khan in 1985.

United States Embassy, Kabul

Ely Eliot Palmer (1887–1977) Ely Eliot Palmer (1887–1977) Consul in Madrid, Buckarest, Vancouver, Jerusalem, Ottawa, Beirut, Sydney; Minister in Kabul 1945–8; Ambassador, 1948. Retired.

Louis Goethe Dreyfus Jr (1889–1973) Consul in Berlin, Budapest, Malaga, Paris, Palermo, Dresden, Copenhagen; Minister to Iran 1939–44, which included responsibility for Afghanistan until the legation was opened in Kabul in 1942; Minister in Iceland 1944–5 and Sweden 1946; Ambassador in Kabul 1949–51. Retired.

Author's Note

Readers may be puzzled by some of the terminology and spellings used in this book, including unfamiliar terms used in British diplomacy and foreign relations in the 1940s, including the distinction between a 'legation' and an 'embassy', and a minister and ambassador. In the nineteenth century, a legation was a diplomatic representative office of lower status than an embassy, headed by a minister, and usually existed where one or both countries was a smaller monarchy or republic. By the mid-twentieth century, this distinction was gradually disappearing and many legations had been upgraded to embassies, headed by ambassadors. Hence the mission in Kabul began as a legation and was upgraded in early 1948. To capture this distinction, I have used the term 'legation' until it was upgraded and thereafter used the term 'embassy'.

Whitehall department names were slightly different in the late 1940s too. Prime Minister Clement Attlee created the Ministry of Defence in 1947, while the War Office continued to administer the Army until the two departments were merged in 1964. After Indian Independence, the Commonwealth Relations Office (CRO) replaced the India Office and Dominions Office. Between 1947 and 1966, it operated as a separate government department from the Foreign Office (FO) with its own Secretary of State and civil servants until the two merged to become the Foreign and Commonwealth Office (FCO). Most of the correspondence between London and Kabul was through the FO, but there were a number of occasions when the CRO became directly involved when India and Pakistan were discussed.

There are multiple ways to spell Afghan words and terms in English, and these inconsistencies run through the British archives and secondary literature on the period too. I have settled on *Pashtun*, *Pashtunistan* and *Wesh Zalmian* because these spellings are most frequently used. I have also referred to Daud Khan – the future President of Afghanistan – without an 'o' in Daud instead of the more commonly used Daoud Khan today, because this is how British diplomats in Kabul and officials in London referred to him in the 1940s.

Finally, I have made some arbitrary decisions about place names. The British archives always refer to Iran as Persia in the 1940s, so I have used the latter throughout. In the case of Russia and the Soviet Union, however, I have used the label Russia up to the Russian Revolution in 1917, and Soviet Union thereafter, but kept the term Russia in the direct quotes from the archives because that was how the Afghans and British referred to the Soviet Union. I concluded it was important to recognise the distinction between British and Afghan fears of the expanding Russian empire in the nineteenth century, and the perceived Soviet Communist threat after the Second World War. As far as the river serving as the boundary between Afghanistan and the Soviet Union/Russia is concerned, the Amu Darya, I have referred to it as the Oxus because that was how it was known historically. For similar reasons, I have always referred to the Afghan-Pakistan border area as the Frontier, with a capital F, because that is how it was written in contemporary correspondence.

Foreword

Once again, I am embarking on something that, as in past years, is part of an experience we call life, but from which I feel I have learned very little ... As regards this venture, it bodes well to be as strange an affair as I could wish and I do confess that I am looking to it to offer a degree of excitement and an opportunity, possibly to introduce a little colour into a career which in a brief civilian life was of little use to me or to anybody else.

Sam Simms, 7 January 1948[1]

These words were written by my grandfather, Sam Simms, just before he set off to Kabul for a two-year posting at the British embassy in January 1948. He had spent most of the war employed on troop ships transporting men and supplies between different battle fronts in Asia, Africa and the Far East. Now aged thirty-nine, unemployed, and married with a sixteen-year-old daughter (my mother), he had decided to re-enlist as an Army Warrant Officer because this seemed the best way to secure a regular income. Kabul had never been part of his plans, however. Soon after arriving at his new base in Thetford in Norfolk, he had applied to the War Office for a transfer. A month later, he was assigned the position of clerk supporting the Military Attaché at the British embassy in Kabul, one Colonel Alexander Stalker Lancaster.

Nearly sixty years later, in 2010, I started my own job in Kabul and, not surprisingly, began to ponder over potential parallels between his experiences and my own. I wondered if we had visited some of the same places and what Kabul had looked like in the 1940s before over thirty-five years of conflict had destroyed many old parts of the city. I also speculated about what was prominent in the minds of embassy staff at that time, and wondered if there had been any significant incidents or decisions affecting

British–Afghan relations. Once I returned to Britain, I began to dig deeper. This book is the result of my quest. Quite unexpectedly, I learnt that my grandfather had been witness to a maelstrom of political and diplomatic activities that had a long-term impact on the future of Afghanistan and the region as a whole. Quite literally, events in the late 1940s helped shape the key building blocks of today's British–Afghan narrative, and underline that many recurrent themes have strong roots in the relatively recent past, some of which Britain itself played a key role in moulding.

When he arrived in Afghanistan, Britain was enjoying unparalleled influence over Afghan policies and international relations. Britain's arms manufacturers equipped the Afghan army and air force; British subsidies helped finance the machinery of government; and Britain's imperial presence in India protected the country from Soviet ambitions in Asia. Britain's 'Great Game' in Asia, using Afghanistan as a buffer to hold back Russian ambitions in the Indian subcontinent, was enjoying a post-Second World War resurgence, twenty-five years after Afghan independence in 1919 had all but killed it. Within two years of Indian independence in 1947, however, the British government's attempts to steer a smooth transition to a new world order in Central Asia during the early years of the Cold War – one involving India, Pakistan and latterly the United States – lay in tatters and Britain's reputation was irrevocably damaged. Any residual capacity to influence the course of future events was marginal thereafter. Meanwhile, when the autocratic Afghan government tried to introduce some of the lessons learned from the democracy movements in South Asia in the late 1940s to help shore up its position, the state risked collapse. Years of dependence on foreign subsidies combined with weak institutions and a stagnant economy meant the state was unable to adapt to change quickly. My research has thus helped me to appreciate why it has proved so difficult to 'rebuild' Afghanistan after the NATO-led invasion in 2001.

I knew some of my grandfather's experiences from stories during my childhood. I remembered descriptions of his frequent trips by road through the Khyber Pass to Peshawar; the adventures of his wild cat, Topaz, which climbed up the curtains and tore at speed through his bungalow, breaking anything in his path; and the terror of getting lost on a solitary walk in the mountains and fearing he would never get back alive. He also spoke enthusiastically about tennis tournaments, dinner parties and grand receptions, as well as music and theatre evenings in the Ambassador's residence, known as the Big House, a massive white colonial edifice which could be seen from all the mountains surrounding Kabul. I knew little else, however. I had no idea what his job involved or the issues current in Afghanistan at the time.

While I was in Kabul, I started to read the letters he had sent to my grandmother regularly, sometimes weekly, from the day he joined the Army in September 1939 in the first week of the war to the time he was finally demobbed in 1951. Nearly a third were from Kabul. As I started to work my way through them, deciphering the writing and gradually building up a picture of his life at the embassy, I soon realised I had found a window into his world.

I was surprised to learn that the embassy had been called a legation when he first arrived, headed by a minister. Later that year, it was upgraded to embassy status and headed by an ambassador as part of a joint initiative with the United States to raise their profiles in Kabul. I was also surprised to discover that there were several similarities between his experiences and mine, albeit sixty years apart. He, like me, had lived in a walled compound cut off from everyday life in Kabul and from close contact with Afghans except those he worked with. Travel around the country was as restrictive then as now, although the main constraint in the 1940s was the lack of motorable roads, not security. Stomach problems were a recurrent problem, and entertainment, like now, was largely self-generated. I also learnt for the first time that he had taken up tennis in Kabul just as I did, although I suspect that he reached a far higher standard. The most noticeable difference was our respective ability to keep in contact with friends and family. I had the luxury of Skype, a mobile phone and email. He relied on pen and paper and a mail system which took at least two weeks to deliver the post to its destination.

By the time I had finished reading his letters, I had not only gained an insight into British embassy life in Kabul in the 1940s, but also learnt something about the people he worked with. Some names stood out. Sir Giles Squire, the Ambassador, had spent most of his career in the Colonial Service in India and Persia and had been in Kabul since 1943. In contrast, his successor, Sir John Gardener, was a permanent Foreign Office staffer who had led an austerity drive from London in 1946/7. Colonel Alexander Lancaster, the Military Attaché, had lived in Kabul for more than ten years and had earned the respect of the Afghan military. According to my grandfather, he was fun socially but not good at delegating tasks. Then there was Lancaster's successor, Colonel John Hume Prendergast, a war hero with the Military Cross, who arrived in September 1948. He valued my grandfather's work and encouraged him to stay the full two years. Finally, nineteen-year-old Ray Brooks, who travelled out to Kabul with my grandfather and worked with him for a year before he returned to Britain. Brooks seems to have succumbed to just about every malady it was possible to get more or less from the day he arrived.

Soon after I arrived in Kabul, I discovered not only that the old embassy compound still existed, but that there had been tentative plans relatively recently to purchase it from the government of Pakistan so that the present British diplomatic mission could move back there.[2] The site had become Pakistani property many years earlier, apparently as part of a three-way deal between Britain, Pakistan and India after Indian independence in 1947. Pakistan had given India its rights to the former British embassy property in Kathmandu in exchange for sole right to the property in Kabul.

Just one month after my arrival, I booked a car and invited two friends to join me on an excursion to visit it. In the 1940s, the compound had been three miles outside Kabul surrounded by open fields. Now, I soon discovered, it is hidden within a crowded residential suburb to the west of the city centre. As we turned a sharp corner, we caught our first glimpse of the main gate, and then the walls surrounding the compound came into view. Although there was a pervasive sense of decay and neglect about the whole place, it was still possible to imagine what the approach originally looked like. We left our vehicle and gingerly stood on upturned stones to peer over the walls where they were beginning to crumble. I had reined in my expectations considerably, but even then I still inexplicably hoped to see the beautiful lawns, the trees and the roses described in the letters, and of course an array of bungalows, perhaps even the one my grandfather had lived in. Instead, we were greeted by the burnt-out ruin of the Big House surrounded by acres of barren wasteland, a visible reminder of Afghanistan's violent recent history. There were no signs of other buildings at all. It was still possible to get a sense of how majestic the Ambassador's residence must have looked in its prime, but it was hard to imagine it could, or indeed ever would, be restored to the magnificence it had once clearly enjoyed.

We asked the armed guards at the fortified gates if we could look around. They did not speak English, but one of them asked a Pakistani official inside the compound to help translate. In spite of tight security and the fact that we had arrived without prior warning, he let us enter and then led us along an internal road closed in by high walls until we reached what had once been, I learnt much later, the staff quarters of the former embassy's hospital compound. This had not only been designed to provide medical care for the expatriate community, but also for Afghans in the surrounding villages as well. Over tea and biscuits, and interspersed with a discussion about the England–Pakistan Test match at the Oval that weekend, he apologised for not being able to take us into the main compound because Pakistan embassy staff were playing cricket in the grounds. He also explained, to my surprise, that his job was to oversee the restoration of the buildings – the

Government of Pakistan planned to move their diplomatic mission to this site once all the work was completed.

Two years later, I returned. The Big House was now the official residence of the Pakistan Ambassador and the whole Pakistan embassy had recently relocated to the compound too. This time round, I organised the visit well in advance with an embassy representative so that we could get inside. He showed us round the former hospital compound, including their new office, which he understood was located in the former British surgeon's house, and then led us along the road between the high walls and through into the main compound. There, I finally saw the Big House just as Squire and Gardener, Lancaster and Prendergast, and my grandfather and Brooks, would have known it. It had been magnificently restored. Instead of the blackened ruin I had seen over the walls, the house now gleamed with fresh white paint, and was surrounded by a network of colonnades and verandas, complete with a sweeping driveway up to the main entrance. Next to the front door was a plaque proclaiming the residence had been officially opened by the Pakistan Prime Minister just two weeks earlier. The rose gardens unfortunately were long gone, but the ornamental pond at the back of the residence and the old water tower set in the compound walls were still visible. Beyond the Big House, however, all traces of other buildings – the office, the tennis courts and the swimming pool – as well as the trees and gardens had long disappeared. We learnt that, undeterred, the Pakistan government planned to seed new lawns and replant the gardens.

When I returned to London in early 2013, I decided it was time to find out what my grandfather and his colleagues were actually doing in Kabul in the late 1940s and why Britain had such a high-status presence there. Since his letters home said virtually nothing about his work or about British–Afghan relations at the time, I decided to start my search by looking for books and articles written in English about Afghanistan in the post-war period. To my complete surprise, I discovered that information about Afghanistan between 1929, when King Amanullah was deposed, and 1979, when Soviet forces invaded, was very limited and usually only a few pages, if any, were devoted to the crucial period 1948 to 1950.[3]

It was evident that if I wanted to know more, I would have to dig out the original embassy papers in the India Office Records at the British Library and in the National Archives in Kew. Inevitably, my eyes were first drawn towards files which potentially contained papers my grandfather had actually written or signed – and failing that, a reference to him or his work. I was to be disappointed. After wading through numerous military papers and drawing a complete blank, I eventually realised that it was unlikely his name would be on any despatches or reports at all because he was a junior clerk. Everything at that time would have been signed off by the Ambassador, the Military Attaché or the Political Counsellor.

Eventually, however, among a pile of papers about the management of the embassy buildings, I finally found two documents which mentioned him by name. Neither was earth-shattering, but they represented my first tangible connection with his life in Kabul from an independent source. The first was in a despatch from the Ambassador, Sir Giles Squire, to the Foreign Office, dated 8 July 1948, reporting that the two Military Attaché clerks, Mr S. Simms and his colleague Mr R. Brooks, were still not 'getting reasonable foreign service allowances ... and that they are both still officially on a rate of pay which is grossly inadequate'.[4] This chimed with frequent complaints in my grandfather's letters about financial difficulties in Kabul. The second reference was in an office circular, dated 16 March 1949, informing staff they would continue to get free treatment at the embassy hospital and clinic even though the new doctor had left at short notice – my grandfather had ticked his name off to show he had seen the paper.[5] I learnt much later exactly why the doctor had left so suddenly – he had arrived with another man's wife and was promptly encouraged to move on by Squire.

As I widened my search through the files, I gradually realised that my grandfather had inadvertently handed me a special gift – an introduction to a story which was as relevant then as it is now. His letters had introduced the embassy and his work colleagues. Now they were leading me towards a unique insight into a critical period in Afghan–British relations with resonance today. My grandfather had provided the outline – the time frame, the place, the cast of characters – and now it was my turn to interpret the rest. I had a head start, too. I could draw on my knowledge of the post-war Labour government and the origins of the Cold War from my history degree many years earlier. The archives began to fill in the gaps.

My grandfather had arrived in Kabul during an economic recession and in the midst of an Afghan government-led initiative to introduce a modicum of democracy in an erstwhile autocratic state. It was extremely uncertain how these two dynamics would play out, especially if rising food prices coupled with increasing opportunities for free speech and association triggered social and political unrest. He had also arrived just as Britain's interest in Afghanistan and influence with the Afghan government was waning following Indian independence in August 1947. After 1947, Britain no longer needed Afghanistan to act as a buffer to protect its empire in India from the Soviet Union, and assumed that Pakistan and India, and latterly the United States, would take over that role. Furthermore, with independence, Britain quickly lost many of the levers of power and resources which had enabled it to have influence.

By January 1950, when my grandfather left, many of the strands in Afghanistan's subsequent troubled history were falling into place. Indian independence triggered a boundary dispute in the Pashtun tribal areas straddling Afghan and erstwhile British Indian territory, now in Pakistan. This still poisons Afghan–Pakistan relations to this day. At the same time, Afghanistan had already become a pawn in India–Pakistan tensions – India's interest in Afghanistan continues to fuel Pakistan's fears of encirclement and helped drive Pakistan's covert support for the Taliban in the 1990s.[6] Meanwhile, as the battle lines of the Cold War were being drawn in 1947–50, Afghanistan's geographic position drew it ever deeper into the superpower rivalry between the Soviet Union and the United States in the 1950s. The Afghans hoped that the Americans would protect their new commercial interests in the Helmand river valley by providing funds, arms and military equipment to fill the vacuum left by Britain. By 1950, Afghanistan was reframing its international alliances, exploiting the Cold War to play the Soviet Union and America off against each other, and turning the hostility between India and Pakistan to its own advantage. As the story of British–Afghan relations began to merge with the early years of the Cold War, I also therefore read some American archival resources to help explain the terms under which Afghanistan was drawn into this new conflict. Meanwhile, some of the seeds of the conflict in Helmand, which has involved British and American troops in recent years, date back to that commercial venture.

Throughout, the story of the former British embassy in Kabul was a recurrent theme. It had been purposely built in the 1920s to symbolise the might of the British empire in Asia. For its residents, it reproduced the atmosphere of a 'country house weekend'.[7] Soon after independence, however, its ownership was contested first by India and then Pakistan. My grandfather must have wondered from one day to the next whether, and indeed when, he would have to leave his bungalow. While the British remained in residence, they could hide from the reality of their declining power and status. Once lost, it would stand as a stark reminder to everyone that Britain's days in Afghanistan were over.

Over subsequent weeks, I decided to try to weave these various strands into a coherent story. The main ingredients were there. All that was needed was the time and patience to pull them together. I had initially hoped my grandfather's letters would drive the narrative, but there was too little of him in the archives and nothing on British–Afghan relations in the letters. I have therefore used his voice, alongside others, to provide local texture and colour to the narrative, and have stuck, more or less, to the same two-year period when he lived in Kabul. Some background information is included to introduce Britain's relationship with Afghanistan up to 1947, but after that, the real story begins with the former embassy compound in its heyday as my grandfather would have known it, and where my own journey began six years ago. It ends with the increasingly bitter and acrimonious disputes about who actually owned the property and why. In between, I have told a series of separate stories, organised around distinct themes, to bring out the multi-layered strands of this complex period. Throughout, I have set each chapter in context, and ensured each story is followed through to its logical conclusion. The chapters can be read out of sequence too, although they do follow a logical order so that the story flows. Towards the end, I have weaved these various strands together and brought them up to the present day.

The files in London of course only tell the British side of the story. I have not been able to access Afghan archives from the period or read any Afghan history books written in local languages.[8] The chapters that follow therefore only tell the British version of events, and a partial picture at best. Foreigners' access to internal palace politics was limited, constrained, as Sir John Gardener explained in 1950, 'by my constant lament that no one of us here can get hold of the facts'.[9] Indeed, 'owing to the secretiveness of the Afghans, coupled with the government's precautions to isolate us, it is very difficult (I could say virtually impossible) for any of us to gain sufficient information thereon to base a reasonably accurate appreciation of the Afghan scene'.[10]

Diplomats therefore had to rely on joining up the dots between conversations with Afghan ministers. Some pieces of information were shared openly with many other embassies, but not all, as tensions on the international stage seeped into relationships in Kabul. Sir Giles Squire avoided German diplomats during the war; the Soviet embassy showed propaganda films which became the talk of the town, especially when they went down badly with the Afghan government and international community alike. In spite of this, the files provide a rich source of material about what the Afghan government wanted the British to know, as well as instances when their guard was down and they perhaps shared more than they intended. Conversations were recorded more or less verbatim in long despatches sent regularly to London. I have quoted directly from many and hope their thoughts and reflections will be of interest to Afghan, British and other readers alike. At the end of the day, it was how the British actually interpreted what the Afghans said that helped frame British policy in Afghanistan, not what was really going on behind the scenes in the royal palace.

In the course of doing this research, I have met or been in contact with some fabulous people who either lived on the embassy compound in the

1940s, or had memories and memorabilia from people who did. I have met Squire's daughters, Hazel and Gillian, who lived with their parents in Kabul and who kindly shared their photographs and recollections. Hazel also shared with me her father's private journal, which provides a rich backdrop to the stories behind the files, and an invaluable insight into what was uppermost in his mind during those crucial years. I have also met Colonel Prendergast's son and son-in-law, both of whom kindly shared their Afghan photograph albums with me. My search also led me to fascinating conversations with a former Ambassador in Pakistan, Sir Nicholas Barrington, who introduced me to a wonderful booklet about the embassy compound written by a later occupant, Katherine Himsworth, in the 1970s. I have also had the pleasure of speaking to a senior minister in President Karzai's government, His Excellency Hedayat Amin Arsala, who as Foreign Minister led the negotiations with Barrington to hand over the compound from the British to the Pakistan government in the 1990s. Last but not least, I have had the unique experience of meeting my grandfather a second time. I now know something of his life in Kabul, the people he worked and socialised with, the issues that must have dominated many office conversations, and the scenery which would have greeted him every day – the austere beauty of the surrounding mountains and the contrasting colours and vitality of the former British embassy.

1

All Change

We do not get much further with our own plans. The complete confusion
in India is likely to lead to this legation being entirely overlooked with
the result that we may well expect to be left on here undisturbed –
though who will pay our salaries is not very clear!

Sir Giles Squire, 15 June 1947[1]

Indian Independence, 15 August 1947
In early 1947, the British government agreed to transfer power in India
by June 1948 and sent Lord Louis Mountbatten of Burma to be the
last Viceroy of India to negotiate the terms. Within a matter of weeks,
however, he recommended that the deadline be brought forward a year
in the midst of escalating violence between Hindus, Muslims and Sikhs.
During May and June, Mountbatten, Mohammed Ali Jinnah, the leader
of the Muslim League, and Jawaharlal Nehru, the leader of the Indian
Congress Party, prepared the terms for Indian independence and then
set a date for just a few weeks hence. At the stroke of midnight on the
night of 14/15 August, the British empire in India would not only cease
to exist, but would also be partitioned between two new dominions, one
predominantly Muslim (Pakistan) and the other predominantly Hindu
(India), bringing an abrupt end to 200 years of British rule. This would be
the first time in history that an imperial government had ever voluntarily
given up its power without war or revolution.[2]

As the deadline drew nearer, Sir Giles Squire, the British Minister at the
legation in Kabul, felt a mixture of amazement that a deal had actually
been struck and fear for the future of the subcontinent. As he recorded in
his journal that June, 'I find it impossible to agree with the cosy optimism
of so many observers who seem to think that everything in the garden

1

will be lovely. So, far from solving anything, this new plan, which aims at Dominion status by 15th August, will bring all difficulties to a head at once.'[3] He had spent his entire working life in the region and understood the delicate balance of power extremely well. Now he wondered whether Britain's withdrawal would trigger a political vacuum that the Soviet Union might try to fill. This was a spectre that had driven Britain's policy in Afghanistan for more than a century, as Chapter Two explains, in the so-called 'Great Game' between the British and Russian empires over hegemony in Asia, causing Britain to invade the country twice and to invest heavily in Afghanistan's security apparatus. If Afghanistan fell to the Russians, so the argument went, the door would be wide open for an invasion of India. As the BBC World Service recounted daily reports of violence on an unimaginable scale, especially in Punjab and Bengal, the legation began to fear this might spread to the North-West Frontier too, just over the border in British India. They were right to be concerned. Kabul was initially insulated from the problems, but by August the violence had begun to disrupt the delivery of petrol to Afghanistan through the Khyber Pass, triggering huge price rises.

On a practical level, Squire and his team also wondered what the changes might mean for the British legation in Kabul. The legation currently reported to the British government in India in Delhi and the India Office in London. All staff had British government of India contracts, and many were Indian Muslims, including the Oriental Secretary and the Commercial Secretary. He also wondered whether the legation would continue to represent India's and Pakistan's interests in Afghanistan until the two new Dominions set up their own diplomatic missions. This would in all likelihood add to everyone's workload while he and others in the meantime tried to navigate a fine line between representing British interests on the one hand and those of Britain's successor governments in India and Pakistan on the other.

The Afghan government was watching the events in India closely too. Indian independence could trigger a power vacuum in the tribal areas along the Afghan–Indian border. At the same time, it potentially opened up the possibility of recovering the empire of their eighteenth century founding leader, Amir Ahmed Shah, which had stretched to Peshawar and beyond, and subsequently been absorbed in the Sikh empire and then the British within decades of his death. A border between Afghanistan and British India been agreed with Sir Mortimer Durand in 1893 and thereafter called the Durand Line. Now they wondered if this could be up for renegotiation.

The Afghans had other reasons to be interested too. Independence from Britain in 1919 had marked their own transition to statehood, but recent events in Persia suggested the Great Game was far from over.

Soviet troops had occupied parts of Persia during the war and showed no signs of leaving the north in 1945, setting up two breakaway republics in spite of an international agreement in 1942 to leave. Although these were later recovered by the Persian government with American, British and United Nations assistance, the whole incident left a strong impression on the Afghans. If the Soviets could do this in Persia, they could potentially do the same in northern Afghanistan too.

The Afghans were also aware that the wartime alliance between Britain, the Soviet Union and the United States was crumbling rapidly and that a new struggle was underway, this time over who would dictate the post-war settlement. The Soviets appeared to be in a pretty strong position. Of the three war-time Allied leaders, only Josef Stalin was still in power by August 1945. In the United States, President Theodore F. D. Roosevelt had died in April and been replaced by his Vice-President, Harry S. Truman. In Britain, Winston Churchill, the popular wartime leader and Prime Minister in a coalition government war effort, had been trounced in a landslide election victory for the Labour Party in July. The new Prime Minister, Clement Attlee, Churchill's wartime deputy, and the new Foreign Secretary, Ernest Bevin, a former trade unionist and Minister for Labour in the war, were fairly unknown quantities as far as the Afghans were concerned.

Over the next eighteen months, the Afghans watched Stalin re-position the Soviet Union in Europe, the Eastern Mediterranean and the Middle East. He staked a claim to retain territories he had acquired through the Soviet-German Non-Aggression Pact in 1939 – notably parts of Finland, Poland and Romania and all the Baltic States – and was securing pro-Soviet governments in the rest of eastern Europe. Soviet troops had occupied eastern Germany and shown no sign of leaving, while the Turkish government was facing intense Soviet pressure to allow military bases on Turkish soil and free passage by Soviet ships through the Black Sea and into the Mediterranean.[4] Soviet-style communism was also becoming a popular political force across western Europe, with communist parties doing extremely well in elections in France and Italy. Meanwhile, the Greek government was fighting a civil war against communist separatists, and to the east Mao Zedong's Red Army was beginning to sweep across China.

The Afghan government therefore anxiously sought reassurance that post-war Britain was still able and willing to provide a security shield against the Soviet Union, just as it was helping the Greek and Turkish governments in Europe. The position was far from clear-cut, however, as Chapter Seven explains. By the end of the war, it was increasingly evident that the Indian independence movement was gaining steam and that some kind of change in the constitutional status of India was on the cards. For the Afghans, this signalled that Britain might ultimately deprioritise Afghan security in the not-too-distant future. Alarm bells started ringing in Kabul. In June 1947, General Daud Khan, the Afghan Minister of War and King Zahir Shah's cousin, sought reassurance from Colonel Lancaster, the legation's Military Attaché, that Britain would not abandon Afghanistan after Indian independence. He also wanted to know if Britain would continue to supply arms and military equipment.[5] A year later, the Prime Minister, Mahmud Khan, asked if Britain was still prepared to assist Afghanistan in the event of a third world war against the Soviets. If so, he wanted to start making plans.[6]

The Afghans were also concerned about the impact of Indian independence on their economy. As a landlocked country, Afghanistan was heavily dependent on overland trade routes. Although they had some trade deals with the Soviet Union, these were vastly outweighed by the volume of trade through India importing essential goods such as petrol and cotton piece goods, and exporting agricultural products which earned crucial foreign exchange. The 1921 Anglo-Afghan Treaty had guaranteed the continued free movement of goods between Afghanistan and India, but what if India became independent? Would that negate the treaty? If so, where would that leave Afghanistan's trading rights? As early as 1944, Ali Mohammed, the Afghan Foreign Minister, had shared his fears with the legation that any change in the constitutional position of India would seriously affect Afghanistan's economic wellbeing, cause acute shortages of vital products, and bring misery to millions.[7] High inflation on imported goods, and severe petrol shortages in July and August 1947 suggested he and others were right to be worried.

Things were not all bleak, however. The Afghans had a Plan B up their sleeves too. If Britain eventually withdrew from the subcontinent, they wondered whether the United States, the new global superpower, could be persuaded to take over their role. Initially, this seemed unlikely. The United States to all intents and purposes appeared to be preparing to withdraw from global affairs as soon as the post-war peace settlement was finalised, just as they had done after the First World War. On 12 March 1947, however, following Britain's announcement that it was withdrawing troops and aid from Greece and Turkey, President Truman announced that the United States would not only support those two countries, but would thenceforth 'support free peoples who are resisting subjugation by armed minorities or outside pressures' anywhere in the world. This was a game-changer. The Truman Doctrine, as it was later called, signalled a shift in United States foreign policy from isolationism towards being a global guarantor of liberty and freedom.

This was good news for Afghanistan too, especially as they had recently succeeded in enticing an American company, Morrison-Knudsen, to sign a multimillion-dollar contract to transform the Helmand river valley into the breadbasket of Afghanistan, picking up from where the Germans and Japanese had left off at the start of the war. The government hoped the contract would bind the United States to a stake in Afghanistan's future for years to come. Even though it was clear by mid-1947, as Chapter Four explains, that the contract had more or less bankrupted the country with little to show for the expenditure to date, the Afghans were confident they now had a friend on their side with more money, more influence and more power than any other country in the world. It was no longer, so the argument went, a life-and-death matter if Britain decided to downsize. Afghanistan could cope.

The Afghans had a Plan C too, although this did not seem quite so straightforward or necessarily rewarding. The establishment of a new post-war international architecture – the United Nations, the World Bank and the International Monetary Fund – coupled with the emergence of international development assistance, offered new opportunities for political, financial and economic support. This was the dawn of a new post-war world order of global interdependence, respect for human rights and mutual entitlements and responsibilities, backed by mechanisms to resolve conflicts and increase cooperation. It was a double-edged sword, however. Henceforth, if the Afghan government repressed its people, the world would take note. Alternatively, if the Afghans wanted international respect, the government would have to heed the new global standards, and if they wanted financial or technical assistance, they would need to be prepared for economic and political conditions.

The country's new, post-war liberal government, led by Mahmud Khan, was open for business too. A few democratic reforms here and open market reforms there would, it was hoped, bring the emerging middle class into the polity and thus deepen support for the regime, and enable the country to draw on the positive lessons from the democracy movements in the Indian subcontinent. It would potentially also do wonders for Afghanistan's reputation on the post-war international stage. The country could put to bed persistent rumours of human rights abuses and perhaps be in a good place to secure financial and technical support from the new international institutions.

The critical question, however, was whether a reforming government in the midst of an economic recession could also afford to adopt a foreign policy position that might put it at odds with Britain's successor state across the Durand Line, especially when Afghanistan also heavily relied on the trade routes to India. The British knew their historic interest in the region, but did not anticipate that in the final run-up to Indian independence, the Afghans would launch a campaign to renegotiate the border and promote the idea of an autonomous Pashtun region – Pashtunistan – created out of the tribal areas straddling the Durand Line, and possibly including the North-West Frontier Province (NWFP) too. When Mountbatten announced that there was to be a plebiscite in NWFP to decide whether the province should join India or Pakistan, the Afghans added 'to the confusion' according to Squire 'by lodging a violent protest against the plan that does not explicitly give the NWFP the option of setting up its own separate government'.[8] Indeed, 'to be quite logical,' Squire recorded in his journal, 'the disappearance of India as a single entity should involve chaos in the NWFP which will also engulf Afghanistan and Kabul, but am continuing to hope for the best and human nature is not apt to prepare for the worst which may never happen.'[9] When the British refused to countenance this option on the ballot form during the plebiscite in July, the course was set, as Chapters Five and Six will explain, for a potentially rocky relationship with Britain's successor state in the tribal areas and NWFP, Pakistan.

As independence approached, Squire was relieved that some of the logistical nuts and bolts plaguing his mind for weeks had been fixed. In July, he had been asked by London to stay on for two more years to ease the transition and he had readily agreed. His Indian staff had been told to opt 'for either India or Pakistan. But except for making me an offer, the Foreign Office have given no indication so far of their intentions here'. He could only assume there would eventually 'be three legations or embassies'.[10] Two weeks later, he finally learnt that 'HMG have offered to continue the whole of its staff which I consider necessary at the same rate of pay and both the new governments have agreed in principle, though Pakistan say that it will not be for long as they hope to set up their own representation shortly'.[11]

The pace picked up in the first couple of weeks of August:

We are really getting down to the change over and are flooded with telegrams, from India regarding our retirement or continuation in service, from the FO [Foreign Office] regarding communications, cyphers etc. It looks as if our connection to the India Office [in London] too is to be severed from 15th August. India has asked us to go on representing her, and has agreed to those of my staff opting for India to be seconded here. As regards Pakistan, we still have no orders, but I intend to carry on much as at present until we hear something definite.[12]

And then he set about making some plans of his own. His daughter, Kristen, was due to arrive in Karachi from London on the 14th, and he decided to leave Kabul on the 10th so that he could meet her. At the last minute however, he changed his plans:

> Partly because I had no reply from the Foreign Office, partly because no one [in Karachi] seemed to have any time to see me, (and Pakistan has announced it wants to have its own representative at once), but chiefly because the Foreign Office has sent out a circular that flag hoisting ceremonies should be held where possible – so we are to have a show on Friday.

He was privately relieved too. The temperature had been hovering around 100 degrees Fahrenheit for four solid days, which would have made the journey unbearable. He sent Joe Morgan, his secretary, to meet Kristen instead. The two of them then drove from Karachi to Quetta, where 'the Rogers put them both up and took them to a club dance. Then on to Kandahar where they spent the night at the consulate and so to Kabul starting at 2.15 am and getting here whilst we were at lunch.'[13]

Since it was Ramadan, the Muslim month of fasting, Pakistan hosted a celebration at the India Club in Kabul on the evening of Thursday 14th, just hours after the formal independence ceremony in Karachi attended by Jinnah and Mountbatten. The next morning, Squire listened to the BBC news from Delhi, and then, since it was a holiday, spent some of the afternoon writing in his journal:

> We celebrate today with mixed feelings. Naturally among all Indians there is great rejoicing, but after the rejoicings, what? Will the British gamble succeed? If it does, our stature in the eyes of the world will greatly recover and the British empire may well continue to grow in world importance. But if it does not, and I myself see little chance that it will, then surely we shall rightly deserve the obloquy of the world for having put our hand to the plough and turned back.

On the whole, he felt Mountbatten had handled the transition well, but 'the details are less encouraging'. He could see problems ahead in NWFP with the 'agitation for an independent Pashtunistan a very dangerous playing with inflammable material', and was concerned about continuing violence in the Punjab, food shortages (especially in India), and the future of the two new dominions as they faced a mountain of challenges in the days, weeks and months ahead.[14]

He then turned his mind back to the main business of the day, at least as far as Britain's outpost in Kabul was concerned – overseeing the final preparations for an official reception at the legation that evening. 'About 300 Indians came and I made a speech after which the new flags were unfurled. The guests then fell on the tea and ate up everything in about five minutes. We had asked just the Heads of Missions and Chief du Protocol and gave some of them drinks afterwards. The flags which were floodlit along with our front tank [pond] looked lovely at night.'[15] The next day, the Indians held their own celebrations.

As to whether the Afghans were right to question if Britain planned to reduce its interest in Afghanistan after Indian independence, the outlook, even for seasoned observers like Squire and Lancaster, was far from clear. Although the Joint Chiefs of Defence Staff in London had confirmed in March 1947 that Afghanistan's territorial integrity was important to Britain,[16] Squire had already guessed that independence could irrevocably change the rules of the game, and had shared his thoughts with London that January. 'If India insists on full independence, it may be that her defence e.g. against Russian aggression, is of no interest to His Majesty's Government and that therefore the maintenance or expansion of British influence in Afghanistan is only of commercial importance.'[17]

The Chiefs of Defence Staff met again on 29 August, just nine days after independence, and concluded that Britain was still interested in preserving Afghanistan's territorial integrity, but thought this time round that it would be a good idea to find out what India and Pakistan could do to help. Afghanistan was now in their backyard, not Britain's.[18] One month later, Ernest Bevin, the Foreign Secretary, informed the Afghan government that their country's security against the Soviet Union was still of the utmost importance and Britain would therefore now work hard to encourage India and Pakistan to ensure this.[19]

Meanwhile, as troubled flared up in Kashmir in the weeks running up to Independence, it was becoming clear that nothing would be straightforward. The Hindu ruler of this predominantly Muslim state refused to join Pakistan at independence and his troops attacked local Muslim farmers. Incensed Pashtun tribesmen from the North-West Frontier marched on Srinagar to wreak revenge. Once the Maharaja decided to join India in October, India and Pakistan came close to war. It began to look just possible that Afghanistan could be left to the mercy of a new Great Game power-play in which India and Pakistan forged separate bilateral alliances with the Soviet Union or the West based on which offered them the better deal.[20] Afghanistan, as before, would be piggy in the middle.

The British government was therefore to find itself caught between a desire on the one hand to scale back its engagement while handing the mantle over others, and concern on the other that it may just have to expend yet more resources to help frame the new rules of a new game, bringing in her new ally, the United States, as and where necessary. By late 1947, however, Britain was in no state to do this. The country was in a dire state economically, and overcommitted internationally. It simply could not afford to take on any additional political, financial or military commitments, which were not a top priority. In these circumstances, the critical questions for those interested in Afghanistan's future were not whether Britain would stay committed, but rather, by how much would Britain scale back, in what way, and by when; and who would take Britain's place?

The Home Front

British policy towards Afghanistan in the late 1940s was as much driven by events at home as in Asia. The war had brought the nation together to fight against a common enemy, thus helping to heal the fractures of the 1930s Great Depression when mass unemployment had brought into sharp relief the gap between the rich and the poor. The war was won by men and women, rich and poor alike, who worked side by side, fought and died together in battle, and experienced bombing raids on the home front which did not discriminate between the haves and the have-nots. They shared the common experience of ration cards and wartime blackouts, as well as the loss of loved ones. This union of spirit was epitomised by the publication of the Beveridge Report in 1942, which focussed on the 'Five Giants on the Road to Recovery' – want, disease, ignorance, squalor and idleness – and recommended the creation of a welfare system with a free national healthcare service, child allowances and full employment (meaning less than 8.5 per cent unemployment). The public loved it. In a poll carried out by the British Institute for Public Opinion in 1943, 83 per cent supported the recommendations, and only 6 per cent opposed them.[21]

In the run-up to the general election in July 1945, one of the critical questions for voters was not whether a particular party supported the Beveridge Report, but which one could be trusted to deliver it in full. Although the Conservative Party backed the main principles behind the report, their reputation was tainted by pre-war mass unemployment and their appeasement policy towards Hitler in 1938–9. As the troops began to send back their postal ballots from various foreign outposts, and people at home went to the polling booths, they thought very carefully about what sort of society peace time Britain should be. On 26 July, the results of the election were announced. Voters had given the Labour Party an overwhelming mandate to deliver peace overseas and build a new society for returning heroes – with state action to ensure full employment, the formation of the National Health Service and state ownership of public industries such as the railways, coal and power. They also believed the Labour Party had the leadership in men like Clement Attlee and Ernest Bevin to deliver this.

In theory, Britain in 1945 was one of the post-war world's three superpowers alongside the United States and Russia. The reality was somewhat different, however. The United States was the only country to emerge from the war with a thriving economy – in less than four years, wartime spending had almost doubled their Gross Domestic Product (GDP).[22] Meanwhile, although the Soviet Union had experienced heavy wartime losses, they showed few signs that this affected their approach to the peace settlement as the Red Army occupied parts of eastern Europe and Germany and began to transport German industrial and military assets to Soviet territory. In Britain, the new government initially thought the country would recover economically pretty quickly because it had a strong industrial base, a global empire, and a huge navy, air force and army to boot. The Royal Air Force alone had 55,469 planes at the end of the war and over a million personnel.[23] Lying behind the victory parades that summer, however, was a stark reality – Britain had thrown just about every resource it had into winning the war and had few reserves to draw on to win the peace.

Britain's challenges at home and abroad were immense. By the end of the war, Britain's debt was at a record level of £3.8 billion. The government had run down Britain's gold and dollar reserves to pay for the war effort, mobilised factories and labour to shift to wartime production, and drawn on resources from across the empire. Britain was in debt to India alone for over £1 billion. In 1941, the country had negotiated a Lend-Lease scheme with the United States to secure supplies of food, munitions and other goods against agreed collateral from Britain. When President Truman abruptly ended Lend-Lease on 21 August 1945 within days of the cease-fire in the Far East, the new Labour government had to face the stark reality that the country was bankrupt. They went cap in hand to Washington to ask for a loan. Without money, the country would not be able to pay for crucial food, fuel and other imports, let alone implement Labour's ambitious social reform agenda. The government was also forced to retain wartime rationing indefinitely.

By the end of the year, an American loan of $3.75 billion had been agreed. The interest rate – at 2 per cent with payments suspended for five years – was good, but the United States insisted that all holders of sterling should be able to convert their pounds into dollars on 15 July 1947. Labour had bought some breathing space, but it was limited. Many feared that the full convertibility of sterling on 'C' Day, as it became known, would cripple the economy. In the meantime, throughout 1946, the economy did not look too bad – exports increased, while the extension of wartime rationing kept demand for imports low – and so the government was able to press ahead with its ambitious reform package.

One of the first issues the government sought to address was the mounting housing crisis. There had been housing shortages before the war. Now an additional 750,000 houses had been destroyed or partially damaged by bombs.[24] The challenge was exacerbated by men returning from the front demanding homes for their wives and children instead of living with their extended families. The government initially distributed prefabricated housing, while thousands squatted in empty properties, many of them military. After 1946, they focussed on building new council homes, with 55,400 completed that year, and a further 137,690 in 1947.[25] Labour's other manifesto promises were beginning to take shape too. The coal industry was nationalised on 1 January 1947, in a move that many hoped would improve the management of precious coal resources as well as labour relations within the industry, which had been fractious even at the height of the war effort. Plans to establish a National Health Service (NHS), providing services free at the point of use, were well underway too – the NHS was finally launched in 1948.

Internationally, Britain's ministers and diplomats were also busy managing a wide number of post-war issues. British diplomats were involved in intense discussions with the United States and the Soviet Union to help frame the peace settlements with Germany, Italy, Austria and Japan. They were also actively engaging with the United Nations, which had been established to create a new post-war world order. The first meeting of the United Nations General Assembly was held in London in January 1946. The government also faced demands for independence from Burma and India, while the British military were not only part of the occupation force in Germany and Austria, but also deployed in Egypt, Libya, Cyprus, Somaliland, Sudan, the Far East and Jamaica. The German commitment alone cost Britain £80 million a year. Elsewhere, British forces were also supporting the Greek army in the Greek civil war, and were trying to maintain peace in Palestine in accordance with their post-First World War mandate in the Middle East. By 1946, however, Britain's protection of Palestinians and Arabs against rising Jewish claims for a homeland was rapidly swimming against the tide. The United States now wanted Britain to allow increased Jewish settlement in Palestine, while the Jews were launching violent attacks against the British position, symbolically blowing up the British headquarters in the King David Hotel in Jerusalem in July 1946.

These international commitments in turn had a negative impact on Britain's labour market and the country's capacity to re-deploy its human resources to peacetime occupations, including transforming factories from war to peacetime production. In 1945, there were 5 million in the armed forces, and a further 5 million working on civil defence and munitions production.[26] The government had demobilised 3 million by mid-1946, but retained 2.2 million in the forces, in addition to the new intakes of eighteen-year-olds in 1945 and 1946, in order to meet their commitments.[27] Until and unless they could significantly reduce the size of the military – and the attendant costs involved – further economic recovery would be constrained.

Then in the winter of 1946/7, Britain had a run of extraordinary bad luck. Just about all heavy industry, as well as the railways and people's homes, were reliant on coal for fuel and heat. Heavy snowfall in January 1947, followed by exceptionally cold weather throughout February, brought fuel supplies to a standstill, ironically just weeks after the nationalisation of the mines. The River Thames froze, the trains stopped, and coal could not be lifted from the mines. The government deployed the RAF to drop food supplies for people and animals in outlying areas. By 15 February, around 2.3 million were unemployed because factories had been forced to close. Homes went without heat, electricity supplies were rationed, and there was a heavy loss of cattle and sheep. Then in March, just as the country was beginning to emerge from the disaster, the snows melted, causing the rivers to overflow and the fens to become submerged. The cost of that winter on ordinary men and women's lives then continued throughout the summer – the domestic use of electricity and gas was banned until September 1947 because there were too few miners to replenish coal stocks any earlier.[28]

It was not at all surprising that in the midst of that awful winter, Attlee and Bevin made some difficult, but pragmatic, decisions to roll back from some of their international commitments and speed up the transfer of power to national governments in the British empire in Asia. They were not in the business of believing the British empire was dead, however. Instead, they simply saw the need to reformulate imperial policy to meet the pressing requirements of the moment. On the one hand, the country lacked the wherewithal to turn the tide against the nationalist movements in Asia and the Jewish uprising in Palestine. At the same time, however, the government was acutely aware of the strategic importance of the Eastern Mediterranean, Middle East and Persian Gulf as a vital source of energy and as a crucial gateway to the Indian Ocean and Britain's colonies in South-East Asia.[29] Given this complex scenario, it made sense to roll back from some, but not all, of their international commitments, so that they could focus their undivided attention on the areas that still mattered to Britain. Britain would thus retain its post-war 'Great Power' status alongside the United States and the Soviet Union, and would now have greater capacity to exercise it.

In Burma, once the Japanese were driven out in 1945, Britain had decided to back Aung Sang's bid for independence. The final agreement was signed in January 1947.[30] Attlee and Bevin also decided that Mountbatten should be approached to take on the role of Viceroy of India to sort out Indian independence, especially as he had already proved his mettle in backing Aung Sang over more conservative pro-British Burmese leaders. Attlee's first attempt to find a political solution to the India question had been to despatch the so-called 'Cabinet Mission' to India in 1946 comprising the Chancellor of the Exchequer, the First Lord of the Admiralty and the Secretary of State for India. This had proposed a federation of states with a central government responsible for foreign policy, defence and communications. When this solution floundered, violence between Hindus, Muslims and Sikhs escalated, which the army were unable to contain. On 13 February 1947, the government agreed that power in India should be transferred by June 1948, and a month later, Mountbatten arrived in Delhi to oversee the process. Bevin and Attlee also asked the United Nations to take over Britain's mandate in Palestine, and announced that Britain would withdraw its 15,000 troops from Greece by 31 March, together with its support to Turkey. They hoped this precipitate action would force the United States' hand and compel them to re-engage globally.

In the months preceding this momentous decision, Foreign Office officials had already been actively reviewing the Soviet Union's post-war intentions, and had concluded it was set on a path of expansion using the ideological spread of communism and the boots of the Red Army as its instrument. A number of British politicians, civil servants and military chiefs had already begun to question Soviet intentions in the last days of the war. In early 1946, the Joint Intelligence Committee, the Foreign Office and the British embassy in Moscow had reassessed the Soviet threat in a paper called 'The Soviet Campaign against this Country and our Response to it', and come to the gloomy prognosis that the Soviet Union and communist ideology posed an active global threat, including to Britain's strategic interests in the Near and Middle East.[31] Although Attlee continued to believe that Britain's relationship with the Soviet Union could be managed through the United Nations, Bevin was more inclined to buy into the Foreign Office view and called for a strategy to stall the spread of Soviet communism. By the end of 1946, Attlee had changed his mind too and was now prepared to call the United States' bluff. He hoped the government would step into Britain's shoes to help address rising threats to global peace and stability.

The strategy paid off. The Truman administration had already reluctantly come to the conclusion some months earlier that the Soviet Union did pose a threat to post-war peace, and that only way to deal with it was to 'contain' its urge to expand and conquer.[32] Two months after Britain announced it was withdrawing from Greece and Turkey, President Truman committed the United States on 12 March 1947 to taking over Britain's role. Thenceforth, Britain and the United States would tackle the global threat together. At the end of the year, the British and American governments also met at the Pentagon to agree a regional division of labour, as Chapter Seven explains. Britain took responsibility for the Persian Gulf, the Indian subcontinent and South-East Asia in recognition of its historic equities in the region.[33] From now on, Afghanistan's role in the emerging Cold War would be viewed against that wider context.

Nearly three months later, on 5 June, the Secretary of State, General George Marshall, announced that the United States would provide economic assistance to aid European recovery. Although the details had not been worked out and the funds did not flow to Britain until 1948, this lifeline ultimately helped lift the British economy out of recession.

In the short term, however, the economy was to meet another crisis before it began to reap the benefits of the Marshall Plan. The American loan was already running out by July 1947, and the flow of dollars and gold out of the country had quadrupled between 1946 and 1947, driven by the need to import American goods and services.[34] Then on 15 July, in accordance with the terms of the loan, Britain introduced the full convertibility of sterling. The result was chaos. Within days, countries rapidly changed their sterling balances for dollars and Britain faced economic ruin. The government retracted convertibility on 20 August – five days after Indian independence – and was then forced to introduce yet more austerity measures to help contain the crisis, this time on tobacco and American foodstuffs.

As the momentous year of 1947 drew to a close, however, Britain's fortunes were beginning to turn a corner, albeit slowly. With the reduction in Britain's international military commitments, it was possible to pump much-needed labour back into domestic production. By the middle of the year, more troops had been demobilised – although this was partially offset by a decision in April to introduce permanent peacetime National Service.[35] By the end of March 1948 there was a net 'inflow' of dollars, and between 1947 and 1952, GDP grew by 3 per cent a year.[36] After 1947, the government would seek to embed its socialist reforms within a slowly recovering economy at home and manage the domestic and international fall-out from the loss of empire, as well as join the United States in a new campaign, the Cold War, which would lead to the creation of the North Atlantic Treaty Organisation (NATO) in 1949 and military engagement in Korea in 1950.

It was against this backdrop that a handful of British diplomats in Kabul, supported by the new British High Commissions in Islamabad and Delhi, and officials in London, worked hard to navigate a path through this complex, multi-layered and ever-changing international context. There was no script to work from, and few givens. Furthermore, they harboured few illusions that Britain's past relationship with Afghanistan would carry them through this bumpy period on the strength of historic affinities alone, in fact possibly quite the reverse.

One Man's Story

My grandfather was among those who came home in 1946. His story over the subsequent year is a microcosm of the views and complex decisions being taken in millions of households across Britain at this time. He came back to Manchester with mixed emotions. On the one hand, he had little money, no job and no home – he was returning to live once again with his wife's extended family. On the other, he was keen to be reacquainted with old friends, visit his favourite theatres and pubs, and see his family again. As a lifelong Conservative, however, and a supporter of the empire, unlike many other troops returning to Britain that year, he thought the Labour government had got its international priorities totally wrong:

> To my small conception, this seems to be a period during which we should have spent less time in pacifying our late enemy and concentrated on the countries which have suffered, including our own, and win them now as our allies for the future, and at the same time, reassure our faithful and patient colonies and Dominions that we are worth bothering about. Then we could have emerged even stronger than at any time in this century. Instead of that, our own country commences to be reconstructed by those small people who are meddling with the very foundations of the empire's system of trade and economics. It must suggest to anybody that we are the people who were at fault and that it took six years of war for us to make the discovery. It seems strange that we can spend fifteen million each day on a war, and the moment it is over, then we haven't

enough money to buy a few tins of milk for the folks at home. Mind you, I'm sorry for German women and children, sorry for any women and children, but here are several people who have a sort of stupid sentiment about the health of their own people at home. I'm tired of this 'We can take it' business. The people in the UK 'had to take it'. No choice at all.[37]

He remained on full pay until the end of the year and was then kept on in a reserve capacity until the end of August 1947. In spite of labour shortages, however, he was unable to find a job. I have no idea why. Perhaps it was because he was a middle-aged man with few qualifications, or perhaps he found home life too dull and could not commit to anything which came his way. I do know, however, from my mother, that it was difficult for him to share rented accommodation once again with his mother-in-law, disabled sister-in-law and her teenage daughter. Like thousands of other men returning from the front, he wanted a home for his immediate family. The solution came from an unexpected source in the summer of 1947, however. A businesswoman friend of my grandmother, Elsie Johnson, offered to sell her one of her large Victorian properties in Sale, Manchester, complete with fee-paying lodgers, for £1,700, as a private arrangement between the two women. She knew that my grandmother had a secure job and had been the main family breadwinner for years, so it was a sound proposition. Over the next few years, my grandmother, with some contributions from my grandfather, managed to pay Elsie back. It was a start. Next, he needed to find a job.

At some point that summer, he decided to re-enlist in the Army. His first day was 1 September 1947. If he needed a reminder that he was doing the right thing, a walk through the camp at Thetford a few weeks later set him straight. 'Money doesn't go anywhere, does it? Half mine has gone already and it's only Saturday. Do you know – in the course of a few hundred yards this evening, two Warrant Officers and a Staff Sergeant asked me for a loan. I thanked them for the gentle flattery and jangled my bobs and pennies as I walked on.'[38] Colonel Lancaster, his new boss in Kabul, was on leave in London that autumn, and so the two of them communicated about what he should plan to bring out with him.

Had a message a few hours ago from Colonel Lancaster who has written quite a friendly little note and enclosed two sheets of instructions and advice about what I shall need in the shape of clothes and money to take with me, and has given me names and addresses at various points in India – Karachi, Peshawar etc. – of various army and civilian people who will give me assistance and advice if I find it necessary … I am writing to Lancaster today because I am not sure exactly what the War

Office are allowing me in the shape of civilian clothing ... I am taking my suit to Bury St Edmunds to repair, anyhow, it may be very useful.[39]

Two weeks later, on Monday 20 October, he finally met Lancaster in person at the War Office. They parted on good terms, with Lancaster's last words being, 'See you in Kabul', and then he finally set off himself, armed with Lancaster's travel tips, on Thursday 8 January 1948.

The Journey to Kabul

Nowadays, it is possible to travel to Kabul from London on a commercial flight via Dubai, Islamabad, Istanbul or Delhi. In the 1940s, however, there was no direct route. The journey took at least a week, first on a plane, which stopped regularly to refuel, then a train journey from Karachi to Peshawar, followed by a two-day journey by road on the British legation lorry, which plied weekly between Peshawar and Kabul through the Khyber Pass. A direct flight from Peshawar or Quetta to Kabul was only organised for important visitors.

My grandfather flew from Heathrow Aerodrome accompanied by a nineteen-year-old man called Raymond Brooks, who was to become his colleague in the Military Attaché's office in Kabul. Their first port of call was Bordeaux, followed by refuelling stops in Italy, Palestine, Basra and Cairo. At the last minute, a stopover in Delhi was cancelled because 'we had a message that I could not get out of there' – another flare-up of communal violence between Hindus, Sikhs and Muslims was restricting movement around the city. They were re-routed to Karachi instead, although things were no better there as it turned out. They arrived on the morning of Sunday 12 January, 'one day after the worst conflicts are over, although no one is supposed to be on the streets between 6 p.m. and 9 a.m. each day'.[40] The severity of the riots that January caused 11,000 Hindus to flee the city for their lives.[41]

As a seasoned traveller, he decided the two-day train journey from Karachi to Peshawar was potentially unsafe and so set about finding a flight instead. He managed to get two seats on the only available plane to Peshawar, Oriental Airways, which set off on Thursday 16th. He sent a running commentary home: 'A Dakota, lovely craft – I warn Ray not to touch it, something might come apart – baggage too heavy – to Lahore – drink tea, then Rawalpindi, get coffee this time and two eggs – to Peshawar. Everyone astonished except man with tuberculosis – he doesn't care what happens. Car to Deans Hotel, Peshawar.'[42] They missed the truck by one day, and had to wait a week before it returned. Later, he confided that he did 'not feel like the Khyber so soon, between you and me, so contrived to get a plane which was just one day too late to catch the legation truck – next goes on Wednesday, 21 January'. My grandfather was in his element. The two of them then spent six days in

> one of the best hotels in India, not hotel rooms in the normal way, they are a series of bungalows with a large garden all around, a nice sitting room in good Indian style with a bedroom adjoining, bathroom etc and not forgetting my personal boy, by name of Arfullah Ahmed, who of course brings tea at the right time, fills the bath to tested temperature, presses the clothes, cleans the shoes, lights the cigar or cigarette, places the shirt over the head, adjusts the tie, and satisfies himself that 'Sahib' is fit to walk out.[43]

The final stage of their journey could not be put off forever, however. One of the passengers on the truck was the King's Messenger, who guarded the diplomatic bags and confided to my grandfather that whenever he used the Oriental Airways plane, he always left his will in the bank just in case. He also revealed that 'he has something in his bag that will poison us both later on, but we will get a bit of fun out of it first. I agreed and we did.'

This hazardous and uncomfortable route through some of the most spectacular scenery in the world has been described by countless travellers. My grandfather provided an evocative account of his own emotional and physical journey from the known to the unknown world in one of his first letters home:

> Slow truck, bumpy road narrow and twisting, open plains dark and nasty – a few mud huts, Afghan graves to left and right for 30 miles or so, marked by pieces of upturned slate or slab of rock – barren plains all the way – nothing human anywhere – night hides most of it till Jalalabad is reached. Afghan Consul [at the British Consulate] provides dinner and a shake down until 3 am on Thursday when the final lap begins. Daybreak picks out a tortuous narrow path perched on the side of a mountain. Look upon the left to a thousand feet of rugged grey rock – to the right, a sheer downward swoop to barren and stony valleys in the distance. In the twists and turns of this miraculous path and knowledgeable Indian driver there is nothing but rock and dust and providence – an overwhelming deathly silence save the chug of our own engine echoing in the solemn spaces. In the breaking dawn at this point I peer up at the endless overhanging rocks and boulders and dark ravines on either side, almost shutting out the misty sky – the small world closes in and the cold air is close and fetid. Mountains now everywhere – mountains in snow and ice, mountains in sombre black – blue mountains – green ridges – grey coves – lashing and angry torrents

rushing at the foot of ghostly chasms – ten thousand peaks and valleys of cold and desolate splendour. Dante's story and pictures of those being whirled into Hades is forced upon us. It all seems as hard and cruel as life itself, and in this sleepy terrain I think this is life at last without pretence or subterfuge. When I've passed through this space of rocky waste, I hope again to meet the sunshine of a happy smile and clear eye. Just shows how a few rocks here and there can interfere with a chap.[44]

His thoughts were mirrored by a contemporary, Mitchell Carse, the Deputy High Commissioner in Peshawar, who visited Kabul in August 1949. For him, the road from Peshawar was the 'most atrocious track I have ever known for motoring purposes – and if its object is to slow up to a walking pace any invading force from this side [Pakistan], then I should say its object will surely be served'.[45] These uniquely personal descriptions capture at once the distinctiveness of the journey to Kabul and also its allure for the British men and women who came to live and work there. As both men turned into the gates of the British embassy in Kabul, wrapped in their separate thoughts, they entered a strange world, isolated from everyday Afghan life and remote from Britain geographically, physically and culturally, but also full of familiar reference points.

2

British–Afghan Relations

The extraordinary and unparalleled anomaly of the relations between Afghanistan and the British government has often been described: how we are bound to defend the Amir's country, yet are forbidden to take a single step for defence within its border, or to send a single officer to reconnoitre the best means for its defence; how we give the Amir an annual subsidy of 18.5 *lakhs* [1,850,000 Indian rupees], yet are not allowed to place a European Agent at his capital, and even one Asiatic agent is kept under strict surveillance; how even our advice is resented; how we give the Amir arms, and yet must make the best of much unfriendly behaviour, and refrain from effectively asserting even the '*droits des limitrophes*'; how our ally, as a condition of governing his subjects, is unable to check their fanaticism. Evidently so singular a position is only tolerated or upheld for peculiarly strong reasons, arising from the belief in the minds of Afghan and British rulers equally that each of them requires and receives some valuable considerations from the other.

Lord Morley, Secretary of State for India, 1906[1]

Introduction
The territory of present-day Afghanistan sits at the crossroads of three major geopolitical regions – the Middle East and especially Persia to the west, Central Asia and the Russian/Soviet empire to the north, and the Indian subcontinent to the south and east – and is made up of three distinct geographic landscapes. The mountains of the Hindu Kush lie to the east, marking the western edge of the Himalayas. This region is mostly barren and unpopulated except where craggy peaks are dotted with occasional remote villages in fertile valleys. The other two regions are

quite different. To the south are vast deserts – including the colloquially named 'Desert of Death'[2] – broken up by irrigated land along the Helmand and Arghandab rivers. The north forms part of the flat, grassy plains of Central Asia and was once part of the historic 'Silk Route' from the Orient to markets on the Mediterranean and in Europe.

At different times in its history, this territory has been conquered and occupied by men such as Alexander the Great and Genghis Khan, as well as the Persians, the Arabs and the Turks, and became the home of three great religions: Buddhism, Islam and Zoroastrianism. Its rulers conquered and occupied territory far into Central Asia, Pakistan and India. Each empire-builder's ambitions were aided by porous borders and distinct geographical regions which were not coterminous with political boundaries. In effect, as one Foreign Office analyst in the 1940s put it, 'if an advance into the mountainous country is undertaken, there is no self-evident point at which to stop'.[3] The territory that now constitutes Afghanistan and its numerous tribes and ethnic groups – the Uzbeks, Tajiks, Turkmens, Hazaras and Pashtuns to name a few – has been ruled at different times under various political systems with only limited connection to today's state. In fact, Afghanistan's 'current form is only one of its many incarnations',[4] while the name Afghanistan, land of the Afghans, 'conjures up a totally false impression of homogeneity'.[5] This label has been used by other communities to describe the country's dominant group, the Pashtuns, although the latter do not necessarily describe themselves as Afghans.

Up to the mid-eighteenth century, the territory had been ruled by a succession of Turko-Mongolian families for more than 900 years. One man, Ahmed Shah, is credited with the establishment of the modern state. Born Ahmed Khan, he was a Pashtun tribal leader and a commander in the Shah of Persia's army. After the Shah was assassinated in 1747, however, Ahmed Khan captured a caravan carrying the Shah's taxes back to Persia and then used this to finance alliances and military campaigns. Over time, he was crowned king, taking the title Shah, and mobilised the Pashtun-speaking tribes to seize territories in Persia, as well as lands in what is now Pakistan (the Punjab, Sind, Balochistan and the city of Peshawar), and Kashmir. Afghanistan, the land of the Pashtuns, was thus born.

In the nineteenth century, Britain and Russia became the latest in the long line of foreign powers seeking to control Afghan territory for their own ends – Britain with its desire to secure the north-west corner of the empire in India from foreign incursion; Russia with successive Tsars' ambitions to extend their rule southwards into the Muslim Khanates in Central Asia. Inevitably, their gazes soon focussed on Afghanistan itself.

Over time, it assumed a unique position – as a buffer state in the 'Great Game' between the two empires as each vied for control and influence.[6] This did not mean that it was left alone – far from it. By the end of the century, and after two Anglo-Afghan wars, Britain controlled Afghan foreign policy, was supplying the Afghan government with money and weapons, and had defined Afghanistan's borders Persia and Russia and with British India along the North-West Frontier.. It was a relatively unique relationship for Britain and Afghanistan, as Lord Morley pointed out in 1906, one very much shaped by Afghan terms and conditions on the one hand and British pragmatism on the other. Although Afghanistan gained independence from Britain in 1919, the legacy of this complex relationship was still strong in the 1940s.

Understanding the Afghan State

Modern-day Afghanistan's four main urban centres loosely define a region with an ancient urban centre – Kabul to the east, near the ancient city of Kapisa (modern-day Bagram), which is associated with Alexander the Great; Mazar-i-Sharif (beside the ancient city of Balkh) to the north near Uzbekistan; Herat to the west, culturally and historically linked to Persia; and Kandahar, in the heart of Pashtun tribal territory to the south, near the border with Pakistan. Each has well-irrigated plains or river valleys producing agricultural surpluses and has remained relatively distinct in character. These four regions were also politically significant at different times in Central Asia's history – Balkh, for instance, was one of the oldest cities in the ancient world, dating back more than 3,000 years, and the home of Zoroastrianism. In more recent history, Kandahar became politically important after Ahmed Shah made it his capital in the mid-eighteenth century, and again in the 1990s, when it became the Taliban's power base. Kabul became politically important when a descendent of Genghis Khan, Babur, chose it as his capital in the late fifteenth century before he moved south and founded the Moghul empire in India. It became the capital of a united Afghanistan in the early nineteenth century when Ahmed Shah's descendants moved there. A fifth ancient city and region, in Afghan minds at least, is Peshawar, now part of Pakistan but once part of Ahmed Shah's territory and his descendants' winter capital until it was lost to the Sikhs in 1834.

Afghanistan is still essentially an agrarian society. Although only 12 per cent of Afghan land is actually arable – and of that only half can be used at any one time due to water shortages[7] – the vast majority of the people live off the land in remote villages far from these urban centres. Their primary loyalty even today is to their kin, tribe or ethnic group, not to the idea of an Afghan nation state. In the 1940s, the British estimated there were probably around 12 million people in the country, made up of around twenty ethnic and kinship groupings, each of which were divided and subdivided based on identity, context and locality.[8] Many had close affinities with communities across Afghanistan's arbitrary international borders.

The largest single group in the 1940s were the Pashtun-speaking tribes – such as the Safis, the Mohmands, the Afridis and the Shinwaris – straddling the border between Afghanistan and the North-West Frontier in British India. They became politically powerful after Ahmed Shah founded a new royal dynasty. The British estimated there were around 2.75 million Pashtuns in Afghan territory (constituting about 20 per cent of the Afghan population) and about 6 million across the border in British India.[9] The differences between the Pashtun-speaking tribes even today are almost as great as what distinguishes them collectively from other tribes or ethnic groups. Each Pashtun tribe is segmented into numerous clans and sub-tribes with huge differences in their social organisation and culture. These often relate to their historical roots and associations, how they make a livelihood and where they live, including whether they were relocated to a different area or migrated to towns. Most speak Pashtun, but not all – those who moved west to Herat or north into Kabul, for instance, speak Dari (the Afghan version of Persian or Farsi), the language of the royal court and government.

Among the remaining population, a few ethnic groups or tribes stand out numerically and culturally, although, like the Pashtuns, what distinguishes them from each other, or defines their identity within an ethnic-linguistic group, is often associated with place and occupation. To this day, the predominantly Persian-speaking Tajiks and the Turkic-speaking Uzbeks and Turkmens to the north still enjoy close associations with ethnic groups across the border in Uzbekistan and Turkmenistan. The centre of Afghanistan, and especially in and around Bamyan, is predominantly populated by the Hazaras, Shia Muslims who are said to be descended from Genghis Khan's army and speak a version of Persian. They have long been considered low down in the social hierarchy and many were forcibly moved to this remote area in the late nineteenth century.

The development of the modern Afghan state has been shaped by the way in which its diverse territories and peoples have been ruled over the centuries, its distinct geographic regions and climate, and the way in which external powers have interacted with it. Like other agrarian societies, particular kinship groups have played a pivotal role in Afghan state-building in much the same way as the Plantagenet and Tudor families in England secured and maintained power through conquest, patronage and the management of dynastic alliances by marriage.[10] Ahmed Shah's establishment of his Afghan empire conforms to that model. He succeeded in gaining control over alternative sources of power and authority, and then cemented his rule through the management of patronage and kinship networks, rewarding his supporters with land and treasure. From the mid-eighteenth century until 1978, all Afghan rulers, including Ahmed Shah, came from either the Muhammadzai or Saddozai clans of the Barakzai tribe within the Durrani Federation, one of three major groupings among the Pashtun tribes. Since the First Anglo-Afghan War (1839–42), virtually all came from the Muhammadzais.[11]

Over time, local people saw there was more to gain from being part of this nascent state, with its guarantee of stability and peace, than being outside it. This was not a modern nation state with a centralised bureaucracy, legal system, police force and ministries responsible for delivering services, however. Rather, this was a state built on mutual gain between ruling elites. They accepted the idea of a 'first among equals' with the right to raise revenue to maintain an army guaranteeing their collective security, but not to rule over them. This system of government had little imprint beyond the cities and towns, and its control diminished towards ill-defined borders, where it competed with other sources of power. To the north, these included the Emirs of Bukhara and Khans of Khiva until they were absorbed into the Russian empire in the 1880s. To the south and east, there were the Sikhs, the Moghuls and, latterly, the British.[12]

Ahmed Shah's state was initially unstable because it depended on the continual conquest of new territory to reward tribal followers and pay his army. He also risked parts breaking away as soon as other would-be rulers offered a higher reward.[13] Once his rule was endorsed by the tribes, however, he began to consolidate his position by building up a regular army paid in cash or grants of land from conquered territories and directly under his leadership. The state became a giant patronage network in which local leaders gained land or money in exchange for providing troops, and later raised taxes on their fiefdoms to pay for an imperial army. Eventually, Ahmed Shah and his descendants were able to reduce their reliance on irregular forces recruited through levies on particular districts, or from tribal armies, known as *lashkars*, and only called up *lashkars* when they needed additional fighting men.

In the years after Ahmed Shah's death in 1772, however, his nascent state lacked sufficiently robust institutions to survive internal squabbling among his various descendants, or to repel new empire-builders on its eastern and southern borders. Ranjit Singh's Sikh empire annexed Kashmir in 1819 and Peshawar in 1834. The British in turn first annexed the Punjab and Frontier territories, and later took Peshawar from the Sikhs in 1849 to protect their own empire in the Indian subcontinent. More territory in what is now Balochistan in Pakistan on the border with Afghanistan and Persia was taken from Afghanistan at the end of the Second Anglo-Afghan War in 1881. The Sikh and British empires effectively sealed off future opportunities for Afghan rulers to reward tribes with conquered territory and the spoils of war. After that, Ahmed Shah's descendants were forced to use different strategies to retain what was left of his empire.

These strategies included the tried and tested policy of divide and rule to ensure that no tribe or individual from within the ruling dynasty accumulated sufficient power or resources to oppose their rule. This approach was often combined with the development of rudimentary structures of government and administration to raise revenue to fund military mobilisation and maintain a degree of control over this disparate kingdom. The tribes and regions, however, were left with a high degree of autonomy. In exchange for owing fealty to the ruling family and providing manpower for the Amir's army, they were left to get on with their lives more or less as before. To supplement their resources, the royal family also accepted funds from outside powers, which were used in turn to buy support, build up state systems, and strengthen the one institution that could guarantee the continuation of the ruling dynasty – a national army owing loyalty to the monarch, and not to any particular faction, region or tribe. The relative emphasis placed on each of these strategies during the nineteenth century was often determined by the way in which Afghanistan became a buffer between the British and Russian empires.

The Great Game

Britain first diplomatic engagement with Afghanistan in 1809 was a precursor of things to come. It was prompted by intelligence that Napoleon planned to invade India through Afghanistan and Persia, and Britain therefore needed to be sure the Afghans would protect the East India Company's investments in the subcontinent. Montstuart Elphinstone, the new emissary, duly arrived at Shah Shuja's winter court in Peshawar in early 1809, accompanied by 200 cavalry, 4,000 infantry, a dozen elephants and 600 camels, leaving no room for doubt in anyone's mind that Britain was a force to be reckoned with.[14] Elphinstone turned out to be an excellent choice. He had a strong aptitude for languages and diplomacy, and an enquiring mind which he used to build up an intriguing picture of the Afghan people and Afghan politics and power structures. This material subsequently formed the basis for his 1815 book *An Account of the kingdom of Caubal*, the first European publication on Afghanistan. Much of his analysis would have been recognisable to subsequent British travelers to the country over the following decades.

During his five-month sojourn, Elphinstone witnessed first-hand the overthrow of Shah Shuja and the continual competition for power and resources both within the ruling dynasty and between them and other tribal leaders. Based on these experiences, he reflected:

> There is some distinction of interests between the king and the nation, and a still greater difference of opinion regarding his legal powers; the king, the Courtiers, and the Moollahs [Mullahs], maintaining that he has all the authority possessed by Asiatic despots; and the people in the tribes considering him as a monarch with very limited prerogatives. This produces a great deal of diversity in the actual exercise of the royal power ... The situation of the Afghan country appears to me to bear a strong resemblance to that of Scotland in ancient times: the direct power of the king over the towns and the country immediately around; the precarious submission of the nearest clans, and the independence of the remote ones; the inordinate power and faction of the nobility most connected with the court; and the relations borne by all the great lords to the crown.[15]

He noted that the tribes expected the king to use revenue raised from tribal levies to build a 'national' army to meet collective security interests, but also observed this came with challenges too. Since 'the king cannot compel the tribes to send the contingencies of men that they are bound to furnish, his army is composed of soldiers who come for pay, or from attachment to their leaders. The failure of the revenue naturally diminishes the species of the army; and the troops that do service, are more at the disposal of their commanders than at the king's.'[16]

In this complex context, however, Elphinstone concluded that Afghanistan did not need an absolutist monarchy. This would be an anathema to the Afghan way of life and damaging to the people. 'The internal government of the tribes answers its end so well, that the utmost disorders of the royal government never derange its operations, nor disturb the lives of the people.' As one old man pointed out to him, 'We are content with discord, we are content with alarms, we are content with blood, but we will never be content with a master.' At the same time, Elphinstone had little confidence that a constitutional monarchy – a compact between the crown and the Afghan people based on consent – would ever emerge:

> There is reason to fear that the societies into which the nation is divided possess within themselves a principle of repulsion and disunion, too strong to be overcome, except by such a force as, while it united the

whole into one solid body, would crush and obliterate the features of every one of the parts.[17]

Over the next three decades, a number of British and Russian adventurers travelled far deeper into Afghanistan than Elphinstone to see the lie of the land for themselves. After Napoleon's retreat from Moscow in 1812, Russia had resumed its slow but inexorable expansion, this time south into Persia's empire in Armenia and Azerbaijan and south-west into the Ottoman empire in the Middle East. By the late 1820s, it seemed just possible that the Russians might even seize Constantinople and Teheran. Lord Ellenborough, the President of the East India Company's Board of Control, and Minister with responsibility for India in the Duke of Wellington's government in London, speculated that Russia therefore posed an active threat to India too. In his despatch to the Governor General of India in 1828, he made it clear that the threat was not so much that the Russians would invade India, but that their approach towards the border of the East India Company's territories would undermine the moral stature of the Company's position with Indian princes and others:

> It is in our interests to take measures for the prevention of any movement on their part beyond their present limits. But the efficiency of such measures must depend upon their being taken promptly, and you being kept constantly informed of everything which passes on the Russian frontier.[18]

This despatch prompted a programme of British intelligence-gathering in Central Asia, often matched head for head by Russians sent by the Tsar. These men were often young army officers or political agents with a gift for languages, a capacity to adopt disguises and a willingness to take unimaginable risks for long periods at a time in remote areas with no support. If it came to it, they were also prepared to pay the ultimate price. Their task was to gather as much information as possible about local cultures and customs and how this massive Central Asian landmass was governed, to map the topography and to ascertain the region's vulnerability to Russian expansionism. Much later, this strategy became known as the Great Game after it was immortalised in Rudyard Kipling's book *Kim*. The term, however, had been coined by the first intelligence-gatherer himself, Lieutenant Arthur Conolly, in a letter to a friend in the 1830s.[19] Over subsequent decades, it came to embrace 'something far more serious than any game and lead to deaths, wars, invasions and colonisation on a massive scale, profoundly changing the lives of hundreds of thousands of inhabitants of Afghanistan and Central Asia'.[20]

In the nineteenth century, the risk to the empire seemed real enough. For the past four centuries, the Russian empire had expanded by 55 square miles a day, amounting to around 20,000 square miles a year. At the beginning of the nineteenth century, the British and Russian empires were separated by 2,000 miles. By the end, it was just a few hundred as Russia absorbed first one then another of the Central Asian khanates or kingdoms of Samarkand, Khiva and Bokhara in the 1860s and 70s.[21] Afghanistan was all that separated the two empires. It therefore became more or less inevitable that the spotlight would soon fall on how best to shore up Afghan defences – either by conquest and occupation, or through a compliant ruler – to create a buffer state to keep the Russians away from India.

The most famous of the early British intelligence-gatherers, as far as Afghanistan was concerned, was Captain Alexander Burnes. He was a young man with tremendous language skills, a quick intelligence and charming manner, which enabled him to win over the various rulers he met on his journey, including Ranjit Singh.[22] His first visit to Kabul was in 1831 on his way to the Khanate of Bokhara to test Russian influence across the Oxus River. Seven years later, in spite of Burnes' reports that the current ruler of Afghanistan, Dost Mohammed, was a man Britain could do business with, the Governor General of India, Lord Auckland, decided in 1838 that he should be deposed and replaced by Britain's 'own' man, Shah Shuja, the very same man who had hosted Elphinstone in Peshawar thirty years earlier. This marked the beginning of Britain's 'Forward Policy' of conquest and occupation.

Although Shah Shuja was placed nominally in charge, real power was vested in the hands of the British Envoy, Sir William Macnaghten, who established a British cantonment on the edge of Kabul.[23] His deputy was none other than Burnes, now newly knighted, who chose to live within the ancient citadel of Kabul, the Bala Hissar. The trigger for rebellion came three years later when the British decided to reduce the subsidies paid to tribal chiefs. Burnes and his brother were slaughtered in the Bala Hissar on 1 November 1841, and Macnaghten was murdered at the end of December by the leader of the rebels himself, Dost Mohammed's son, Wazir Akbar Khan, in the midst of negotiations to resolve the situation. A truce was agreed on 1 January 1842. This allowed the British and Indian army, and their wives and children, to leave Kabul and make for the Khyber Pass. It was a bitterly cold winter that year, however. Hundreds died en route from the cold, and then the army itself was attacked near the village of Gandamak and suffered one of the worst defeats in British military history. Only one British soldier, Dr William Brydon, escaped to recount the tale at the British fort at Jalalabad near the Khyber Pass.

Britain sent an army to avenge their fallen comrades and decided, once the point was made, to put the previous Amir, Dost Mohammed, back on the throne, supported by British weapons and money. During the remainder of his reign, Dost Mohammed recovered some of the territory which had been lost by his predecessors, including Kandahar in 1856 and Herat in 1863, and extended his northern frontier to the Oxus River. Meanwhile, the British kept a close eye on events in Afghanistan. They switched to a new policy – later known as Masterly Inactivity – to ensure British interests were secured with minimal outlay of men and money, while also making clear that they would revert to a Forward Policy if those interests were ever threatened.

There were four important legacies from the First Anglo-Afghan War. The first was that Britain's new policy enabled the Amirs to consolidate their rule within defined state borders and with sufficient funds to impose their authority. Thereafter, the Amirs' own resources were supplemented with British money rather than increasing their dependence on taxes from the local populace or investing in enterprises, which would have generated economic growth but potentially represented high risk. This money not only helped build a professional army, but also an administrative system which reached into the five provinces, led increasingly by men who owed their position to the Amir, rather than to the Amirs' sons who had previously run them as personal fiefdoms. At the beginning of the twentieth century, power and resources were still concentrated in the hands of the ruling family and their close allies.

The second significant impact of the war was that it had exposed the Amirs' dependence on tribal *lashkars* and popular mobilisation to supplement the regular army in order to expel external aggressors. Subsequent Amirs would find it harder to exert control over tribesmen who increasingly expected a share of the spoils. Military success had therefore strengthened the royal family's negotiating position with Britain, but had come at a cost internally. Over the next hundred years, and 'with each succeeding crisis and popular military mobilisation, the restoration of state authority became harder and disputes over who had the right to rule the state became fiercer'.[24] This issue became particularly acute in 1929 when the Pashtun tribes helped overthrow an Amir they disliked and then placed a new royal family, the Yahya Khels, in the palace a year later. The new dynasty knew they owed their position to the tribes, and their response to Indian independence in 1947 was in part coloured by this relationship of mutual dependency.

The third legacy was that it marked the beginning of Britain's hegemony in Afghanistan and the consolidation of the Great Game. Over time, this was to be recognised by outside powers too. As the Russian empire moved further south into Central Asia, the British and Russians reached an agreement in 1873 that the area south of the Oxus River would be Afghan territory and lay within Britain's sphere of influence. The British also agreed with the Persians that a low-lying area known as the Seistan, located along the Afghan–Persian border, should be ceded to Persia. Afghanistan began to have clearly defined international borders for the first time.

The fourth legacy was that it convinced the British that 'Peshawar should be the North-West Frontier of their Raj'.[25] It was crucial to have a strategic base to protect this vulnerable border region of the empire from foreign incursions and tribal unrest. From now on, therefore, any claims by future Amirs to recover Ahmed Shah's empire would be repulsed. Afghanistan's historic claim to these areas would resurface in the run-up to Indian independence a century later.

There was another legacy of the war too, a very personal one. Arthur Conolly, the man who had first coined the term 'the Great Game', was to become a direct casualty of Britain's defeat at Gandamak. Three years earlier, he had travelled to Bokhara in an attempt to secure the freedom of a fellow British officer from Emir of Bokhara's prison. Once the fallibility of the imperial British army had been exposed at Gandamak, the Emir no longer feared British retribution and had them both publicly executed in June 1842.[26]

The Second Anglo-Afghan War and Its Aftermath

Nearly forty years later, amid fears of Russian expansionism and concerns about whether British interests were being respected in Kabul, Britain sent troops back into Afghanistan. At the Treaty of Gandamak in 1879, the Afghans agreed to hand over territory on the North-West Frontier, including the Khyber Pass, to British India, and to conduct foreign policy in accordance with the wishes of the Government of India. They also agreed to host a new British mission in Kabul, this time based in the Bala Hissar, headed by a British citizen, Sir Louis Cavagnari. In return, he was to receive an annual subsidy of £60,000. Within a matter of weeks, however, on 3 September 1879, Cavagnari, his staff and guards were slaughtered in the new mission by mutinying Afghan troops, angry that they had not been paid by the Amir and blaming the British for their situation. This incident led to the second phase of the Second Anglo-Afghan War. Once again, the Amir's army was joined by volunteer *lashkars* and defeated the British army, this time at the battle of Maiwand, which is immortalised as a great victory in Afghan history to this day.

After subsequent losses on both sides, the British struck a deal in 1880 with the next Amir, Abdur Rahman Khan, who was a grandson of Dost Mohammed and had spent eleven years in exile as the guest of the Russian government. By now, the British had concluded that the most effective way to secure India was to define a clearly demarcated border between India and Afghanistan and to help Abdul Rahman build a robust state with sufficient coercive resources to maintain stability and contain unrest. Although this came at a price, it largely suited both parties for the next forty years. The Amir agreed that Britain would control Afghan foreign relations, that territories on the North-West Frontier already ceded to Britain in the Treaty would remain in British hands,[27] and that Britain could have diplomatic representatives in Kabul. As a concession to the Amir, they were to be Indian Muslims, not British. In exchange, the Amir would receive, as agreed at Gandamak with his predecessor, a yearly subsidy of £60,000, and would have total independence in the management of the internal affairs of his kingdom. Britain also guaranteed to protect Afghanistan's territorial integrity against any foreign aggressors.

During Abdur Rahman's reign, the rest of Afghanistan's frontiers were finalised with British assistance. The Persian–Afghan frontier was agreed in 1891 and the northern frontier with Russia along the line of the Oxus River was finalised in a series of agreements in 1873, 1885 and 1895. In 1893, Sir Mortimer Durand and the Amir also agreed the limits of Afghan territory on India's North-West frontier – along the so called Durand Line – thus giving up historic Afghan claims to Pashtun territory, including the city of Peshawar, in British India.[28] In recognition of the Amir's willingness to enter into these negotiations, the Amir's annual allowance was raised from 12 to 18 *lakh* rupees a year (1.8 million rupees). British funds effectively gave Abdur Rahman the freedom and the finances to impose his rule over Pashtun and non-Pashtun tribes alike within clearly defined Afghan borders.

By the time Abdur Rahman died in 1901, he had left a significant legacy, much of which was achieved through ruthless determination to build the Afghan state, irrespective of the cost to its various peoples. As he explained in his autobiography, 'when I first succeeded to the throne of Kabul, my life was not a bed of roses. Here began my first severe fight against my own relations, my own subjects, my own people.'[29] He destroyed old state structures, which had allowed major urban centres and surrounding regions, such as Kandahar and Herat, to remain virtually independent because they could raise sufficient revenue to finance their own armies. He replaced state governors with men answerable to himself, split provinces into districts and sub-districts to break up local power bases, and when people resisted the extension of central control he used

British weapons and money to help impose his rule by force. He increased the state's revenue base by creating a unified tax system and imposing direct taxation on regions that had not been taxed directly before. He then used the income raised to strengthen the coercive instruments at his disposal – the army and police force – which were in turn used to spy on, torture and kill his opponents. In the course of enforcing his authority, he faced over forty uprisings but tackled each through a divide-and-rule approach – directly suppressing some groups, buying friendship with others and then turning them against his opponents. He also regularly moved populations to other parts of the country to reduce their power base, and exiled powerful individuals and families who challenged his position. Unsurprisingly, he is known in Afghan history as the Iron Amir.

To complement his reforms, he adapted existing social structures to meet his needs. He established a new formal body, the *Loya Jirga*, based on the tribal *Loya Jirga* or Great Council, which had been called by his predecessors to endorse key decisions in a national emergency. His *Loya Jirga*'s role was to approve decisions the Amir chose to present to it, and had a much broader membership, drawn not just from Pashtun leaders, but also from three other distinct groups – the Muhammadzai sardars (tribal commanders from his own Pashtun sub-tribe), village leaders or tribal elders from across the country, and religious representatives. The inclusion of the Muhammadzai sardars in the new *Loya Jirga*, supplemented by cash stipends, effectively neutralised his kinsmen, the one group who enjoyed a strong local power base and potentially had the capacity to challenge his rule. In addition, he co-opted Islam to validate his rule – Sharia courts, for instance, were established in all provinces using procedures he had drawn up personally.

His approach, however, came at a cost. Rule was imposed by coercion, not consent. The resources and power of the state remained in the hands of a narrow elite, which excluded and marginalised competitors rather than co-opting their support. For most people, the state was either oppressive and exploitative, or absent and irrelevant. Although he raised more revenue from taxes on land and trade than any Amir had ever done before and thus reduced his dependence on foreign subsidies, he did not use these resources to invest in the social and economic development of the country. Little was done to develop education or health systems, or to transform the economy from subsistence agriculture to the production of high value, revenue earning, export goods. As a result, while India and Persia were investing in education, infrastructure and communications which transformed their economies in the late nineteenth century, the Amir refused foreign offers to construct railways or telegraph lines, forbade foreign investment, and left Afghanistan's rich mineral resources virtually untouched, believing the country's isolation from the rest of the world would guarantee its security. It was arguably a missed opportunity. As one recent commentator has written, 'Abdur Rahman thus laid the foundation for the country's long-term economic stagnation and poverty, even though in terms of population density and available resources it had a stronger potential for growth than many of its neighbours.'[30]

The Iron Amir had also built a state that could survive while the ruling dynasty maintained absolute control over power and resources, but not one that was sufficiently robust to withstand any serious political challenges. To maintain power, it was easier to crush dissent than accommodate it in a more open political system, but this strategy could become problematic if and when the regime became less repressive. At the same time, although British subsidies only constituted around a fifth of government expenditure on the military and police during the Amir's reign, the proportion of foreign money in the state's budget was to increase substantially in subsequent years. As the costs of running the state expanded in the twentieth century and Afghanistan's own revenue base failed to keep up with demand, reliance on foreign assistance became increasingly important.[31]

The Iron Amir also left a complex legacy with regard to the country's relations with the outside world. The Amir had recognised Afghanistan's geographic vulnerability, delicately poised between the British and Russian empires – or as he put it, 'a goat between two lions, or a grain of wheat between two strong millstones of the grinding mill'[32] – and had opted for a policy of careful neutrality. Of the two, however, he feared the Russians more than the British:

> The Russian policy of aggression is slow and steady, but firm and unchangeable … Their habit of forward movement resembles the habit of an elephant, who examines a spot thoroughly before he places his foot upon it, and when once he puts his weight there is no going back, and no taking another step in a hurry until he has put his full weight on the first foot, and has smashed everything that lies under it.[33]

Set in this context, the 1880 and 1893 Anglo-Afghan agreements made complete sense, giving the Amir the freedom and the resources to impose his will within a defined territory. They would, however, become a source of resentment in later years. The next generation wondered why their foreign relations should be managed by Britain, and resented the fact that the Pashtun-speaking tribes, once part of Ahmed Shah's empire, were now divided by the Durand Line. Their ideas gradually coalesced into the Young Afghan movement with an emphasis on Afghan nationalism and a nationalist identity, above and beyond the differences of tribe, ethnicity, gender or class.

Amir Habibullah, who succeeded his father in 1901, basically continued the same form of government, but with two exceptions. First, he allowed the descendants of Muhammadzai families exiled by his father to return to Afghanistan, and thus allowed some new foreign ideas to permeate Kabul politics. These returning exiles included the Yahya Khels or Musahiban family, who had been living in India and France and were to play a pivotal role in Afghan politics from 1930 to 1978.[34] Secondly, he decided Afghanistan needed an educated elite with the skills to run the expanding number of state institutions. He founded the country's first secondary school, Habiba College, in 1904, and the Royal Military College in 1904–6 under the supervision of a Turkish colonel. This met the immediate needs of the government, but over time a well of resentment began to build up among young, urban, educated Afghans, who increasingly wanted more authority to make decisions about state affairs and did not see why they should continue to be excluded.

Meanwhile, resentment about the British simmered below the surface. Britain may have sorted out the imperatives of empire by making Afghanistan, in effect, a vassal state, but did not fully appreciate the extent to which the Afghans disliked being a 'goat between two lions'. The Anglo-Russian Convention, signed in 1907, underlined the extent to which they were simply a pawn in others' power politics. The two imperial governments agreed that Britain would retain full control over Afghan foreign policy, while Russia would have equal commercial opportunities. Meanwhile Persia was to be divided into northern and south-eastern 'spheres of influence', with the north for Russia, and the south-east for Britain. Habibullah was not consulted about the provisions for Afghanistan, refused to sign it and soon afterwards began to purchase arms from outside the British empire, looking west towards the Ottomans as his natural ally.[35]

Throughout the First World War, however, Habibullah maintained Afghan neutrality in spite of inducements from German diplomats who offered land in India in return for the use of Afghan territory as a springboard for a German invasion of the British empire. Years later, during the Second World War, the British Minister, Sir Giles Squire, was told by the Afghan Prime Minister that when he had been a young man at Habibullah's court, he had asked the Amir why he had not accepted the German offer. Habibullah had replied that he did not think Germany would win and he would not go back on his word to the Viceroy of India to stay neutral.[36]

Independent Afghanistan

On 2 February 1919, Habibullah wrote to the Viceroy of India asking for independence. Eighteen days later, he was assassinated on a hunting trip outside Kabul and was succeeded by his son, Amanullah, the leader of the Young Afghan movement. He swiftly exploited the post-war regional power vacuum – the Russian Revolution and Britain's preoccupation with peace negotiations – and declared independence. The Third Anglo-Afghan War was short-lived, from 3 May to 3 June 1919. Britain swiftly sued for peace and granted independence – there had been little appetite for another protracted conflict so soon after the Armistice in Europe, while nearer to home British troops returning from the front were already being deployed in Ireland to suppress a separate battle for independence. Although this war may have been of limited significance for Britain, in Afghanistan it was hailed as a third great victory by David against Goliath and the combined might of the British army and air force. It produced a war hero too in General Nadir Khan, a member of the previously exiled Yahya Khel family, who would come to prominence in Afghan politics a decade later.

During the 1920s and 30s, British–Afghan relations were re-established on a new footing. In the Anglo-Afghan Treaty of 1921, the two countries agreed to exchange diplomatic relations and Britain was granted the right to buy land for its new mission. They reaffirmed the Durand Line as the border, and under Articles 6 and 7, Afghanistan was permitted the free movement of goods and materials with British India and exemption from customs duties, subject to the right by Britain to stop the transit of munitions to Afghanistan if the Afghan government demonstrated hostile behaviour towards India. Significantly, there was no undertaking by Britain to pay a subsidy or assist Afghan development. This treaty would be examined repeatedly after 1947 when Afghanistan challenged Pakistan's right to inherit the Durand Line from Britain under the terms of this treaty, and Pakistan later challenged Afghanistan's right to move goods and materials freely over the border.

The first British diplomatic representative to Afghanistan since Sir Louis Cavagnari's ill-fated appointment arrived in 1922, and an Afghan diplomat was sent to the new Afghan mission in London. Thenceforth, as a Foreign Office report written in 1949 recounts, 'the policy which His Majesty's Government decided to pursue in Afghanistan was to try to live down the suspicion and hatred engendered in the minds of the people by eighty years of unhappy relations, and at the same time to educate the Afghans to a true appreciation of their obligations to the Indian Frontier'.[37] It was an uphill struggle, however. Even in the late 1940s, when relations with Afghan ministers were fairly close, the Foreign Office was still acutely aware that

this attitude is not shared by the inhabitants, most of whom still harbour resentment against Great Britain for her (to them) unjustified aggression in the Afghan wars. This attitude is more noticeable in the provinces than in Kabul, and is reflected in the coldness, and sometimes even hostility, which has been shown in the past to His Majesty's consular officers in Kandahar and Jalalabad ... Little by little, the unpleasant associations of the past are being forgotten, but in a country like Afghanistan, tradition dies hard.[38]

Meanwhile, Amanullah and his successors sought new friends to counterbalance Soviet and British influence. He specifically cultivated Middle Eastern, Persian and Turkish diplomatic relations, but also sought alliances with Germany, Italy, France and the United States because they either had an anti-British or anti-Russian stance, or sufficiently deep pockets to provide financial assistance. He was also prepared to sign a treaty with the new communist regime in Russia, the Soviet Union, in 1921, guaranteeing subsidies and economic assistance. Whereas his predecessors had purchased arms more or less exclusively from Britain, he now also bought them from the Soviet Union, Italy, Turkey and Germany. Germany was particularly favoured because the country had fought against Britain and the Russians, and had been an ally of Muslim Turkey in the First World War.[39] American interest in Afghanistan's overtures proved lukewarm, but Germany and Italy became important political and economic allies. By August 1924, seventy-two German experts and their families were resident in Afghanistan, the largest number of nationals from any foreign country. By 1938, their number had risen to 270.[40]

The British still tried to retain their influence in this new world, offering loans to purchase weapons and airplanes and funding survey projects for road construction. When these were not accepted, they offered them as gifts, but now the Afghans were in a position to pick and choose. The funds were rarely used, partly because some officials were unaware the money was available, and partly because others knew about them but were reluctant to be beholden to Britain once again.[41]

Amanullah is also remembered for his attempts to modernise the country, influenced by the ideas of a man called Mahmud Tarzi, who had spent many years reviewing the experiences in the Ottoman empire and Europe and then reformulating these in a way that was consistent with Afghan values. Tarzi became the driving force behind the Young Afghan movement, which placed Afghan nationalism above differences defined by tribe and ethnicity, and supported female education and equality between citizens within a constitutional framework. Amanullah's attempts to introduce these reforms into Afghanistan in the 1920s, however, ultimately cost him his throne in 1929.

Amanullah built on his grandfather's work by creating a legal basis for state power through the introduction of the first Afghan constitution in 1923. This established an appointed Council of State or Cabinet, made the *Loya Jirga* the highest representative body in the country, and subordinated the king's authority to the law. He also promulgated written administrative regulations for government departments, ended allowances to the tribes, abolished slavery and forced labour, granted the Hazaras full citizenship and extended some rights to women. In the field of education, he initiated a scheme to send a handful of students from elite families for studies abroad each year, built a primary school in each district, set up the first high school for girls in 1921, and established three secondary schools in Kabul, each funded by a different country – France, Germany and Britain. Ghazni College, the English medium school, was staffed by Indians and opened in 1927.

In order to pay for these initiatives, he tried to transform the Afghan economy and tax system. All taxes now had to be paid in cash, and the level of direct tax on land and livestock was increased. He also opened the country to foreign trade and started projects to shift the economy away from reliance on agriculture to capital-led development, initiating state-led industrialisation to replace imports. To assist with this, he established the first joint-stock companies, instituted full private property in arable land and pasture, and drew up plans to set up a central bank.

Amanullah's reforms, however, while well-meaning, were introduced far too quickly for the vast majority of Afghans who were physically and culturally distant from the narrow political milieu of Kabul life. The reforms also struck at the heart of the Afghan establishment and Afghan society. The Mullahs disliked his policies to restrict the use of religious symbols, such as wearing long beards. The Pashtuns were alienated because he had ended tribal subsidies and interfered with the sanctity of a man's household in his changes to the status of women. The peasants in the north were angry about increased taxes. The rank and file in the army were upset because Amanullah had changed their remuneration from being wholly cash-based to a mixture of cash and payment in kind (free food and shelter), and as a result many ended up with neither sufficient money nor food.

The final straw came when Amanullah returned from a seven-month fundraising tour of the Middle East, Europe and the United States in 1928 and tried to rush through yet more reforms based on his experiences overseas. He had been particularly impressed with his visits to two Muslim countries, Turkey and Persia, where Kemal Ataturk and Reza Shah Pahlavi respectively were transforming their states through a secular reform agenda. He did not appreciate how different the Afghan context was, however, and lacked the skills and patience to negotiate his way through the inevitable opposition any imposed changes would provoke.

A tribal revolt broke out among the Shinwari tribe in the east, which the army lacked the capacity to suppress. In the north, a rebellion led by a Tajik bandit, Habibullah Kalakani – popularly known as the Bacha Saqua or the water carrier's son – swiftly shifted from a mob robbing the rich to give to the poor towards a cause with a political meaning. His men marched towards Kabul and met the royal army three miles outside the capital, just outside the British legation. After intense fighting in late December and early January 1929, Amanullah fled the country through India. The Bacha Saqua then ruled the country for the next nine months.[42]

This period in Afghan history and Britain's role in it is controversial to this day. Many still believe the Bacha Saqua was supported by Britain and received medical help from the legation when he was wounded.[43] Some also believe the British government actually facilitated Amanullah's departure too because they were concerned the country was heading towards anarchy, resented his victory in the Third Anglo-Afghan War, and were concerned about Soviet activities along the border.[44] Britain certainly helped Amanullah's brother to escape, but in other respects tried to tread a neutral path. For instance, during this period T. E. Lawrence, better known as Lawrence of Arabia, was based incognito at the RAF's most forward air base, Miranshah in Waziristan, just ten miles from the Afghan border. When the British Minister, Francis Humphrys, realised that Lawrence's cover was blown and that this was fuelling speculation in the Indian and international press that he was supporting the Shinwari revolt, he requested Lawrence's immediate recall to Britain on 3 January. This was swiftly granted – Lawrence left for Lahore on the 8th, and sailed for England on the 12th.[45] Whatever the case, the hero of the Third Anglo-Afghan War, General Mohammed Nadir Khan, was accorded safe passage through the North-West Frontier and into Afghanistan by the British a few months later, supported by an army of Pashtun tribal *lashkars*. Once he reached Kabul, Nadir Khan captured the Bacha Saqua and had him executed. Nadir Khan then summoned a *Loya Jirga*, which proclaimed him King in October 1929. Thereafter, he was known as Nadir Shah, using the term 'Shah' to distance himself from associations with the former Amir's stronger claim to the throne.

He inherited a number of problems – not least a nascent administrative system, a weak resource base and a demoralised army. On top of these, he also needed to reward the four Frontier tribes who had helped him secure the throne. He made his younger half-brother, Mohammed Hashim Khan, Prime Minister, and swiftly turned to Afghanistan's friends – Germany, France, Italy and Britain – for financial assistance.

Britain alone provided £175,000, plus a gift of 10,000 rifles and accompanying ammunition, which was used to equip the Kabul garrison.[46] William Kerr Fraser-Tytler, who had been based at the British legation during this period, reflected many years later that Nadir Shah did a very good job. 'The combination of the King and his brother produced a well nigh perfect form of benevolent autocracy, which in the state of Afghan society in 1929, was the only possible form of government.'[47]

Once Nadir Shah had sufficient resources, he exempted the four tribes who had helped him claim the throne from military conscription and tax. He introduced a new constitution in 1931, which 'established the kingship in the line of Mohammad Nadir Shah, created a facade of parliamentary government while leaving control in the hands of the royal family, kept the judiciary primarily under the religious leaders, created a semi-socialist economic framework with the principle of free enterprise accepted, and guaranteed theoretical individual equality'.[48] The National Assembly or parliament was to consist of a twenty-plus-member Council of Nobles selected by the King, and a Lower House elected every three years based on male universal suffrage. On paper, the Assembly had wide-ranging powers, including approval of the budget and all new laws, but in practice its role was more symbolic than actual. The government told it how to vote and potential Assembly candidates were screened first. The constitution also stated that every provincial centre should have an elected Provincial Advisory Committee, invited each Ministry to send representatives to the provinces, and required all towns with populations over 18,000 to elect a municipal council. It marked a start in transforming Afghanistan's creaking political and administrative system.

Afghanistan's first steps towards higher education began in Nadir Shah's reign too with the establishment of a Faculty of Medicine in 1932 under French sponsorship. As far as the economy was concerned, however, Nadir Shah did not continue Amanullah's efforts to promote state-led industrialisation to replace the country's dependence on imports. Instead, he protected the peasant economy, and shifted the tax base from land and livestock, which would have alienated rural elites, to the export trade in primary products – karakul lamb skins, fresh and dried fruit, and cotton. To achieve this, the Yahya Khels wooed the merchant classes, and tied them to government-controlled monopolies known as *shirkats*. The government also invested in infrastructure – a new airport, a theatre, and better communications and transport infrastructure.

To support these efforts, Nadir Shah also invited Abdul Majid Zabuli, who had founded the first joint-stock company in Afghanistan in 1924, to help prepare a plan for economic recovery and development. He founded Afghanistan's first national bank, the Bank-i-Milli, and its trading arm, the Ashami company, in the 1930s and remained the major shareholder until the bank was nationalised in 1975. From then on, Afghanistan had a bank that could issue paper currency, provide credit and nurture business talent, and thus no longer had to rely on the arrival of rupees from India or roubles from the Soviet Union on the back of donkeys and camels.[49] In return for chartering the bank, the government demanded an ownership share and later created Da Afghanistan Bank in 1939 as a rival institution.[50]

Nadir Shah's reforms had a long-term impact on incentives to diversify the economy, on the vulnerability of the country to external economic shocks, and on the level of state revenue and expenditure relative to GDP. Between 1945 and 1952, the proportion of state expenditure to GDP in Afghanistan was as low as 3–4 per cent, which was just about sufficient to run a minimal state machinery, but not to make the state visible and relevant to most of the Afghan people through a network of public servants and services.[51] The rapid shift in the revenue base was marked too. In 1931, land and livestock taxes amounted to nearly a third of Afghanistan's total revenue, which was already half their share under Amanullah. By 1953 these taxes constituted just 18 per cent of total domestic revenue, while 40 per cent came from taxes on foreign trade.[52] In 1958, their share had fallen to just 7 per cent. By the 1960s, foreign trade constituted nearly 80 per cent of all taxes. This shift away from land and livestock taxes towards an export-led cash economy meant that between 1945 and 1952 only 3 per cent of GDP was actually extracted from the state, which was incredibly low. By the early 1970s, when Afghanistan was compared with another forty-eight poor countries, the ratio of tax revenues to estimated taxable income was only lower in Nepal.[53]

These reforms solved Nadir Shah's immediate problem – keeping the rural community on board – but were to come at a cost in later years because they did not encourage capital accumulation through the expansion and diversification of productive activities in industry or agriculture. Afghanistan therefore became increasingly vulnerable to shifts in the global prices for primary products, as well as highly dependent on foreign subsidies and ready access to essential imports such as petrol and cotton. At the same time, Afghanistan's elite continued to remain remote from ordinary people. They had little incentive to build state machinery because they were not dependent on internal taxation to replenish state resources. Nadir Shah and his successors had therefore merely diversified their resource base, generating additional revenue from exports to add to irregular foreign subsidies, but done little to build a more robust Afghan state. Abdul Majid was to admit this error publically himself in later years: 'Our greater mistake ... has been to borrow from foreigners more and more without carrying out administrative reforms, without training technicians and specialists, without mobilising our internal resources.[54]

Just three years after seizing the throne and six months after his eldest brother, Aziz Khan, the Afghan Ambassador in Germany, was assassinated by a pro-Amanullah activist in Berlin, Nadir Shah himself was assassinated on 8 November 1933. Unlike previous times in Afghanistan's history, however, when the late king's brothers had often competed for the throne, Nadir Shah's family did the reverse and ensured the continuity of the Yahya Khel dynasty. Nadir Shah's nineteen-year-old son Zahir Shah ascended the throne, his half-brother Hashim Khan stayed on as Prime Minister, and his half-brothers Shah Mahmud Khan and Shah Wali Khan took leading positions in the government and military.[55] The next twenty years in Afghan history is unsurprisingly known as the 'Rule of the Uncles'.

The Rule of the Uncles

Shah Wali Khan was born around 1885, Hashim Khan around 1886 and Mahmud Khan around 1894. All three had spent their formative years and twenties in the military with the rank of general (although none of them had any formal military training), and two had gained administrative experience at a relatively young age as civil and military governors of provinces – Mahmud Khan in Southern Province in September 1919, and Hashim as general of the armed forces in Herat and then as Governor of Jalalabad in 1919 and Governor of Eastern Province in 1920. Although all three had seen military action in the Frontier areas, Shah Wali Khan was perhaps the most successful in the field. He defeated the Bacha Saqua's troops near the British legation on 13 October 1929, thus enabling his brother, Nadir, to claim the throne. In the 1920s and '30s, all three assumed political roles – Hashim as Afghan Minister in Moscow, where he had been deeply suspicious of Soviet intentions towards his country, and then as Prime Minister from 1929; Mahmud as Commander-in-Chief and Minister of War in the 1930s; and Shah Wali Khan as Afghan Minister in London in 1930, and in Paris, off and on, from 1931 to 1946. The three also stood in for each other whenever one was overseas. Shah Wali Khan, for instance, covered for Hashim Khan as Prime Minister when the latter was medically indisposed in 1936.[56] Over time, Shah Wali became the public face of the family, attending major ceremonies at home and abroad while his brothers ran the government.[57]

The brothers were distinctive in other respects too – unlike earlier Afghan ministers and military commanders, they had spent time abroad, both in India and Europe. They variously spoke Russian (Hashim and Mahmud) and French (Shah Wali) fluently, and over time improved their English considerably. Although Shah Wali was perhaps the greatest anglophile of the three – one son was sent to Harrow and another studied at the Guards Staff College – Mahmud's connections with the United States and Britain grew in the 1940s. He sent one son to Harvard, and considered sending his three younger sons to Harrow after he visited his nephew there in 1948.[58]

The five brothers – Hashim, Mahmud and Shah Wali, plus the late Nadir Shah and Aziz Khan – were also closely tied to each other and to Amir Amanullah through marriage. Shah Wali was married to Amir Amanullah's sister, a son married Zahir Shah's daughter in 1950 and another married one of Mahmud's daughters. Hashim's own marriage plan with Amanullah's daughter in 1926, however, was thwarted when Amanullah married her to a cousin. He never married, and instead invested his hopes for the next generation on his two nephews Daud Khan and Naim Khan, the sons of the late Aziz Khan, the only one of the five brothers with whom he shared the same mother.

Daud and Naim Khan were born around 1909 and 1911 respectively and married their cousins, the daughters of Nadir Shah and thus the sisters of Zahir Shah. These two men came to increasing political prominence in the late 1940s, although like their uncles before them they assumed senior positions in the military and in government at relatively young ages. Daud became military commander of Eastern Province when he was about twenty-three in 1932 and civilian governor two years later. In 1935 he was appointed military and civilian governor of Kandahar, which gave him control of most of southern Afghanistan and enabled him to strengthen a Pashtun nationalist identity among local intellectuals and tribesmen.[59] In 1939, his uncle made him Commander of the Central Forces in Kabul in 1939, and then he became Minister for War in 1946. Naim on the other hand, unusually for the family, started his career in foreign affairs, becoming first Director General of Political Affairs and Under-Secretary in the Foreign Office, then Acting Foreign Minister whenever the minister was away. He also had a spell as Afghan Minister in Rome when he was about twenty-two years old. In 1939, he became Minister of Education, then stood in for his uncle Hashim as

Prime Minister when the latter had a serious heart attack in 1943, and became Afghan Minister in London from 1946 to 1948. Daud and Naim Khan were to dominate Afghan politics from the early 1950s until they were assassinated in the palace with many members of their families on 28 April 1978.

Although the royal family controlled just about all the top jobs, there were two other Afghans who played prominent roles in the 1930s and '40s and feature heavily in the correspondence with London. The first was Abdul Majid, the architect of Afghanistan's banking system in the 1930s and economic liberalisation in the 1940s. He was born into a Pashtun merchant family in Zabul around 1902. He had worked in the customs office in Herat initially and then went to Moscow in 1920 to head his father's import-export company and expand its economic activities. When relations soured there, he transferred his operations to Berlin in 1929 and married a German. His role as adviser to Hashim Khan was formalised when he became Minister of Trade in 1938 and then Minister for National Economy in 1939 after the ministry was renamed. Today, he is remembered both as Afghanistan's greatest entrepreneur and, controversially, as the man whose bank squeezed small traders out of the market in the 1930s and whose deal with the American Morrison-Knudsen company in 1946 to transform the Helmand river valley was perhaps a bridge too far, as Chapters Four and Nine will discuss.

The second was the country's Foreign Minister from 1938 to 1953, Ali Mohammed, a Tajik from Badakhshan in northern Afghanistan, who had benefited from Amir Habibullah's education reforms at the turn of the century. He was born around 1891, attended Habibia College in Kabul, and then rose quite quickly in the civil service – from a teacher in 1920 to Inspector of Schools in 1922, Vice Minister of Education in 1924, Afghan Minister in Rome in 1928, Minister of Commerce in 1929, then Minister of Education and Acting Foreign Secretary in the 1930s. From 1933 to 1937 he had been the Afghan Minister in London, and he spoke English fluently before returning to Kabul to become Foreign Minister. He was to become an important player in British–Afghan diplomacy throughout this period.

Hashim Khan played a significant role in Afghan affairs from 1929 until he retired as Prime Minister in 1946. He repressed dissent, revived Abdur Rahman's network of spies and secret police system, built an army sufficiently strong to repress tribal revolts, and carefully nurtured the cult of monarchy around Zahir Shah and his late brother Nadir Shah. By the time he left office, all power was in the hands of the ruling dynasty. A description of Hashim prepared by the British legation provides an insight into how they assessed Hashim's personal and professional style at the time:

> A real patriot and a tremendous worker, he laboured to improve the stability of the country. Insisted on a high standard of efficiency and was high handed with officials who respected and feared him. Trusted very few of his fellow countrymen which made him even more unpopular ... Is personally quiet and dignified though his temper is short and he can be outspoken and ruthless when aroused. His manners are charming – he has a quick sense of humour and an ability to come to quick decisions ... Understands English well and speaks it fairly.[60]

He was also a cautious reformer. He carefully nurtured some of Amanullah's reforms, especially in education, but left the sanctity of male patriarchy within households intact. He also supported entrepreneurs who could help swell the state's coffers through the production and sale of primary products. An example of one of these men was Abdul Aziz Londoni, who was named after his successful import-export trade in karakul skins in Britain after the First World War. He oversaw the draining of an erstwhile marshy malarial swamp in Kunduz in northern Afghanistan and established the Afghan Cotton Company there as part of an initiative to transform primary goods into finished products and thus add to their market value.[61]

Britain's Fortunes Pick Up

Throughout the 1930s, Britain failed to take advantage of potential opportunities to regain their political and economic position in the country. Although the government agreed to a loan of £500,000 when Hashim Khan and the President of the Afghan National Bank, Abdul Majid, visited London in 1937, Britain was slow to respond to other requests. The Afghans turned to Germany, Czechoslovakia and Italy after the British prevaricated for too long. The British government in India also refused to provide a substantial loan to support Afghan efforts to expand irrigation and agricultural productivity along the Helmand river valley. On this occasion, they were unwilling 'to be associated with a venture which might result in Afghanistan competing with India in the world markets', and instead offered to do an economic survey and consider a loan based on the findings. Unfortunately, as the Foreign Office Research Department later realised, 'this decision, while doubtless sound from a purely economic standpoint, ignored the political aspect of such a survey, for the Afghan government shrank from disclosing the details of their revenue and expenditure to a foreigner, and as a result, refused the offer and turned elsewhere for help'.[62] Germany and Japan were only too willing to oblige.

The Second World War was to change Britain's fortunes in Afghanistan dramatically. Initially, the Soviet Union was allied with Germany, and Afghanistan therefore once again posed a potential risk as a staging post from which to launch an assault on British India and Allied interests in the east. Once Hitler turned his guns on the Soviet Union in June 1941, however, and the Soviets switched sides and joined the Allies, the dynamics changed. Britain and the Soviet Union were initially concerned about access to oil and the need for a southern supply route to the Soviet Union since most of Europe was occupied by the Germans. They first focussed on Persia, demanding that the country declare its neutrality and expel all non-diplomatic Axis citizens. When the government was slow to act, British and Soviet forces occupied Persia in August 1941, forced the abdication of Reza Shah and replaced him with his young son.[63] They then turned their attention to Afghanistan and demanded the same of the Afghan government.

Given what had happened in Persia, Hashim Khan decided to comply with their demands and called a *Loya Jirga* in October 1941 to endorse his recommendation, since he knew this would be unpopular and he needed wider buy-in. His appeal was successful, but did little to stem wider Afghan sympathy with the Axis powers because they were anti-British and anti-Soviet and supported the Indian independence movement. Indeed, many Afghans saw Britain and the Soviet Union behaving once again as colonial dictators. So much so, in fact, that Hashim Khan refused to accept half a million pounds from the British government a few weeks later.[64] Meanwhile, Kabul newspapers increasingly featured articles calling for self-determination for Pashtuns on the British side of the Durand Line, which would give Afghanistan direct access to the sea and thus freedom from dependence on transit arrangements with other states.[65]

One of the immediate impacts of the decision was that contact between foreigners and Afghans became severely curtailed. A British visitor to Afghanistan in 1940 recorded one incident. 'Mohammad Aziz of Bangalore and the Lahore School of Art, was employed at the Kabul Art School ... He sold a picture to the Oriental Secretary of the legation, and later called to collect his money. Within half an hour of his return to Yusaf's house [where he stayed], he was rung up, in my presence, by the police and cross examined. He is a British citizen.'[66] Similarly, although the embassy legation offered free medical care to Afghans regardless of their status, many were increasingly deterred from attending. Major Legard, the legation's surgeon, provided an account of the restrictions to London in 1943:

> From July '42, patients reported extra police posted along the roads leading to the legation and were arresting people coming from the direction of the dispensary. The Commander of the Afghan police guard (there are 5 posts around the legation walls, manned by about 50 Afghan police) deny having received orders to prevent people attending. But many extra police have been employed to do this. Rumours that some were flogged, but in all cases, medicines [were] taken from them. By September, the only Afghans attending, apart from legation staff, were the Afghan police guard, their relatives and their friends. As a result, attendance now down to 15–20 daily. But demand is high – any excursions my assistants or I make into the city call forth requests for treatment.[67]

Meanwhile, the Germans and Italians recruited native agents and made contact with tribal groups on the Afghan side of the Durand Line to destabilise the North-West Frontier. Kabul itself became a hot-bed of political intrigue as the government played court to both sides. The German Minister in Kabul offered help to restore part of Ahmed Shah's empire, including Karachi, in return for Afghan help in stirring up trouble for the British among the Frontier tribes.[68] The vulnerability of British India was underlined when Subhas Chandra Bose, the head of the Indian National army who was working with the Axis powers to gain Indian independence by force, escaped from British surveillance and made his way overland to Kabul disguised as a Pashtun. From there, aided by the German and Italian legations, he escaped to Moscow and thence to Berlin.

Towards the end of the war, Squire asked Hashim Khan how he had managed to maintain Afghan neutrality in the face of such huge pressures to join the Axis Powers. He replied that he was a man of his word, just as Habibullah had been in the First World War.[69] Squire also recalled a conversation with the Italian Minister in Kabul:

> I remember the Italian Minister telling me soon after the Italians had changed sides how, after the fall of Crete, he had himself gone to the Prime Minister in an endeavour to persuade him to join the Axis, and had said, 'Your Highness, the Germans have captured Crete. The British, who are supposed to be a naval power, have been quite unable to stand up to the German air force.' The Prime Minister replied, 'Your

Excellency, you tell me that the German air force has captured Crete. Crete I believe is a small island in the Mediterranean. But surely it is England you are fighting. Have you captured England yet?'[70]

Squire remarked ruefully to an audience in London in 1951 that Hashim Khan's commitment to neutrality 'was, of course, of the greatest advantage to us, and I do not think it has ever been generally and adequately recognised'.[71]

The war brought Afghanistan to the United States' attention too. Although they had officially recognised Afghanistan in 1921, they delayed establishing diplomatic relations until 1935. Thereafter, the United States Ambassador in Persia was additionally accorded the status of diplomatic representative in Kabul. A rethink began once the prospect of a combined German and Soviet invasion of the Indian subcontinent reared its head. State Department officials, however, continued to advise against setting up a diplomatic mission in Kabul, drawing on recent experiences in Ethiopia where they had required British help to evacuate their mission after the Italian occupation:

> In view of the fanatical character of the Afghans and the record which the country has for internal disturbances, our officers there would be exposed to far greater dangers than in Ethiopia and their evacuation would be equally difficult. In case of trouble, our legation would be thrown on the British for protection as happened in Ethiopia. That occurrence, it will be recalled, subjected the Department to considerable criticism in and out of Congress. It should be mentioned in this connection that, during the last century, the personnel of two British missions at Kabul were completely annihilated.[72]

In 1942, however, long after the urgent need had passed and the Soviet Union had joined the Allies, and seven years after exchanging diplomatic relations, the United States finally opened a legation in Kabul. Its brief: to secure a potential supply route through Afghanistan to support the Soviet Union and China should the Germans from the west and Japan from the east cut them off.[73] The Afghan government had finally secured American involvement in the country.

Post-War Afghanistan

In the late 1940s, Afghanistan still looked very much as it had done when the British first arrived in the early nineteenth century. 85 per cent of the population still depended on the rural economy and lived in remote rural areas, which were generally inaccessible to any but the most adventurous traveller on horseback or donkey. They continued to do so right up until the Soviet invasion in 1979.[74] At the same time, communications between Afghanistan and its neighbours were still fairly rudimentary. The first motor road over the Hindu Kush joining Kabul with Mazar-i-Sharif in the north, and Kandahar in the south, only opened in 1932. A few other tracks, including the route between Kabul and the Khyber Pass, were motorable in the summer months, but frequently became blocked by snow or mud slides in the winter.

Afghanistan's urban population remained relatively small, confined to the large towns of Kandahar, Herat, Kabul and Mazar-i-Sharif or smaller towns like Jalalabad close to the Khyber Pass. Urban Afghans, however, and especially those from well-to-do homes, now had a chance to get educated and find non-agricultural work. In just twenty years between 1930 and 1950, educational opportunities expanded massively. In 1932, there were only twenty-two schools in the country, teaching 1,350 pupils.[75] By 1950, 5,000 pupils were in secondary and 461 in tertiary education, while between twenty and thirty students from elite families were sent abroad each year to study.[76] From 1947, the urban elite could also send their sons to Kabul University too, which was formed when the Faculty of Medicine was joined with other faculties which had been established in the 1930s and 1940s, each with a foreign sponsor.[77] This was a drop in the ocean, however – only 8 per cent of the overall Afghan population was literate in 1948 and only 10 per cent of school-age girls were in education.[78]

Against this background of slow reform and continuity with the past, however, a number of other forces were simmering below the surface. The war had exposed the fault lines in the Afghan economy. Once the international markets for primary products became severely disrupted, demand for Afghan products fell, contributing to a fall in government revenue by 6.2 per cent between 1935 and 1950. Over the same period, GDP fell by 0.7 per cent, and the price of essential imports – oil and petrol, and manufactured goods, such as capital equipment, armaments and military stores – increased, triggering 20 per cent inflation.[79] At the same time, the removal of the German engineers from Helmand reduced labouring opportunities and halted work on the country's ambitious irrigation scheme, which was intended to raise agricultural production.

The single most important export in the 1930s had been karakul lambskins, which constituted between 40 per cent and 50 per cent of all Afghan exports between 1936 and 1946.[80] In 1939, however, only 29,176 skins were exported to London, one of the chief outlets for karakul, as a result of increases in the cost of shipping insurance, British wartime taxes on luxury items and declining demand.[81] The situation was similar in Afghanistan's other main market, the United States.[82] Abdul Majid reported in April 1947 that the price of karakul lambskins in the United States had fallen from $13–14 a skin in March 1946, to just $9 a year later. Nearly two million skins remained unsold from the 1944/5 market, and the whole of 1946's production was still lying in go-downs.[83] Although some of the foreign exchange shortfall from karakul sales had been made up through increasing exports of fruits and nuts to India during the war to feed the troops – thus providing the rupees needed to buy Indian cotton piece goods – this was insufficient to bridge the gap.

A severe drought in 1946/7 made matters even worse, reducing the grain harvest and increasing prices. In response, the government decided to use more than a third of its dollar balances for the first time to purchase 15,000 tons of foreign wheat, on this occasion from the United States.[84] At the same time, just about all export markets for Afghan products were in freefall. Wool purchased by the government from traders over the previous four years was still lying unsold in the northern provinces, carpets and furs were no longer in high demand internationally, while a post-war fall in the price of pistachio nuts and dried fruit in the Indian market began to have a severe impact on Afghan farmers. Unsurprisingly, by 1947, the government was finding it hard to find sufficient rupees to buy their normal supply of cotton piece goods from India, and they only just managed to find sufficient exchange to pay the first instalment of 1.5 million rupees for arms and equipment from British India in a deal negotiated by Colonel Lancaster in 1946. In May 1947, Squire told London that the government's five- and ten-year development plans were now on hold.[85]

On the political stage, however, the situation was buoyant. Hashim Khan retired as Prime Minister in 1946 following a heart attack, and handed the baton to his brother, Mahmud Khan. In the 1930s and '40s, Hashim Khan's answer to the growing number of Pashtun intellectuals who promoted the Pashtun language and a degree of political reform, had been violent repression. Mahmud, on the other hand, was a known liberal and seemed determined to tread a different path. He soon released some political dissidents from prison and indicated that he was interested in creating space for this new non-royal educated elite in government, albeit on terms dictated by the royal family. The change had an impact on contacts between Afghans and foreigners too. European women married to Afghans were thereafter allowed to go out without being in strict purdah, and women from the British, French and United States missions were allowed to volunteer in Afghan charities.[86]

Attendance at the hospital increased too – in 1947, the medical team saw 8,990 patients and admitted forty-one to the hospital – but this was considerably lower than the 60,000 patients who had passed through its doors in 1941.[87]

Only time would tell if these changes would help Afghanistan navigate a steady course through the challenges ahead – Indian independence and the emerging Cold War on the one hand, and a weak economy and a more vocal opposition on the other.

3

The British Embassy in Kabul

The legation is about three and a half miles from Kabul itself and we are actually in a wall-surrounded compound of about twenty-odd acres, and beyond the wall, we are again encircled by mountains entirely. As you know, I like figures, and this distance is a little over 9000 miles from London, 5600 feet up the mountains, and at the moment, it is 24 degrees below freezing point after a new fall of some five inches of snow ... I can say that Kabul itself is about the most forbidding place I have ever seen and it is set in one of the most remote countries in the world.

Sam Simms, 10 February 1948

Introduction

Kabul became the capital of modern Afghanistan soon after Ahmed Shah's death in the late eighteenth century when his descendants moved there from Kandahar. By the 1940s, it was still relatively small. In the words of the travel writer Robert Byron, who visited Kabul in 1933, it was clustered 'round a few bare rocky hills which rise up abruptly from the verdant plain and act as defences. Snow-covered mountains decorate the distance, the parliament sits in a cornfield, and long avenues shade the town's approaches.'[1]

Kabul was once a walled city with seven gates. Today, only one gate remains but the walls can still be seen in places along the crest of the hills surrounding the city. To the south of the old town, on the right bank of the Kabul River is the Bala Hissar, the historical citadel where Burnes was killed in 1841 and Cavagnari in 1879 in the First and Second Afghan Wars respectively. It is still a prominent landmark.[2] It was once home to Babur, a young descendent of Genghis Khan in search of his fortune, who captured Kabul in 1504 and made it his capital before moving south twenty years later to found the Moghul empire in India. Babur had been drawn to Kabul by its defensive location in a central plateau surrounded

53

by the mountains of the Hindu Kush, its relatively mild climate and fertile soils permitting the production of a wide variety of fruit, vegetables and flowers, and its ready access to passes through the Hindu Kush going north to Central Asia and south to India. After he died near Agra in India, his descendants brought his body back to Kabul in the 1540s and laid it to rest in accordance with his dying wish, in his beloved terraced gardens beside the river. Babur's gardens later became a popular venue for casual walks and picnics for Kabulis and foreigners alike, and still are to this day.

By the end of the nineteenth century, the only visible sign of Britain's presence in Kabul was the small Christian cemetery located at the north-western edge of what was once the British Sherpur cantonment. The cantonment was besieged in 1879 during the Second Anglo-Afghan War, and the cemetery therefore contains memorials to some of the soldiers who died there. The site of the cantonment was later occupied by the Afghan military and is now a residential area. Meanwhile, the Bala Hissar had become a military fortress and the royal family was living in a number of palaces in and around Kabul. Amir Abdur Rahman built several, including the Arg or Palace on the northern bank of the river near the site of the 1830s British cantonment. The moat is gone, but the high walls (three quarters of a mile by half a mile) still enclose extensive grounds. The surrounding area formed the nucleus of Kabul new town which was being laid out in the 1940s. The Arg is now occupied by the present Afghan President and the President's Secretariat offices, while the Dilkusha Palace, which was once used for Ambassadors to present their credentials to the King, is used for state receptions. One of the grandest palaces was later built by his grandson, Amir Amanullah, at Dar-al-Aman as part of a grand scheme to construct a new capital outside the existing town. Here, a huge French-style palace surrounded by fountains and gardens was erected in the 1920s, and alongside it Amanullah built the Kabul Museum with support from French archaeologists to house treasures excavated from different sites across the country. Robert Byron visited Dar-al-Aman and was particularly struck by Amanullah's vision. The palace was 'joined to Kabul by one of the most beautiful avenues in the world, four miles long, dead straight, as broad as the Great West Road, and lined with tall white-stemmed poplars. In front of the poplars run streams confined by grass margins'.[3]

In contrast, the old town was (and is) densely populated, but still benefited, as the *British Gazetteer* noted in 1912, from Kabul's spectacular location. 'The city itself, wedged in as it is between two hills, its confined streets, want of proper drainage and proximity to extensive marshes, would seem to labour under strong disadvantages, but in compensation, it has the benefits of fine atmosphere, excellent water and provisions, with delightful environs.'[4] Although the medieval bazaar of the fabled Silk Road had been destroyed by the British after the First Anglo-Afghan War – as retribution for their defeat at Gandamak – it had soon been replaced by a new bazaar welcoming traders from all over Asia. Kabul was a city of stark contrasts, however – as a British journalist, Andrew Roth, wrote in 1950 – combining a veneer of modernity with a pattern of life that had remained unchanged for centuries:

> It is only in Kabul, the capital and trading centre of Afghanistan, that the twentieth century has left its slight impression. Kabul has a well laid-out modern suburb ... but most of it has the charm – and stench – of an ancient Oriental city. It has a few paved streets, but the rest are a mass of mud in winter and a swirl of dust in summer ... Some piped water is brought in, but most people have to use open water ditches for their drinking water. There is no sewage disposal system. Kabul has one outdated hotel and one cinema showing five to ten year-old pictures, which are interrupted every few minutes while the translation is screened. The eyes of a Kabul carpenter bulge with envy at the sight of a common claw hammer. People tell the time by a cannon which is set off every noon after consulting a sun dial. The mass of the people live in medieval poverty, both in town and country.[5]

Although Kabul had always attracted travellers and traders from across Asia, the first Europeans had only arrived in the early nineteenth century. The British community was one of the largest in the 1940s, but their numbers were still relatively small. These included members of the RAF Training Mission and their families, teachers employed by the British Council to work at Ghazni College, a Mr Sills, who was an adviser to the government's Textile Purchasing Commission, and a handful of British and Indian engineers, who floated between India and Kabul working for a British firm, Associated Consulting Engineers (India). In 1950, when the Foreign Office requested the figures, there were fifty-nine British citizens in Kabul, of which thirty-one were at the embassy (twelve men, ten women and nine children), thirteen at the British Council (five men, five women and three children), and fifteen with the RAF mission and other organisations (seven men, three women and five children).[6]

The number, however, only told part of the story. As a reminder to anyone who dared question Britain's continued imperial stature after Afghan independence in 1919, they only had to look at Britain's diplomatic compound, which was as distinctive from the air as the Amirs' palaces. This vast complex of colonial buildings projected Britain's symbolic power better than any army could have done.

Within its walls, British diplomats and their families lived the lives of English country gentlemen and women, playing tennis and croquet, tending their rose gardens, grooming their horses, sipping afternoon tea with a plentiful supply of cakes, hosting bridge evenings, and entertaining guests at play readings, cocktail receptions and white-tie dinners. Everything about their way of life underlined their physical and cultural separation from the day-to-day lives of ordinary Afghan men and women. There was another way of looking at the British establishment in the 1940s, however. These men and women were very aware that the political situation in Afghanistan was potentially volatile and could blow up in their faces at any time. The first two British missions had been destroyed in the First and Second Anglo-Afghan Wars. Who was to say this could not happen to the third? The current mission had already been caught in the crossfire between the Bacha Saqua's men and Amir Amanullah's forces in 1928/9 and the staff had been evacuated to Peshawar after being under attack for several days. They were therefore willing to take unimaginable risks.

Most of them had also lived and worked in the Indian empire or the Persian Gulf for most, if not all, their professional lives. True, they basked in this English country-house lifestyle, but they had also acquired a very deep knowledge of local politics and culture too. Many spoke the local languages, were interested in how Afghan people lived and what they thought, and were prepared to travel long distances on horseback for weeks at a time to reach remote areas and report back to London what intelligence they had gathered. They knew how to build strong relationships with the elite group of men who controlled Afghan politics from the royal palace, and drink tea with local villagers, and at the same time survive frequent bouts of food poisoning and endless small talk at cocktail parties. Their intensely personal experiences are therefore as much the backdrop to British policy in Afghanistan as the official records in the archives.

The British Legation

Under the terms of the 1921 Anglo-Afghan Treaty, Britain had been accorded the right to purchase land and build a legation headed by a British Minister. When it came to designing it, Lord George Curzon, the Foreign Secretary and a former Viceroy of India, reputedly made it clear that the minister in Kabul should be 'the best housed person in Asia', using the grandeur of the new legation to symbolically replace 'two or more battalions on the Khyber'.[7] It was to leave no doubt in anyone's mind that Britain was still the dominant power in Asia, irrespective of Afghanistan's new legal status as an independent nation.

The first British Minister, Sir Francis Humphrys, took Curzon's instructions to heart and arranged for the purchase of 25 acres of land three miles outside Kabul, using the Mission's Indian Oriental Secretary as intermediary.[8] An architect and a chief engineer came up from Delhi, and just about all the building materials were despatched from Peshawar in traction engines over the Lataban Pass.[9] The site was divided in two, with the hospital compound to the right of the main gates and the main compound with the minister's residence, the 'Big House', and other residences. The two compounds were separated by an internal road with high walls either side, apparently to stop diseases spreading from one side of the compound to the other.[10] Over the course of two to three years, a self-contained settlement was constructed with most of the residences, utilities and offices on the main compound, and the hospital and dispensary on the other.

Everything about the Big House, from its design and location to its extensive gardens and carefully chosen contents, announced in the 1920s that the British were back in business. It was built in the colonial style with white colonnades surrounded by large verandas opening onto extensive lawns and gardens. Many of the fixtures and fittings, including the doorknobs, the engraved cutlery and crockery and the full-size portraits of King George V and Queen Mary, were sent from London.[11] On the ground floor, there was a ballroom complete with a grand piano, a dining room, billiard room and cinema, as well as some private rooms for the minister's family, including a small dining room, a lounge, and a study overlooking the gardens where the minister did all his work. The library was on the first floor and was noted for its unique collection of books about Afghanistan and Central Asia.[12] Along the corridors were seven bedrooms and four bathrooms, and a private room which housed the stenographer's equipment to send ciphers to London.[13] The house also came complete with a resident ghost, reputed to belong to the skeleton found when the swimming pool was built by Squire in the 1940s. Gillian, one of his daughters, recalls it was seen by the doctor, Ronnie Macrae, and the nurse, Armine Sandeman, her tutor (and Armine's sister), Heather, and many of the house servants.

The gardens received equally lavish treatment too. They were originally designed by horticultural experts from Delhi, while the grass seed and many of the plants and shrubs were sent out from Britain. The centrepiece was an ornamental pond – which still exists – fed by a large *jui* or irrigation channel. According to a booklet produced in the 1970s,

> the *jui* in its heyday was a hazard for the unwary, especially after dark. Its victims included the head of an Iron Curtain Mission who disappeared into it while attending a film show in the embassy garden, and, even more dramatically, a Foreign Office inspector who surprised his hosts late one evening by appearing at their front door completely waterlogged and covered with weed, his briefcase disgorging streams of muddy water.[14]

When Robert Byron stayed at the Big House, he concluded that 'the gardens here are too pleasant to leave, full of sweet williams, Canterbury bells, and columbines, planted among the lawns and terraces and shady arbours; it might be England till one notices the purple mountain behind the big white house'. The gardens were prized among the Afghans too. On the morning after the King's birthday party on 3 June, Byron noticed visiting cards from the Minister of Court's gardener attached to the rose bushes and wryly reflected that 'British diplomacy in Kabul just now hangs on the Minister's roses ... Now all the other [Afghan] ministers want cuttings too, and are also in a turmoil over the peonies, which have been promised them for next year.'[15]

Besides the Big House, the two largest residences were occupied by the Military Attaché and the Political Counsellor/First Secretary, while a number of smaller bungalows were built for clerks, complete with gardens and servant quarters. My grandfather wrote regularly about his new home. Soon after he arrived, he acquired a servant, Ghulam Ali, who brought him an 'uncalled for mixture that afternoon' – a pot of tea and a bottle of rum which one of his colleagues had given as a welcoming gift. He also quickly focussed on making one room habitable, using furniture hired from the legation store. By 10 February, the room was furnished with a bed, dressing table, two armchairs, a table in the centre, 'on which I write as now, with a nice cloth on it to match the curtains which Colonel Lancaster has given me, another table by the fireplace on which are my books and a few newspapers from the UK, and a small coffee table on which is perched upon occasion my tea or coffee'. Three months later, he provided more details:

There are three windows looking out in one direction, and in addition, French windows looking out upon the veranda. From each window, I can see nothing but foliage of one kind or another. The only sound is the rustle of leaves when a sudden wind stirs them and the buss of insects becoming more alive as summer approaches.[16]

He had apparently always had his eye on another bungalow, and when that became available later in the year he moved in and then set about decorating it in a somewhat innovative way:

The walls of the new bungalow are plain cream and although I have a few pictures, it's still a bit plain. I found a book of birds, in colour, and I've spent hours cutting them out with a pair of scissors, the silhouette business, and I've stuck odd bits on the wall, so now there are kestrels and woodpeckers perched around. Incidentally, I'm thinking of buying a parrot if I find one with good vivid plumage. At the moment, I'm working out a system of thin wire which is going to be fashioned into a frame for lampshades – then all I have to do is get the cloth and have them covered.[17]

The need for lamps was addressed a few weeks later when Doctor Macrae's wife gave him two just before they left for a private medical practice in Canada. He was also given some curtains by Colonel Lancaster: 'nice plain pale green, which just fits the windows. Also gave me a large curtain for the door, same shade, but I have since found it makes a really nice bedspread – it's the first time I've seen a bed spread with rings on the bottom – had my toe in one of these the other morning and damn near broke my neck getting out of bed.'[18]

Within the compound walls, there was a water tower with a clock (which still exists), and hidden to one side, a sewage system and water-treatment plant, a power house and fuel depot, and garages and stables. The compound also included sports and leisure facilities – four tennis courts, the swimming pool, and a squash court, which was at one end of the Big House. The hospital compound was substantial too. It had been built to provide medical services for legation staff as well as local Afghans to encourage them to accept a large compound, and a British one to boot, in their midst, complete with unveiled women wandering in and out. In 1941 alone, the medical team saw nearly 60,000 Afghan patients.[19]

To run the entire establishment, the legation employed nearly 150 Afghans, sixty of whom maintained the buildings and managed the ancillary services. These included two grooms for the horses; six permanent gardeners, which increased to fourteen in the summer; six in the garage, with a further six responsible for maintaining the vehicles (the legation truck and the minister's two official cars, a Snipe and a Hillman); seven hospital staff; four running the powerhouse; two coolies in the sanitation plant; eight handymen who were responsible for clearing the snow, mixing building materials, working blow-lamps on frozen pipes and supporting camping trips on tours outside Kabul; thirteen messengers and two couriers, who were responsible for delivering papers and messages around the compound and in Kabul; thirteen *chowkidars* (guards) and two watchmen at the hospital; and a total of fifteen pumping the septic tank and acting as firemen and firemen's mates. In the summer, an additional twenty to twenty-five men were employed on a daily rate to do annual repairs.[20]

Practicalities
The compound may have looked magnificent and projected a powerful statement about British prestige in Asia, but it also had its detractors. One

British Minister, Sir Francis Verner Wylie, left nothing to the imagination in his scathing despatch to the Foreign Office in 1943:

> It is unfortunately most violently divorced from its local background. [The impression of] Kabul town ... is one of dirt, dilapidation, slovenliness and extreme poverty ... The British legation by contrast is of a startling white ... There was no need for, and there is as much disadvantage in the British Minister being housed in a fashion which is outrageously out of relation to the architectural background or the capacity in which he resides and to the buildings which house – and for Kabul house adequately – the representatives of a number of other great powers. Granted that our position in Kabul is perhaps a special one. Even so, there was no need to emphasise the fact at any rate in this startling degree.[21]

His successor, Sir Giles Squire, however, thought somewhat differently:

> These buildings, far exceeding in magnificence anything previously dreamed of or yet constructed in Afghanistan, may have been the envy of many Afghan and foreigner alike, but they have certainly enormously enhanced the prestige of the British Minister and the government which he represents. Although Kabul housed three ambassadors, it was an invitation to dine at the British legation which was, and still is, the hallmark of having socially 'arrived'.[22]

There were some practical problems with the compound too. It may have looked splendid, but it had significant design faults. The architect, for one, had not taken into account the differences between the Kabul and Delhi climates, especially the Kabul winters, and had designed all the buildings to face east, as in India. My grandfather refers to the cold several times in his letters. On his first morning, he was greeted by frozen pipes and a bathroom flooded with two inches of frosty water. As a result, he had washed in a 'small tin of hot water in which one hand at a time was inserted'.[23] In preparation for his second Kabul winter, he bought a quilt for his bed and a sheepskin jacket: 'Many nights last winter, I never felt warm at all, the only things that saved the situation were wearing in bed the pyjama jacket plus a shirt, plus a pullover with a leather jerkin on top.'[24]

This design fault was compounded by the fact that the central heating system collapsed irretrievably after Indian independence. The radiators had used coal from India, but when rail communications became disrupted between India and Pakistan after Partition, the supply ceased.

Even in the 1970s, residents reported that the 'bedrooms were so cold that shoes froze to the floor and the sound of blow-lamps being used to thaw out the outside drainpipes became a familiar one in the early morning'.[25] The problem was never fully resolved. A Foreign Office inspector in 1977 found the houses and offices had 'little insulation, the water and waste systems freeze up in winter, the drains become blocked quite often … the single-glazed window frames and poor quality doors let in the winter cold, and they are impossible to heat properly with the mixture of oil stoves, wood fires and electric appliances of various types with which they are supplied'. The report was not very complimentary about the general state of the houses either. 'The houses are substandard and among the worst we have seen anywhere we have visited or served.'[26]

The distance of the legation from Kabul was problematic too, especially in bad weather since the road was unpaved and unlit. My grandfather recounts one memorable journey in April:

> I've just been out of the compound for the third time in the past seven weeks I think – borrowed a bike and rode into Kabul to do a little shopping, bought a half a pound of tea. The last time I went to Kabul it was snowing heavily all the way with wind and driving snow between the mountains and got back to the bungalow some two and a half hours later with toothpaste and very wet clothes. Time before that, it was pouring with rain and I got soaked while the other members of the party stayed put indoors. But I like a storm.[27]

The wolves were another concern. These roamed around at night, especially in the winter when they were driven down from the hills by the cold. James A. Michener, the American writer, morbidly captured the image of these wolves killing a vulnerable old Afghan man on this route in his novel *Caravans*, no doubt based on stories he had heard during his travels in Afghanistan in the late 1950s.[28] Even a decade later, unmarried female staff were expected back by 10 p.m. before the wolves came out.[29]

To cap it all, the legation also experienced the most extraordinary bad luck. No one had anticipated when the land was bought in the 1920s alongside one of the main roads into Kabul that it would become caught up in not one, but two major battles. As the Bacha Saqua's men advanced on Kabul in December 1928, they literally met King Amanullah's army outside the compound. On the 14th, Sir Francis Humphrys, pipe in hand, went out of the gates to secure reassurance that the compound and its residents would not be attacked.[30] In the ensuring battle, however, the legation received several direct hits. On the night of the 17th alone, the Military

Attaché's house was hit and bullets strafed the Big House where all the staff had taken shelter. Over the next ten days, the fighting was more or less relentless. Throughout, as Lady Humphrys recorded in her diary, 'our garden man has continued to drive his two donkeys about our garden each day with complete unconcern, but the day has come when there is only one donkey left'.[31] On the 21st at 5 p.m. she reported 'bullets in squash court, three in bedroom, several in east corridors, many in gallery, three near my bed, three in our bathroom, one missing the Minister by six inches'. By the time it was all over, two Afghan servants, a horse and a donkey had been killed, and four Afghans had been injured. The final tally of shells was sixty-six direct hits on the legation, eleven of which hit the Big House, while the number of bullets was too great to count.[32]

Organising an evacuation was not easy either. In a lull in the fighting on 23 December, Humphrys led the women and children out of the compound at 5.30 in the morning for a 2-mile walk to the Italian legation. From there, they took a vehicle to the airport where Royal Air Force planes stayed on the ground for just twenty minutes and then flew them to Peshawar.[33] The fighting around the compound did not end there, however. Nine months later on 8 October 1929, General Shah Wali Khan led an attack on Kabul to help secure the throne for his elder brother, Nadir Khan. Again, the legation was in the thick of the fighting, this time defended by a number of Afghan staff led by Nazir Rahmat Khan, who tried to prevent the worst of the looting.[34] After being warned by the general that the fighting was about to start, he gathered all the *chowkidars* and the guards together, and assigned three of them to stay in a tent outside the Oriental Secretary's house. During the subsequent fighting, some people broke into this house to loot it, and three of the guards died trying to stop them. On 10 October, a group tried to take away the horses. The guards killed three of the raiding party and then at 11 p.m. the same night, a party of forty Wazir tribesmen broke in. Rahmat recounted, 'I persuaded them not to loot it by killing sheep and entertaining them.'[35]

The British community moved back into the legation a few months later, but never quite forgot these experiences.[36] Meanwhile, the contingency plans for future evacuations were only updated after Indian independence – prompted by the realisation that if the trigger was unrest between Afghanistan and Pakistan, then an escape plan through Peshawar or Quetta might be unviable. Unfortunately, the only alternative was via Persia, but the distance was too great for a round trip without refuelling. Kabul lacked sufficient stocks, and so the Air Ministry in London started to explore whether aviation fuel supplies could be kept in Kabul or Kandahar for emergencies.[37]

The Residents

Up to Indian independence, the legation was staffed by a mixture of British, Indian, Anglo-Indian and Afghan staff, mirroring the way in which other government offices were run across the Indian empire. The core team comprised the Minister, Military Attaché, Doctor, Political Counsellor, First Secretary, Oriental Secretary and Commercial Secretary. Three of these posts – the Political Counsellor, the Oriental Secretary and the Commercial Secretary – were filled by Indian Muslims. In addition, there were a further nineteen British, Indian or Anglo-Indian office staff, including the Military Attaché's clerks (my grandfather's and Ray Brooks' positions), an archivist, two interpreters, and a number of stenographers and cipher clerks. The legation also ran consular offices in Kandahar and Jalalabad, which were managed by Indian Muslims. Many of the Indian Muslim staff left to join Pakistan at Independence, including the Political Counsellor, Oriental Secretary and Commercial Secretary, as well as the two Consuls. In spite of this, the legation was still responsible for sixty official and unofficial Pakistani staff in 1950.[38]

A high proportion of the British staff had served as colonial political or military officers in the Indian empire or Persian Gulf, and their wives and families had invariably accompanied them. Some of the older members of the legation had seen action in the First World War, while others had recently been demobbed from the Second and were keen to return to normal life again. They spoke a number of the local languages in Afghanistan fluently and were as much at ease sitting on the ground drinking tea with Afghan villagers in remote valleys or riding through the North-West Frontier as they were conversing in Dari with the Afghan King and his ministers at court.

The head of the mission for most of this period was Sir Giles Squire. He had first arrived in Kabul in 1943 after seven years in Persia, first as Consul-General at Mershed for five years, and then as Political Counsellor in Teheran for two. At an earlier stage in his career, he served in Balochistan in British India. Soon after he arrived in Kabul, he was joined by his wife, Lady Irene Squire, a former teacher, whom he had first courted in Hyderabad and married in Bombay. At different points during their stay in Kabul, they were accompanied by their daughters, Hazel, Kristen and Gillian, and Gillian's teacher, Heather Sandeman. As a reward for his services, he received a knighthood in 1946 from the Viceroy of India, Field Marshal Viscount Wavell, in Delhi. He had been due to leave Kabul in 1947, but was asked to stay on until 1949 to provide continuity to help manage the transition after Indian independence.

Squire's experiences during the First World War had a profound impact on his life. He had spent a year at Oxford studying Classics before joining up, and was seriously wounded at Gallipoli by a bullet close to his heart, which seriously impaired his breathing in later life. Once Squire recovered sufficiently he was sent back to the front, this time to Persia, which changed the course of his professional life. He fell in love with the country and its people, and once the war was over switched his degree to study Persian at Christ Church, Oxford. By the time he arrived in Kabul, he could also understand Pashtu, Hindi, Urdu and Russian, and according to his daughter, Gillian, a further five non-Asian languages too. His fluency in Persian stood him in good stead in Kabul.

To those who knew him, Squire was 'a typical man of the Manse', a devout Christian imbued the values of his religious upbringing, with a fairly traditional and conservative view of how things should be done.[39] Sir Olaf Caroe, who who met Squire many times while he was Governor of the North-West Frontier Province, described him as:

> The type of civil servant that leaves a deeper mark on affairs than his seniors or even his compeers suspect, and wins the affection of his juniors by fairness and an equitable temperament. A typical son of the Rectory, he was noticeably quiet and unassuming in manner, but concealed behind a modest exterior a firmness and sincerity of purpose that revealed itself to all who knew him ... He refrained from saying more than he meant or meaning more than he said. As a companion, he was always gentle and kindly and – a little unexpectedly – a most redoubtable opponent on the tennis court.[40]

My grandfather provides a hint of the man behind the formal exterior too. On his first Friday in Kabul, 'Lady Squire asked me to tea at 5 o'clock if possible, to which I replied I would be happy to accept. Thus have spent two hours at tea this evening and have talked most of the time. Sir Giles was interested in places I've been because he wants to settle somewhere. He is also interested in poking quiet and indirect fun at the expense of Bevin and company'.[41] Clearly, he was not a Labour government supporter either.

With his fluency in Persian, Squire was able to build personal relationships with some of the most influential men in Afghanistan, including Hashim and Mahmud Khan. Indeed, Hashim Khan once told Caroe 'how steady and reliable Squire's advice had always been on occasions of difficulty'.[42] Both brothers used to invite Squire and his family to their homes and gardens at Paghman, Amanullah's hill station outside Kabul, although as Hazel, Squire's daughter, recalls, they never met the women. His closest friendship was with the Foreign Minister, Ali Mohammed, a fluent English speaker who enjoyed reading English literature. Gillian and Hazel recall that Ali Mohammed regularly came over to the legation to play bridge with their father, and that he once brought Gillian a present, a model motorboat to sail in the ornamental pond at the back of the Big House.

Squire's daughters describe another side of his character too, that of a kind caring man with a deep sense of duty and compassion. When the Soviet Union occupied eastern Europe after the war, Squire helped a Czech family in Kabul to get passports to go to Canada, and he personally hired a man from the Polish embassy, Bruno Talatski, to help keep the legation gardens under control, paying him a salary from his own pocket. When Squire finally left Kabul in September 1949, Talatski and his wife left too, and Squire gave him half the money he needed to buy a farm in Zimbabwe (then Rhodesia). A few years later, Squire bought a farm nearby and called it 'Asmania', the name of the mountain behind the legation.

Other members of the legation had long associations with British India and the North-West Frontier too. Doctor Ronnie Macrae was an Indian Army Medical Officer, and the Second Secretary (Oriental), Donald Jackson, and Second Secretary, Patrick Keen, came from the Indian Political Service. Keen's personal profile was fairly typical. He was born in Simla, the son of an Indian Army general, and had lived and worked on the North-West Frontier since the 1920s. He had spoken Urdu since childhood, learnt Pashtu from his bearer (house servant), and then learnt Dari while he was posted to the legation in Kabul in 1938.[43] After war service in India and Persia, he returned to Kabul in 1948, where his fluent language skills were to prove invaluable as subsequent events would show.

Squire's replacement in late 1949 was a very different man altogether, however. Sir John Gardener was a permanent foreign service officer through and through.[44] He arrived in Kabul on 3 September, just months after receiving a Knighthood and fresh from his post as head of the Foreign Office's Establishment Department in London. He was therefore more familiar with Britain's diplomatic mission in Kabul as a costly drain on the public purse than as an outpost of empire. He too had served in the First World War, while most of his subsequent work had been with the Levant Consular Service working in North Africa and the Middle East and Persia, where he became fluent in Persian.

The two men my grandfather worked most closely with, though, were Lieutenant Colonel Alexander Stalker Lancaster, and Lancaster's replacement, Acting Lieutenant Colonel John Hume Prendergast. Both were former Indian Army officers, and it was their reporting, alongside Squire's and Gardener's, that provided the bedrock of the political analysis sent to London during this period, a carry-over from the days of the Raj. In spite of several remonstrances from the Foreign Office, this responsibility was not transferred to the Political Counsellor until 1950.

Lancaster's knowledge of Afghanistan and the Afghans was exceptional. He had lived and worked as Military Attaché in Kabul since December 1935, save for a short break in 1938 at the end of his first posting. By the time he left Kabul at the age of fifty-six, he had visited most of the country – some of which had never encountered a Britisher before – and had compiled a detailed ethnography of Afghanistan's tribes and ethnic groups right down to the level of sub-tribal affiliations and kinship relationships. He had also researched the country's military history thoroughly, including producing a detailed assessment of its military assets and capability, and developed a copious knowledge of the country's economy and political system.[45] There are a couple of descriptions of him from his time at the legation that give some idea of the kind of man he was. In August 1941, the then British Minister, Sir W. Kerr Fraser-Tytler, recommended him for a CBE, describing him as

> a peculiar fellow with a personality which possibly does not attract people on first acquaintance. But his work here has been of great value, his knowledge of the country and of the people, his patience in dealing with them and his influence with the senior members of the military staff, and above all, his very shrewd judgement of the trend of events has been remarkable.

A later report by Squire in May 1946 underlined the quality of his relationships with senior members of the Afghan military, aided no doubt by his fluent Dari. 'His knowledge of the country and its people is encyclopaedic. By tact and patience, he has established such a special position for himself as friend and unofficial adviser to the Afghan Ministry of War[46] that it would be very difficult to do without him.'[47] In fact, when Daud Khan, the Minister, heard he was about to leave, he personally asked if Lancaster could stay for a further two years.[48] Lancaster kept in touch with his Afghan friends for years afterwards, and some of those prized letters are now among his papers in the National Army Museum in London. One letter, sent in April 1954 by the then Minister of War, General Mohammed Arif, speaks volumes:

> You would undoubtedly believe that since you left Afghanistan, I've always remembered you and your happy days in this country and most particularly our trip to India and Burma. I am always asking after your health and well being from those who are coming from your end and more especially from British Military Attachés in Kabul ... I would feel very

delighted if you could possibly extend your travel and pay a visit to the old shooting and fishing haunts in this country and renew old friendships.[49]

Squire's daughters remember their father and others calling him the 'Duke' because he had a nose shaped like the Duke of Wellington's. They also thought he drank rather a lot because his nose had gone red, and described him as a 'crusty old bachelor' because as teenagers they found him a little difficult to talk to.

Lancaster and my grandfather seem to have got on rather well, at least socially. During a dinner together in May 1948:

> He [Lancaster] told me that one of his best laughs had been a few weeks previously when the Minister [Squire] was talking about the wolves in the Afghan winter, when I had said 'Wolves, I'm very interested in those, they're the chaps I've been trying to keep from my door for years'. He also recalled the time when a lady was in the course of introductions to me and she said 'Oh, you are army' with a slight raising of tone and eyebrow, and I said, 'Yes, Madam, army! I'm really a very fortunate person in as much that if I do manage to deport myself creditably, everyone will be suitably astonished or if I do happen to be downright vulgar, no-one will be prompted to notice because they won't really expect anything better.' Anyhow, a good evening and he knows very well I don't mind that kind of a 'do'.[50]

At work, however, it was a different matter. The colonel supported some of my grandfather's recommendations: 'At the tail end of my chat with Colonel Lancaster, I fetched in young Ray Brooks and told the old man that he should at least be given the rank of sergeant. Lancaster agreed and the recommendation is now on its way to town.'[51] In other respects, however, he was dissatisfied. 'Now that I've sorted out the filing system etc and the position is clearer in the office, I am convinced that all that is needed is a good copy typist with a good memory for papers and files. So you will see that I am not very satisfied.'[52]

Lancaster's replacement, Colonel Prendergast, arrived with his family in September 1948 and seemed a good fit. He was born in Lahore to a major-general in the Indian army, and an uncle, Captain George Hume, had actually marched to Kabul during the Third Anglo-Afghan War.[53] By the time Prendergast arrived at the embassy, he was just about to turn thirty-eight and had a distinguished military career behind him, including years of service on the North-West Frontier. While he may not have climbed as high up the ranks as his father, his bravery in the face of danger was remarkable. He was awarded his first Military Cross in 1937 for a successful assault on a group of tribesmen in North Waziristan. Three years later, he received a Bar on his Military Cross for bravery in Norway.[54] After that, he returned to India and became an instructor in mountain warfare in Poona in India. By 1941, however, he was back on the front line and in 1942–3 took part in the Arakan campaign on the Burmese border, later taking part in the advance on Mandalay. For his services in the final stages of the Burma Campaign, he was awarded the Distinguished Service Order.[55]

By January 1947, Prendergast was at the Staff College at Quetta on a one-year course to prepare him for promotion. As he later reflected:

After my return from Burma, I faced up to the fact that in order to prosper in the army, any army, I must go to the Staff College to become what is termed an 'educated officer'. It was the military eleven plus and no amount of command fighting in war would take its place in peace time, and although I had been forged in intense heat, I lacked the stamp on the yet white hot metal.[56]

The course ended suddenly at Indian independence and Prendergast found himself helping to police Quetta in the midst of communal riots. He managed to help his Christian *ayah* (children's nanny) and his Hindu gardener and sweeper to escape to India, and waited anxiously as his Muslim cook, Moosa, first waited for his sons to arrive from Delhi and then tried, and failed, to return home to Kashmir as the fighting escalated there. By November, Prendergast was on a ship sailing to Britain and about to face a new career in the British army away from his beloved India. A few months later however, he unexpectedly found himself put forward for the post of Military Attaché in Kabul and leapt at the opportunity of returning to the Sub-Continent. Their former Ayah met them at Bombay and Moosa at Karachi, and then he set off for Kabul in his own car with family and servants in tow, arriving much earlier than expected and in full military uniform. Lancaster hurriedly advised him that wearing his uniform like that would not go down at all well with the Afghans.[57]

My grandfather soon welcomed the change. Prendergast had clearly benefitted from his Staff College training as he brought more rigour to the office and paid attention to staff development. By late September, he was writing home confidently: 'I am much relieved by the change ... new avenues are opening up to me, with more and more work and added responsibility.'[58] He decided it was worth staying on in Afghanistan a little longer rather than ask the War Office for another post. Squire, however, had some concerns about Prendergast's suitability for the post because he had limited desk experience, while Gardener and Prendergast did not get on at all.[59] Prendergast provides a damning account of Gardener in his autobiography, ranging from his apparently ill-judged arrival speech – he upset the Afghan Chef de Protocol with his 'torrent of Persian ... which fell like a dead balloon' – to the way he was viewed by the embassy:

> This undistinguished little man was to be our head. I cannot recall anything particular about the two years of his ambassadorship, except that he was unpopular with his staff and always tetchy. My masters at the War Office and I did not have much to do with him. He was so undistinguished that it was difficult not to overshadow him at parties and he had the unfortunate habit of getting slightly tipsy and showing it.[60]

Prendergast himself found Lancaster a difficult act to follow and initially felt very much in his shadow:

> I found the 'Duke' a fussy little bachelor, held in much awe by the officers of the embassy. He had certainly achieved much. He had ... gained the confidence of the Afghan leaders who were intensely suspicious – an almost impossible feat. He did this by playing endless bridge with them, and through the years had pieced together little tit-bits of information. I felt inadequate, for I have never been keen on that smoke-clouded, sedentary game. Besides this, he was great friends with the Turkish Military Mission, bridge players all, who were training the army, and was able through them to work out the detailed structure of the armed forces ... After years of this atmosphere, Lancaster had become as secretive as the Afghans and suspected every member of staff of indiscretion: indiscretion about what? I was to ask myself later. It must have been a terrible wrench for him to leave Kabul ... although by then he had obviously been there far too long.[61]

Within a few weeks, however, Prendergast felt more confident. He had carved out his own place, focussing on improving the lot of the men in the RAF training mission in Kabul, and using his love of fishing as an entry point into the inner sanctums of the palace.

Work and Play during an 'English Country House Weekend'

The lifestyle of the diplomatic community in Kabul was at once stifling and insular, and fun and adventurous. Their day-to-day activities were also under the spotlight of the Afghan government, which kept a close eye on what foreigners did, monitoring their telephone lines through an exchange in the Ministry of Foreign Affairs, restricting links with junior Afghan officials, and requiring prior permission and a police escort for all visits out of Kabul – ostensibly to protect diplomats from would-be attackers.

A British embassy booklet produced in the 1970s describes the peculiarities of this distinctly English scene: 'The history of the compound is a very English one. It depicts a curious and almost permanent atmosphere of an English country house weekend, with time for gardening, cricket, and above all parties, despite the obvious privations of a small community in an isolated post.'[62] The daily life of legation residents combined office work, formal diplomatic occasions and strong codes of social behaviour (much of which had been imported from Britain), with an array of parties, tennis matches, horse riding, skiing, film nights, amateur dramatics and lots of drinking, livened up by the odd romance – my grandfather's colleague, Ray Brooks, was briefly smitten by Squire's daughter, Kristen. They worked five and a half days a week with Wednesday afternoons and every Friday off. Although Sunday was a working day, their religious needs were not neglected – a Christian minister came from Peshawar once a month.

At times, and especially for the more senior members of the mission, the constant whirl of socialising was as much about work as pleasure. These events were often the closest the diplomatic community came to meeting Afghan ministers in a more relaxed context, while many social occasions at other diplomatic missions were simply extensions of the day job. Mitchell Carse's four-day official visit from Peshawar in August 1949 provides an insight into what was involved. During lunch in the Big House, he met the Afghan Ambassador to Delhi, Najibullah Khan. Later the same day, he met the Pakistani Ambassador, Ibrahim Ismail Chundrigar, and members of his staff at a tennis party at the Pakistan embassy, and at supper he met the Counsellor and Military Attaché from the Indian embassy. The following day he met the Afghan Prime Minister, Foreign Minister and the Minister of Court, as well as other members of the diplomatic community – although not the Pakistan Ambassador – at an exhibition of Indian Art.[63]

Even film nights at the legation – on the lawn in summer, and in the Big House during winter – combined entertainment with politics. Residents were shown the film on the first night, the diplomatic community on the second, and Afghan ministers and officials on the third. The films were sent up from India and included patriotic stalwarts like *Henry V* and *Caesar and Cleopatra*, or wartime movies such as *This Happy Breed* and *Theirs Is the Glory*. Not all film nights were a huge success, however. Squire's daughter, Gillian, recalls at least one occasion when a British comedy did not translate well in an Asian context – Afghan ministers found it difficult to understand the comedy in Noel Coward's *Blythe Spirit*, about a man with two wives, one dead and one alive, given that polygamy was so common in Afghanistan. The plot simply did not make sense.

One of the most politically significant events in the life of this legation happened on Tuesday 25 May 1948 when it was upgraded to embassy status. Squire was transformed overnight from minister to ambassador after a lavish ceremony at the Dilkusha Palace replete with ritual and Afghan 'informality'. At 10.15 a.m. sharp, Squire and the other senior members of the legation were collected by the Afghan Chef-du-Protocol, and then driven in two government cars to the palace. When they arrived, Squire inspected the Guard of Honour, and was then escorted by the Minister of Court at 11 a.m. to the Audience Chamber where the King was standing with the Foreign Minister. Squire presented his credentials as incoming Ambassador and read out his prepared speech. The King gave a formal reply, they shook hands, and then Squire sat down with the King, Foreign Minister and Minister of Court for a longer, private conversation in Dari – during which the King revealed he was keen to find out if Squire had caught any trout during his recent visit to Mazar-i-Sharif. The formal part of the day ended with a wreath-laying ceremony at the mausoleum for King Nadir Shah. After that, Squire and his team returned to the newly upgraded embassy to be greeted by all the staff.[64] My grandfather picks up the story. 'About midday, I went along to the Big House (had to pack up all the files and all the rubbish) to shake hands and congratulate him.' Later that day, Squire hosted a tennis tournament.[65]

It was the kind of life you either took to, dipped in and out of, or disliked intensely. Lady Squire laid on tennis tea parties whenever there was a tournament against other embassies. If the weather was bad the tennis courts were turned over to deck quoits and in the winter to an ice rink, while the children used to toboggan down the slope towards the pool.[66] My grandfather spent many of his leisure hours on those courts. The more adventurous climbed the mountains behind the mission and skied down them in winter. Patrick Keen recalled that 'one year I was actually on my skis, at least for a short period, every day from December 7th until March the 17th'.[67] Hazel remembers bringing two cocktail dresses to Kabul when she visited for three months in 1946. She had thought them terribly grand, but after more than sixty events, the novelty of dressing up had considerably worn off.

Those who were confident around horses also went riding before breakfast on Seistan (Squire's black stallion), Bamyan (Lancaster's horse), or Snowball, Dunne and Chestnut. The most adventurous riders were the Squire family, Macrae and Lancaster. They went every summer on trips lasting anything between two days and three weeks, accompanied by Afghan servants, who erected the tents, tended the horses and cooked the meals. Some trips were pretty arduous. When Lancaster toured north-east Afghanistan with Macrae between 4 and 23 June in 1948, for instance, they took five hours to cover the first 71.5 miles by car, and then rode between 12 and 26 miles a day, accompanied by eight armed, mounted police and fourteen baggage ponies.[68] In his report for Military Intelligence in London, he interspersed information about local conditions with a rambling account of the various ponies and donkeys hired along the route, especially those that the police and baggage handlers could not control.

These trips often combined a holiday with a spot of intelligence-gathering. Lancaster's aim on that particular occasion had been to explore whether Soviet troops could move over the Hindu Kush through previously unexplored passes. He also included 'the prospect of some brown trout fishing in the rivers north of the Hindu Kush and a hint from the former Prime Minister, HRH Muhammad Hashim Khan, that I should carry out a tour in northern Afghanistan in order to assess the affect [*sic*] Russian propaganda is having on the inhabitants'. One of Prendergast's journeys was 'to get near the Oxus at the end of the month under the guise of being a fanatical trout fisherman and shot, which is not far from the truth'.[69] Prendergast's children were taught at an early age how to be intelligence agents too – John Prendergast recalls being taught how to use his fishing rod to calculate the width of a bridge.

Others, like my grandfather, spent most of their time in Kabul. Many of his letters provide an insight into how he and others felt about life on an endless 'country house weekend'. He did a deal with Squire's daughter Kristen, a talented musician, to 'play the piano at a fixed time with the window open so that I could listen to it from my bungalow – so I've heard echoing over trees and bushes bits of Chopin and Mozart and others. I know the idea was received so well because it was something new – as she said, it is quite unique'. He also loved the tennis, playing at every opportunity after work in the summer and on Fridays and Wednesdays in the winter when the weather was good. He loved his daily routine, 'getting back around five o'clock, having a bath, hot or cold, cleaning up oneself generally, changing into flannels and sports jacket, lighting the fire, and a time spent anticipating a pot of tea, and of course, plenty of reading, writing these letters and receiving them each week'.[70] My grandmother also got into the habit of sending the *Daily Express* to him regularly and he used to cycle to Dilbar cafe in Kabul on Sundays after work to read the *Sunday Express* even though it was often six weeks old. As he explained, 'I can assure you that the date is not important. The pleasure in being confronted with a pile of unread papers is something very real and I think not widely understood by many who have not found themselves in like positions.'[71]

There were periods when he loved the social whirl of drinks and receptions too:

8 April 1948, round of parties – just left a tea party given by the Head of Chancery for the christening of their daughter. Tea party tomorrow, Friday, at the Ambassador's. Next Wednesday, the Russians have a party. Just now, one of the Foreign Office blokes came round with a bottle of sherry and said 'I'm thirty-one today' so I drank the bottle with him. To the Persian legation 'do' the other Sunday and escaped within three hours.[72]

At other times, however, he chose to shut himself away. 'Have been very busy lately avoiding the confounded parties – Ambassador's picnic last Sunday, dodged that – two lunches during the week – went the same way – three evening affairs – tonight, tomorrow, Sunday – America, India, Pakistan – dodged the lot. I've had enough.'[73] He was certainly not the only one who felt this way at times. After finishing work one Friday afternoon in April, he had felt 'as free as the air to do what I like as long as I don't want to do anything. On that topic, the cypher fellow came into my room the other night, followed by his dog as usual, and he said that about the only bit of pleasure he found in this place was that dog. So I said, "What about me? I haven't even got a dog."'[74]

Life was not without its health challenges either. Food poisoning was a common occurrence, while a mild illness could easily escalate into something more serious. My grandfather managed to see the humorous side of at least one of his health adventures:

I was at the Russian party and after four hours of an excellent propaganda film it was time to eat. By this time, I'm feeling very groggy and what makes it worse is I know what is wrong. Anyway, when in doubt, have a drink, so I have a couple of brandies and later a vodka – only I knew why I had them mixed with water or soda. Had one or two more brandies and escaped as soon as I could, and on the way back was glad to think I had some candles knowing well that sleep would not be a good thing even if that were possible – I rather knew it wouldn't be. So I sat down and read and waited for the pain, and it came in very good style, and at intervals I'm doubled up and stretched out ... so I get over to the cupboard and have a swig of a drop of Booths that's got to last about six weeks.[75]

There was one advantage to being ill, however – it relieved him of 'five of these beastly parties'. By August, he had worked out why he kept getting sick. He put it down to the tinned milk. 'So since the last bout, I'm taking tea without milk and finding it far more pleasant too, and have also discovered why the Russians have become such an awkward lot of people – it's because they can't get lemons to put in their tea which explains the whole thing.'[76] As for Ray Brooks, he seemed to 'wind his way through the medicinal dictionary' and was more or less constantly ill from the outset. My grandfather reported two incidents when Brooks literally keeled over suddenly at the office, and in November 1948 alone, he had a 'combination of sand-fly fever, jaundice and pleurisy'.[77] Given this track record, Brooks was no doubt relieved to leave Kabul after only a year.

There was another side to this community too. It lived by a set of social mores in which deviance was difficult to tolerate. When Brooks' successor as clerk to the Military Attaché, one Lance Corporal Redshaw, got Patrick Keen's nanny pregnant in 1949, both were sent packing.[78] The biggest scandal during this period, however, involved Dr Macrae's replacement, Colonel Harrington. Squire had arranged for the new nurse, Armine Sandeman, to stay with Dr Harrington and his sister when they arrived in late 1948. Unfortunately, Harrington's 'sister' turned out to be his lover, a Mrs Hancock, who had left her husband to accompany him. Armine therefore stayed in the Big House while Squire told Mrs Hancock to leave. This she promptly did, but only as far as Kabul where she moved in with a family, the Blyths, and then continued to visit the embassy daily. Matters were made worse by Harrington's difficult character. According to Squire, he was 'a rather unpleasant man with a bad temper which is not improved by his having been unable to get away with his plan. What will be the outcome we do not know, but it has certainly been a most unpleasant episode which is by no means yet at an end.'[79]

The Foreign Office soon advised Squire that Harrington could be sacked. The final straw came after Harrington's unreliability and his violent temper finally trumped his professionalism as a doctor. When three babies were born in the hospital, 'the last with only Armine in attendance, Harrington having gone off in a vile temper to the town … and not getting back until after midnight when it was all over,' it was time to settle the matter once and for all, especially as 'in a small place like Kabul, his unpleasantness has loomed unduly large'.[80] His contract was terminated on 21 March, less than four months after he had arrived. Thereafter, his role was taken over by the assistant surgeon, Khan Sahib Barkat Ali, a long-serving member of the hospital team who had previously split his medical work with commercial duties, backed up by support from a French doctor, Madame Boulenger, for more serious cases.

This, then, provides the context within which Squire and his team tried to interpret Afghan policy, relay their assessments back to London, Delhi and Islamabad, and communicate British policy to the Afghans. It was an incredibly insular existence, permeated by British values, lifestyles and behaviours. At the same time however, and in spite of the Afghan government's efforts to control foreign access to information, these two rather isolated communities found a way to communicate with and respect each other, spend some leisure time together and to become friends. Each in their different ways tried to understand the 'other' and to find common ground so that they could navigate a steady course through the rocky weeks and months ahead following Indian Independence.

4

Afghanistan in Transition

Although the 1931 Constitution provides theoretically for a parliamentary government, the Government of Afghanistan has in fact been exercised by the ruling clan, the Yahya Khel. These have ruled harshly, venally but, until recently, with reasonable effect ... However, even the people of remote Afghanistan are beginning to doubt whether they should fatalistically accept the possession of power and wealth as the birthright of the few ... The established regime is narrowly balanced, and its stability depends largely on its wisdom and strength in dealing with internal security, economic development and democratic reforms.

British embassy briefing note, 1951[1]

Introduction

By the time my grandfather arrived in Afghanistan, the country was just beginning to experience its first taste of political reform since the 1920s. Hashim Khan, the Prime Minister since 1929, had resigned in 1946 and handed over to his more liberal younger brother, Mahmud Khan. Change was in the air, but the jury was out as to whether this would put the country on a more stable and prosperous footing, or simply expose the underlying fault lines in the Afghan state, which had thwarted the previous reformer, Amir Amanullah, in the 1920s.

From the outset, Mahmud confronted challenges on just about every front. At home, Afghanistan was in the midst of a protracted economic recession, which increased the price of food and essential imported goods such as petrol, and had a knock-on effect on government revenue. He also had to assess the extent to which political reforms demanded by the next generation of Afghans were viable in the Afghan context. There were a number of choices. The ranged from giving Afghanistan's small, educated middle class entry to the previously closed political elite within and around the palace, to introducing some democratic processes such as free elections and an uncensored media, and even allowing opposition parties to evolve. Each came with risks, and had an added edge during this period too. Within the royal family, the next generation, Mahmud's nephews Daud and Naim Khan, were increasingly putting their own stamp on politics, sometimes at odds with Mahmud's views. Meanwhile, internationally, Mahmud also needed to navigate a steady course through Indian independence, the gradual unraveling of the wartime pact between Britain and the United States on the one hand and the Soviet Union on the other, and the new international world order of the United Nations and development assistance. Each in turn would have an impact on regional alliances, access to trading opportunities and the flow of concessional finance.

If handled well, Afghanistan might just emerge a stronger, more secure and economically vibrant state with a robust set of foreign policy alliances guaranteeing stability and territorial integrity, enabling economic growth and addressing some of the long-standing grievances which had festered during the Great Game. If the government put a foot wrong, however, it could face armed rebellion and economic collapse at home, and become a pawn once again in others' ambitions overseas with none of its own foreign policy goals met.

Mahmud Khan's government made two moves early on that were to shape the future course of his premiership. The first was to restate historic claims to Pashtun territory across the Durand Line in British India, if and when India became independent. This appealed to Afghans who believed Ahmed Shah's eighteenth-century empire should be recovered, and met the royal family's need to reward the Frontier tribes that had helped it secure the Afghan throne in 1929. It also made sense economically for Afghanistan to gain direct access to the sea. His second was to release some of his brother's political prisoners as the first stage in a process to introduce democratic reforms. Time would tell whether these two decisions would provide the catalyst needed for sustained political and economic development and security, or set Afghanistan and British–Afghan relations on a very different course altogether.

The Palace's New Broom

Mahmud had a very different personality from his brother. Whereas Hashim was quick to make decisions and form opinions about people, those who knew Mahmud personally recall he was much more gentle and warm-hearted.[2] He was also more inclined to learn from the democracy movements which had been sweeping across British India and Burma in the 1940s and to adapt them to the Afghan context, rather than label all political opponents as traitors. The first attempt at organising a political movement (as opposed to a violent uprising) had been between 1903 and 1909, led by a small group around the palace advocating for replacing the absolutist monarchy with a constitutional one. The group was easily suppressed after seven of the leaders were executed.[3] The second movement, the Young Afghans under Mahmud Tarzi's intellectual leadership, was first co-opted by Amir Amanullah and then, when he was forced to abdicate, dispersed under Hashim Khan's brutal crackdowns on dissent. Surely, speculated Mahmud and his cabinet, it should not be too difficult to co-opt the new democrats this time round for mutual gain, harnessing their education, ideas and skills for both the good of the country and the Yahya Khel regime.

The British legation, however, was wary from the outset. They believed, from experience, that the country was at its most stable when controlled by a strong autocratic ruler, who guaranteed peace and tribal autonomy in exchange for unqualified allegiance and support. As Mahmud Khan began to introduce his reforms, they were therefore at once sceptical that it was possible to democratise Afghanistan in the absence of an educated and politicised population, and fearful that successive economic crises might derail the democratisation experiment and destabilise the state. What made matters more worrying was that they were not wholly convinced Mahmud was the man for the top job, describing him to London as

> an opportunist rather than a man with a consistent policy and not likely to prove a good administrator especially as he is given to favouritism and susceptible to flattery. Consequently, gives the appearance of packing his Administration with non-entities and 'yes-men' ... Is inclined to be vain, but has good manners and considerable charm ... Fond of games but is a bad loser.[4]

Mahmud may have been more reform-minded than his brother, but he was also very aware that change needed to be introduced gradually, respecting tradition and the conservative values of the vast majority of the population. A central part of that process was continuing to use his nephew, King Zahir Shah, to reinforce through ritual the legitimacy of the Yahya Khels' rule, irrespective of which member of Zahir Shah's family actually ran the country on a day-to-day basis. A glimpse into how monarch and government were mutually reinforced through ritual and obeisance is provided in Gardener's account of the King's return to Kabul from France in April 1950 after medical treatment for an eye infection:

> The roads leading to the airfield were crowded with an orderly mass of spectators: townsmen, tribesmen and organised groups of students, marshalled by a large number of soldiers and policemen. Just as I was going into the airfield with my staff, His Royal Highness Shah Mahmud, Regent and Prime Minister, arrived and greeted us all personally. As he walked ahead of us towards the reception point, he was loudly cheered by those people – certain mullahs and tribes people, pensioners, government officials and students – who had been allowed inside the airfield ... At the reception point, two battalions of strong-looking, but by our standards rather slovenly, troops were drawn up as a guard of honour. The Regent and Prince Daud (War Minister) went forward to meet the King's plane as it taxied in: a Lebanese Airways Dakota, and manned by the same Air France crew that took him to Paris in October. His staff and baggage followed in two of Ibn Saud's personal planes, which, (I learnt from my Saudi Arabian colleagues) had been lent to him at Riyadh ... The Afghan Air Force escort which had gone out to Kandahar to meet and bring in the royal planes flew over the airfield in salute.[5]

Mahmud's reforms were also grounded in necessity. Gardener was given a rare insight into Mahmud's thinking at this time during an extensive and rather unexpected discussion with Ali Mohammed in July 1951.[6] The royal family had 'realised the vital and universal strength of democracy and the need to train it and harness it to the service of the country'. They knew this would be really challenging, especially 'as the Afghans by their nature (and especially the Pashtun component, the most vigorous one) found it practically impossible to work for the common interest'. Moreover, 'the low standard of education, and material well-being also militated against the successful working of democracy, for poor, ignorant people readily become the creatures of schemers for power, both external and internal'. The government had, however, taken its new obligations as a member of the United Nations and signatory of the Human Rights Convention seriously and had therefore wanted to develop a more progressive relationship with political opponents.

Behind the scenes, he also explained that the royal family had been concerned that it lacked sufficient leaders and administrators from within its own ranks to modernise the country and had therefore needed to recruit external support to staff key positions. This was self-evident to

Afghan observers already. During this period, all three of the King's uncles went overseas for medical treatment. Hashim Khan, after his heart attack, was out of the country for much of the time between 1946 and 1950. Shah Wali Khan went for treatment in Paris in September 1949, reportedly because he had temporarily lost his memory,[7] and Mahmud Khan himself was away from January to September 1951. Health problems also bedevilled Abdul Majid, the mastermind of Afghanistan's economic reforms. He was in the United States for medical treatment for nearly a year in 1948/9.

The family therefore needed new blood, but were not yet prepared to open the doors to the next generation – Hashim, Shah Wali and Mahmud Khan's nephews King Zahir Shah, Prince Naim and Prince Daud Khan. Gardener was already aware that Naim and Daud had been personally groomed by Hashim to take over the top jobs when they were ready. By 1948, it was also increasingly evident, to British minds at least, that Daud had now supplanted Naim in his uncle's good books. One report back to London thought it had the answer: 'It was at one time believed that he [Naim] was destined to succeed his uncle as Prime Minister, but it is doubtful if he has either the brains, physical fitness or strength of character for the task.'[8]

Getting Down to Business

The reforms seemed to go well initially. Mahmud released a number of the political prisoners who had been put behind bars by his brother, and as a sign of his personal commitment appointed Abdul Hadi Khan, who had been in prison for the past fifteen years, as the King's Chief Private Secretary. Mahmud also delegated more power to his ministerial team rather than accruing all power for himself. Once it became clear that alternative ideas would not be crushed, the Young Afghans were revitalised by a new political grouping, *Wesh Zalmian*, the Movement of Awakened Youth, which began to grow in 1947 when a number of press articles were published. Although the core of *Wesh Zalmian* was nationalist Pashtun, it initially drew intellectuals from across Afghanistan's diverse cultural and ethnic groups. In 1948, it became a formal organisation with around 100 members and published a manifesto calling for legal rights for women, the eradication of bribery and corruption, social justice and social welfare.[9]

There were also hopes that the government's investment in the Helmand river valley would reap economic dividends in the near future. Work by German and Japanese engineers had been halted during the Second World War when the Soviet Union and Britain forced the Afghans to expel Axis nationals. In 1946, the government used $16 million of its foreign exchange to hire an American engineering company, Morrison Knudsen, to build a comprehensive irrigation and power-generation system in the Helmand valley. The contract included two dams on the Helmand and Arghandab rivers, a hydro-electric power station, large-scale irrigation channels, and a network of access roads. This decision made sense on paper. The Helmand watershed drained 40 per cent of Afghanistan's land area, directly affecting about one-fifth of the entire Afghan population.[10] Once completed, the largely barren Helmand valley in the heart of Pashtun tribal territory would be transformed into productive arable land, while the dams would generate sufficient electricity across the region, including Kandahar, to drive economic growth and reduce dependence on foreign subsidies. Furthermore, Morrison Knudsen seemed to be the best company in the world to deliver this. Their work on the massive Hoover Dam in the United States, including the successful re-routing of the Colorado River to support this, had provided mass employment in the midst of the 1930s Great Depression, and transformed a once unproductive region into an economic powerhouse.

This was a high-risk strategy, however. If the investment paid off, it promised to turn around the Afghan economy, diversify production and kick-start much-needed economic growth. If it took too long to complete and the costs overran initial expectations, however, it threatened to eat into Afghanistan's precious foreign exchange and plunge the country into an economic and political crisis.

Although it soon became apparent that all was not well within the royal family, Mahmud Khan felt sufficiently confident in his position to make it clear who was in charge. Prince Daud had replaced him as Minister of War in 1946 and was upset when Mahmud continued to meddle in his empire. The first skirmish occurred when Mahmud opposed Daud's plan to replace the Governor of the Eastern Provinces with one of his friends. The second, according to Lancaster's sources in the army, led to a complete breakdown in the relationship. Mahmud had stopped Daud from retiring military officers who were illiterate or inefficient because a fair share of them came from the tribes. Their removal, in Mahmud's view, would cause unnecessary disquiet along the Frontier. Daud did not see it quite like that – he promptly went on strike and refused to attend to his ministerial duties for several months.[11] In the summer of 1948, Mahmud removed Daud in a Cabinet reshuffle and sent him as Ambassador to Paris, while Daud's brother, Naim Khan, became the first Afghan Ambassador in Washington. The Prime Minister had bought some political space for his reforms, but Squire was not terribly optimistic in his reporting to London in June 1948:

> It looks as if the government, when finally reconstituted, will in the main be one of non-entities; certainly it contains no-one of outstanding ability and it is difficult to see how it can possibly hold the country together, though Ali Mohammed, the Foreign Minister, will continue to exercise a steadying influence over foreign policy. Certainly the ex-Prime Minister takes a very gloomy view of the whole position and can see no-one other than his favourite nephew, Daud Khan, who is at all capable of controlling the situation. Capable executive officers are becoming increasingly hard to find and the administration is becoming every day more inefficient and more corrupt. The Prime Minister, though kindly and well-meaning, has neither the ability nor the strength of character to govern.[12]

With his nephews safely out of the way, the international community watched Mahmud Khan introduce yet more political reforms, this time focussed on making existing political institutions – the National Assembly and Municipal Councils – more representative. In the run-up to the Kabul Municipality election in June 1948, at least five men had been arrested for opposing the government's practice to date of appointing the mayors.[13] After this election, however, Mahmud Khan allowed the elected representatives themselves to vote for their own mayor. They selected a complete outsider – the German-educated Director of the General Electric Company, Ghulam Muhammad Farhad. Once this process passed peacefully, the government extended the policy to other municipalities.

A year later, in 1949, Mahmud decided that the elections for the seventh National Assembly, which had been instituted in the 1931 Constitution, would be more open and inclusive than ever before. This time the government did not nominate or approve candidates in advance; rather, Provincial Governors were given a free hand to put forward candidates of their own choosing. There was a risk that the newly elected representatives would have more affinity with their locality and the Governor than with the central government, but it was a risk Mahmud was prepared to take. The voting process was more open too – each Governor called together hundreds of men to vote on a particular day, while in Herat, Kabul and Kandahar, people were allowed to select their representatives by ballot.[14]

The seventh National Assembly (1949–52) therefore became the most representative and least pro-government parliament that Afghanistan had ever witnessed and is now commonly referred to as the 'Liberal Parliament'. Five members of *Wesh Zalmian*, the Movement of Awakened

Youth, were elected, including Dr Abdul Rahman Mahmudi, a Hazara, who had been among the protesters imprisoned in the run-up to the municipal elections, and Mir Ghulam Mohammed Ghobar, a Tajik and well-known political activist and erstwhile political prisoner, historian and poet. They called themselves the *Jabha-ye-Melli*, or National Front. A further eleven representatives allied with the Front in the Assembly, and between thirty and forty others supported their agenda. Although Mahmudi and Ghobar soon split from this Pashtun-dominated group, the very fact that the original five had stood on a unified reformist platform, and then formed a political faction within the Assembly itself, marked a significant shift in Afghanistan's political history. Their departure from the faction also sparked an internal debate about how far this Pashtun grouping could challenge the Pashtun-dominated government without being viewed as an opposition party, the core of democratic politics.[15] A year later, some of these charismatic leaders began to form political parties too. This next stage in the Liberal Parliament's story is covered in Chapter Nine.

At the same time, urban Afghans began to get greater access to the outside world. Kabul University students formed a Students Union in 1950, which toured the country in April and May debating issues ranging from communist ideology to the role of religion in a Muslim state.[16] Some translations of articles from foreign newspapers began to appear in the two official newspapers (*Anis* and *Islah*) and the first cinema opened in Kabul showing two films a week, one in Urdu and one in English. The ones in English were mostly cowboy films from the United States that had been obtained from India. The Ministry of Education also asked the British embassy to loan two of its films, *Henry V* and *Antony and Cleopatra*, to show to all senior students from the principal schools in Kabul at the Kabul cinema.[17] In Kandahar, a girls' school and a cinema were also opened in the face of strong opposition from local Mullahs. Alongside these changes, Afghanistan also experienced its first industrial action in 1949/50 amongst textile workers and miners demanding better pay and the right to organise. Although both were crushed pretty quickly – the miners were sacked and the textile workers in Pul-e-Khumri were punished with a pay cut – these actions marked a significant, albeit limited, extension of the political movement beyond the intellectual elite.[18]

Alongside these political changes, Abdul Majid began to initiate some economic reforms too, designed to open up Afghanistan's planned economy to freer trade, reduce the rate of inflation and boost growth. He started by introducing reforms to reduce the influence of government monopolies and provide better opportunities for private sector trading. To halt the disruptions caused by the war, the Bank-i-Milli (national bank) induced traders with idle funds to invest them and took increased control over the eighty-four *shirkats* through amalgamation and joint management boards.[19] The *shirkats* were government-supervised monopolies, whose shares were owned by the wealthiest Afghans, most of whom were in the royal family. In March 1948, Abdul Majid also began tentative steps towards ending the government-controlled monopoly on the sale of karakul and announced that a trader or group of traders could thenceforth sell consignments exceeding 25,000 skins directly themselves. Other aspects of the trade, however, remained unchanged – the actual export and sale of skins abroad still had to be done through branches of Afghanistan's central bank, the Da Afghanistan Bank, which was established by Abdul Majid in 1939, and any foreign exchange realised was still controlled by the bank, with only 20 per cent ultimately going to the exporters. The net effect of the reforms was mixed, according to British embassy observers. Only the extremely rich had consignments of at least 25,000 skins, but since the market for karakul had declined, there were limited export opportunities in any case.[20]

In May 1948, Abdul Majid announced a plan to end the government monopoly on the procurement and distribution of cotton piece goods, which was currently in the hands of the government's Central Cooperative Depot. Thenceforth, the depot's mandate was restricted to the procurement of piece goods for government servants, while the rest was opened up to the public. Companies possessing at least £2,000 in capital and who could form a group would be able to secure 60 per cent of the trade, with the remaining 40 per cent in the hands of small private traders organised as groups in smaller companies. As before, the British were sceptical that this change would enable small traders to enter the market, reporting to London that 'if these plans are put into effect, it will mean that for all practical purposes, one government monopoly company will have been replaced by three, and that the small trader will remain virtually excluded'.[21]

The government also began to explore options to extract Afghanistan's considerable mineral wealth on a commercial scale. An American geologist employed by the government took samples of Afghan chrome, talc, lead and zinc ore to the United States in early 1949. The Afghans also made a tentative approach to the French to help them develop their nascent oil industry, although, as the British observed, 'the development of the country's oil resources will probably have to wait until political conditions in the world are somewhat more favourable'.[22] The likelihood of the Afghans being able to develop their oil reserves commercially, let alone exporting them through Pakistan, the Soviet Union or Persia, seemed extremely remote.

Entering Choppy Waters

This reforming zeal went well to start with, but soon Afghanistan's weak economic position, and tensions over the pace and scale of political reform caught up with it. Neither the government nor Morrison Knudsen had fully appreciated the sheer scale of the enterprise nor the wisdom of trying to enfold an entire region within a single project.[23] Nor had they taken sufficient account of the wider geopolitical significance of the Helmand River. Although it flowed nearly 300 miles through Afghanistan, it ended in two lakes and a saline marsh in the Persian Seistan. This meant that although any change in the course of the river or the flow of water into the Seistan might well be good for Afghanistan, it could negatively affect the livelihoods of poor Persian farmers. The Persians therefore wanted to know what was going on.

The first hurdle for Morrison Knudsen was the logistical difficulty involved in operating in a remote area where all the equipment and fuel needed to be brought in overland from Karachi, often on poor – or, more often than not, non-existent – roads. Although the first engineers and construction workers arrived in the summer of 1946, it therefore took them several months to complete the initial surveys, so that by 1947, the only things to show for the investment were two roads from Pakistan to Kabul and Kandahar and the newly constructed living quarters for American staff. Given this, it was hardly surprising that the Afghans had little to show for their investment two years into the contract.

It was not long before the government began to complain about the impact of the project on the Afghan economy too and claim they had been duped by skilled American businessmen into a contract which was more beneficial to the company than to Afghanistan. In May 1947, Ali Mohammed told Squire that their American dollar reserve 'had already been dissipated and that the Afghans are at their wits ends to know which way to turn'. Given that the legation had estimated that these reserves would last for five years, this came as quite a shock.[24] A year later, Ali Mohammed complained again that the government had expected the total contract to cost $16 million spread over four years, but now the whole amount had been exhausted in just two and a half years and the work had hardly started.[25]

Squire did some digging and eventually found out that the contract had committed the government to a three-year advance payment, thus giving the company the freedom to spend whatever it required to implement agreed projects as well as charge an additional 8 per cent profit.[26] In communications with London, he left no doubt at all about where his own sympathies lay. All public works in British India, he explained, had used local labour as much as possible with the minimum of foreign expert supervision. This ensured that the bulk of the money went back into the country and did not drain national resources. 'A poor country like Afghanistan cannot afford to support the large number of Americans, already numbering well over a hundred, who are now working in the country.' Indeed, 'I was recently told of an ordinary American mechanic who boasted that in Afghanistan he was living entirely at the company's expense, and in addition drawing a salary equivalent to £2,000 a year, and that in five years' time, he proposed to retire on his savings.'[27]

Meanwhile, Afghan criticism of the company's performance and, in particular, the number of American staff living in luxury on large salaries grew apace. Ex-Prime Minister Hashim Khan weighed in too, asking Squire in July 1948 'why should American workmen in the Jalalabad area live in air-conditioned houses with electric light when we ourselves have to put up with ordinary oil lamps?'[28] Even the normally reticent United States Ambassador, Ely Palmer, started to be more talkative about the challenges, prompted, Squire concluded, by 'the widespread criticism that the company's extravagance and, more particularly, the frequent changes in its personnel have evoked throughout Afghanistan'.[29]

It was not surprising therefore that the Afghans began to ask for significant loans and credit from the United States and Britain to help them out of their economic quagmire. In 1946, they asked Britain for a loan or credit for £10–20 million to fund their Ten Year Development Plan. A year later, with the plan already overtaken by the scale of debt, they asked for £20–30 million, and then in 1948 for £1.5 million to enable them to order capital equipment such as road, textile and cotton machinery from British companies.[30] Similar requests were passed to the United States.

As criticism of company waste heated up, another problem was brewing over the border with Persia concerning the flow of Helmand River water into the Seistan. Historically, the main problem had been flooding, but every thirty to forty years there was a severe drought and Persia invariably blamed Afghanistan for this, accusing them of diverting the water for their own use. Following two previous droughts, British India Service officers had negotiated agreements in 1877 and 1905 – the Goldsmid and McMahon Awards – between the Persian and Afghan governments to divide the Seistan and demarcate the boundary between the two countries.[31] In 1946/7, as luck would have it, a severe drought affected the Seistan once again, triggering renewed tensions. When the Persians kicked up a fuss this time round, the Afghans threatened to take the matter to the United Nations in early 1948, irrespective of concerns that this could trigger Soviet involvement.[32] By July, there were growing concerns that the Persians might refer the matter to the United Nations too.[33]

Although the British had been sceptical of the Helmand project from the start, they now tried to help out because 'it is very much in our interests that the dispute should be settled since Russian propaganda is already making capital out of it, and friction between the Afghans and the Persians will only weaken the resistance of each country to Soviet infiltration'.[34] Quite unexpectedly, however, they found themselves pushed to the sidelines by an American government uninterested in the colonial deals of a bygone era. State Department officials made it clear that they felt the previous settlements were no longer relevant and had caused too much 'bad blood' in the past anyway. Instead, they preferred to focus on the future prospects for Persia and Afghanistan, drawing on experiences from the Nile, the Rio Grande and the Colorado rivers where agreements had been made between at least two concerned states, to the benefit of all parties.[35] This perspective, however, not only failed to take into account the locally specific topography of Central Asia and the Middle East, but also the politics, including the fact that the earlier agreements were important frames of reference for both the Afghan and the Persian governments. The Afghan Minister for Public Works, Kabir Khan Ludin, asked the British for copies of the original agreements because his government's documents had been destroyed in the fighting in Kabul in 1929. Later, the Persians asked Britain for original copies too. Indeed, Ali Mohammed told Squire that both he and Ludin felt that 'even if the Americans worked for ten years, they would never produce anything half so good as the McMahon Report'.[36]

To help out, the British launched a search party for the records since they had begun to suspect that part of the problem was that the Afghans and the Persians were quoting from different versions. One copy was found in London, a second in the British embassy in Tehran, and a third in Delhi, now owned by the new Indian government.[37] They were swiftly dispatched. It was clear, however, that there was little more they could do except 'assist in every way in promoting a settlement, while at the same time avoiding giving the Americans the impression that we desire to interfere'.[38]

By the summer, the United States had come up with the idea of a neutral Technical Commission, which would investigate the short-, medium- and long-term aspects of the whole issue. Its members would be mutually agreed based on a list prepared in Washington. The British remained sceptical, however. Squire told London that he could not 'see how the precedents of the Colorado or the Rio Grande or even the Nile are going to be of any great use in solving this particular problem'. If the project was ultimately to work, it would require vast expenditures by Afghanistan and Persia to build storage dams and control the flow of water in the river, money 'which they can ill afford, for a project which, even if it could be shown to be economically sound, would, in the political circumstances existing, stand no chance whatever of being successful'.[39] The Technical Commission comprising a Canadian, a Chilean and an American finally set off in 1950.[40] It reported a year later, recommending that a settlement should be made based on the situation five years hence when new data had been collected. Afghanistan accepted the report in November 1952, but the Persians took their time over opening negotiations.[41]

Meanwhile, on the political front, the opening up of municipal elections in 1948 to a new breed of politicians who owed little allegiance to the palace on the one hand and had limited political experience on the other began to underline the challenges of transitioning from an autocratic state to a more open democratic system. Initially, Mahmud Khan's political reforms appeared to go well. On a personal level, the newly elected Mayor of Kabul, Ghulam Mohammed, seemed a breath of fresh air. Squire spoke warmly about him. 'Such enthusiasm has he inspired that voluntary and apparently unsolicited subscriptions are now pouring into the municipal coffers for the improvement of the Afghan capital, an extraordinary tribute to his personality and honesty.'[42] Colonel Prendergast was impressed too. 'He is eccentric in that he walks everywhere and makes his family do so too, in a country where anyone who holds an important office travels in a large American car. He gives money to the poor freely although he is not wealthy.'[43]

On the flipside, Ghulam Mohammed's actions were beginning to anger many. One of Kabul's most famous landmarks was the covered market. In the middle of the winter of 1948/9, however, the mayor had it pulled down in spite of the impact this would have on people's livelihoods at a time when they could least afford it. A protest went to the Prime Minister. The mayor, however, made it clear that he, not the Prime Minister, was in charge now. He had demolished it because it was airless and unsanitary, and since the municipality was now his concern and not the government's, he was the one with the responsibility to improve it, not them.[44] Throughout, he openly criticised government policy and allegedly the royal family too – apparently, the embassy discovered, remarking that King Amanullah should not have been deposed.[45]

His actions even prompted a reaction from the King, who usually kept out of politics. Once it became clear that the fate of the bazaar was part of a grand masterplan to rebuild much of the old city, Zahir Shah decided enough was enough. During his Durbar (or audience) on 15 January 1949, he congratulated the mayor for his work, but advised him to spread his reform programme over two years, not one. He then suggested he went abroad for a while to complete negotiations to purchase machinery for General Electric.[46] The respite was short-lived, however. By May, the mayor was back from the United States and had turned his attention to a large-scale road improvement system. This created havoc across the city as homes were destroyed, services were disrupted and businesses were forced to relocate. Colonel Prendergast heard that the mayor had personally upset the Deputy Director of the Agricultural Department, whose electricity supply had been cut off by the roadworks. When he complained, the mayor told him he was too busy finding homes for poor people whose homes had been destroyed by the construction work and could not spare time to consider the needs of a man who owned three houses. When the man got angry, the embassy heard that he was manhandled by the mayor's assistants and then hauled before the Prime Minister, who thereupon sent him to hospital to deal with his wounds.[47] On top of all this, the mayor also introduced a new rule that everyone should drive on the right in Kabul, leading inevitably to mass confusion – diplomats wondered idly if and when the rule would extend to the provinces.[48] In the end it proved to be a popular move, however, distinguishing Afghanistan from the British period, and the whole country eventually moved to driving on the right.[49]

Although the mayor's antics were somewhat awkward for the government and a political opposition movement was beginning to take shape in the run-up to the Liberal Parliament's election, the main threats to Mahmud's position in 1949 came from elsewhere. Namely Afghanistan's parlous economic condition and his decision in 1947 to lay claim to Pashtun territories on the other side of the Durand Line and promote the idea of Pashtunistan, a land for the Pashtun people. This policy put Afghanistan on a collision course with Britain's successor state across the Durand Line, Pakistan, and at the same time threatened access to the country's main trade route through Pakistan and India. As Chapter Six will explain in more detail, things reached a crisis point in June 1949 when a Pakistan Air Force plane inadvertently dropped bombs on Pashtun tribesmen just inside Afghan territory. Although Afghan claims were subsequently recognised by an international team, the incident severely damaged Mahmud's political reputation. He had maintained the peace but not advanced Afghanistan's Pashtunistan policy one iota. It was to leave the door open for Afghan nationalists like Mahmud's nephews, Daud and Naim Khan, to claim that they, not he, would carry the nationalist banner forward in future.

In November 1949, a few months after Abdul Majid returned to Kabul after a long medical sojourn in the United States, Mahmud Khan restructured the way the business of government was organised, 'presumably in an attempt to integrate and rationalise the economic policy of the country', speculated the British embassy.[50] Mahmud also brought his wayward nephews back into the fold.

This time round, the government was reorganised into three clusters, each headed by a senior figure.[51] Daud resumed his post as Minister of War, but now his power was boosted by responsibility for the Ministries of Interior and Communications and the Tribal Directorate too, thus giving him significant control of the army, the police and the tribes, the three most potent forces in the country. Naim became Minister of Public Works under an economic and financial grouping – finance, public works, mines and agriculture – led by Abdul Majid. A third grouping of more minor ministries – including health and education – was headed by the former Ambassador to London, Faiz Mohammed Zakria. A new institution was introduced too, the Supreme Council of Government (*Shora'i Ali-ye-Daulat*), headed by the Prime Minister and consisting of the First and Second Assistant Prime Ministers (positions currently held by the Foreign and Interior Ministers), the heads of the ministerial clusters, and two other ministers. Its mandate was to consider general affairs of state, decide the aims of the country, and consider and approve plans recommended by different ministerial clusters. Given that this body would operate in addition to the existing Supreme Council of Ministers, Gardener concluded that the ruling oligarchy had simply established yet another layer to insulate themselves from the demands of the newly enfranchised populace.[52]

Meanwhile, although the new government looked strong on paper, 'its efficiency as a team', Gardener observed in a cable to London, 'is very much open to question and its present composition may merely mark one stage towards the elimination of Shah Mahmud Khan and the establishment of a government basing itself more on the ideas of former Prime Minister, Hashim Khan, Daud Khan being the chosen instrument of the latter'.[53] Back in London, Foreign Office officials concluded it was 'in fact the old pack re-dealt, but the strong men are kept at home', underlining that the 'Afghan government have decided that the internal situation is far more pressing than their attempts to enlist support for the Pashtunistan issue'.[54]

Creeping British Paralysis

Throughout this period, the British tried to find ways to help the Afghan government chart a steady course through these complex challenges. They fell back on what they had always known about the country – namely that it needed a regular flow of resources and access to international markets to survive. Without these, discord in the palace, a nascent opposition movement, tribal unrest and rising food prices would either topple the regime or push it to promote a foreign policy position, Pashtunistan, which would shore up support at home but potentially destabilise the region. In a worst-case scenario, they feared the regime would collapse and the Soviet Union would exploit the power vacuum, while Pakistan would become embroiled in interminable conflict along the Frontier. When the British examined what levers they had to hand, however, their options were limited – their commercial relationship with Afghanistan was now pretty weak while British resources were already extremely stretched.

By 1947, Britain's position in the Afghan economy had fallen rapidly. That year alone, anticipated Afghan orders for aircraft, wireless and telephone equipment, and textile machinery failed to materialise.[55] By 1948, sales to Afghanistan were only around £400,000 with few new contracts in sight, while Afghan exports to Britain were virtually zero. In early 1948, Marconi withdrew its engineer from Kabul because a new contract for radio equipment was unlikely,[56] and later in the year, Mr Sills, a technical expert in the Textile Purchasing Commission, returned home when the government's plans to purchase textile machinery ground to a halt. In November, contracts for the British firm of Associated Consulting Engineers (India) to produce estimates to supply hydro-electric power to the Panjshir valley, expand the woollen mills in Kabul and Kandahar, and set up a brick and tile factory, were shelved too.[57]

British officials were not concerned about the impact on the British economy since Afghanistan, with annual revenues below £4 million, was too small to provide a lucrative market for British products and services.[58] In any case, most Afghan development plans rarely reached beyond the planning stage, as Squire noted wryly: 'The government are very prone to spend much time on the preparation of elaborate plans without any serious intention of putting them into effect.'[59] The legation had already decided that the post of Commercial Secretary should be cut when India became independent in August 1947.[60] In fact, if anyone was concerned about the decline of Britain's economic fortunes in Afghanistan in 1948, it was the Americans. Ambassador Palmer told Ali Mohammed in November that the United States was disappointed not only that the contract with Associated Consulting Engineers (India) had been suspended, but also that Mr Sills was leaving. From his point of view, 'whoever supplied the textile machinery, it would be a tragedy if Sills were not here to help to install it and see that it was properly used'.[61]

Helping Afghanistan became an increasingly thankless task, however, as first one then another hurdle was placed in the way. Foreign Secretary

Bevin, ever mindful of the impact of Afghanistan's weak economy on stability in the region, was keen to find a means to help strengthen it. Unfortunately, his wishes were blocked at every turn by Treasury officials who refused to consider a loan in anything other than commercial terms. This meant what when the Afghan government repeatedly asked for financial assistance after the war, they found that Britain had little, if anything, to offer. When the Afghans asked for a £10–20 million loan in 1946, Bevin directed that this request should be given appropriate attention and told the Afghan Ambassador to London that he attached 'great importance to the maintenance of Afghan independence, in the face of possible Soviet pressure and penetration'. After the meeting, he 'therefore directed that the question of a possible loan should be further carefully considered'.[62] The Treasury, however, took a different view. They believed Afghanistan should be directed to the newly formed World Bank rather than turn to Britain which was already unable to fund its existing loan requests, including from the French, as well as struggling to pay for its imports.

They also rejected a second loan request in 1947 because Britain was 'hard put to it to meet our inevitable overseas commitments, and there is no margin for additional ones of this nature'. This time, they hoped the new governments of Pakistan and India would be able to provide assistance, or the United States. Failing that, they hoped the United States would refer them to the World Bank. In any case, the Treasury argued, the maximum amount that Britain could provide would be so negligible that it would be unlikely to generate any political good will anyway.[63]

When the Afghans made a third request in 1948, the Foreign Office decided to pull out all the stops to secure Treasury support. They, like the State Department in Washington, had been examining the spread of communist-led insurgencies across South-East Asia and were concluding, as Chapter Seven explains, that the best way to stop these trends was by removing the conditions – poverty, unemployment, despair – that bred them. In many ways, Afghanistan seemed to be in a similar situation, but in the Afghan case, they concluded the country was unstable because its economy was weak, not because it was threatened by communist ideology. This time round, the Foreign Office therefore swiftly underlined the political importance of the loan before the Treasury or the Board of Trade responded from a narrow commercial perspective, underlining that since Indian independence the 'Afghan government have had an impression that we are losing interest in their affairs. It is true that our concern is now more remote, but Afghanistan is in a strategically important position, and the maintenance of the stability and integrity of the present friendly regime is still definitely a United Kingdom interest. Some kind of financial assistance would bring this fact home very effectively to the Afghans, thereby maintaining our prestige and influence.'

They also explained why Afghanistan could not apply to Pakistan for a loan, and pointed out that any attempt by Afghanistan to seek financial assistance from India instead would simply fuel India–Pakistan tensions.[64] The Treasury, however, remained sceptical:

> The matter was discussed again at a Cabinet Defence Committee meeting on 19 April 1949 at which Ministers were asked to consider what Britain should do if Afghanistan and Pakistan went to war. Ministers concluded Afghanistan's Pashtunistan policy was probably driven by a need to distract attention away from the country's deepening economic crisis and directed officials to find out what could be done to increase Afghan exports, especially but not exclusively to Britain, to help the country recover.[65]

Some steps were already underway. The embassy in Kabul had been exploring whether Britain could help resolve Afghan transit problems through Pakistan. The Ministry of Food was in the midst of negotiations with the Afghan National Bank's representative in London to increase the import of dried fruit. Separate work was also in hand to encourage the Board of Trade to agree an import licensing concession on all imported karakul skins, and was exploring options to import Afghan wool. The first shipment of karakul under the new scheme actually arrived in mid-1949, earning the Afghans £16,000. From Kabul, the embassy also suggested Britain could consider importing new mineral finds such as lead, zinc, chrome, beryl ores and talc.[66]

When officials investigated further, however, they found they could do next to nothing to increase non-karakul exports from Afghanistan. Some of their efforts soon bordered on the farcical. First, they explored whether dried fruit could be imported into Britain, but realised relatively quickly that the fruit would require a higher standard of sorting, packaging and grading, as well as higher levels of hygiene than existed at present. When samples of fruits and nuts were finally sent to the Ministry of Food from Kabul, the reaction in London was lukewarm – there was limited demand in Britain for the type of dried fruit Afghanistan produced.

Hopes were then raised that increasing imports of Afghan wool might be the answer. This plan fell flat before it even got off the ground. The government had no control over wool imports, so officials needed to get the Liverpool Wool Brokers Association on side. This unfortunately raised a new set of problems. It was already known that Afghan wool was of mixed quality and that Soviet traders rejected a certain amount each year. On top of that, the Association had no contacts in Afghanistan and was therefore unlikely to get in touch with Afghan traders unless the British government acted as an intermediary. To help get the ball rolling, the Board of Trade asked the Association to send a purchasing representative to Kabul, but they then met another brick wall – the Association simply refused to pay. It was not long before the board understood why. 'A fairly large proportion of exports of "Pakistani" wool originates from Afghanistan', and so 'this might well prove to be a case of "swings and roundabouts"'.[67]

The Board refused to give up, however, and concluded at this point that the only way to get a representative out to Kabul would be if the British government paid for it. A request was submitted to the Treasury – who promptly refused on the grounds that since Pakistan had recently relaxed its exchange controls, this would assist Afghan exports without any British involvement at all. In any case, as the Treasury went on to argue, there were no grounds to believe a visit would be successful:

> The Afghans seem only slightly more willing to send wool on consignment to the United Kingdom (with no guarantee of sale) than the wool trade here is to encourage the trade from this end ... Our view therefore is that it would be quite unjustifiable for His Majesty's Government to undertake an expenditure ... for this speculative purpose. If either of the parties is sufficiently interested to pay for the visit then there may be some hope of its proving useful. If not, then we think it would be money thrown away.[68]

Officials then approached the Afghan government to pay for the visit. Wisely, the Afghans first sent wool samples to the Wool Association to see if this was a runner. A few months later, the whole initiative stalled when the Afghan government discovered they had no spare wool stocks to sell to Britain before April 1950 in any case. By then, the British embassy assumed, any surplus would be mopped up in a Soviet trade deal so there was little point now in actively pursuing opportunities in Britain.

Attempts to import minerals from Afghanistan did not fare any better either. Leaving no stone unturned, the British embassy sent samples of chrome ore, beryl, manganese ore with silver content, and ordinary manganese to Britain for testing. Positive news came back from the Ministry of Supply in London – although beryl was not needed at present, the chrome was good quality and could be used in Britain. Existing supplies came from South Africa but the ministry would welcome a quote from Afghanistan for delivery in 1951. It seemed finally as though at least one success story would come from Britain's attempts to help the Afghan economy. The United States offered to purchase some too. Then came disappointing news from Gardener in March 1950. Although the Afghan Minister of Mines could in theory supply 5,000 tons of chrome ore up to the end of 1950, there were three problems. First, his ministry was unable to transport supplies to the border because of petrol shortages in Afghanistan. Second, even if they could deliver the chrome as far as Peshawar, it would be difficult to transport it any further because transit through Pakistan was problematic. Third, 'difficulties with Pakistan have so affected the normal flow of Afghan trade that his ministry is now left with practically no dynamite' to extract the chrome ore from the ground.[69]

The Americans Come to the Rescue

As British avenues were drying up, the focus now shifted to the United States, which had been quietly building up an economic relationship with Afghanistan alongside the Morrison Knudsen contract. The Afghans had avoided developing a trading monopoly with any single country since independence, but by the late 1940s the United States accounted for over two-thirds of imports.[70] Although United States interests were very much tied up with making the Helmand project a success, Squire speculated that the Afghans also hoped to turn this to their own advantage:

> American interest in Afghanistan, initiated and developed through the purely commercial activities of the Morrison-Knudsen company, will be sustained through direct American government assistance, and it is my belief that the achievement of such assistance has all along been the Afghan government's principal objective, as they hoped thereby to secure stronger American backing against any possible menace from the North.[71]

When the Afghans first approached the United States for a loan in 1947, Palmer privately told Squire that he backed the request and would forward it to Washington, provided it was used for 'the completion of the Morrison-Knudsen operations should the Afghan dollar resource be exhausted before their work was accomplished'. Thinking back on that conversation, Squire did not think Palmer 'anticipated, any more than I did, that this would happen before the company had even started to carry out any one of the projects for which their services had been engaged'.[72]

Meanwhile in Washington, Abdul Majid kept up the pressure for an untied loan to fund his economic plans and improve Afghanistan's balance of payments.

It was an uphill struggle, however. Mahmud Khan moaned to Squire in June 1948 that 'when he had been in America last year, the American government had put him off with kind words, saying that it was very difficult to get anything through Congress unless the Afghans knew Congressmen personally'. Now, he complained, the United States seemed to be fobbing them off again. Indeed, 'America appeared to be helping all foreign countries except Afghanistan.'[73] Supplying Berlin with essential food and supplies by air was to be their latest endeavour after Stalin closed all land routes to the city within days of this correspondence.

In Kabul, however, Palmer had already decided to get the ball rolling by asking the government what security they could provide to guarantee repayment of a commercial loan.[74] Squire was sceptical and thought Palmer 'appeared to ignore the fact that the country has no assets which she could hypothecate as security for any loan'.[75] In the end, the exercise was quashed when it quickly became apparent there was little information to collect in any case. The government had limited data sources to draw on, let alone the capacity to analyse it. Once Palmer realised this, he sent a senior official from the Department of National Economy to the United States to learn how to set up a statistics office in Kabul.[76]

When the Afghans were subsequently advised by the State Department to put their loan request through their incoming Ambassador to the United States, Naim Khan, rather than through the Minister of National Economy, Abdul Majid, the British were relieved to see that the Americans finally seemed to be looking at the political, as well as the financial, dimensions of the issue.[77] As William Ledwidge, the Afghan Desk Officer in the Foreign Office, realised:

> It is certainly more than likely that the Americans will refuse to lend anything to Afghanistan as a strictly business proposition. But there is an obvious political advantage in keeping the Afghans as independent as possible economically of Russia, and it is no doubt for this reason that the State Department want to receive an official request from the new Afghan Ambassador who is now in Paris on the way to Post. They can then put forward the political case for helping Afghanistan.[78]

The State Department in turn passed the request to the United States Export-Import Bank. This bank had been established in 1934 by President Franklin D. Roosevelt as the official export credit agency of the United States with a mandate to help finance and facilitate exports and imports between the United States and other countries during periods of economic crisis when the private banking sector was unwilling or unable to provide credit or take on the risk. It was ideally placed to consider the Afghan request, although it took another year before the loan was in the bag. Palmer's replacement in Kabul, Louis Dreyfus, kept up the pressure, setting out his concerns privately to the State Department in September 1949:

> Justly or unjustly, Morrison-Knudsen cannot avoid being [the] scapegoat for Afghan critical situation. Abandoned Morrison-Knudsen camps will stand as monuments of American inefficiency. Arghandab and Kajaki dams would be monuments of American ability. Only [a] loan making possible continued Morrison-Knudsen employment and completion [of] Helmand can avoid reduced US prestige and cooling of present cordial Afghan-US relations.[79]

A $21 million loan from the Export-Import Bank, repayable at 3.5 per cent interest over fifteen years, was finally announced on 23 November 1949, tied, against Abdul Majid's express wishes,

> to assist in financing the United States costs of equipment, materials and services, including off-shore purchases of fuel oils and lubricants, required for construction of the Kajaki Dam and completion of the Boghra canal system in the Helmand river valley and for such supplemental additional river developments and irrigation projects in the Helmand and Arghandab valleys as any balance of the credit may permit.[80]

It received a mixed reception in Kabul. Although the Afghan government had overruled Abdul Majid's desire for an untied loan to help finance Afghanistan's own development plans,[81] their displeasure about the terms of the loan was evident from the way the news was received in Kabul. It was hotly debated in the National Assembly and several members openly opposed it. Dreyfus told Gardener that he had tried to get a word of thanks from the government, but 'failing to get the Minister for Foreign Affairs', he had 'telephoned to the Minister of National Economy, and the latter's only comment was merely "Is it all arranged now? When do we get the money?"' As Gardener reported to London, 'Mr Dreyfus had thought that at all events, some expression of gratitude would have been shown ... But the credit has been accepted in Kabul in a very cool and matter of fact way and we feel the Americans are mortified.'[82]

Others had mixed feelings too. The British were pleased that the United States had finally made a political as well as an economic commitment to Afghanistan. They were annoyed, however, that no political conditions had been attached requiring Afghanistan to back down on its anti-Pakistan/Pashtunistan campaign, and felt that this would undermine any subsequent British negotiations to lend money with conditions.[83] The Pakistani Ambassador in Kabul in turn feared this injection of capital would free up other Afghan money to be spent on pro-Pashtunistan agitation,[84] and the Persian Ambassador in Washington sent a memorandum to the State Department setting out his government's mixed feelings too. He was satisfied that the loan provided concrete evidence of United States interest in the Middle East and South Asia, but was upset that his country had not been consulted first given that construction work in Helmand could have an impact on the Technical Commission's progress.[85]

Britain's own deliberations about whether or not to support yet another request for a loan became caught up in the fallout from the Export-Import Bank loan. Once Abdul Majid returned to Kabul in mid-1949, he had approached the embassy once again with a new financial plan. This time he proposed that Afghanistan would buy capital equipment from Britain to the value of £4 million, half of which could be paid in dollars if Britain bought more Afghan exports, the other half requiring credit with a two-year grace period, and with the balance paid in sterling over six years at 5 per cent interest.[86] Although the fiscal projections did not add up from a purely commercial perspective, the Foreign Office was initially keen to encourage the Treasury to take into account the political desirability of helping Afghanistan. Initial reactions were hesitant, but not necessarily negative. During a cross-Whitehall meeting in the Treasury on 18 November 1949, officials 'agreed that political considerations would not in this case justify the acceptance of a thoroughly bad commercial proposition, but if it were merely a case of doubt as to whether the Afghans might be able to repay in full within the stated time, the political considerations would justify the acceptance of some risk'.[87]

The Treasury, however, were not prepared to come to any firmer conclusions until the terms of the American loan were announced the following week. As the details began to trickle out, Gardener became more and more concerned that Afghanistan would not only struggle to repay the Americans – especially as the likely return on the Helmand scheme was still years away – but would also be unable to service other loans, even if these were more suited to the country's needs. The tone of his report left London in no doubt about his concerns:

> You will see that I regard the United States loan as not so good for Afghanistan, or even the United States of America, who doubtless gave it to extricate Morrison Knudsen from a hole not solely of their own making. We must avoid this thing in future.

As 1949 drew to a close, the picture was mixed. Mahmud's liberalising reforms had been pushed through, but the government's long-term commitment to change was uncertain, especially as Mahmud had recently restructured his cabinet and ceded some power to the next generation of the royal family, Daud and Naim Khan. A large loan had been secured from the United States. True, it was tied to the Helmand project and the government still needed financial assistance to support the rest of the economy – but it was a start. Although the United States had given few indications that it planned to bind Afghanistan within the emerging Western coalition to contain Soviet expansionism, but it seemed a small step, to Afghan minds at least, to move from the Helmand loan to a much broader and deeper relationship. Meanwhile, a nationalist Pashtunistan policy had alienated Britain's successor state in Pakistan, the one country with whom Britain had expected Afghanistan to find common cause against a Soviet threat. It still seemed possible, however, in late 1949 that this dispute could be resolved in the foreseeable future. Afghanistan therefore appeared to be just about weathering the storm, but it was unclear whether this would hold or if the country would simply lurch from one crisis to another in the coming months and years ahead.

In the meantime, it was becoming blatantly obvious that Britain itself had woefully few financial levers left to influence Afghan internal affairs or its choice of regional policies, both of which had previously been intimately tied up with the financial, political and military resources of the Indian empire.

Unfortunately, within a matter of weeks the instability at the heart of the Afghan state became increasingly apparent when the newly restructured Cabinet sought to find means to tackle the country's worst economic crisis since the war – the imposition of a petrol blockade by Pakistan on 1 January 1950. This had a catastrophic effect on the economy, fuelled social unrest, triggered questions about the long-term viability of the current political system, and challenged the wisdom of pursuing a nationalist foreign policy in Pashtunistan to reclaim past blood and treasure while the state remained vulnerable to policies imposed by others. The next two chapters look at the Pashtunistan question in more detail, including Britain's attempts to resolve this legacy of empire.

5

Afghan Demands on
the Frontier

It soon became apparent that the British were leaving India ... Who was going to defend them against the Russians? Who was going to take the place of the British empire? What sort of relations could they have with the states of India and Pakistan, so unfriendly to one another? They had, however, no time to solve the problem because what Mr Winston Churchill has called 'Operation Scuttle' left them only a few weeks in which to consider all its implications.

Sir Giles Squire, 1951[1]

Introduction
Indian independence on 15 August 1947 and the Partition of the empire between two new dominions, the predominantly Muslim Pakistan and the predominantly Hindu India, had a huge impact on Afghanistan and on Afghan foreign policy. Meanwhile, the inherent weaknesses in the new state of Pakistan at independence had an influence on their approach to the North-West Frontier and their willingness to collaborate with Afghanistan to find a solution. During that summer, however, no one anticipated that the decisions taken by Britain, Afghanistan and Pakistan between 1947 and 1950 would leave an indelible legacy, which would fuel the Cold War in Asia and have an impact on regional politics and stability to this day.

Initially, the British were baffled when the Afghans demanded a right to be involved in making decisions about the future of the North-West Frontier, and viewed it as a distraction from the main event – namely sorting out the status of India and Pakistan. They thought their claims would fade away after independence. Looking back with the benefit of hindsight just four years later in 1951, Squire told an audience in London that Indian independence had put the Afghans in an impossible situation. It presented a challenge because they thought they would need to find new allies to protect them from the Soviet Union if Britain withdrew, and an opportunity because it opened up the possibility of recovering part of Ahmed Shah's eighteenth-century empire beyond the North-West Frontier. The Afghans, he pointed out, always believed that 'the only solution of the Frontier problem was for the two governments concerned to get together and try to disarm and civilise these tribes and make them law-abiding members of society'. Unfortunately, 'the negotiations had not gone very far when the decision of the British government to leave India was announced'.[2]

Meanwhile, the new government in Pakistan had its own concerns to grapple with in the weeks and months after independence, and had not factored a dispute on the North-West Frontier into the mix either. They had inherited a 'moth-eaten' territory, as Jinnah called it, divided into two parts – West and East Pakistan (now Bangladesh) – which were separated by several thousand miles of Indian land. Virtually up to the last minute, no one anticipated that India would be partitioned, and as a result, the territories of what now became Pakistan lacked a coherent administrative system and a fully resourced army with sufficient finances to manage it. The main machinery of government under colonial rule had been in Delhi, not Karachi, while the only tie between East and West Pakistan was their shared Muslim faith. The new country was crippled economically too. Pakistan inherited only 10 per cent of the subcontinent's industrial base, and its raw materials, such as cotton, were now separated from key markets like the cotton mills in Bombay and Ahmedabad.[3] In the first few months, the new government, not surprisingly, relied on continued support from British officials to help them manage the transition period.

The Pakistan government also needed to focus on building up their military strength, which was an uphill struggle too. At independence, Pakistan should have inherited 17.5 per cent of the assets of undivided India, but only just over 23,000 of the 160,000 tons of ordinance allotted to Pakistan by the Joint Defence Council was delivered, and only six armoured regiments to India's forty, and eight artillery and infantry regiments to India's forty and twenty-one respectively. The challenges were exacerbated by the fact that the pre-independence armaments industries were located in India, not Pakistan. In the short term, the new government therefore employed nearly 500 British officers to meet shortfalls in the technical branches of army and at senior levels, and allocated three-quarters of all expenditure in their first budget to the military.[4]

In the months that followed, Afghan demands gradually became clearer, but by then they had become caught up in Pakistan–India rivalries,

Pakistan's desire to keep the North-West Frontier region as part of Pakistan, and complex legal wrangles in London about what constituted statehood. By the time Squire left Kabul in late 1949, it had become abundantly apparent that Britain had underestimated Afghanistan's determination to establish a Pashtun homeland straddling the border area between Afghan and former British government of India territory. It was also clear by then too that there were no easy solutions. The evolution of Afghan policy and Britain's various attempts to understand and address it at different points during this crucial two-year period sheds light on the post-independence origins of this complex issue and how positions subsequently became entrenched and fractious.

Trouble on the North-West Frontier

The area under contention was called the North-West Frontier by the British because it literally comprised the frontier region between British Indian territory and Afghanistan. In the mid-eighteenth century, the area had been part of Amir Ahmed Shah's Afghan empire, but after his death, the territory controlled by his successors slowly receded. The Treaty of Gandamak in 1879 marked the last in a series of treaties under which Afghanistan ceded territories to British India in exchange for a yearly subsidy. Just over a decade later, in 1893, Sir Mortimer Durand negotiated an agreement between Amir Abdur Rahman and the British government in India, 'fixing the limits of their respective spheres of influence', and 'the eastern and southern Frontier of His Highness's (The Amir's) dominions'.[5] The Durand Line, as it became known, was then defined on the ground in 1894 and 1895, covering 1,584 miles.

It was an uncomfortable arrangement, however. The line did not reflect locally defined boundaries, or put to bed Afghanistan's historic claims to lands in north India, including to the city of Peshawar – indeed, many Afghans simply viewed the agreement as a temporary suspension of their claim for the sake of political expediency. There were few geographic markers, like rivers, to work from and so a number of tribes – such as the Mohmands, Afridis and Wazirs – found themselves straddling the Durand Line and then used that status to play both governments off against each other to suit their own interests, particularly when it came to settling disputes and receiving allowances. Meanwhile, Amir Abdur Rahman himself realised that while the deal met the needs of the hour, it would in all likelihood store up problems in the future. He had signed the agreement with Durand because it had been a pragmatic solution to a thorny problem, buying him the time and the resources – in the form of British guns and money – to meet his immediate goal, building a strong Afghan state under his rule. As he explained in his autobiography, however:

> If you should cut them [Pashtun tribal territories], they will neither be of any use to you nor to me. You will always be engaged in fighting or other trouble with them, and they will always go on plundering. As long as your government is strong and in peace, you will be able to keep them quiet by a strong hand, but if at any time a foreign enemy appears on the borders of India, these frontier tribes will be your worst enemies.[6]

Given this complex situation, it was hardly surprising that the legal status of the Durand Line would come under intense scrutiny in the late 1940s.

In 1901, the British Indian side of the Frontier was divided into two parts, which were carved out of the Punjab. The first were the five Settled Districts or Administered Area of the North-West Frontier Province (NWFP), which accounted for two-fifths of the territory and were home to around 4 million Pashtuns. The remaining 2 million Pashtuns resided in the so-called 'unsettled' and 'unadministered' areas to the west, located between NWFP and the Durand Line. Pashtun tribes were predominant in the 'unsettled' areas, but were neither politically nor economically dominant in the 'settled' areas where much of the commerce and many of the professions, including the bureaucracy, was in the hands of non-Pashtun Muslims, Hindus and Sikhs.

The 1921 Anglo-Afghan Treaty confirmed the Durand Line as the frontier. As a 1949 Foreign Office Research Department report pointed out, 'thus that [which] was formerly merely a "limit" to spheres of influence now became the international boundary laid down by agreement between the Afghan government and His Majesty's Government'.[7] The treaty included two important clauses – one acknowledging the interests of Britain and Afghanistan in the tribal areas close to the Durand Line; the second, Article 11, stating that the two 'hereby undertake each to inform the other in future of any military operations of major importance which may appear necessary for the maintenance of order among the Frontier tribes residing within their respective spheres'.[8] Britain therefore officially acknowledged in 1921 that Afghanistan had an equal stake in the future of the Frontier area.

The un-administered tribal areas never became officially part of British India. The tribes enjoyed the category of 'British protected persons' living under customary law administered by tribal assembles or *jirgas*. Their relations with the rest of India were agreed through a series of treaties, agreements and allowances, and not through the laws of the British government in India. The Afridis of the Khyber Pass, for instance, undertook not to impose transit dues on travellers in exchange for financial subsidies and arms. Thereafter, the tribes were more or less left to their own devices. Fifteen years later, when the settled areas of NWFP were accorded the right to set up an elected legislative assembly under the Government of India Act of 1935, the tribal areas remained distinct. They were placed under the direct responsibility of the Governor General and thenceforth his representatives, British political agents, negotiated agreements, distributed allowances in exchange for peace, and deployed troops when the need arose. The 1935 Act effectively meant that the tribal areas were now part of India, but crucially they were not part of directly administered British India. This distinction was to be a key issue in the arguments deployed by the Afghans in the 1940s.

The Afghan government's own relationship with the Pashtun tribes on their side of the Durand Line was equally complex. Since Pashtun tribesmen had played a key role in toppling Amanullah in 1928, and had helped Nadir Shah to claim the throne a year later, the present Afghan royal family knew its security was highly dependent on their continued support. Like the British, they too paid allowances to the tribes, including to some on the other side of the line too. After Afghan independence, relations with British India in the Frontier area were mixed. By the 1940s, however, things had improved considerably – most recently, in 1945, the British had prevented the Mohmand tribe on the Indian side of the Durand Line from joining the Safis across the border, who had rebelled against the Afghan government's proposal to change the way tribes provided conscripts to the army. The British also hastened the supply of military equipment and ammunition to help the Afghan army defeat the rebellion. Prime Minister Hashim Khan later conveyed his appreciation during a meeting with the legation's Political Counsellor:

> The events of the last summer had had one pleasing result. They had proved that we could speak frankly to each as friends, even brothers, about our mutual problems and consequently, a hitherto unknown degree of cooperation [between] the governments of India and Afghanistan had been achieved ... The government of India had nobly and promptly come to their aid (by restraining the Mohmands in the presumptive area, and by the emergent supply of military equipment and munitions). A few years ago, he said, the Afghans would not have dreamt of approaching us so openly and frankly ... and the government of India would not have dreamt of pouring valuable military equipment into the country.[9]

Historically, the Afghans had regularly reminded the British since 1893 that they hoped the tribal areas would be returned to them if and when

Britain left Asia. At the beginning of the Second World War, this had seemed a hypothetical discussion. Towards the end of the war however, as demands for Indian independence gathered pace, the Afghans speculated that India might just gain independence in the not too distant future and decided to put a few markers down. Squire recorded an account of one such meeting with Ali Mohammed in November 1944:

> The Foreign Minister said that while the Afghan government were prepared fully to respect their treaty obligations in regard to the Indian boundary so long as British control in India is maintained ... no Afghan government could possibly contemplate the handing over of areas populated by people of Afghan origin with the present Indian boundary to a Hindu government, or for that matter to a Muslim government. His Majesty's Minister [Squire] suggested the removal of all British control from India was so remote that it was scarcely necessary to raise the point at this stage.[10]

In the months that followed, however, the Afghans began to widen their arguments. They requested that the people in the territories ceded to Britain under the 1879 Treaty of Gandamak – in Balochistan and NWFP – be given the opportunity to decide for themselves whether they wanted to join Afghanistan or become a separate state if the status of India changed. This would, they argued, be in line with preparations for the separation of Burma and Ceylon from India.[11] By mid-March 1946, they began to raise questions about the future of the 'unsettled' tribes along the Frontier and the 'settled' tribes in NWFP.[12] While Squire was happy to concede that this made sense geographically and politically, he was not at all convinced, as he told Ali Mohammed, that the tribes themselves would welcome this proposal, especially as it would cut them off from the financial benefits they currently enjoyed under the British government in India.[13]

In response to the reports from Kabul, officials in London thought it might be helpful to examine the issues further. They looked at all the arguments put forward so far by the Afghan government, consulted Squire and his team in Kabul, and then wrote briefing papers for a Cabinet meeting in March 1946. These conceded that the Afghan royal family could in all likelihood be deposed if it acquiesced quietly to the transfer of Pashtun territory to a new government in India, particularly a Hindu-majority one. They also agreed that the Afghans had legitimate concerns about security in the tribal belt if the British left India:

> The reality is here that the Afghan government find it impossible to visualise an Indian government strong enough, without British support,

to prevent the North-West Frontier dissolving into anarchy and chaos with fatal consequences to themselves ... [A Hindu–Muslim struggle in India] would constitute an open invitation to tribal irruption both on the Islamic appeal, and on the purely barbaric motives of loot and destruction; continuing because the anarchic Pashtun is quick to sense indecision or weakening of authority. The destructive vitality of the purely Muslim belt thus emerges as a major factor in a constitutional settlement in India.

On the other hand, although they completely dismissed Afghan arguments that the tribes were looking to the Afghan government for a lead, they privately agreed that these issues needed to be taken into account in planning for any future handover of power.[14]

Fifteen months later, in a simultaneous broadcast in Delhi and London on 3 June 1947, Attlee, Jinnah, Nehru and Mountbatten announced that India would become independent. The statement included the possibility of a plebiscite (or referendum) for the inhabitants of NWFP to decide whether to join Pakistan or India, and a provision for the tribes in the non-administered tribal areas along the Durand Line to negotiate their future relations with whatever successor government would be concerned with the Frontier.

By pure coincidence, this broadcast was made on the same day that the Afghan government issued an aide-memoire setting out their concerns and outlining their 'ask' of the British government. They explained they were worried about Soviet intentions and tribal disturbances in the event of a power vacuum, and feared disruptions in the supply of petrol, kerosene, sugar and textiles from India after independence. In view of this, they requested Britain to sort out the status of the tribal territories before the new successor government was established.[15] When the Afghans heard the broadcast, they felt betrayed. Unsurprisingly, Hashim Khan told Squire on 30 June 1947 that he had never been as disappointed as now by the British refusal to restore the Pashtun areas of north-west India to Afghanistan. He had expected the whole issue to be resolved before independence. Now, 'he could only conclude that this was a further example of the British determination to ruin Afghanistan, which he had hoped during all his time as Prime Minister to exorcise'.[16]

The British quickly dismissed the Afghan line of argument linking the Frontier question to Soviet intentions – indeed, they questioned whether this fear was real or imagined and suspected it was simply sabre rattling to frighten Britain and encourage the United States to get engaged.[17] Beyond this, however, British officials and diplomats in London, Kabul and Delhi privately agreed with the Afghans. They were all too aware how volatile the tribes could be and realised that a power vacuum could trigger serious unrest. For this reason, they had also been making efforts to understand tribal perspectives as well.

The evidence, however, suggested there were no straightforward solutions. For instance, in one *Jirga* between Afridi tribesmen and the then Governor of NWFP, Sir George Cunningham, on 15 March 1947, the Afridi said they considered themselves closer to Afghanistan than to India because of their shared Muslim faith, but that the Khyber Pass should come to them and not to the Muslim League or any other body, and that their territory should be independent. As Foreign Office analysts examined a range of sources, they were forced to conclude that 'while the spiritual allegiance of the tribes is due to Kabul, their economic allegiance is essentially bound up with India, to which they look for all necessary imports of food, clothing, arms, kerosene etc and for a market for their exports'.[18] Taking all things into consideration, continuing the status quo under Britain's successor government in India seemed to make most sense.

The British responded formally to the aide-memoire on 4 July. Their tone was somewhat curt, reminding the Afghans that they were extremely busy on other matters. As far as the border was concerned, they were prioritising two issues – protecting the territorial integrity of the new states of Pakistan and India, and maintaining peace in the tribal areas between the lapse of British authority and the time when a new government took over. They were not prepared to accommodate Afghan concerns or to open up a much broader discussion of the type the Afghan government had in mind. The territory in question was 'an integral part of India,' and Britain could not

> admit the right of any foreign governments to intervene in matters which are the sole concern of the inhabitants of the territories in question ... The Pashtuns in the tribal areas are left entirely free [under the 3 June statement] to negotiate their future relations with whatever successor government is concerned with the Frontier ... As regards the settled districts of the North-West Frontier Province, the people are to be given the opportunity freely to express their wishes regarding their future, but the geographic factors that govern the security of India cannot be overlooked. If the districts of the North-West Frontier Province were to attempt to form themselves into a small independent state, they could not possibly safeguard their own security and would be a source of weakness to India.

The future status of Pashtun tribesmen had finally been clearly set out. Those in the 'unsettled' or 'un-administered' tribal areas would have their opportunity to renegotiate their treaty and allowance arrangements with Britain's successor government in the area. Those in NWFP would have a plebiscite to choose between Pakistan and India. A third option, independence, had been specifically ruled out.[19] This answer, not surprisingly, failed to satisfy the Afghans. They quickly shifted their focus to the plebiscite and Ali Mohammed sent a six-page letter on 11 July arguing that the settled districts in NWFP should be given two additional choices, independence or joining Afghanistan.[20] Interestingly, the Afghans did not focus attention then, as the following sections will show, on the plans for the unsettled tribal areas, in spite of the fact that it may, in retrospect, have been just possible for the tribes at that time to negotiate new agreements with Afghanistan, rather than with Britain's successor government.

The NWFP Plebiscite

The decision to allow the people of NWFP to decide whether to join Pakistan or India resulted from the unique nature of NWFP politics in the 1930s and 1940s, and not from pressure from Afghanistan. A Pashtun nationalist movement did indeed exist in NWFP in the 1940s, but this did not align with Afghan policy or mobilise Afghan propaganda to achieve its ends in the run up to the plebiscite. To understand these dynamics, it is necessary to step back a little and explain what was going on in NWFP at the time.

By 1947, Muslim leaders in NWFP had become very different from Pashtun tribesmen in the unsettled areas. Two schools had been established in Peshawar which specifically catered for the sons of tribal leaders, landowners and other influential families. Many had subsequently taken up professional posts or joined the Indian Civil Service and Indian Army, where they were well represented in the officer ranks. Within this context, a Pashtun political leader called Abdul Ghaffar Khan had been keen to further the political, social and economic prospects of the Pashtuns as a distinct cultural identity, one embracing reform and change, not locked into the past. He created a Pashtun journal in 1928 and a new political party, the Afghan *Jirga*, in 1929, which stood for independence from Britain, Hindu–Muslim unity and reform of Pashtun society.[21] Three months later, he created a parallel organisation, the *Khudai Khidmatgars* (Servants of God), which soon overshadowed the Afghan *Jirga*.[22] Abdul Ghaffar Khan's appeal spread much further than the Pashtuns, however. Although he addressed himself to Pashtuns, he used this term in a much wider sense, referring to everyone living in Pashtun society or NWFP who supported social, political and economic reform, thus breaking down the distinction between Pashtuns, non-Pashtun Muslims and other religious and ethnic/tribal groups.[23] This approach was to prove critical when arguments were deployed in the run up to the 1947 plebiscite to head off union with the Punjabi Muslims. His brother, Dr Khan Sahib, joined the movement a few years later on return from his medical studies in Britain.

In 1931, the *Khudai Khidmatgars* formally allied themselves with the India Congress Party, a seemingly unusual match since NWFP was predominantly Muslim and Congress predominantly Hindu. It suited both, however, since it offered opportunities for financial backing and a stronger base for their respective anti-British campaigns.[24] The Khan brothers' strategy began to bear fruit, especially when the 1935 Government of India Act granted NWFP the status of a governor's province, recognising the rights of the settled tribes to the same political privileges and institutions as those enjoyed in the rest of India. Frontier Congress won the first Assembly elections and Dr Khan Sahib became Chief Minister, in spite of the Muslim League's manifesto calling for Muslim solidarity against Congress. People had voted for the party that seemed most likely to address local concerns.

The Muslim League won the 1943 election, but later failed to capture and maintain public support. Their government fell in a vote of no confidence in March 1945. The Governor of NWFP then asked Dr Khan Sahib to form a ministry once again, and Frontier Congress won the elections the following year. This time, however, the new government was shaky from the start. When Nehru visited in October 1946, he found himself heckled by the crowds and there were fears for his safety. As the Muslim League stepped up its campaign of civil disobedience against Britain, and Hindu–Muslim communal violence began to spread across the province, many Muslims in NWFP became increasingly attracted to Jinnah's idea of a separate Muslim-majority nation. The new governor, Sir Olaf Caroe, argued that the only way to end the violence would be to hold new elections to the NWFP Assembly. Nehru, however, bitterly opposed this proposal, concerned that an election would look as though Congress had bowed to Muslim League pressure. When Mountbatten visited the province on 28–29 April, he saw for himself just how bad the violence had become and concluded elections were no longer practical. Given this situation, he later concluded, the only way forward was to hold a plebiscite so that the people themselves could decide whether they wanted to be part of Pakistan or India, rather than leave the matter to be settled by a vote in the Assembly, the approach in Punjab and Bengal.[25]

That summer, amid rumours that India might be partitioned, the Khan brothers, the *Khudai Khidmatgars*, and other Frontier Congress Party members started to demand the creation of an autonomous Pashtun state,

Pashtunistan, and made a number of statements in press conferences to this effect. On 15 May, for instance, Dr Khan Sahib told reporters: 'Pashtuns will never be dominated by anybody, but in a sovereign state of NWFP we shall join hands with others having due regard to their interests as well as those of India as a whole.' What that meant in practice was far from clear however. It certainly reflected Pashtun fears of Punjabi domination in the name of the Muslim religion,[26] but beyond that, it may simply have been a bargaining tool to maximise NWFP political leverage in any successor administration. A letter apparently exists from Dr Khan Sahib to Nehru, dated 16 June, arguing that behind the demand for Pashtunistan lay the idea that NWFP would have full provincial autonomy within the Indian Union, not Pakistan.[27] In contrast, one commentator has speculated that the idea of Pashtunistan may just have represented the ideal of a Pashtun society liberated from blood feuds.[28] Whatever the case, Frontier Congress and the *Khudai Khidmatgars* announced on 21 June that an 'independent government of all the Pashtuns should be established'. Afghanistan was not mentioned.

The British refused to countenance the idea of an autonomous or independent Pashtunistan in any form. They had earlier proposed a 'Plan Balkan' idea for India, which would have enabled all eleven provinces, as well as the 562 Princely States, to opt for independent status, but this had been rejected. By June, all parties, including the Muslim League, had agreed that India would be partitioned into just two entities. If one province now had the option of breaking away and forming a third, then others might try to do so too.

The timing of the plebiscite was therefore crucial. If it was held before the Provincial Assemblies in Punjab and Bengal voted to partition their provinces between India and Pakistan, this would leave open the door for NWFP voters to opt to join India. Once the Punjab Assembly had voted for Pakistan, however, which seemed highly likely, it would be virtually impossible for NWFP to be part of India since it would be geographically cut off from it by Punjab. The plebiscite was therefore scheduled to take place after these assemblies had voted. Frontier Congress members felt betrayed by Nehru and the rest of Congress' leadership. Three weeks before polling began, Abdul Ghaffar Khan declared that Frontier Congress would boycott it and continue to work peacefully for Pashtunistan.[29]

Polling took place over two weeks in July. When the ballots were counted, 292,118 people had voted for Pakistan, and 2,874 in favour of India. This landslide victory was tempered by the fact that only 55 per cent of the total electorate had actually voted – the boycott by Frontier Congress had played a big part in that. Nevertheless, the result was clear – 51 per cent of the electorate had voted to join Pakistan. It was not a great result, but at least the Muslim League could take comfort from the fact that it had doubled its vote since the Provincial Assembly elections a year earlier.[30]

Afghan Hopes Thwarted

From his vantage point in Kabul, Squire had been frustrated by the way Congress Party had used NWFP for its own political ends, and concerned about the Afghan government's role in muddying the waters. He had actively encouraged the Afghans to back down:

> We have latterly been kept very busy with the Afghan campaign about the NWFP Referendum. There has been a lot of telegraphing and they have been clearly told to mind their own business. It has all been very stupid and has aroused a good deal of mistrust in India, coinciding as it did with what appeared to be an unscrupulous stunt on the part of Congress to try and make the inevitable Pakistan unworkable in a shameless evasion of the condition explicitly laid down by the Congress itself that no secession either of the states or of units such as Bengal should be tolerated – the Afghan campaign received a very poor reception. I had to speak very straight to MFA [Minister of Foreign Affairs] and then to the PM. I think they got frightened and have now dropped their propaganda, and Shah Mahmud is today arriving in Delhi en route for the United States to see his son and will talk with the Viceroy [Mountbatten] and I hope also with Jinnah.[31]

As for Squire's hope that Mahmud Khan's differences with Indian leaders could be resolved during a face-to-face meeting in Delhi, this was to be dashed by an unfortunate sequence of events which left a bad taste in the mouth of all concerned. The idea of a meeting between Shah Mahmud, Jinnah and Nehru had been mooted privately by the British for some time. The initiative was welcomed by the Americans too – behind the scenes, they were becoming increasingly concerned that instability along the Frontier would threaten the supply of goods, equipment and fuel for the Helmand project. Some fancy footwork, however, was required to make the meeting come about, without raising expectations or provoking ill-feeling all round. If Mahmud Khan received an invitation to visit Delhi, that would perhaps, feared the British, suggest the Afghans actually had a valid case. On the other hand, the optics would look completely different if the meeting came about because he was planning to travel through Delhi in any case on his way from Karachi to London and Washington.[32]

All went well to begin with. The Prime Minister was invited to stay at Mountbatten's house in Delhi as the Viceroy's personal guest and invitations to dinner were sent out to Indian leaders, including Nehru, Jinnah and Liaquat Ali Khan. But then the best-laid plans, and all the diplomatic positioning around it, went awry, thwarted by a 'contretemps', as Mountbatten put it.[33] The Prime Minister's plane arrived in Delhi too late for him to get to the dinner, and then, rather than going to the Viceroy's residence, he had promptly got on another plane back to Karachi to catch his scheduled flight to London. British diplomats tried to fathom out how this had happened. In the meantime, they faced constant reproaches from the Americans who wanted to know if Mahmud Khan had been accorded appropriate VIP facilities in Delhi, and whether the British had considered procuring a plane to take him direct to Karachi after the meeting. Indeed, had the British accorded his visit sufficient importance at all?

It took a further two months to get to the bottom of what had really happened, by which time a great deal of ill-feeling had been passed around. It turned out that the Prime Minister's flight from Peshawar had been delayed by engine trouble and the pilot had decided it was safer to stay overnight in Lahore rather than fly to Delhi in the dark. The Viceroy had actually arranged for a special plane to collect him from Lahore, but this had been cancelled at the last minute once it became clear he would be too late for the meeting. In addition, the Prime Minister been accorded all due courtesies at Delhi Airport by the Viceroy's Military Secretary himself.[34]

If the Prime Minister felt angry about this incident, however, he did not show it when he reached London. He met King George VI on 30 July, was a guest for dinner with the Foreign Secretary, Ernest Bevin, that evening, and had lunch with Prime Minister, Clement Attlee, at No. 10 on 31 July. He arranged to have a follow-up round of meetings on his way back to Kabul that November, when he would be in London to attend the royal wedding between Princess Elizabeth and Philip of Greece at Westminster Abbey.

Any hopes that Shah Mahmud's meetings in London and Washington would end Afghan agitation about Pashtunistan were, however, premature. When the Deputy Speaker of the NWFP Assembly visited Kabul in early August, Squire suspected that Congress planned to harness Afghan support to undermine Pakistan:

Meanwhile, the Afghan campaign goes on stimulated by a visit from one Girdhari Lal Puri, a Cambridge graduate and Deputy Speaker of the NWFP Legislative Assembly and obviously here on a mission for the local Congress Party. That party seems to be preparing trouble in the NWF when the new Pakistan government turns out the Khan brothers, and seems to be trying to enlist tribal and Afghan support for the disturbances they propose to make.

He was relieved however that 'the Pakistan government seem confident that they will be able to cope with the situation'.[35] One cause for his optimism was Jinnah's press statement on 31 July:

> As regards the tribal areas, I am very happy to acknowledge the great support they have freely given to their fellow Muslims in their demand for an independent state. I wish to assure them on behalf of the Provisional Government of Pakistan that we would like to continue after August 15th all Treaties, Agreements and Allowances until such time as representatives of the tribes and of the Pakistan government have met and negotiated new arrangements ... The Government of Pakistan has no desire whatever to interfere in any way with the traditional independence of the tribal areas.[36]

So there it was. A clear announcement to one and all that the post-independence Pakistan government intended to ensure the smooth transition of governance in the tribal areas from the British to the new government in Karachi. Within a two-week period, Pakistan had not only gained NWFP through a plebiscite, but also sorted out how it would absorb the un-administered tribal areas too. Neither the British nor the Pakistanis realised at this point how committed the Afghans would remain to the Pashtunistan cause. Thereafter, they would try even harder to get their demands met.

Independence
On Independence Day, 15 August, Squire's views were mixed: 'Certainly we have reached our goal and have divested ourselves of responsibility for India far more successfully and with far less bloodshed than could possibly have been predicted 6 months ago.' Things were still, however, a little rough around the edges:

> So much for the general picture. The details are less promising. What will happen on the Frontier we do not know. The Congress government [in NWFP] will have to be turned out, but how successfully they will resist remains to be seen. Afghanistan seems to have been cooperating with them in their common agitation for an independent Pashtunistan ... but

it may be that the Afghans have not themselves been very serious and that their agitation will have no tangible results.[37]

Just over a week later, however, the Afghans announced their intention to increase their agitation, not lessen it, and make life more, not less, comfortable for Pakistan. This time round, King Zahir Shah himself took up the cause. On 24 August, he sent a public letter via the government-controlled newspaper *Anis* to the new Governor General of Pakistan, Jinnah, asking him to ensure the 'independence of trans-border Afghans'. On the following day, the King also used the annual Afghanistan Independence Day celebrations to declare:

> Our hearts are with those Afghan brethren who are struggling for their lawful rights ... Once their legitimate rights are secured in principle and to the satisfaction of the people of those areas, we will welcome any coordination in conditions of life and cooperation between them and their Pakistan brethren and the Pakistan state.[38]

Then in early October, Afghanistan cast a lone vote in New York opposing Pakistan's admission to the United Nations and threatened to raise the question of Pashtunistan in the United Nations General Assembly. At the time, British officials concluded the Afghan representative in New York had acted independently without consulting Mahmud Khan. Squire felt Afghanistan had not handled the situation well, but felt fairly relaxed about things overall. 'Afghanistan,' he wrote in his journal on the 11th, 'is still peaceful and friendly, but has made a bad "gaff" by opposing Pakistan in the United Nations Organisation and greatly harmed her relations with Pakistan, but she is behaving well with the tribes, who are unusually quiet. Whether she will be able to continue the process of gradual rapprochement under the new conditions remains to be seen.'

Shah Mahmud's return visit to London on his way back to Kabul took on new importance. During his meeting with Bevin on 28 November, he asked for British help to secure autonomous status for the tribal areas in Pakistan and underlined his concern about the stability of the area. Bevin politely refused but agreed to meet him again before he left London. A telegram was despatched to Karachi to inform the Pakistan government what had been discussed, confirming that Britain had refused to mediate, but would be happy to do so if Pakistan so wished.[39]

Throughout the rest of November and on into December, British officials tried to make sense of Mahmud Khan's position so that they were fully prepared for his next round of meetings in London. They were still unclear what geographic area Mahmud Khan actually meant when he talked about 'autonomous status for the tribes'. Did he only mean the un-administered tribal areas along the Frontier, or did he also include the settled, administered area of NWFP too? They pored over the information they had received to date from Kabul and the minutes from previous meetings with Afghan government representatives in London. In the end, the Foreign Office concluded he meant the 'un-administered' territory lying between the Durand Line and the administrative borders of the settled districts in Balochistan and NWFP during the British period, and probably not NWFP, even though the Afghans had taken an active interest in the July plebiscite.[40]

The legal position, it seemed, was less clear cut, however. On 15 August, the tribal areas had been released from their commitments to British India and restored to independent status until the Pakistan government established its own treaties and agreements with them.[41] Although this suggested a break in the transfer of governance from Britain to Pakistan, advice from Foreign Office legal advisers on 5 November confirmed that Pakistan had indeed inherited Britain's rights and duties under the Anglo-Afghan Treaty of 1921 with respect to the tribal areas. The Pakistan government's subsequent treaties and agreements with the tribes, in line with Jinnah's 31 July statement, reaffirmed this. Separately, British officials had also been receiving reports that the tribes were comfortable with these arrangements, and that, although some supported the idea of Pashtunistan, this was not causing undue problems.

General Sir Geoffrey Allen Percival Scoones in the Commonwealth Relations Office in Whitehall had a slightly different take on the situation, however. He was an experienced military officer who had enjoyed a lengthy career in India, including on the North-West Frontier, and therefore had a good understanding of the local situation.[42] He wondered whether the real reason behind Mahmud Khan's Pashtunistan policy was to make the tribes more powerful because he knew Pakistan did not have sufficient resources to keep the tribes in check in the same way the British had done. By pushing the Pashtunistan cause, Scoones speculated, Mahmud Khan believed he could kill two birds with one stone. He could reward the tribes on the Pakistan side of the Durand Line (especially the Wazirs and the Mahsuds), who had played a crucial role in helping the present royal family secure its position in 1929. At the same time, he could also reduce the likelihood of a tribal uprising which might quickly get out of hand. In Scoones' view, therefore, Mahmud Khan's ultimate aim was to reach a satisfactory deal with Pakistan to secure the border area against instability, but 'what is required, and what is lacking at present, is a common [Afghan-Pakistan] policy towards them [the tribes] and a common system of control. His Majesty's Government can take no executive action in this matter, but may be able to create the atmosphere for talks on these lines by getting Pakistan to face the issue'.[43]

The Cabinet meeting chaired by Attlee on 9 December concluded that there was no immediate threat of serious trouble in the tribal areas and that the only long-term solution to the problem would be for Pakistan, India and Afghanistan to work together. The 'great difficulty in translating this idea into practice at the present time' was recognised, but Britain should stay well out of the discussions and not get involved in any form of mediation between the respective parties. This point, the Cabinet agreed, should be made clear to all three governments.[44]

Accordingly, when Sir Orme Sargent, Permanent Under-Secretary at the Foreign Office, met Mahmud Khan on 12 December, he focussed on the condition of the tribes, and not on Afghan demands for Pashtunistan. Sargent told Mahmud about Pakistan's agreements with the tribes after Independence, and pointed out that the signs for the future looked fairly good. He had also heard several reports that the tribes were content with the arrangements and reassured the Prime Minister that there were no signs of unrest. Mahmud Khan, in response, said he was not so sure. He did not believe the matter could be solved bilaterally by Afghanistan and Pakistan. He was happy for the main points of the meeting to be shared with the Pakistan government – indeed, these would be useful for his forthcoming meetings with Jinnah in Karachi – but he stressed Britain needed to stay engaged.[45]

Any confidence British officials may have felt after their meeting with Mahmud Khan was swiftly dispelled a month later. When the new United States Ambassador to Pakistan, Paul Alling, passed through London in January 1948, he told them that during his previous post in the State Department, he had learnt Mahmud himself had been behind the Afghan refusal to recognise Pakistan as a member of the UN. It was not, as the British had assumed, due to the Afghan representative to the UN acting on his own initiative. This point is still contentious, and the Afghans refute this version of events to this day.[46] Unfortunately, the damage was done. Perceptions and rumours became facts, irrespective of whether Mahmud Khan had sanctioned his representative's actions or not. Thereafter, the British believed 'that Shah Mahmud, despite our considerable efforts to win his good will and cooperation, both before his visit to America and on his way back, is the main complicating factor in the present situation'.[47]

The Afghan–Pakistan–India Nexus: Trouble in Kashmir

Relations between Jinnah's Muslim League and Nehru's Congress Party remained acrimonious after independence and soon found expression in a bloody struggle over the future of the Princely State of Kashmir. Afghan claims for Pashtunistan gradually became caught up in this wider geopolitical context.

After the 3 June announcement on Partition, attention had shifted to the future status of the 562 Princely States, which had made separate treaties with Britain during the days of the empire. It was decided that they should either join India, where most of them were located, or Pakistan, in exchange for an annual allowance from the relevant government. Kashmir was one of three that held out.[48] The whys and wherefores of the Kashmir crisis are not covered in detail here. Lots of controversy surrounds it. What is not disputed is that the mostly Muslim population of Kashmir at independence wanted to be part of Pakistan, but the ruler, a Hindu Maharajah, was still undecided. As tensions grew, the Maharaja's troops launched a violent assault against Muslims, especially in Poonch and Jammu. Thousands were killed and many more were displaced. Large areas of Gilgit, Hunza and Nagar unilaterally seceded from Kashmir to join Pakistan. At the end of October, the Maharaja finally signed the instrument of accession to India, which then provided cover for Nehru to send Indian troops into Kashmir to defend Indian territory.[49] Meanwhile, the British estimated that about 300,000 tribesmen from the North-West Frontier and a further 25,000 from Balochistan had stormed into Kashmir to support the Poonchis and then set off towards Srinagar, the capital of Kashmir, to force the issue.[50] Communal violence, looting and outbreaks of fighting continued for months. By mid-November, Liaquat Ali Khan, Pakistan's new Prime Minister, thought the matter should be referred to the United Nations. Two months later, Nehru did too. It took another year, however, before a ceasefire was finally declared on 1 January 1949.[51]

As the tribesmen set off to Kashmir in the autumn of 1947, Britain's immediate concerns were that their departure would provoke instability in the tribal areas, which could in all likelihood be exacerbated by any political vacuum during the transition from British to Pakistani rule. The tribes could engage in widespread looting on both sides of the Durand Line and later use arms and ammunition brought back from Kashmir to ferment more unrest. The Afghan government were equally concerned.[52] Both governments knew that stability in the tribal region was dependent on allowances and agreements, backed up by the threat or use of military force. For that reason, the former British government in India had maintained a large troop presence on the Frontier ready to intervene if any inter- or intra-tribal aggression got out of hand. The Afghan military had been trained and equipped to deal with such an eventuality too. Now, worryingly, the War Office in Whitehall was beginning to collect intelligence that the number of troops deployed by Pakistan on the Frontier had declined significantly.

According to this intelligence, the number of battalions employed on the Frontier had dropped from about fifty in 1939 to around thirty in 1947. This was hardly surprising since the military forces of British India had been divided at Partition and Pakistan now had only forty-five battalions in total to cover the whole state.[53] Mountbatten had already been concerned before 15 August that Pakistan might not allocate sufficient troops to the area and had warned Jinnah about this, explaining in no uncertain terms that 'there is no doubt but that it is impossible to avoid a very considerable risk on the Frontier during the period immediately after the transfer of power'.[54] More worrying news emerged on 14 November. Jinnah announced the withdrawal of Pakistani troops from North and South Waziristan to 'eliminate all suspicions in [the] brotherhood of Islam of which [the] tribes and Pakistan were both members, and he hoped that by the moving of the troops, the bonds of friendship would be stronger than ever'. Jinnah had, it seemed, calculated that since the tribes had pledged their loyalty to Pakistan and signed formal agreements in return for allowances, they would cause little trouble. The British Deputy High Commission in Peshawar reported that the number of battalions had now gone down to around nine.[55]

Although British military intelligence estimated that Pakistan's military capability was more than double that of Afghanistan's,[56] the War Office retained serious doubts that Pakistan would be able to cope with any major unrest in the tribal areas, especially if their tribes were joined by those on the other side of the Durand Line. They also concluded that it was highly unlikely that the Indian government would come to Pakistan's assistance. Afghanistan was the unknown variable so they sought Squire's and Lancaster's advice: 'If tribes on [the] Pakistan side of Durand Line started hostile movement against [the] settled districts [in NWFP], how far do you think the Afghan government would support them in deference to "national feeling"? Could [the] Afghan government be relied on, in their own interests, to restrain their tribes from joining in [an] attack?' The reply from Squire was not terribly promising. He pointed out that the Afghan government were fully aware of the risk, and were hoping that if the tribes moved, it would be to the east into Pakistan, and not west into Afghan territory.[57]

Gradually, however, the British legation began to suspect that the Afghans were playing a far more subtle game than they had at first realised and were exploiting the Kashmir crisis to progress their own Pashtunistan policy. According to Squire, Kashmir pushed all the right buttons. It was not merely about gaining territory. It represented 'another plank in India's programme of encirclement'. India and Afghanistan were therefore natural allies against Pakistan. Agitation in the tribal areas would force Pakistan to shift some of its attention away from Kashmir and thus give India more room for manoeuvre. Squire and his team also suspected the Afghans were spreading anti-Pakistan propaganda to keep the tribes' minds focussed on Pashtunistan, not Kashmir. As Squire explained to London, 'possibly Shah Mahmud, who has always been primarily interested in the tribes, thinks that it will pay him best to divert their attention to the Pashtunistan question in preference to that of Kashmir'.[58] News from New York seemed to confirm this. The Afghan Representative to the United Nations had presented a letter to the President of the Security Council asking to be allowed to participate in discussions on Kashmir which related to the Frontier tribesmen. Conscious this could only serve to add fuel to the existing fire, London instructed its representatives in New York and Kabul to discourage Afghan participation:

> We certainly do not wish to complicate an already involved situation by giving Afghans [an] opportunity to air their views on Pashtunistan which would not only irritate Pakistan but reduce [the] chances of Pakistan and India reaching a settlement … We therefore hope that no encouragement will be given at this stage to [the] Afghan demand to intervene in the proceedings before the Security Council.[59]

Afghanistan also appeared to be exploiting deteriorating relations between India and Pakistan in its wider diplomatic strategy too. India initially showed no interest in establishing diplomatic relations with Afghanistan, preferring to let the British legation continue representing its interests, in the short term at least. For Pakistan, however, with its long border with Afghanistan, exchanging diplomatic relations was a priority. Negotiations got off to a bad start from the outset. The man sent by Jinnah to establish official relations that September, Saidullah Khan, irritated the Afghans and the international community alike. He eventually 'got his way and an agreement to open embassies but the Afghans are very annoyed about the way it has been done and I am sure that they will avoid having Saidullah Khan back as Ambassador if they can do so'. Moreover, recorded Squire, 'we have found S.K. very difficult too. He writes very long letters asking for things I have already refused, and ignoring my reasons for refusing. We definitely hope that he will not return though about this we are not optimistic. He has put everyone's backs up by refusing all invitations when he will not be the senior guest!'[60]

Once Saidullah Khan left Kabul, Afghanistan tried to peg an agreement on exchanging diplomatic relations to a deal on Pashtunistan, while Pakistan argued that relations should be exchanged before any bilateral agreement between the two countries was discussed.[61] The situation became even more rancorous in December 1947 when it was announced that India and Afghanistan had agreed to exchange diplomatic relations.[62] Behind the scenes, British and American diplomats in Kabul and Karachi tried to encourage both parties to sort this out without preconditions and to stop their propaganda campaigns against each other. They also suggested to the Pakistan government that their relations with Afghanistan might improve if they concluded a bilateral treaty covering a number of non-controversial matters, such as transit rights and trade.[63] Afghanistan finally agreed to exchange relations with Pakistan, without conditions, in February. The Afghans had made their point, however. Henceforth, India was to be their ally of choice, not Pakistan.

If the British were beginning to suspect Afghanistan and India were playing a double game against Pakistan, the arrival of Girdhari Lal Puri as a member of the new Indian embassy in April 1948 seemed to confirm their suspicions. This was the very same man who had visited Kabul the previous summer and had used his position as a member of the Frontier Congress Party and Speaker of the NWFP Legislative Assembly to stir up pro-Pashtunistan propaganda. The Foreign Office recalled that Squire had 'considered him most dangerous as he was working for tribal disturbances and Afghan intervention in support of [the] North-West Frontier Province Congress Ministry. He supplied [the] Afghan Press with anti-Pakistan articles from the Indian Press. Puri's appointment seems likely to heighten the intrigue between India and Afghanistan and hence make re-establishment of normal relations between India and Pakistan more difficult.'[64] Within a month of his arrival, Pakistan intelligence reports shared with Britain claimed he was already paying the tribes to make trouble for Pakistan and to deter them from going to Kashmir.[65]

Just over a year later, in April 1949, the British were given a unique insight into Pakistani thinking at this time. General Walter Cawthorn, Deputy Chief of Staff in the Pakistan Army, was officially given copies of internal government papers over the past year to share with London.[66] These showed that Pakistani ministers and officials were drawing similar conclusions to the British. Pakistan too, it seemed, viewed Indian interest in Afghanistan as purely instrumental – to fuel disturbances in the tribal areas against Pakistan. As one document conjectured, 'India is anxious that in the event of a renewal of fighting in Kashmir, Afghanistan should at least give indirect help by preventing the tribesmen from going to Kashmir and by creating disturbances in the tribal area.' The Afghan government understood Indian motives and was purposely using these to exploit India–Pakistan tension over Kashmir for their own ends. One note written by General Iskander Mirza, the Secretary of Defence, on 28 February 1949, reflected ruefully that the only winner in a war between Afghanistan and Pakistan would be India. Indeed, 'war between the two countries will encourage India, which for the time being is our enemy number one, and will compromise our effort in Kashmir to such an extent that we might lose this most vital area.'

Hurt Pride: Afghan–Pakistan Negotiations 1948/9

The internal government papers also explained that throughout 1948 Pakistan had sought to keep a lid on the simmering Pashtunistan dispute so that they could concentrate all their energies on dealing with India in Kashmir. This approach, it turned out, was to prove fairly successful. Although there were continuing diplomatic scuffles between Afghanistan and Pakistan throughout 1948, these remained fairly contained and did not spark a crisis which could have destabilised the region still further.

Afghanistan sent Najibullah Khan, the former Director General in the Foreign Ministry and a noted supporter of Pashtunistan, to Karachi in November 1947 to negotiate with the Pakistan government. Early reports received by Squire suggested things were 'going on well in Karachi though we have as yet no definite news of any results. Saidullah Khan has been entirely discredited and has not even been invited to Karachi for the discussions, and Pakistan is most anxious to make amends for his atrocious behaviours. Najibullah has at any rate received a very friendly reception.'[67] After this promising start, however, things deteriorated rapidly. Najibullah took it upon himself to send a draft treaty to the Pakistan government in December. Article 3 set out a plan to recreate an autonomous Pashtun region:

> The Government of Pakistan with the desire that all people included in the Federation of Pakistan may enjoy their material and moral security, recognise the Afghans inhabited between the Durand Line and the River Indus, and their land which covers the Tribal Areas, the North-West Frontier Province of Old India, and the areas of Quetta, Pishin, Kakaristan, Tortat in Tortarin and Speentarin, as a single nation with distinct entity and identity, and a complete political and administrative autonomy is granted to them and their country inside the constituent frame of the Union of the Federation of Pakistan and under its own authority, and their land will be admitted into a single autonomous country called (blank) and the City of Peshawar will be established as its capital.[68]

He showed the draft to the British High Commissioner in Karachi, Sir Lawrence Grafftey-Smith. During the course of a long conversation,

1. Sam and Rene Simms in the 1930s. (Author's collection)

2. Sam Simms in Peshawar, 1940s.
(Author's collection)

3. Sam Simms in the army, 1940s.
(Author's collection)

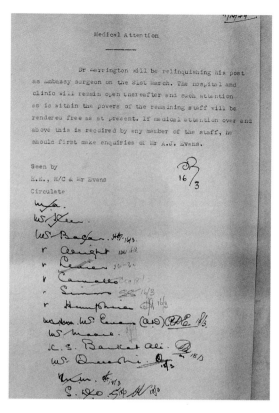

Right: 4. An internal embassy circular informing staff about changes in the use of the hospital, one of only two references to my grandfather in the files. Sam Simms has ticked his name. (National Archives, 16 March 1949, FO983/36)

Below: 5. An aerial view of the compound, showing the Big House in the centre, the hospital compound bottom right and the bungalows above, and the water tower, garage and stables to the left. Taken by Squadron Leader Reid from the RAF Training Mission. (Courtesy of Hazel Hastings)

6. The entrance to the British compound where Minister Sir Francis Humphrys negotiated with the Bacha Saqua and his men in December 1928 to ensure the legation was not attacked in the ensuring battle with Amir Amanullah's advancing army. (Courtesy of Annemarie Wilson)

7. The Ambassador's residence, known as the Big House, in the 1940s. (Courtesy of Hazel Hastings)

8. The Big House in 1969.

Above: 9. Another view of the Big House in 1969.

Below: 10. The gardens at the back of the Big House in 1969. These were often used for official parties and film shows.

11. The Military Attaché's residence. (Courtesy of Hazel Hastings)

12. A bungalow in the compound. Although this picture was taken in the 1970s, my grandfather's home probably looked very similar to this one. (Courtesy of Annemarie Wilson)

13. The embassy stables. (Courtesy of Hazel Hastings)

14. A 1970s photograph of the embassy swimming pool, which was built by Squire in the 1940s. (Courtesy of Annemarie Wilson)

15. The tennis courts in 1969.

16. The ruined Big House in 2010, after coming under attack in the Mujahedin period. (Author's collection)

17. The hospital compound in 2012, following its remodelling in the 1970s and later renovation by the Pakistan government. The British had considered reopening their embassy there after 9/11. (Courtesy of Jackie French)

18. The site of the bungalows, tennis courts, swimming pool and gardens in 2012 behind the Big House. (Courtesy of Jackie French)

19. The front of the Big House after renovation by Pakistan government. It is now the residence of the Pakistan Ambassador. (Author's collection)

20. A 2012 photograph of Zahir Shah's Soviet-made Zil limousines parked outside the Kabul Museum. (Author's collection)

21. A 2012 view of the back of the Big House showing the original ornamental pond in the foreground. (Author's collection)

22. Amir Amanullah's palace at Dar-ul-Aman in 2011, abandoned and later bombed during the takeover of Kabul in November/December 2001. (Author's collection)

23. A 2011 photograph of Nadir Shah's tomb, which was built in the 1940s by his son Zahir Shah and his brothers, where Sir Giles Squire and all incoming ambassadors paid their respects after their formal accreditation ceremony. It is now Zahir Shah's mausoleum too. (Author's collection)

24. The British Cemetery in Kabul in 2012, located on the site of Britain's Sherpur Cantonment, which was attacked during the Second Afghan War. (Courtesy of Louise Walker)

25. The Second Anglo-Afghan War graves in the wall of the cemetery. (Author's collection)

26. The cemetery's memorial to the men and women who died in Afghanistan since 2001 as part of the International Security and Assistance Force (NATO). (Courtesy of Louise Walker)

27. The Kajaki Dam, part of the Helmand scheme, which was completed in 1953. (Courtesy of Mark Harvey)

28. Irrigated land in the Helmand river valley in 2009. (Courtesy of Mark Harvey)

29. Part of the repaired irrigation network in Nad-e-Ali district, Helmand, which was completed with British financial support in 2009. (Courtesy of Mark Harvey)

30. Hazel Hastings (*née* Squire) and the author. (Courtesy of Robert Hastings)

he explained that 'what the Afghan government feared was an incident in the tribal areas leading to a conflict between the two countries, and what they hoped for was the satisfaction of national feeling among the tribesmen by the creation of an autonomous state within the Pakistan Federation guaranteeing to all "Afghans" in Pakistan security from dispersal or hostile discrimination and complete political and administrative autonomy'. In response, Grafftey-Smith made it quite clear to Najibullah that his ideas were a non-starter: 'I could hardly believe Pakistan would wish to adopt at his suggestion a regime which the British government had not found it expedient to establish in many years' experience of the Frontier conditions, to which Najibullah replied that a Muslim State could do things which a foreign Christian authority could not.'[69]

Pakistan's first response was fairly dismissive and, not surprisingly, considerably upset Najibullah since it made no reference to any future form of tribal administration on the Frontier. Najibullah dejectedly told Grafftey-Smith that it looked as though it had been drafted by Sir Henry Dobbs himself, the man who had negotiated the 1921 Anglo-Afghan Treaty and confirmed the Durand Line as the border.[70] A second reply was sent on 1 January, signed by Prime Minister Liaquat Ali Khan Khan. This time, Najibullah was reminded that Jinnah had assured the tribes that Pakistan would continue to respect all treaties, agreements and allowances until representatives of the tribes and the government had met to negotiate new agreements. These had now been completed amicably. He was also reminded about a recent announcement by Jinnah stating that 'so far as the Pashtuns in [the] North-West Frontier Province are concerned, I have no doubt they will enjoy in Pakistan [the] fullest freedom to develop their social, cultural and economic institutions. They would have the same self-government as any other part or province of Pakistan.' The response, however, did seem to offer one small glimmer of hope, or at least Najibullah thought so. Liaquat Ali Khan confirmed that the constitutional relationship between the central government and the provinces would be framed by the new Constitutional Assembly with representatives from all parts of Pakistan. Any province would have the right to raise a question there about its future constitution.[71]

Najibullah apparently interpreted this to mean Pakistan had agreed to grant autonomous government to the Pashtuns and that all Afghans east of the Durand Line could join a single government if they so wished. He also thought it indicated that the territory could have a new name, thus signalling its separate national identity. Liaquat Ali Khan put the matter straight during a meeting with Najibullah on 3 January. He asked Najibullah to bear in mind three facts:

1. Pakistan is a single country, and all who live in it are Pakistanis and as such, free and equal citizens of a trustee sovereign state with equal rights, privileges and responsibilities.
2. All Pakistani provinces enjoy the same rights and same degree of autonomy.
3. The Constitution of Pakistan will be framed by the Constituent Assembly, which is a sovereign body and only it has the powers to alter the names of any of the component units of Pakistan.

He also pointed out that the tribal areas enjoyed a unique position. If they themselves wanted to join the settled administered districts in NWFP, the Constituent Assembly would accord due weight to this request. At the end of the meeting, he politely reminded Najibullah that all these issues related exclusively to Pakistan's domestic affairs and were of no concern to any other country.[72] A formal letter was then sent to Najibullah's office summarising the points covered to avoid any further misinterpretation of the government's position. A few days after the letter was delivered, a rather uncomfortable meeting took place between Jinnah and Mahmud Khan in Karachi, during which the latter made it clear that he had disliked the tone and substance of the communications with Najibullah. The British High Commission subsequently learnt that the letter had been withdrawn.[73]

Najibullah's position in Karachi from then on was untenable. Once diplomatic relations with Pakistan were formalised a few weeks later, Mahmud Khan made his brother, Shah Wali Khan, the first Afghan Ambassador to Pakistan. As Najibullah departed Karachi, he made one more statement before the game was up, this time directed against Britain. In a radio broadcast on 3 February, he claimed that between 1943 and 1947, the Afghan government had been in direct negotiations with Britain about the 'actual and future political destiny of the Afghans living between the Durand Line and the River Indus'. In spite of Afghanistan's obvious interest in the issues, however, Britain, he claimed, had gone ahead and set up the two new dominions without Afghan wishes being taken into account.[74] Back in Kabul, the legation hurriedly checked back through their files to see if there was any evidence that bore this claim out. They found nothing. There were no smoking guns suggesting that either Squire or his predecessors had ever encouraged the Afghans to intervene in the area east of the Durand Line in the event Britain relinquished her authority in India. This information was then also relayed to the Pakistan government so that they could be assured that Britain was not playing a double game.[75]

Over the following months, the simmering dispute seemed to have turned a corner. Shah Wali Khan got on well with Jinnah, whom he had known for some time, and the Pakistan government began to address Afghan complaints about delays in transporting goods to Afghanistan from the docks in Karachi. That August, Pakistan was invited to send a delegation to Afghanistan's annual Independence Day celebrations. The delegation was led by the Minister of Communications, Abdur Rab Nishtar. Unfortunately, the visit was not an unqualified success. When the Pakistan delegation arrived, 'Afghan officials', reported Squire to London, 'objected to the unauthorised wearing of a uniform by the crew of the Pakistan Air Force plane which brought Sardar Abdur Rab Nishtar, [and] gave rise to bitter comment among the lower ranks of Afghan and Pakistani officials'.[76] The last day of the celebrations were marred by a 'contretemps', as Squire described it, during a football match. 'The Pakistan team lost their temper with what they considered unfair refereeing and walked off the field ten minutes before time, whereupon the Afghans who were one goal down proceeded to kick the ball through their opponents' goal twice to win the match.'[77]

There were also signs in December 1948 that Pakistan was prepared to meet at least one Afghan demand – changing the name of NWFP. During one of their frequent meetings, Mohammed Ikramullah, Secretary at the Ministry of Foreign Affairs, told Grafftey-Smith that he had explored the idea of encouraging NWFP representatives on the Constituent Assembly to present a private bill to change the province's name. When he had talked to two of the three representatives, however – the third was in jail – he had met a brick wall. They had insisted there was no demand within the province for a new name and refused to cooperate with their political opponents in Karachi on this issue.[78] The Pakistan government, London concluded, 'displays an entirely proper attitude'.[79]

Tensions Mount while Britain and Pakistan Compare Notes
In spite of simmering tensions, Squire still felt sufficiently confident to write in his journal on Sunday 1 February 1949 that 'there is nothing much to report about Afghan affairs. Her relations with Pakistan are still not firmly settled though they are no worse.'[80] Although the Afghans had begun to open up new lines of argument which put Britain centre stage once again, no one anticipated that Afghan–Pakistan relations were about to deteriorate irrevocably within a matter of weeks.

Things started to flare up again when the Afghan Ambassador to London, Faiz Mohammed Zakria, questioned the validity, of the 1947 NWFP plebiscite since nearly 50 per cent of the population had abstained from casting their vote. He also argued that the treaties concerning the Durand Line had been with Britain, not Pakistan, and that therefore the focus for negotiations should be with London, not Karachi. Britain, he argued, should now return all the lands taken from Afghanistan in the nineteenth century after the First and Second Afghan Wars, and specifically the territory which had been 'illegally' passed to Pakistan:

> Great Britain took this territory from Amir Dost Mohammed, the King of Afghanistan, and a further portion was seized during the second British invasion of Afghanistan. The government and people of Afghanistan request Great Britain to render that same justice which they have rendered to the peoples of India, Pakistan, Burma and Ceylon, which nations have received their freedom and acknowledgement of their national status, to the Pashtuns, that they too should receive their freedom and have their national status acknowledged. Otherwise, great troubles will arise between Pakistan and the Pashtuns, in which Afghanistan, without her own volition, will inevitably be involved.[81]

In March, tensions were fuelled by an alleged diplomatic incident involving staff from the Afghan embassy in Karachi and by increasing anti-Pakistan propaganda in Kabul. A reporter from the *Dawn* newspaper and other passers-by saw an eighteen-year-old Pakistani woman and her child abducted from the street and driven away in an Afghan embassy car. Since Shah Wali Khan was in Kabul at the time, the reporter approached the Chargé D'Affaires, Mr Makhmoor, for a statement. Makhmoor went to *Dawn*'s offices and then apparently became involved in a heated argument with the journalists. Not surprisingly, the whole incident appeared in *Dawn* the next day. Makhmoor was promptly summoned to the Ministry of Foreign Affairs and asked to hand over the driver for questioning, but before further investigations could take place he and the rest of the Afghan embassy had taken the train to Peshawar and returned to Afghanistan with, it seems, the woman and child in tow.[82] The incident became the talk of the diplomatic community in both Karachi and Kabul, but no one ever got to the bottom of it. It did little to improve Afghan–Pakistan relations.

In a second incident, Kabul Radio reported that Pakistani air raids had killed 'hundreds of innocent Afghan men, women and children'. If the media had waited for verification, they would have learnt that a Pakistani plane had been used to disperse a gang attacking a military post in

Waziristan.[83] Then, a few days later, Kabul Radio claimed that the purpose of the Pakistan government was to 'annihilate the Afghan race'.[84] When the Governor General of Pakistan said the tribal areas were 'an integral part of Pakistan', Shah Wali Khan told Squire this had 'stultified all the negotiations of the past three years'. The whole Afghan government 'were incensed and that they would make no further attempts to restrain either their press or their people'. Squire reminded him that action may be bad for Afghanistan and that Pakistan was a member of the Commonwealth, but 'this provoked a further outburst that His Majesty's Government, while not being prepared to accept any responsibility for the present problem which was a British origin, would apparently help to prevent Afghanistan from obtaining justice, and that in any case destruction was better than dishonour'.[85]

Within a matter of days, news began to filter out that the Afghan government was planning to hold a *Loya Jirga* of all the tribes on 15 April. In preparation, the Afghan Ambassadors from London, Karachi and Delhi were being recalled to Kabul for discussions. Since the last time a *Loya Jirga* had been held was in 1941 to endorse Afghan neutrality in the Second World War, the British wondered what the government planned to ask them to agree to this time around. Would they be asked to declare war, or was this simply a ruse to frighten Pakistan? Whatever the case, it was quite clear that the British embassy needed to get to the bottom of what was going on and then try to dispel tensions before the whole situation got further out of control.

Squire and his team now became critical intermediaries between the Afghan and British governments. They pulled together as much information as they could about the Afghan position to see if there were any concessions Pakistan could make – short of giving up the tribal areas – which would be sufficient to calm things down. Grafftey-Smith shared much of the analysis with the Pakistan government to help find a way out of the impasse. Although there were some private concerns that Anglo-Pakistani collaboration, if it came out, 'would merely provide "proof" to the Afghans that Pakistan was nothing but British in another form', the overall message from the Pakistan government was that they wanted Britain to stay engaged and to help resolve this legacy of empire. The Pakistan government in turn shared more information with Britain.

As they compared notes, Britain and Pakistan found themselves on the same page. In one of the documents sent to London by General Cawthorn, General Iskander Mirza, the Secretary of Defence, had written on 28 February 1949 that he believed Afghanistan lacked both the capacity to embark on hostilities with Pakistan and the economic means to win over the tribes financially. Afghan ammunition stocks were low and the air force was negligible, the economy was in poor shape and Afghan petrol reserves would be exhausted within a month. He believed the Afghan government knew this too since a war would 'bring about complete disintegration in Afghanistan, thus paving the way to Bolshevik infiltration'. Indeed, 'I will be very surprised if the province of Mazar-i-Sharif will not turn to Bolshevism lock, stock and barrel'. In view of this assessment, Mirza recommended that Pakistan should encourage Britain and the United States to provide Afghanistan with a loan. Failing that, Pakistan should offer a small loan themselves, as well as improve transit facilities. On no account, he argued, should they support alternative contenders to the Afghan throne, including the sons of ex-Amir Amanullah, since this would simply antagonise Afghanistan.

Squire reports from Kabul were in a similar vein. He thought that anti-Pakistan propaganda was in part a smokescreen to deflect attention away from the country's growing economic crisis and an increasingly unpopular government. He also agreed with Mirza's view that Afghan ministers themselves knew they lacked sufficient support from the tribes.[86]

London, Kabul and Karachi also concurred that a degree of hurt Afghan pride was mixed in with these stark realities. Liaquat Ali Khan told Grafftey-Smith the gist of a difficult conversation he had had with Shah Wali Khan after the Governor General's comment that the tribes were an integral part of Pakistan. He had asked him 'whether [the] Afghan government really wanted [the] tribal territories on [the] Pakistan side of Durand Line. Shah Wali Khan had thrown up his hands in horror at this suggestion saying that [the] Afghan government could not possibly afford to subsidise [the] tribes as Pakistan was doing.' Thereupon, Liaquat Ali Khan 'had suggested that there was some impropriety in Afghan interference in these territories'. As Grafftey-Smith subsequently reported to London, the Prime Minister 'declared to me roundly that he could, if he wished, bring [the] present Afghan dynasty toppling and that [the] Afghans knew he could do so. Unfortunately, they also knew that he would not attempt such a thing.'[87]

As Squire surveyed the Afghan position from his vantage point in Kabul, he concluded that the protagonists, with the possible exception of Ali Mohammed, the Minister of Foreign Affairs,

> seem to have lost their heads completely ... [The Prime Minister] is, I think, incapable of thinking for himself, is surrounded by 'yes-men' and is very much under the influence of Faiz Mohammed Zakria [Ambassador in London]. Shah Wali, whom I have normally found reasonable and open to arguments, is rabid on the subject of Pakistan. That a member of the royal family and uncle of the King should have been treated with such scant respect by Pakistan that his request should have

been summarily rejected is extremely galling to him. Any suggestion to these three that Afghanistan's present policy will be suicidal is countered with the reply that death is a hundred times better than dishonour. The most dangerous of the three is undoubtedly Faiz Mohammed Zakria ... If Ali Mohammed is successful in getting him sent back to his post in London, there may yet be a chance of the situation being retrieved.[88]

Squire, on the other hand, possessed a deeper understanding than most about what was driving Afghan policy, even if he thought it ill-advised. Robert Scott, the Head of South Asia Department in the Foreign Office therefore asked for his advice: 'South-East Asia Department has various crises on its hands at the moment – Java, Burma, Indochina – but (perhaps because I know least about it!), I must confess I find none as intriguing and baffling as the mystery of the behaviour of your Afghan friends. If you have time to enlighten my darkness by telling me the story as you see it – motive, plot, criminal, accomplices and your forecast of the ending – I shall be most grateful.'[89]

Squire's sent a comprehensive response explaining, in his view, that Afghan policy was entirely domestically inspired.[90] 'This is not to say that Russia and some elements in India may not be only too glad to fish in troubled waters, but the Afghan government hotly repudiate, and I think with complete sincerity, any suggestion that they are working under foreign tuition.' Economic and domestic difficulties played a part, but the main driver was the tribal question itself. Volume two of Amir Abdur Rahman's autobiography was considered the Afghan 'political bible' and the policies he laid out for his successors had been followed ever since. The Afghans also looked at what the Amir had actually agreed with the Viceroy, Lord Lansdowne, in 1892 and 1893, including the comments he had written in the margins of letters, and not just the formal treaties themselves. The Afghan Ambassador to London was to explain the significance of this point to the Foreign Office in June. In the meantime, Squire also explained that the present royal family's dependence on the Pashtun tribes for their legitimacy went much deeper than that. All Afghan regimes since Ahmed Shah had been dependent on tribal support. Amir Amanullah had learnt this to his cost in 1928, and Nadir Shah had only succeeded in claiming the throne once he had won over 'our' tribes. That was why Afghan rulers had resisted all attempts by the former British government of India ever since to get them to dissociate themselves from the tribes or to discontinue paying allowances to their headmen.

Squire also suggested that the Afghans were still trying to adjust to the new rules. In the past, when Britain had taken military action against the tribes, the Afghan government had complained and the British had told them to stop whingeing, and that was that. Now when they complained about the Pakistan government's actions – such as the air attack in Waziristan or the Governor-General's statement – it took on a more sinister meaning than perhaps the Afghans had intended. Indeed, 'the Afghans cannot understand why they should now be receiving such very different treatment from that to which through all these years they have been accustomed, and it is perhaps too much to expect that they should be either temperate or logical'.

London took note, started reading the autobiography, and shared it with others, including the United States embassy. One member of the latter, Lewis Jones, wrote back to say 'your analysis of Afghan motives came as a flash of lightening. I am now reading the autobiography.'[91] The Pakistanis asked for the original copies of the Durand Agreement, including the original correspondence. When Ikramullah, Secretary at the Ministry of Foreign Affairs, received them while staying in Claridge's in London, he sent his heartfelt thanks to the Foreign Office: 'After all these papers, we should be able to deal with the Afghan question more thoroughly than the Afghans themselves.'[92]

Around the same time, the Afghans started to explain their position in these terms too. Ali Mohammed wrote to the Pakistani Ambassador in Kabul on 24 April explaining the Amir had agreed:

> Not to interfere in the independence of these tribes and therefore withdrew his forces from their territory, but it did not mean that Amir Abdur Rahman Khan had accepted the free Frontier tribes as British subjects. The Afghan government has never accepted the free Frontier as having been under British or Pakistan sovereignty ... [Furthermore] it may be understood that if the independence of the free tribes is recognised, the Afghan government will never stand in the way of the Pakistan government's relations with and legitimate advantages from the free Frontier, and the government of Pakistan can also expect cooperation from Afghanistan. But without these conditions, Afghanistan cannot enter into negotiations with the government of Pakistan to admit Pakistan's rule over the free Frontier or to accept them as Pakistani subjects.[93]

In June, Faiz Mohammed Zakria, the Afghan Ambassador in London, told Foreign Office officials that Lord Lansdowne had referred to the tribal areas as 'no man's land', and told Amir Abdul Rahman to move Afghans from the area because Britain recognised it as 'independent'. The Amir, on the strength of this, had then agreed to Lord Lansdowne's suggestion to set up a commission to delimit the Frontier. What the British had not appreciated was that the Afghans interpreted the word 'independent' to mean something different from its current definition. Then, it had been used by the British themselves to denote parts of India not directly under British administration, like the 'independent' Princely States, even though they were still seen as part of British India under a series of treaties. In view of this, the Amir had therefore taken the term to mean that the tribal areas were truly independent even though they were temporarily part of British India. The Durand Line was not therefore a border between Afghanistan and British India, but rather a 'border beyond which the Afghans could not interfere in the tribal area'.[94] The land between the Durand Line and the Indus River was 'independent' tribal territory, and Pakistan had not therefore inherited any rights to it under the terms of the 1921 Anglo-Afghan Treaty.

Over the months to come, the Afghans raised these points about the independent status of the tribal areas, and the conditions under which they had accepted the Durand Line as the Frontier time and again. The British now understood it. The explanation had been incredibly helpful. Instead of solving the problem, however, it had created a new one. At the same time, British officials still believed Pakistan had inherited Britain's rights and obligations in the tribal areas in accordance with the 1921 Treaty, and that this had been confirmed once Pakistan had entered into agreements with the tribes in November and December 1947.[95]

Contested Rights and Obligations

Pakistan decided it was about time to become more proactive. They first asked Britain to state categorically that the 1921 Anglo-Afghan Treaty was binding and that the Durand Line was the border between Afghanistan and Pakistan. After this, they pressed Britain to make it clear to the Afghans that Britain would take action if the boundary was violated militarily or politically. While the British were prepared to consider the first request, the second one raised the stakes considerably. No one had given any serious thought as to what level of support Britain would be prepared to give Pakistan if relations with Afghanistan deteriorated still further. Officials went back to the drawing board. After a flurry of telegrams between Kabul, Karachi and London, they decided that the best way forward would be to identify the Afghan bottom line, and if possible, ensure this was met so tensions were defused. There seemed to be two outstanding issues to resolve, both of which recognised mutual rights and responsibilities:

1. Pakistan needed to recognise Afghan interest in their tribal areas,
2. Afghanistan needed to accept the Durand Line as the frontier with Pakistan.

Having clarified this, they decided to use every opportunity to put these points across to both sides. When the Pakistan government, for instance, asked to see Britain's files on relations with India for 1935–47 and the 1892/3 correspondence on the Durand Line, they used this to demonstrate the value of a collaborative Afghan–Pakistan relationship in the border area:

> When the Pakistan government get the documents we are collecting for them, they will see that we in the past, while consistently maintaining [the] Durand Line to be international Frontier, recognised that Afghan government have interest in [the] conditions of tribes on both sides of it (letter from British representative to Afghan Foreign Minister attached to 1921 Treaty). We tried to avoid action embarrassing [the] Afghan government and endanger its stability, because we believed a stable and friendly Afghan government [was] essential to peace of tribal areas. For example, we tried to stop movements in our tribal territory hostile to Afghan government and we recognised that [the] civilisation and economic development of tribes must be gradual and cautious if it were not to produce reaction in Afghanistan with which Afghan government could not deal. We assured the Afghan government that these considerations greatly influenced our policy and this enabled us to obtain their acquiescence to it.[96]

The Foreign Office also concluded it would be a good idea to do more homework on the legal position. First, whether Pakistan had indeed inherited Britain's rights and responsibilities with respect to the tribes, and thus Britain's unwritten obligation to collaborate with Afghanistan along the border. Second, whether Pakistan had inherited Britain's rights and responsibilities under the 1921 Anglo-Afghan Treaty, including recognition of the Durand Line as the border given that the legal status of one of the parties to the treaty, Britain, had changed. If not, then everything was up for grabs. Earlier Foreign Office legal advice in November 1947 had concluded that changes in the legal status of the parties had not affected the Frontier provisions of the treaty.[97] But what if this was wrong? What if it was the tribes who had inherited Britain's rights in respect of the Durand Line at independence and Pakistan had only acquired the benefits of the 1921 Anglo-Afghan Treaty through subsequent agreements with the tribes? If this was the case, could Britain still expect Afghanistan to accept the Durand Line as their border with Pakistan?

Grafftey-Smith kicked off the process. He asked Liaquat Ali Khan in April 1949 if he could recall what had been agreed with the tribes eighteen months earlier. The Prime Minister remembered that Sir George

Cunningham, Jinnah's Governor of NWFP through the transition period – and a former Governor under British times too – had held a series of *Jirgas* with the tribes in the autumn of 1947. During these, the tribes had solemnly transferred to Pakistan their pre-Partition relations with, and obligations towards His Majesty's Government. In return, the Pakistan government had guaranteed to protect them and to continue the payment of subsidies. The Prime Minister therefore interpreted these joint undertakings to mean the 'accession' of the tribal territories to Pakistan.[98]

Officials in London decided to track down Cunningham themselves. He had left Pakistan suddenly in April 1948 because his blood pressure had become dangerously high,[99] but was now fighting fit and on a fishing holiday in Aberdeenshire. He confirmed he had held *Jirgas* in November and December 1947 with the Afridi, Ahmedzai Wazirs, Mahsuds and Mohmands, as well as the North Waziristan and Upper Kurran tribes – 'the only tribes that affect the question of Pakistan relations'. All had sworn allegiance to Pakistan and stated they wished to have exactly the same relations with Pakistan as they had enjoyed with the British government. He had not recorded any of the agreements in writing since he had 'always taken a solemn affirmation in tribal Jirga to be binding on a tribe, and in my experience written agreements with tribes have been used much more by the tribes themselves to insist on benefits from government than by government to insist on performance of obligations by the tribes'. After his departure, he understood that Pakistani political agents had finalised written agreements with the leading tribes.[100] Sir Ambrose Dundas, Cunningham's successor in NWFP in 1948–9, later provided some local colour to this statement. The tribes had joined Pakistan 'voluntarily, excitedly and enthusiastically as they did everything else; tremendous feasts were held over it, and quite a lot of people were killed, which was always the sign of a successful party in that part of the world.'[101]

As for Cunningham himself, he decided to add his own thoughts to the wider debate in an article published in *The Statesman* on 4 June 1949. In his opinion, the idea of Pashtunistan had more or less died down by the time he left Pakistan. Indeed, 'union with Afghanistan never, so far as I could see, entered the minds of either tribesmen, [or] villagers of the settled Districts'. In fact, the only period when it could have had some support would have been in late summer 1940 when German and Italian agents in Kabul were 'playing loudly on this theme, and their money flowed freely towards the border'. Even then, however, 'the tribes preferred to look the other way'.[102]

The correspondence with Cunningham satisfied British officials that even if the tribes had been in legal limbo on 15 August 1947, they clearly became part of Pakistan a few months later. Next, the Foreign Office asked its legal advisers whether the legal definition of Pakistan under the 1947 India Independence Act affected the status of the 1921 Treaty and thus the validity of the international frontier in international law. After examining all the evidence again, the advisers concluded that under the Independence Act, Pakistan had been defined as consisting of certain provinces, but may not have been granted responsibility for the un-administered tribal areas on 15 August 1947.[103] The advice posed a conundrum. If it was right, then the legality or otherwise of the Durand Line as the border was now in doubt. After further reflection, the Foreign Office concluded the advice did not materially affect the current situation. 'This does not mean to say that the Durand Line ceased to be the international Frontier of Afghanistan. The new situation did not give Afghanistan any right to extend her territories to include the tribal areas without the consent of the tribes, any more than it gave Pakistan the right to do so.' At the same time, it did not affect the substance of Pakistan's case either:

> Whether or not there was a period following the division of India when Afghanistan could have accepted a voluntary request for incorporation from the tribal areas, the tribes did not make any such request, and in fact, in the Jirgas ... requested and obtained affiliation with Pakistan. This gives Pakistan the conduct of their foreign relations and enables Pakistan to claim the observance of the boundary on their behalf.

The significant additional factor provided by the advice, officials concluded, was that Pakistan should accept Afghanistan had a legitimate political, though not necessarily a legal, interest in the welfare of tribes east of the Durand Line by virtue of the 1921 Anglo-Afghan Treaty, in the same way as the British had done. Pakistan had not only inherited Britain's rights in the tribal areas, but also Britain's obligation to acknowledge Afghan interest. Given this, the two key issues requiring resolution were still on the table: '(a) That Afghanistan recognises the validity of the Durand Line as the international boundary, and (b) that Pakistan recognises that Afghanistan has an interest in the tribes east of the Line.'[104]

The likelihood of shifting either side's point of view appeared increasingly remote, however. Britain had little immediate hope that Pakistan would recognise Afghan interest in the tribal areas. Liaquat Ali Khan told Grafftey-Smith on 3 April that Pakistan would not discuss the tribal areas east of the Durand Line with Afghanistan, let alone permit the Afghan government to ask them about it.[105] Meanwhile, increased Pakistan engagement in the tribal areas made it abundantly clear that they were there to stay. The tribes were being given more opportunities to join the regular armed forces and economic inducements to accept a more settled agricultural existence – presumably, the Foreign Office concluded, to encourage them to join the settled districts in NWFP.[106] Alongside these carrots, the government was keeping its fresh troops close to hand so they could be deployed on the Frontier in an emergency instead of using them to relieve units in Kashmir. It was becoming abundantly clear that Pakistan had no intention of meeting Afghan claims halfway.

Pakistan then played a card that had been floating around for some time. In early April, and just days before he was due to attend the Commonwealth Prime Ministers' Conference in London, Liaquat Ali Khan suggested that tensions would decline if the Afghans were reminded that Britain had obligations to Pakistan as a fellow member of the Commonwealth. In preparation for his imminent arrival, Ernest Bevin asked for advice, and London, Kabul, Karachi and Delhi went into overdrive to work out what to say.

Liaquat Ali Khan Visits London

Squire had already been instructed by London to inform the Afghans that if they threatened Pakistan or took any hostile actions, Afghanistan should be in no doubt that Britain's loyalties lay with Pakistan, a fellow member of the Commonwealth. He had conveyed this message to Shah Wali Khan over lunch on 16 March, and made the same point during meetings with other members of the government on 19 and 29 March and 10 April. After that, he decided to back off a little to allow tempers to cool. He thought it was wise, however, to continue to remind them of Afghanistan's obligation as a member of the United Nations to seek resolution through peaceful negotiations or to use the International Court. If necessary, he also decided to warn them that they were damaging the country's reputation internationally. He asked other diplomatic missions to urge caution as well, and said that the Turkish and Belgian Ambassadors had already taken that line with the government.[107]

London had also advised Pakistan that 'as part of our normal practice we considered it desirable to inform other Commonwealth governments of the existence of this dispute and of our attitude to it'. The Pakistan government agreed this was a good idea and a note was sent accordingly to all Commonwealth countries (India, Pakistan, Ceylon, Canada, New Zealand, Australia and South Africa) on 17 April, setting out Britain's support for Pakistan:

We consider that Pakistan has an unassailable case since [the] tribal areas in dispute are on the Pakistan side of the internationally recognised

Frontier line, the validity of which Afghanistan herself has acknowledged in the Treaty of 1921 with the British government. Shortly after [the] establishment of Pakistan in August 1947, agreements which had existed up till then between the British government and the tribes in these tribal areas were renewed between [the] Pakistan government and the tribes. Thus the position of the Pakistan government in respect of the tribal areas and the international Frontier bordering those areas is precisely that of the British government up till August 1947. We deplore continuance of Afghan agitation, particularly as it is directed against another member of the Commonwealth.[108]

As officials began to prepare their briefing pack for Bevin and a forthcoming Cabinet Defence Committee meeting on 19 April, the complexity of the task at hand became ever greater. There were no straightforward answers. Pakistan and India had recently joined the Commonwealth, but there were no obligations for members to go to each other's defence. On the other hand, however, Commonwealth countries, including people from the former empire in India, had fought on Britain's side in the two world wars and would in all likelihood be prepared to help in any future conflict against the Soviet Union to defeat the spread of communism. On these grounds alone therefore, Britain probably had a moral obligation to support Pakistan.

There was another dimension, too. In the run-up to the Prime Ministers' meeting, Nehru had hinted that India might leave the Commonwealth if certain conditions were not met – he wanted the name changed from the British Commonwealth to the Commonwealth of Nations, and recognition that republics (i.e. India), as well as states owing allegiance to the British Crown, could be members.[109] The relationship between India and Pakistan, and between India and other Commonwealth members, therefore took on increased importance. If Britain sought Pakistan's help against the Soviet Union, and Pakistan provided forward air bases, what would Britain do if India left the Commonwealth and Pakistan then expected Britain to commit to protecting Pakistan against India? This scenario, the briefing pack pointed out, trumped any simmering dispute between Pakistan and Afghanistan:

The medal has two sides. If war broke out in Europe between Russia and the Atlantic Powers, we would hope that some Commonwealth countries (besides Canada) would join us in the struggle and the probability is that New Zealand and Australia at any rate would in fact do so. The Union of South Africa might also come in, because of their fear of communism. The decision of Pakistan, Ceylon and

India would be dictated by their own view of their own interests. It would be important to us that Pakistan should come in, because we should want defence bases in her territory for use against Russia. But Pakistan's decision would be greatly influenced by the consideration whether, in coming to our help, they would gain a greater assurance than they have at present that, in the event of their needing assistance themselves, we would recognise a reciprocal obligation ... [But] to do so would have very serious implications in the event of India leaving the Commonwealth and subsequently attacking Pakistan. It is of that eventuality that Pakistan is chiefly afraid, and against which they would most value from us a guarantee. This, however, would constitute a very onerous obligation indeed and we clearly cannot undertake it.[110]

One other aspect in this conundrum needed exploring: would India help Pakistan if Afghanistan attacked them? And if India did make an offer, would Pakistan accept their help? The Foreign Office decided to consult Sir Archibald Nye, the new British High Commissioner in Delhi, to see if he could shed any light on the issue. He replied swiftly. In his view, if Nehru and others in his government had more information about why Britain was supporting Pakistan, this would help defuse tensions between India and Pakistan, and in turn, 'there would be much better hope of the Indians giving the Afghans sound advice'.[111] In any case, he for one did not believe Nehru had personally authorised agitation amongst the tribes:

In view of Pandit Nehru's categoric public statements on the subject, and in view of what we know of his character, I am satisfied that the government are neither instigating nor conniving at this agitation, although the possibility cannot be excluded that individual Indians acting on their own initiative may be doing so without the knowledge of the government of India.

If Britain were to ask them to urge moderation on the Afghans, however, they would want it acknowledged that the same point would be made to the Pakistan government too. Nye therefore advised against asking India to encourage the Afghan government to be more cautious.

The briefing papers then turned to an assessment of Afghan policy intentions, their current economic crisis, and a detailed analysis of the relative military capacities of Afghanistan and Pakistan. The War Office believed that Pakistan would only be able to defend itself against an Afghan attack if the latter failed to secure the active assistance of the tribes on the Pakistani side of the Durand Line.

If the tribes did support Afghanistan, though, then Pakistan would probably ask for British assistance, especially for planes to destroy targets in Afghanistan and to support the army's ground operations, which would be an extremely expensive 'ask'. The Pakistan Air Force would need one fighter/bomber wing of three squadrons each of eight or twelve aircraft, one flight of long-range reconnaissance aircraft, one flight of transport aircraft to support the fighter/bomber wing and the Pakistan army, and one mobile signals section or unit along with servicing facilities.[112]

The War Office had its own concerns about whether British military assistance should, or indeed could, be provided. From a practical point of view, many of Britain's military supplies were already committed to the Berlin Airlift after the Soviets had cut off land routes to the city the previous summer. In the past, the War Office had been able to draw on surplus equipment and arms from India, but that was now out of the question. The Director of the Joint Intelligence Bureau in the Ministry of Defence warned that any arms given to Pakistan could also be used against India. This meant that the United States would need to be consulted 'because arms supplied by us to Pakistan would have to come from, or be replaced by, arms from the United States, without whose full support our own arms position might be compromised'.[113]

Attlee chaired the Defence Committee meeting at 6 p.m. on Tuesday 19 April.[114] Committee members, including Bevin, pored over the extensive briefing material, weighed up the possibilities, and then, amazingly, discovered it was possible to make a decision about not taking a decision, at least not just yet. 'It would be a mistake at this stage to encourage the Prime Minister of Pakistan to think that we were prepared to enter into unconditional and binding commitments in the event of war.' Britain should establish what Pakistan's intentions actually were before deciding British policy, while more could be done to encourage Afghanistan to back down by helping them address some of their domestic difficulties than by escalating the problem. The Afghan government had already asked for help to find overseas markets for their goods, to purchase supplies of arms and ammunition for internal security, and to secure a £1.5 million loan. Given this, the Committee argued, 'it should not be difficult to make such forms of assistance contingent upon the pursuance of a more moderate policy on the North-West Frontier'.[115] The matter was then passed back to the bureaucrats to crack on and find ways to give Afghanistan financial, economic and military support.

Once the meeting was over, officials reflected whether the advice had actually moved the debate forward at all. Afghanistan's request for a loan had already been refused, as Chapter Four explained. The Afghan National Bank in London was already aware Britain was trying to facilitate more imports of lambskins, wool and dried fruit to earn sterling. Furthermore, as Chapter Seven explains, Britain was already failing to meet its pre-Indian independence commitment to supply arms from Indian supplies to Afghanistan, and was certainly not in a position to make any new ones. This proposal, like the others, was therefore a non-starter.

At 10.45 a.m. on 25 April, Bevin met Liaquat Ali Khan, Foreign Minister, Sir Zafarullah Khan, and the Secretary of the Foreign Affairs Ministry, Mohammed Ikramullah. Many of the issues raised by the Pakistan team echoed the points raised in the internal memos shared by General Cawthorn. They reaffirmed they themselves had no problem with re-naming NWFP but stressed that the people in the area needed to decide for themselves – the government could not impose it on them. They also confirmed that Pakistan had continued to pay allowances to the tribes in accordance with the new agreements and treaties, and that the tribes had remained loyal to Pakistan throughout.

Liaquat Ali Khan said he believed the real issue behind Afghanistan's foreign policy was the critical state of the Afghan economy. It was poorly managed and stifled by the royal family's control over a number of monopolies, which had caused much resentment among Afghan entrepreneurs since others could not compete. The Afghans also had problems in the north because they could not afford to invest in the same level of services enjoyed by people on the Soviet side of the border. He also mentioned his heated discussion with Shah Wali Khan in Karachi, and told Bevin that 'Afghanistan's actions were producing a ridiculous situation in which the Afghans, sitting in Kabul, were calling the tune, but expecting the Pakistan government to pay'. For his part, Zafarullah Khan did not think Afghanistan 'would be so foolish as to go to war when they knew they were in the wrong, but they might incite the tribes to make trouble'. Liaquat Ali Khan's intense frustration was evident when he turned to Bevin and said, 'I tell you I am not boasting. I could upset that dynasty. It only means spending a little money. But I do not want to. It would only benefit Russia.'

Then came the million dollar question. Did the Pakistan government, asked Bevin, need Britain's help?

The answer, fortunately, was no. Zafarullah Khan thought the best thing Britain could do was use its embassy in Kabul to influence the government. Bevin therefore shared the dates and times of Squire's meetings, read out extracts showing the various arguments Squire had used, and recommended the three countries (Pakistan, Afghanistan and Britain) should have a tripartite discussion once tempers had cooled – Pakistan readily agreed. In the meantime, Britain would continue to look at opportunities to help the Afghan economy.[116]

And that was where things were left until an unfortunate incident in June 1949 lit a spark that would prove more or less impossible to extinguish.

6

Pashtunistan: Positions Harden

The North-West Frontier, for a hundred years the bane of the British government in India and the cause of the expenditure of thousands of lives and millions of money, is now proving as troublesome to the successor state of Pakistan as it did to British India; and Pakistan labours under the handicap of possessing much smaller resources with which to cope with the problem. There have been times in the past when the North-West Frontier taxed the military strength of united India, and today Pakistan must deal with the same problem with merely a fragment of that strength.

Foreign Office Research Department, 1950[1]

Introduction

Over the next few weeks, there were some signs that the dispute could turn a corner. The Pakistani Ambassador, Ismail Ibrahim Chundrigar, told the Afghans that his government was prepared to negotiate if they in turn ceased their anti-Pakistan propaganda campaign. Persia also offered to act as a third-party mediator.[2] However, every piece of positive news was unfortunately trumped by constant worrying news from the region. Pakistan initially spent the same amount of money on the tribal areas as British India, but by May 1949 *The Times* was reporting that the amount was now in excess of Afghanistan's total budget.[3] Foreign Office officials feared that Pakistan's 'economic "forward" policy can hardly end in anything except tribal discontent with Afghanistan's backwardness – or at least with her inability to provide the tribes with a welfare state'.[4] Then there was an ugly scene at Lahore Airport in early June when the Afghan Ambassadors to Paris and Washington were shown 'gross discourtesy'. According to the Afghan Foreign Minister, a 'junior and somewhat dirty

Pakistan official, after ascertaining their identity, demanded rudely to see their passports, and when the Ambassadors demurred, had all their luggage unloaded from the aircraft'.[5]

Things came to a head when reports began to circulate that Mohammed Amin Jan, one of more than two dozen half-brothers of ex-Amir Amanullah, was about to cross the border into Afghanistan accompanied by hundreds of followers and with the backing of the Pakistan government. When a Pakistan Air Force plane dropped some bombs on tribesmen near the border near Khost on 12 June, the two countries seemed close to war as each claimed the bombs had landed on their side of the Durand Line. The Indian media wasted no time in pointing the finger of blame at Pakistan.[6]

The Moghulgai incident, as it became known, was a turning point in more ways than one. Although the immediate issue was eventually resolved, thereafter the likelihood of finding a long-term solution to the Pashtunistan question became increasingly remote. It brought an end to the simmering war of words and introduced a harder edge to Afghan–Pakistan relations. From then on, Afghan demands for an independent Pashtunistan became more pronounced, while the Pakistan government not only refused to countenance any proposal which would compromise the country's territorial integrity but also became increasingly prepared to use economic measures against Afghanistan to reinforce this message.

The Moghulgai incident also marked a turning point for Britain. It was the last occasion in which Britain was able to play a more or less unilateral role in influencing Afghanistan-Pakistan relations to reduce tensions along the Frontier. Thereafter, the government had to leverage other voices to articulate its position, while other embassies in Kabul began to take a more proactive role.

Amin Jan and the Moghulgai Incident

Amin Jan was a long-standing political opponent of Zahir Shah's claim to the throne and had arrived on the North-West Frontier in late 1948. The news caused jitters in Afghanistan. Cunningham's replacement in NWFP, Sir Ambrose Dundas, advised Ikramullah in early December that Amin Jan was currently not, and probably would not, cause trouble until and unless the Afghan government's 'own advertised interest in him results in considerable inflation of his own importance'.[7] The Afghan government, however, thought otherwise. The King told Squire a week later that: 'His government looked to us with our long experience of dealing with Frontier tribes to use our influence with Pakistan in this matter. The Pakistan government could not deny all responsibility for allowing undesirable persons hostile to Afghanistan into tribal territory.'[8] Ali Mohammed reiterated the King's view that Amin Jan was being funded by Pakistan officials, and then asked Britain to encourage Pakistan to announce publically that Amin Jan had arrived in Waziristan in the 'un-administered' tribal areas without their connivance.[9]

Over the coming months, Amin Jan's movements were closely watched. Ikramullah took the opportunity in the margins of the Commonwealth Prime Ministers' conference in late April to tell Britain his government was doing everything it could to avoid stoking up trouble on the Frontier, and that included providing no support to any of the eighty-two people resident in Pakistan with a claim to the Afghan throne.[10] Behind the scenes, however, Foreign Office officials in London and the embassy in Kabul were beginning to wonder if the Pakistan government was according due respect to Afghan sensitivities. Indeed, perhaps they had not been 'magnanimous enough to concede the appearance of deference to Afghan wishes in order to preserve the substance of authority on the NWFP'.[11]

Then, at the end of May, news emerged that Amin Jan had held a *Jirga* of the Mahsuds. Although some reports said that only 400 of the anticipated 1,500 men had turned up, the fact that he was there, was meeting the very tribes that had helped place Nadir Shah on the throne in 1929, and was now moving towards the Afghan border, sent alarm bells ringing in Karachi, Kabul and London. The Afghan government swiftly moved troops to Khost to deter him and his followers from crossing the border.[12]

Although Foreign Office officials privately thought that Pakistan should have taken more concerted action, including by air, before things reached this point – which had been common practice before Indian independence – they focussed their attention now on what could be done to defuse the tension. When they reminded Pakistan that it was their responsibility to prevent Amin Jan and his men from crossing the border, however, they learnt that the government had already been carefully assessing what action to take. They had been mindful that any action on their part might trigger a full-scale war, especially if Amin Jan had been on his way to Kabul at the invitation of the Afghan government. As a precautionary measure, therefore, they had put pressure on tribal *maliks* (leaders) and allowance holders to call back tribesmen who had joined Amir Jan, and had distributed leaflets to discourage more from joining them. As for Amin Jan himself, they had offered him safe conduct and an allowance if he agreed to settle in Pakistan, but outside NWFP.[13] Separately, although the British only found out about this later, they had also sent an instruction to their Ambassador in Kabul, Chundrigar, telling him to warn the Afghans that Amin Jan was heading to the border. Unfortunately, Chundrigar did not receive the message in time, and therefore 'failed to convey the warning to the Afghan authorities before himself receiving a note of protest on 6 June'.[14]

By 9 June, the Afghans had reinforced three garrisons on Amin Jan's line of approach. The latter therefore abandoned his plan and retreated with just thirty men, having told others to go home and prepare for service in Kashmir soon.[15] Three days later, however, on 12 June, in the midst of heightened tensions, the problem reached crisis point. Reports came in that a Pakistan Air Force plane had fired on a crowd, killing fifteen and wounding a further twenty-six. Afghanistan was quick to claim that this incident had occurred inside Afghan territory at Moghulgai. Furthermore, the bombs had actually been dropped on the Afghans who had assembled to resist the expected attack from Amin Jan, and had just been told to disperse because the immediate threat was now over.[16] Pakistan quickly claimed that three Pakistan aircraft had been patrolling in tribal territory and had seen a concentration of about 500 men in Dawagar area in North Waziristan on the Pakistan side of the Durand Line. The aircraft had then proceeded to drop leaflets calling for the men to disperse. Unfortunately, one plane had been fired on and had then taken retaliatory action in Pakistan territory.[17]

Although the Pakistan Defence Department continued to state publicly that the incident had occurred in Pakistan, the Afghans were convinced that the bombs had landed in Afghanistan and Pakistan should have accepted responsibility without hesitation. The British were pretty convinced too. A British pilot from the RAF Training Mission had flown the Afghan Minister of War to the site on the 13th. They had been shown cannon shells, which seemed to confirm local accounts of the incident, and the minister had consoled bereaved relatives.[18] Three days later, the government sent a note to the Foreign Office in London claiming Pakistan had

induce Mohammed Amin to attack Afghan territory with a small force of Pakistanis, but Mohammed Amin's army soon dwindled and left him alone with some few of his Pakistan friends to go back to his former residence in Southern Waziristan. In order to distract attention from their failure in this policy of intriguing with Mohammed Amin, the Pakistan authorities sent aeroplanes over the Afghan borders into Moghulgai, lying within Afghan territory, to attack the people who were opposing the ex-King's brother, and there dropped five bombs, killing fifteen, and injuring twelve people.[19]

To verify their assertion, the government decided to invite Military Attachés from diplomatic missions in Kabul, except from the Soviet Union and Pakistan, to visit Moghulgai. The Prime Minister also told Squire that an apology from Pakistan would help improve relations and he wondered if Britain could help encourage Pakistan to do this if the investigation proved their pilot was at fault.[20]

Meanwhile, behind the scenes, the Pakistan government had started its own investigation, and privately shared the process with Grafftey-Smith. Sir Zafarullah Khan, had asked Liaquat Ali Khan if an Afghan government representative and the British and American Military Attachés could visit the Pakistan side of the border to see evidence that the attack had occurred on Pakistan soil. Meanwhile, Liaquat Ali Khan himself was personally questioning political officers from the area to see if they had made a mistake or even lied.[21] None of this was shared publicly, however. Instead, Liaquat Ali Khan formally asked Afghanistan if they wanted to set up a joint Pakistan–Afghanistan commission to investigate both sides of the border. If that was not an option, then he was happy using international observers instead.[22]

Back in Kabul, the government was busy assembling an international inspection team with representatives from Britain, the United States, India, Egypt, Turkey, Persia, France, Italy, Saudi Arabia and Jordan. Since Prendergast was on leave, the British representative was Second Secretary Patrick Keen, a fluent Pashtun speaker. They were joined by the Afghan Acting Chief of the General Staff, the Director General Political in the Ministry of Foreign Affairs, two members of the National Assembly and a journalist from the Afghan media. At the last minute, the Afghans allowed Squadron Leader Lee-Evans from the RAF Training Mission to pilot one of the three Avro Anson planes flying the team to the border area on 21 June. All eyes now focussed on what the team would find in Moghulgai.

The Visit to Moghulgai

Keen wrote a detailed report of his visit and took several photographs, which were later sent to London. Together these provide a rich insight into what he and others saw that day.[23] The party landed at Khost at 9.15 a.m. and were met beside the landing strip by 1,000 tribesmen and a guard of honour comprising 150 Afghan soldiers and a band. The Chief of the General Staff first led the party along the guard of honour and then in front of the tribesmen, 'all of whom started yelling their greetings and firing their rifles into the air. At the end of the procession, we were surrounded by a section of the tribes and an old grey beard on crutches, presumably one of the more influential tribal *maliks*, was brought forward to address us'. He told them he was very glad the tribesmen were being given the opportunity to explain what had happened and that they had held back from taking direct action themselves because they wanted to see what would come out of the team's visit. The team also met General Hazarullah Khan, commander of the troops in Khost, who had actually been an eyewitness to the event himself.

From the airstrip, the party left in cars and jeeps for the next stage of their journey, accompanied by General Ghulam Rasoul Khan, the Supreme Civil and Military Governor of Southern Province, and Lee-Evans, who somehow managed to find a spare seat in one of the vehicles. After a forty-minute 15-mile drive, they switched to horses and spent the next fifty-five minutes riding to the first site where they saw three largish bomb fragments. Lee-Evans thought these could have come from a 100-pounder. The bomb had not exploded on impact and so the tribesmen had lit a fire around it to make it explode about four hours later. At 12.40 p.m., and after another twenty minutes' riding, they reached Moghulgai itself where a *shamiana* (a large tent with open sides) had been erected. Here they stopped for lunch, watched by hundreds of tribesmen who had assembled around the tent and on the surrounding hills. There were no signs of buildings in the vicinity but Keen saw lots of 'chapes', which were temporary shelters often built by tribesmen in that area as protection against the sun.

Over lunch, General Hazarullah Khan described the events of 12 June. He had gone to thank the tribes for their support against Amin Jan and to ask them to disperse. A reconnaissance plane had flown overhead at 6.30 a.m., and then at around 10.30 a.m. a second plane had arrived and attacked the tribesmen who were closely packed together for the meeting. The general had realised the plane was coming in to attack and had shouted to the tribesmen to lie down. He could not, however, describe the markings on the plane's wings, which would have identified where it was from, nor did he know what type of plane it was. According to him, twenty-one had been killed and a further twenty-five wounded. After lunch, the team were shown fragments of the bombs and a 'dried-up hand, blackened and shrivelled', and then got back on their horses to ride to the area where the tribesmen said the bombs had actually landed. Here they saw seven bomb craters in an area of about 40 square yards. Stones had been propped up near the craters and on each was stuck a piece of paper with the name of the individual killed on that spot. Fragments of clothing could be seen lying around. Keen and a few others from the party then rode up to higher ground to try to locate the border. It was impossible, reported Keen:

The general impression which I got which was also confirmed by Squadron Leader Lee-Evans, both during my time in Moghulgai and while circling near Khost in our aircraft, was that any pilot would find it extremely difficult to pin point his position on a map with any degree of certainty in the area to the south of Moghulgai.

Keen was also handed a leaflet, written in Pashtu, allegedly dropped by the plane. It said the tribesmen should disperse, 'by order of the Pakistan government', because they were supporting an un-Islamic movement aimed at attacking the interests of Pakistan, and warned they would be bombed if they did not move. Keen was told that the leaflets had been collected up and sent to the Ministry of Foreign Affairs in Kabul. The party then rode back to the *shamiana* where they received another eyewitness account, this time from a local *malik* or tribal elder called Abdus Samad Khan Khostwal. He told them that approximately 1,100 tribesmen had been gathered that morning. Moreover, 'no true Pashtun could leave an incident of this description unavenged and he then proceeded to say that eventually they would take a thousand Pakistani lives for every one of their men who had been killed'. Others in the party felt the old man had been quoting words put into his mouth, but Keen, who was not reliant on an interpreter, told them that he was fairly confident the *malik* was speaking his own mind. Some of the tribesmen assembled in the clearing then started a tribal dance accompanied by drums, while tribesmen surrounding the dancers 'started firing their rifles in the air and this was picked up by all the others on the surrounding hills until volleys of rifle fire were reverberating in all directions. This, combined with the numbers of men I had actually seen, gave me the impression that there must have been at least a thousand tribesmen assembled in the Moghulgai area while we were there.'

The party arrived back at Khost at 6.30 p.m. and were entertained in the grounds of the governor's house where tents had been pitched complete with carpets, camp beds, bedding and mosquito nets. They had a six-course dinner and afterwards sat for an hour listening to a portable wireless, broadcasting a programme from Kabul Radio. As Keen recalled, 'the main item on the programme was a semi-comic play, every other word of which hurled abuse or flung mud at Pakistan'.

Keen also managed to have a private chat with the Ministry of Foreign Affairs representative away from prying ears. He told Keen candidly that his government could not really control the tribes and feared serious repercussions from this affair if the tribes got out of hand and attempted to take revenge on Pakistan. The government had partly succeeded in holding them back so far because they had already given the tribesmen some money as compensation, but were not confident that they could continue to do so. His points chimed with what Britain already suspected, but it was useful nevertheless to hear it directly from someone inside the government.

After a huge breakfast the next morning, they were taken to Khost Military Hospital to see fourteen of the wounded and concluded their injuries were pretty consistent with being hit by bomb splinters. Then they boarded the waiting planes and arrived back at Kabul at 10 a.m. on 22 June. It had been an incredibly busy and illuminating twenty-six hours. Keen was convinced that the tribesmen's stories were true: 'On the basis of this evidence, I would say that a prima facie genuine case has been established by the Afghans which justified the framing of a charge.' In addition, he believed the presence of the *chapes* on the hills provided additional evidence that the area had been used as the gathering place for tribesmen, who had come specifically to halt Amin Jan's advance and force him back across the border.

Each member of the inspection team prepared reports to send to their respective capitals. Notes were compared and different points of evidence given greater or lesser weight. The United States representative felt the visit had been much more tense than Keen described and that the tribesmen would attack Pakistan if nothing was done.[24] The Turkish Ambassador told Squire that his representative had found the evidence inconclusive except for the 'isolated bomb' which he believed was genuine. He planned to tell the Pakistani Ambassador that he believed, on balance, that the incident had occurred within Afghan territory and that Pakistan should admit liability and pay compensation.[25] Squire decided Keen should meet the Pakistan Ambassador and gave him Keen's report, minus the record of Keen's conversation with the Foreign Ministry representative.

Squire suggested to the American Ambassador that neither of them should express an opinion publicly, at least not just yet. Other missions did likewise. When Squire sent Keen's report to London, he made it clear that he believed the Afghan version of events. Their story had not materially changed since the day after the bombing and it was unlikely that they would have purposely placed the isolated bomb, for effect, so far from the main attack. It just did not add up. He also agreed with Keen that the absence of any physical features in the landscape would have made it difficult for any pilot to know which side of the border he was on. Given this,

It seems to me that, in the absence of any very clear explanation by Pakistan, world opinion will also be inclined to accept the Afghan point-of-view. Indeed, the facts are sufficiently damning. As seen through Afghan eyes, the Pakistan government have harboured a pretender to the Afghan throne in their midst for eight months. They have not prevented him from raising an army to invade Afghanistan, and when the Afghans gather to oppose his passage, they are bombed by Pakistan.[26]

Privately, he also recorded in his journal his personal opinion that the Pakistan government had 'made matters worse by abusing the Afghans for a ludicrous distortion of the facts and for having encouraged a *lashkar* to invade Pakistan'.[27]

Meanwhile, Kabul gossipmongers wondered what the Soviet embassy thought about the whole incident, especially as the Afghan government had purposely excluded them from the Moghulgai visit. The first solid news came at the end of July when the Soviet Military Attaché, while feigning disinterest, tried to pump the Indian embassy for information. 'The Indian Military Attaché says that the Russian expressed regret that he had been unable to go, asked searching questions on what had been seen there, and said in the same breath "we are not interested".'[28]

Britain Tries to Manage the Fallout

Back in London, officials were gearing up to provide an oral answer on 30 June to a Parliamentary Question from Phillips Price MP to the Secretary of State for Commonwealth Relations, Phillip Noel-Baker. The timing and nature of the question could not have been worse. Price wanted to know 'whether, in view of the increasingly hostile attitude of the Afghan government to the NWFP, he will take steps to assure Pakistan that she can count on our full support in the event of armed aggression'. It was a no-win situation. Whatever the Secretary of State said was unlikely to please both parties to the dispute, and they would now hear officially which side Britain was on. They may have had their suspicions, but up to this point Britain had been able to present itself as an honest broker dealing responsibly with a legacy of empire. Within a matter of days, British diplomats' finely tuned diplomacy over the past two years would be undermined in either Kabul or Karachi, depending on how the answer was crafted. The response also needed to be carefully worded to ensure expectations were not raised in Pakistan that Britain would come to their assistance in the event of an attack. There was a further complication too – the answer could also provoke a hostile reception in India. Various drafts of the answer were therefore exchanged more or less daily between London and Karachi, Kabul and Delhi in the run up to the 30 June statement in the House of Commons.

Bevin had meetings scheduled with the Pakistan High Commissioner on 28 June, and the Afghan Ambassador on 29 June.[29] He knew Pakistan was still unhappy at the way a deal had been struck to accommodate Nehru's demands at the April Commonwealth Prime Ministers' meeting and so tried to be conciliatory as far as possible. He therefore began his first meeting with the usual points about Pakistan having inherited Britain's rights on the Frontier. He then went on to say that although he did not believe the attack had been intentional, he was inclined to believe it had occurred on the Afghan side of the border. He asked Pakistan to reiterate its offer for a joint Pakistan–Afghanistan enquiry and to pay compensation if the Afghan version of events proved correct.[30]

A day later, in his meeting with the Afghan Ambassador, Bevin began with a verbal response to the Afghan note of 16 June which had blamed Pakistan for the Moghulgai incident. He reiterated that Pakistan was Britain's heir to the rights and duties in the NWFP, but also made clear that he did not believe Pakistan had assisted Amin Jan. Indeed, on the contrary, he had heard they had tried to stop his activities. Given this, he recommended that the Afghan government should accept Pakistan's proposal for a joint Afghan–Pakistan enquiry. Faiz Mohammed Zakria, however, said that his government did not accept Pakistan's succession to Britain's rights in the 'independent' tribal areas, and could not therefore sit down to negotiate until the Pakistan government recognised that fact:

> Britain had taken territory by force from Afghanistan, and Afghanistan could not recognise that the territory in question had passed to Pakistan after the British had left India ... Where could Afghanistan go for justice; here was Britain building up the new nation of Pakistan and killing the old nation of Afghanistan.

Bevin was having none of it: 'It was impossible to make discussions conditional on such an admission. The only basis for talks must be mutual recognition of Pakistan's status as our successor ... [He warned] him that the agitation he had been stirring up in Muslim countries was dangerous and might lead to most serious consequences, not only affecting Pakistan but endangering the present regime in Afghanistan with consequences no one could foresee, but which could only profit others.'[31] The meeting, not surprisingly, closed without finding a way to bring the two parties closer together.

On the next day, Thursday 30 June, Noel-Baker stood up in the House of Commons and set out Britain's position publicly for the first time:

> It is His Majesty's Government's view that Pakistan is in international law the inheritor of the rights and duties of the old Government of India and of His Majesty's Government in the United Kingdom in these territories and that the Durand line is the international border. Both now and at all times, His Majesty's Government are fully conscious of their duty in the light of Pakistan's position both as a fellow member of the

Commonwealth and of the United Nations ... and are convinced – and are confident that this view is shared by the Government of Pakistan – that there is no outstanding question between Pakistan and Afghanistan which cannot be settled by peaceful means on the basis of the legal position I have stated. They are also confident that there could be no question of armed aggression by Afghanistan who is a fellow member of the United Nations.

This answer was followed swiftly by a question from Mr Grammans MP asking whether Pakistan could rely on Britain's help in the event of aggressive action taking place. The Secretary of State replied: 'The Commonwealth ... does not work by pledges given in advance about hypothetical situations. They are not asked for, and not given.'[32]

So Britain had backed Pakistan's claims over Afghanistan's, which pleased Pakistan, but made an ambiguous statement about whether Britain would, or would not, back a Commonwealth member if the need arose.

In Afghanistan, the response to the parliamentary question was initially bellicose. In the National Assembly, representatives asserted that they were using their right under Article 14 of the 1921 Anglo-Afghan Treaty to denounce the treaty and the 'imaginary' Durand Line, while the government considered sending a special delegation around the world, headed by the Foreign Minister, to explain how Afghanistan felt about the situation. Privately, however, Ali Mohammed told Squire that he was not keen to rush into any action that might be detrimental to Afghanistan's cause and was actually grateful that Britain had finally, as he put it, given an 'authoritative opinion'. He wanted to reflect on that before taking further action.[33]

Faiz Mohammed Zakria, in London, took a different view. When he met Bevin again on 15 July, he reiterated that Pakistan had not inherited Britain's rights in the 'independent' tribal areas between the Durand Line and the settled administered area. Indeed, he wondered why 'Britain had the power and the right to give back to India and to Pakistan what she had originally taken from them, but could not give them what she had taken from someone else, namely Afghanistan'. There was one piece of good news – the idea of a special delegation had been canceled – but as he left the meeting, he put his trump card on the table. Afghanistan might now begin looking for other friends, perhaps even the Soviet Union.[34]

The reaction from India, on the other hand, was measured and reflective, providing some assurance that the Indian government was concerned about peace across the Indian subcontinent and did not want to rock the boat. Although the High Commissioner in London had protested that his government had not been consulted about the proposed reply, the Indian Foreign Minister, Sir Girija Shankar Bajpai, took a slightly different approach when he met the British High Commissioner in Delhi on 16 July. He explained that India fully accepted Pakistan's rights in the whole Frontier area, including NWFP and Balochistan. Indeed, 'the Indian view was this was quite indubitably Pakistan territory and that the Afghans had no right to interfere at all. It would be just as ridiculous for the Afghans to claim a voice in regard to the future of these areas even though the inhabitants might be Pathans as for India to lay claim to Afghanistan on the basis of Ashoka's empire' which had extended across the Indian subcontinent and the Hindu Kush in the second century BC. He did feel, however, that Afghanistan's rights in the tribal areas should be recognised and explained that the Indian government had been trying to find a way for them to come to a mutual understanding with Pakistan.

Bajpai was, however, evasive about whether India accepted the validity of the Durand Line or not, explaining that he did not think it would be helpful for India to make a statement one way or the other at this juncture. India was very concerned about accusations of exacerbating the problem when in fact they had been urging Afghanistan to be cautious and he hoped Britain would do the same with Pakistan, since they could not. Peace in the region mattered to India too:

> It was quite clear to him that only the Soviet Union could profit from existing discord between Afghanistan and Pakistan ... The dispute between India and Pakistan [over Kashmir] coupled with the Afghan–Pakistan dispute if they were not solved would prevent any effective defence organisation on the North West Frontier and ensure that the Indian sub-continent was a weak neighbour to the Soviet Union for a long time to come.[35]

Finding Closure on Moghulgai

The Afghans accepted Pakistan's proposal for a joint commission and a team duly arrived in Kabul in mid-July, headed by Abdur Rab Nishtar, the Minister of Communications, who had attended Afghanistan's independence celebrations the year before. The team set off to Moghulgai on the 17th, flown this time by Afghan pilots to ensure that Pakistan got a good impression of the Afghan Air Force. The British RAF pilots had been kept well out of sight at the airport – although Lee-Evans had actually been told twice that he would be leading the party down to Khost, he was stood down at the eleventh hour, just before the Pakistani team arrived.[36] During this visit, the Pakistan delegation saw sufficient evidence to convince them that the incident had indeed occurred on Afghan soil. It was not a wholehearted success, however, as Squire wrote sadly in his journal: 'The delegation has been up for a week investigating the Moghulgai incident, and although it is understood that Pakistan will climb down, it does not appear that they will do so at all gracefully or spontaneously and another opportunity of a rapprochement seems to have been lost.'[37]

While everyone waited for the publication of the commission's findings, the Pakistan government had been continuing its internal investigation. A court of enquiry had been convened by the Commander of the Pakistan Air Force, and Grafftey-Smith was shown a report of the proceedings. This found that the aircraft had been fired on while dropping leaflets, and in response the pilot had taken retaliatory action with one attack consisting of seven 60-pound rockets. The pilot believed he had fired these 1,000 yards inside Pakistan territory, but while pulling out of this attack it was just possible he had strayed into Afghanistan. The enquiry also found that the two cannon attacks (with 120 rounds of ammunition) had definitely been fired inside Pakistan at targets within Pakistan, but since this occurred very close to the Durand Line, some may have penetrated across the border. The court concluded the pilot had taken 'retaliatory' action in Afghanistan, but 'offensive' action in Pakistan, and found him to blame for not being certain of his position. They did not believe, however, that the attack was deliberate.[38]

Meanwhile, the Afghan National Assembly issued a press release on 25 July announcing that it no longer recognised the Durand Line and demanded reparations for Moghulgai.[39] A few days later, on 3 August, the government announced it hoped to see the creation of an independent Pashtunistan. These developments provoked concern across the diplomatic community. The United States asked Britain if it could see the written statements from the tribes stating their willingness to be part of Pakistan,[40] and the Pakistan Minister of Foreign Affairs, Sir Zafarullah Khan, wrote to Attlee on 26 July saying, 'It is utterly impossible for us at this stage to determine what precisely they [Afghanistan] are after.'[41] The British were puzzled too, but increasingly believed the Afghans would back down in their present campaign if they received some assurance from Pakistan that their interest in the tribal areas was recognised.[42]

Over in India, the pensive mood continued. Bajpai told the High Commissioner he was 'doubtful that the Afghans were capable in their present mood of profiting from any advice and he concluded somewhat gloomily that the only policy seemed to be to play for time and to hope that the Afghans would calm down.'[43] In another meeting, he said that he regarded the Afghan Ambassador in Delhi 'as being one of the more dangerous Afghan extremists and very much on a par with the Afghan Ambassador in London'.[44] Although it was clear India did not intend to get involved in the crisis, Britain decided to reconsider how much information they should actually share with them from now on. Officials were accordingly advised not to 'say too much to the Government of India at present, especially on the line to take on Pakistan, since there is a risk that, in order to worsen our relations with Pakistan, the Indians might allow the Pakistanis to know that they and we had been consulting together about this.'[45]

Over the following weeks, the tensions seemed to ease off. Pakistan suspended all anti-Afghan press comments for a week, and then Afghanistan did likewise. Squire was soon able to inform London that although Ministers were much taken up with the propaganda war, the incident was no longer a hot topic of conversation among ordinary people: 'The whole campaign in fact seems most unreal. I am told that whereas a month ago the Kabul bazaars seemed to think that war between Afghanistan and Pakistan was inevitable – no one quite knew why – they now seem to think that relations between the two countries are quite friendly.'[46] The breakthrough finally came on 30 July when the formal report of the joint commission was published. It announced:

> The incident took place at Moghulgai at a spot which is about 2100 yards from the nearest point of the border. The action of the pilot in flying over Afghanistan territory and firing on people collected at Moghulgai was not intentional, but due to a bona fide mistake. We are of the opinion that the Pakistan government and officials are in no way responsible for this incident.[47]

Pakistan accepted the Afghan figures – dead, twenty-three; missing, one; and injured, twenty-four – and offered compensation. Both parties then agreed to maintain the ban on propaganda through the media. The Afghan government felt vindicated, and lost no time in issuing a press statement in Karachi on 5 August, proclaiming that the report 'confirms how the Afghan government's statements can at all times be verified when subjected to unprejudiced examination; but the utterance of falsehoods and the imperialist policy of whose who may practice them have involved, and always will involve in the future, all mankind in misery and bloodshed'.[48]

Unfortunately, although the immediate crisis was now over, Afghan–Pakistan relations remained strained. This was not helped by the fact that Pakistan failed to offer a satisfactory apology. Squire was deeply disappointed. Although 'the incident has been settled, another opportunity of healing the breach has been lost by the complete failure of Pakistan to make any apology whatsoever. They have admitted that Afghan territory was bombed by mistake and say that no Pakistan official was to blame!'[49] When he began his farewell round of meetings in Kabul in early September, his friend Ali Mohammed told him that the only apology he had received from Pakistan had come in the form of a personal letter from the Pakistan Ambassador. He thought at the very least that he should have received a formal apology from the government itself and an assurance that the pilot responsible would be disciplined.[50]

Squire mentioned the matter to Sir Zafarullah Khan personally when he passed through Karachi on his way back to London on 7 September. The Foreign Minister replied: 'Pakistan was quite big enough to apologise for the Moghalgai incident, and would do so three times over if an expression of regret was not enough for the Afghan government. He declared that he was willing to go to Kabul himself for discussions if that would help.'[51]

There is an interesting postscript to the Moghulgai incident. Squadron Leader Lee-Evans had drawn pictures of the markings he had seen on the debris during his visit to Moghulgai. He suspected the debris was from bombs, but was not 100 per cent certain. When the Commandant of the Afghan Air Force later asked him if it was possible to identify where the missiles had been manufactured and who they had been supplied to, he sent the drawings to London.[52] In September, the Air Ministry confirmed they could identify some of the debris. The fragments were the remains of a rocket projectile made by a British company based in Dalston in London. They qualified this, however, by saying that a complete rocket could be made up of components from a number of different manufacturers, but this did not of course detract from the fact that the debris from the rocket was essentially British-made. They also confirmed that the cartridge had been made in Britain too, by a company called ICL Ltd, based in Standish, in 1944.[53] Armed with this somewhat sensitive and potentially embarrassing information, the Foreign Office advised Lee-Evans to be cautious:

> It would appear from the foregoing that there is *prima facie* evidence that some of the ammunition expended in this incident was of British manufacture. Though this of course provides no firm evidence that it was a Pakistan plane which was responsible for the bombing incident, it might serve as an additional irritant to Afghan–Pakistan relations if revealed to the Afghans. Unless the Commandant of the Air Force raises the matter with you again, we think it might be preferable not to pursue it. If, however, the Afghans enquire what was the result of your approach to us, you are at liberty to give them the information …

but adding that on the details available, there is no evidence to show to whom the ammunition was supplied.[54]

Reverberations

If Squire and his team had hoped that the peaceful resolution of the crisis would help pave the way for more positive Afghan–Pakistan relations in the future, they were mistaken. If anything, Afghan ambitions for Pashtunistan seemed to expand thereafter, not lessen. Whereas in 1947/8 the government would probably have accepted Pakistan's formal recognition of an Afghan role in the tribal areas, now they increasingly asserted that they, and they alone, were championing the Pashtun tribes' cause irrespective of where they lived. Squire speculated that some of this repositioning might be because Mahmud Khan's personal status had been compromised by his handling of the Moghulgai incident: 'Rumours have begun to circulate of serious differences in the Cabinet and of the Prime Minister's probable resignation ... There seems to be increasing resentment against the Prime Minister's inept handling of the situation and his obstinacy in refusing to take any step that may impair his personal popularity.'[55]

Two men in particular stood out: Mahmud's nephews Naim Khan and Daud Khan, both strong nationalists. Naim Khan suggested to Squire in August that Pashtunistan should be created as a separate dominion in the Commonwealth following the outcome of a referendum. The Commonwealth, perhaps with Afghan cooperation, could then guarantee its security. Squire nipped that idea swiftly in the bud:

> In my view, his present proposal was as reasonable as would be a demand from France that there should be an immediate plebiscite in London and the home counties of England to decide whether they wished to remain as they are at present, an integral part of England, or whether they would like to form themselves into a separate State. He was rebuffed but not convinced.[56]

A day later, on 16 August, Ali Mohammed told Squire that while Afghanistan did not want to renounce the 1921 Treaty immediately, 'they consider that any negotiations that take place between them and Pakistan must be on the basis that the Durand Line is not necessarily valid'. Squire therefore suggested to London that the only potential solution in the foreseeable future was to convince the Afghan government that the tribes themselves were happy with the current arrangements.[57]

Meanwhile in Karachi, the Pakistan government seemed to be deliberately winding up the Afghans. In a statement on 15 August, Liaquat Ali Khan said that, as the biggest Muslim state in the world, Pakistan had obligations as an 'elder brother towards his younger brothers'. If necessary, an elder brother should even mildly rebuke his younger brother, but 'always with a feeling of fraternal love'. This did not go down at all well in Kabul, as Squire noted. 'The Afghan press has always adopted the very superior attitude that Pakistan, as a newly created state, is its younger brother and that in view of its lack of experience of world affairs, it is itself in need of help and advice from Afghanistan.' A report in *Anis* on 17 August said that 'if mere numbers are to be the criterion of seniority then England itself should be considered of less importance than Pakistan'.[58]

In the meantime, Squire's worst fears were beginning to be realised. Britain's standing with the Afghan government began to decline considerably after Noel-Baker's speech in Parliament. Up to that point, the Afghans believed the British had not taken sides because they believed the Afghan case was strong. Now, his answer had 'blasted all their hopes'. Thenceforth, the Afghan government became less inclined to seek advice from the British or take note of their warnings.[59] When Squire finally left Afghanistan on Monday 5 September after six years, his farewell from the government was muted. He met the King 'to make my official adieu,' and found him 'quite affable but nothing more'. After that:

> I said my farewells to the various Afghan officials during the last few days and gave little silver tokens to the Prime Minister and Minister of Foreign Affairs. In return, I got a carpet and a marble flower vase. I cannot help suspecting that I should have got neither if I had not myself taken the initiative – so sadly have our relations with the government deteriorated during the last months.[60]

Just before he left Kabul for good that morning, he walked around the embassy gardens one last time accompanied by the Saudi, American and Persian Ambassadors who had come to see him off. He must have felt some regret that the one Afghan whom he viewed as a 'real friend as well as a constant bridge partner', Ali Mohammed, was not there too.

When the new Desk Officer for Afghanistan in the Foreign Office, Richard Blackham, surveyed South Asian affairs later that September, his conclusions were bleak. Positions on both sides of the dispute were increasingly entrenched, while Pakistan's frustrations with India seemed to be seeping inexorably into their dealings with the 'recalcitrant'

Afghans. What had appeared to be a relatively easy issue to solve in 1947, now seemed to have morphed into an intractable problem.

> It looks as though both sides were tired of the truce and are prepared to go hammer and tongs at one another any moment. The Pakistanis have revived the idea of economic counter measures, which would be their way of declaring that there was no hope of a peaceful settlement and Afghanistan could only be brought to heal by force. Unfortunately, the intransigence is by no means all on the Afghan side; the Pakistanis are being very pig-headed over Afghan interests on the Frontier tribes, which cannot be lightly disregarded, and take no account of the obvious truth that friction can only benefit Russia. At the moment, however, the Pakistanis are so obsessed by their isolation, by their fear of India, and their frustration at their own somewhat ineffective international position that they may do anything they think calculated to retrieve their prestige, and getting tough with the Afghans may seem a likely starter ... There is nothing we can do to help in this particular issue at the moment.[61]

This was the context in which Squire's successor, Sir John Gardener, arrived in Kabul in late September, fresh from London and with limited experience in the region. By the time the Afghan government offered to reopen talks with Pakistan a month later, the prospects for a diplomatic solution looked increasingly dim. As a pre-condition, they made clear they were only interested in talks if there was no prior announcement about the continuing validity of the 1921 Treaty. A month later, Pakistan said it was ready to discuss every issue, including cooperation on the tribes and improving economic relations, except the question of Pakistan's sovereignty over the tribes. Privately, the government told Grafftey-Smith they suspected Afghanistan's overture was simply a ruse. The Afghans knew the negotiations would not yield the outcomes they wanted, and so 'after [the] failure of negotiations, [the] Afghan government would then announce to [the] Afghan people that they had begged at Pakistan's door and had been turned away, and would appeal for national support for a stronger policy towards Pakistan'.[62]

Within weeks, the dispute entered a new phase. Pakistan introduced trade sanctions restricting the flow of goods to and from Afghanistan, while the Afghan government endorsed and promoted Pashtun symbols and new institutions to underline there was more to Pashtunistan than mere words.

Economic Sanctions

During 1949, Pakistan started to explore whether there were ways to curtail some of Afghanistan's trading privileges under the 1921 Treaty, including exemptions from customs duties on selected items, without actually violating the treaty itself. This was a potentially risky approach given that Pakistan at the same time expected Afghanistan to adhere to another provision in the treaty, namely accepting the Durand Line as the Frontier. A precedent had already been set by the Indian government soon after independence when they imposed a 25 per cent import tax on Afghan fruit and goods exported to India from Karachi. They had also placed Afghan goods in transit through Pakistan to India in the same category as Pakistani exports, and hence liable to import duties. Pakistan in turn imposed an import duty on dried fruit from Afghanistan.[63] Over the next year, the emphasis shifted to the transportation of petrol to Afghanistan as first one restriction then another was placed upon it. Ostensibly, these restrictions were introduced to ensure compliance with standards and concessions elsewhere, but many Afghans as well as the international community suspected they stemmed from a desire to pressurise Afghanistan to abandon its position on Pashtunistan.

For Afghanistan, any changes to these trading rights was potentially catastrophic. As a land-locked state, they were heavily dependent on access to overland trade routes to reach international markets. Most of that trade had been through British India since the nineteenth century because transport links to Persia were poor, and trade through the Soviet Union was both logistically difficult due to poor transport infrastructure, and strictly controlled through a series of trade agreements designed to restrict Soviet influence in the country. If Pakistan decided to impose trade sanctions, Afghanistan would not only lose access to essential imports such as oil, petrol and cotton piece goods, but also to foreign exchange through the sale of exported agricultural products. They had already experienced the impact of rail disruptions in 1947/8 when violent sectarian riots in the Punjab cut transport links – subsequently, many Kandahar fruit merchants were ruined.

Things escalated after the Moghulgai incident. One of the first signs that Pakistan was beginning to pile on the pressure came at the beginning of September when military supplies arrived in Karachi from Czechoslovakia for onward shipment to Kabul. Pakistan's Ambassador in Kabul, Chundrigar, told Squire that he was wondering whether the treaty could be invoked to prevent the shipment leaving Karachi since Article 6 stated that arms could only be transported to Afghanistan if they did not pose an immediate danger to the former Government of India.[64] In this instance the Pakistan government did agree to release the shipment, but this debate had opened the door to a wider examination of Afghanistan's trading privileges under the treaty.

When Gardener passed through Pakistan on his way to Kabul, he was reassured by the government that Afghanistan still enjoyed all the rights in trade and commerce accorded under the 1921 Treaty. He also learnt that earlier holdups caused by the dislocation of the railways and docks at Partition had now been resolved.[65] A few days later, however, on 29 September, the Pakistan Ministry of Communications announced that the government had decided, with immediate effect, to withdraw a 50 per cent concession on petrol transported to Kabul from Karachi via Peshawar and Chaman. This concession, the ministry explained, had originally been introduced in 1938 by the former Government of India to combat a Soviet campaign to increase their petrol sales in Afghanistan. Now it was being removed because there was no equivalent concession for petrol consumed in Pakistan and it was simply not viable to continue this for Afghanistan. Furthermore, they pointed out, India had already withdrawn a similar concession on certain traffic booked on Indian railways for export to Afghanistan.[66] Then, in mid-November, the Pakistan government announced that trade and tax concessions on specific items under the treaty – petrol, cement, certain electrical equipment – were no longer justified and they were considering withdrawing them too. They were also considering imposing a duty on imports from Afghanistan, including fruit, because if Pakistan continued to offer such exemptions, this could, they argued, lay them open to a charge by India of discrimination under the terms of the General Agreement on Tariffs and Trade (GATT).[67]

Britain became increasingly alarmed. They knew the crippling impact these changes would have on the Afghan economy. All eyes therefore focussed on Washington where the Export-Import Bank was in the final stages of preparing the $21 million loan for Afghanistan. Britain and Pakistan hoped it would include political conditions too, requiring Afghanistan to come to a deal with Pakistan,[68] but when it was publicly announced in mid-December, no strings were attached. Furthermore, there was no mention in the margins of the announcement about the importance of protecting the integrity of the Frontier or Pakistan's sovereignty. British officials felt a key opportunity to put pressure on Afghanistan had been lost.[69]

Then, a week or so later, most Afghans, as well as the diplomatic community in Kabul, heard for the first time that Pakistan intended to impose a blanket ban on all Afghan petrol tankers transporting supplies of petrol from Peshawar to Kabul on 1 January 1950 because Afghan tankers did not comply with Pakistan's health and safety standards. It seemed they posed a fire risk at oil and petrol terminals. Since more than half of Afghanistan's petrol supplies were transported through Pakistan, this threatened to throw the country into a deep political and economic crisis. The diplomatic community immediately consulted their informants to find out why this decision had been taken and whether it had come as a surprise to the Afghans. They eventually found out that three oil companies (Burma Shell, Standard Vacuum and Caltex) had written to the Pakistan government the previous January asking that the Afghans be given six months to improve the safety standards of their tankers in accordance with rules set out in 1937. Now that specialised safety equipment was more readily available on the market, they wanted to ensure that sub-standard Afghan tankers would not cause their depots to explode while they were refuelling. Furthermore, the Afghan government had apparently been informed, but done nothing about it. Indeed, the Burma Shell agent in Peshawar had himself written to the Afghan National Bank in March to inform them that Afghan tankers taking fuel from Burma Shell depots in Peshawar and Chaman would need to be modified.[70] Other oil companies had done likewise, giving the Afghan authorities a full six months to comply.[71]

Now, as Pakistan explained in the press, they were merely enforcing an earlier decision, and it was not their fault the Afghans had ignored their warning. To all intents and purposes, however, the Pakistan ban, irrespective of the rights and wrongs of the safety issue, was interpreted as a political move to crush Afghan demands for Pashtunistan. An article published in *Anis* on 27 December 1949 gave full vent to Afghan frustration:

> A government which is bent on usurping by force the lawful rights of seven million free Afghans and depriving them of their independence and nationality must of course adopt the same attitude towards the other twelve million Afghans who demand the rights of their brethren. Anyway at this point, we only wish to proclaim to the world – who is the aggressor? Who is the usurper? Which government is it that is acting contrary to all international and moral laws? ... In any case, we declare to the brave and zealous Afghan nation that Pakistan has begun to play with petrol. Petrol is inflammable, and this game will bring great dangers in its wake.[72]

As soon as news filtered out, the impact began to bite. There was a run on the country's limited reserves and a black market in petrol started before the year was out. By January 1950, petrol was strictly rationed. Over the coming months, food prices rose, transport came to a standstill and the south experienced food shortages because supplies could not be delivered from surplus areas in the north. Flights on the new fortnightly air service between Kabul and Teheran on Iranian Airways were suspended indefinitely. Embassies were affected too – their petrol supplies were rationed at 70 gallons a month, irrespective of their geographical location or courier needs. This initially hit the British hard since they needed at least 60 gallons a week to run the courier service between Kabul and Peshawar alone. Gardener eventually managed to import additional petrol privately with the help of the Pakistanis – probably because they used this service too.[73]

In the meantime, Britain learnt that the three oil companies were already regretting their decision:

> This has now to some extent recoiled on their own heads as they have been informed by the [Pakistan] Explosives Directorate that if Afghan vehicles not conforming to the regulations are found in their petrol depots, the companies will lose their bulk storage licences. The companies naturally regret the loss of business entailed in the stoppage and are anxious that they should not be blamed for it by Afghanistan.[74]

Meanwhile, although the Afghan government had immediately sent a special representative to Peshawar to arrange for the conversion of their tankers,[75] Grafftey-Smith in Karachi suspected that Pakistan was being deliberately obstructive. He had heard from the British representative in Peshawar that although five lorries were now serviceable, officials in Karachi were stalling by asking for one set of particulars after another. It seemed clear to him that 'although the Afghans have only themselves to blame for the predicament in which they are now placed, the Pakistanis are not likely to be in a hurry to help them to get out of it unless there is a radical change for the better in Afghan–Pakistan relations'.[76]

There was one bit of positive news for Afghanistan, however. The petrol crisis began to have an impact on the way foreign missions in Kabul viewed Pakistan. To date, Pakistan had enjoyed considerable support over the Pashtunistan question and many had joined Britain in asking the Afghan government to back down, but now the tide of sympathy shifted back to Afghanistan. The critical question, however, was how long they would sustain their support if the Afghans continued their Pashtunistan campaign regardless.

The British swung into action, using one of the few tools left at their disposal: diplomacy. Grafftey-Smith wrote to Ikramullah at the Foreign Ministry to warn him that the 'lack of petrol supplies is antagonising feeling in many of the foreign embassies and legations in Kabul whose goodwill has hitherto been very valuable to Pakistan'.[77] The American embassy in

Karachi made similar representations and was told by Liaquat Ali Khan that supplies would resume once the vehicles had been inspected.[78] These warnings seem to have been heeded. Grafftey-Smith was shown a copy of a letter from the Foreign Ministry to the Afghan government in late March saying they were trying to speed up the approval process:

> In view of the fact that supply of petrol to Afghanistan has been seriously affected, the Government of Pakistan have ignored the fact that the plans are incomplete and have directed the Chief Inspector of Explosives to proceed immediately to Peshawar for inspection of the lorries and ask your people in Peshawar to supply on the spot the information that has not been given in these plans. We should be grateful if in future when plans are sent to us, the information now wanting in these plans is supplied.[79]

Soon afterwards, five tankers were approved and petrol was issued to them. The problem was not over, however – not by a long way. Even though the five tankers had passed the safety standards, an additional stumbling block was then placed in the way. New permits and visas were required for Afghan drivers for every round trip to and from Peshawar on the grounds, Pakistan argued, that their own nationals were discriminated against in Afghanistan – Pakistani drivers, it seemed, were only allowed to stay in Kabul for three days, whereas Afghan drivers could stay in Pakistan for eight.[80] A series of tit-for-tat diplomatic notes were sent between the two governments and shared with the diplomatic community.[81]

Six months into the crisis, the Afghan Prime Minister and the Foreign Minister, as well as the editor of *Islah*, shared their intense frustrations with Gardener. They were irritated that although the harvest had been plentiful, it had become impossible to transport foodstuffs from the north to deficit areas south of the Hindu Kush. The cost of living had risen too – the price of wheat alone had increased from 10–14 afghanis for 16 lbs in June 1949 to 17–18 afghanis, and for sugar from 32 to 41. They were doubly frustrated because just when Afghanistan was pulling out of its post-war recession it had been plunged back into economic crisis. They also explained that, for their part, they were doing everything in their power to resolve the situation. A representative had recently been sent to Peshawar and Karachi to find out exactly what was needed to make all the tankers comply with the rules and to ensure visas were issued on a reciprocal basis. He had also been instructed to ask the oil companies if they could sell Afghanistan any second-hand tankers that complied with the rules and to find out what the exact specifications were so that the government could order an additional six tankers from Vauxhall Motors.

Gardener was asked to ensure Vauxhall Motors delivered the tankers swiftly, and that they took on responsibility for appropriate licensing from the Pakistani authorities.[82] Gardener then hurriedly wrote to the British High Commission in Karachi to ask them to intercede with the Pakistan government. 'The present Afghan proposals,' as far as he was concerned, 'would appear to come into the class of topics which Pakistan is ready to discuss with Afghanistan and which would tend to ensure internal security in Afghanistan which is presumably a Pakistan interest.'[83]

Meanwhile the Pakistan Foreign Ministry was sharing its own frustrations with the British. They had, it seemed, offered to help the Afghans get their vehicles altered even though that meant using valuable imported safety material that they needed themselves. It was difficult to justify this to the Pakistani people – the sheer amount of vitriol levelled at the government by the Afghan press had hardened public opinion and it now 'acts as a limiting factor, however much we may like to ignore the Afghan Goebbels'. Furthermore, 'vituperation continues unabated but now it is being consistently tied up with incitement to violence. In view of the manifestation of Afghan attitude, the common man in this country finds some difficulty in comprehending our solicitude for the ordinary man in Afghanistan, who tolerates a regime which is showing such enmity towards us.'[84]

By the end of the year, the immediate crisis was over. Pakistan had begun to construct petrol tankers for the Afghans using material that Pakistan itself had imported using its own foreign exchange. The government had also provided facilities at Peshawar to repair another six tankers, and approved thirty lorries with a total carrying capacity of 32,000 gallons.[85] The fallout from the crisis, however, had grave consequences for Afghan–Pakistan relations and for Afghanistan's domestic and foreign policies more generally.

It deepened mistrust between the two governments, but also touched the lives of ordinary men and women across Afghanistan. The petrol shortages had hit their pockets, while the press campaign served to channel their anger towards Pakistan. Thereafter, the Pashtunistan dispute increasingly became a national issue, not just one affecting the interests of the Pashtun tribes. The dispute also led to a Cabinet crisis, unleashed anti-government sentiment, and prompted the Afghans to take serious steps towards finding a viable and reliable alternative trade route to reduce their dependence on Pakistan – the Soviet Union was the obvious choice – and then locking in a new friend with a common enemy. They turned to India.

By early 1950, a new trade deal had been agreed with the Soviet Union, which included petrol supplies, and an Indo-Afghan Treaty of Friendship had been signed in Delhi, which essentially replaced the 1921 Anglo-Afghan Treaty. Gardener's views leave little doubt that the real value of this treaty lay less in its formal provisions, since these were fairly anodyne, than in its political significance as a means to strengthen Afghanistan's hand over Pakistan. 'The particular point is that it puts Afghanistan in a position to denounce her treaty with us without sacrificing any of its advantages vis-a-vis India. After the denunciation, she would declare that the Durand Line no longer had any legal existence.'[86] Britain's plans for a post-Indian independence settlement were unravelling fast.

Pashtunistan – Real or Imaginary?

Meanwhile, within Afghanistan, the Moghulgai incident had helped trigger a significant Cabinet reshuffle in November 1949. Daud and Naim Khan returned, and now Daud not only resumed his post as Minister of War but was also given strategic oversight of the Ministry of Interior and a new Tribal Directorate. Naim became Minister of Public Works. A harder nationalist line on Pashtunistan became more or less inevitable. In view of this, the Foreign Office now asked the embassy to provide more detailed information about what had been going on over the past few months in the Afghan tribal areas.

A worrying picture was emerging. The embassy reported back that they had been noticing attempts to whip up Pashtunistan sentiment among the tribes since the summer. In May 1949, a Pashtunistan flag had appeared at the Frontier. In early September, tribal representatives had held a *Jirga* in Kabul and decided that Pashtunistan's boundaries lay between the Durand Line and the Indus River. On 20 October, the newspapers reported that the Afridi tribe had completed an election to a Pashtunistan National Assembly (PNA). In early November, Daud visited the Tribal Directorate to talk to a deputation of tribal elders advising them of the value of tribal unity, and then in November and December, two more regional sections of the PNA were formed. In both, the regional sections announced they would henceforth manage the tribes' internal and external affairs until the formation of the central PNA. A month later, on 16 January 1950, the press reported that a Waziristan section of the PNA had been formed demanding that the Pakistan government withdraw its troops and agents from Waziristan. The mullahs were involved as well. On 30 January, the Jamiat in Kabul read the whole of the Koran as 'a thank offering for the formation of the Islamic State of Pashtunistan'.[87] Newspapers also reported that money was being raised across the country, and the Kabul press started printing daily lists of subscribers to the Pashtun cause, including Prince Daud himself. The amount had reached 1 million Afghanis (£20,000) by early January.[88]

When British officials started to look more closely at what was going on, however, they found a mixed picture. There was little evidence that the tribes in NWFP regretted their decision to join Pakistan, but things seemed to be a little less clear-cut among the tribes in the unsettled, un-administered areas. The political goal of Pashtunistan was not, however, the overriding factor. Instead, they were driven by many of the same motivations as before independence: allowances, military contracts and other economic opportunities. Pakistan had initially withdrawn its regular army units from the area and replaced them with Frontier militias in order to concentrate their most experienced men in Kashmir. This had been fine while Pakistan tribesmen could make money in Kashmir, but now the conflict was over, it was unclear how returning tribesmen would react to the changed situation at home. For years, they had relied on lucrative military contracts for supplies and labour, which had supplemented their resources. As those contracts dried up, it was just possible this would trigger unrest.[89]

Mitchell Carse in Peshawar, however, was less concerned. Pakistan not only had the resources to pay the tribes the same allowances as Britain had done, but had also increased the number of tribesmen recruited into the military above pre-Partition levels and continued their 'forward' economic policy in the tribal areas with offers of medical facilities and schools.[90] The Afghans, in contrast, were not in a position to compete, at least not in financial terms. They could whip up some political momentum by creating a Pashtunistan National Assembly, but could not prove to the tribes that Afghanistan offered a better financial deal. In addition, according to Carse, some tribes were also beginning to engage directly with the Pakistan government to meet their political needs – for instance, tribal sections of Bajaurs and Mohmands had asked the government for assurances that Pakistan would continue to pay allowances and would come to their assistance if they attacked an enemy that they could not deal with themselves.[91]

When the Foreign Office put Carse's report alongside the news from Kabul, they therefore questioned the extent to which the tribes actually backed the Pashtunistan cause, notwithstanding the creation of the new assembles:

It must be allowed that much of it has an authentic ring and might make one believe in the existence of a strong independence movement were it not for the fact that our own information (from the Deputy High Commissioner in Peshawar) suggests that there is virtually no support for Afghan objectives among the tribesmen, most of whose leaders realise that Pakistan is, in the long run, in a better position to help them; meanwhile they are in the happy position perhaps of taking bribes or subsidies from both sides.[92]

News about the Pashtun assemblies got short shrift from the Pakistan government too. The opportunity to make a public statement came when Dr Omar Hyat Malik posed a question in the Legislative Assembly. He asked how Pakistan intended to respond to an alleged statement by the Afghan Ambassador in Delhi that the Pashtuns sought a 'free Pashtunistan' to liberate them from oppression by Pakistan. In response, on 9 January 1950, Liaquat Ali Khan stated that the comment was 'entirely a figment of the imagination of certain individuals in Afghanistan ... and could only have been amusing if it had not been so patently mischievous'. The people of NWFP and the tribal areas were loyal to Pakistan. Furthermore, 'the alleged members of the assemblies have no influence or status in our tribal territory and a few of these persons, on their return from Kabul, have been arrested by the local tribes and have been handed over to the political authorities as traitors to the people and the Government of Pakistan'.

When asked a follow-up question about what he was doing to counteract the allegations, Liaquat Ali Khan explained that his government had been restrained to date. They had been trying to keep friendly relations with a fellow Muslim state, but he also reminded the Assembly that Afghanistan had been the only nation to block Pakistan's membership of the United Nations, and had been hostile to Pakistan ever since. His government had been trying to discuss areas of common interest with Afghanistan for some time, particularly the educational and economic development of the tribal areas, but the Afghans had not been interested. Pakistan therefore 'can only infer that the Government of Afghanistan are not so much concerned with the moral and material welfare of the people of the border areas as with securing for themselves political advantage in their own country or diverting the attention of their own people from the political and economic deterioration of Afghanistan'. He still hoped to negotiate with Afghanistan, but 'not one inch of our land will be surrendered to anybody come what may'.[93]

Where Next?

By the time my grandfather left Afghanistan in January 1950, the pattern for future Afghan–Pakistan relations had become fairly well entrenched, with arguments on both sides increasingly bellicose and diametrically opposed. It was also clear that Britain's capacity to influence the situation was declining rapidly. Officials and ministers did not give up trying, however. They hoped the forthcoming Commonwealth Foreign Ministers' Meeting in Colombo, Ceylon (Sri Lanka), in mid-January 1950 would provide an opportunity to come to a joint agreement with Pakistan on the way forward and to explore India's views about the whole situation. The omens did not look good from the start, however, since Afghanistan had just finalised the Treaty of Friendship with India.

In advance of the meeting, Ikramullah told Grafftey-Smith that Afghan–Pakistan relations were

> one of the many matters in which Pakistan looks for strong support from His Majesty's Government and one of the few in which support can be given without offending another Commonwealth country. I hope that it will be possible for United Kingdom delegates to take a positively sympathetic and constructive line in discussion with Pakistan delegates at Colombo about Afghanistan.[94]

By now, however, the Foreign Office suspected that the Afghans wanted concessions in both the tribal areas and NWFP, and no longer recognised Pakistan's rights in either territory:

> Afghanistan, while disclaiming territorial ambitions, persists in the demand for 'Pashtunistan' ... though what is really implied by this term is far from clear. Officially the demand amounted to little more than a proposal that the North West Frontier Province be given this new name and be permitted to enjoy autonomous status within Pakistan, and that the Tribal Areas be regarded as independent; suggestions of plebiscites ... are also advanced. But whether Afghan aspirations are in actuality so moderate as this is a matter on which Pakistan may have its doubts; for while officially the Afghans claim for the North West Frontier Province only a change of name and a guarantee against absorption into the Punjab, with also a special measure of local autonomy, press and wireless propaganda from Kabul appears to make no real distinction between the Province and the Tribal Areas and to demand independence for both ... The evidence of the Afghan attitude is conflicting, but it is fairly apparent that the Afghans do not wish Pakistan to retain any real authority in the Province, any more than in the Tribal Areas.[95]

Whether the Afghan government had the capacity to act on these demands, other than through a war of words, was another matter entirely. Foreign Office analysts concluded that Afghan policy was still unclear because the government had to satisfy a number of different constituencies at home. True, they needed to keep the Pashtun tribes on board, but they also had to take into account the interests of the non-Pashtun-speaking people – including Turkmens, Tajiks, Hazaras and Uzbeks – who collectively comprised the majority of the Afghan population. These groups were not particularly keen to see the Pashtuns increase their strength in the country, and wanted their own needs catered for as well, especially as they saw their Uzbek, Tajik and Turkmen kinsmen across the border in the Soviet Union much better-off economically than themselves. Oil and petrol shortages only served to add to their grievances. On top of this, Afghanistan also had an insecure border with the Soviet Union and a potentially insecure border with Persia, especially if the Persians felt the Persian-speaking people in Afghanistan, and especially around Herat, were getting a bad deal. In sum, Afghanistan lacked the capacity at present to do more than rattle sabres: 'With so many almost irreconcilable desiderata, it is not surprising that the Afghan government had failed to evolve any satisfactory policy.'[96]

Bevin met Ghulam Mohammed, the Pakistan Minister of Finance, and Ikramullah on 16 January at Temple Trees in Colombo. Ghulam and Ikramullah thought the Indo-Afghan Treaty of Friendship had encouraged Afghanistan to be more difficult and feared that some of the money from the United States loan had found its way into purchasing arms. They also shared a report they had received from a Czech representative in the Afghan Ministry of War stating that the Soviets were promising to give the Afghans $7.5 million worth of arms and equipment. On top of this, they were aware, like the British, that the Afghans were now claiming the whole of NWFP was part of Pashtunistan, not just the tribal areas, and asked Bevin to make a public statement once again that Britain supported Pakistan.

Bevin's response had a markedly different tone on this occasion, reflecting the fact that, while he could publicly support Pakistan's position, Britain no longer had the power to control events. It was also increasingly clear that the Afghan–Pakistan dispute was becoming a serious international issue in its own right, and not a sideshow. Bevin therefore said he would no longer discourage them from referring the matter to the United Nations.[97]

Britain did not give up entirely, however. A few weeks later, Britain and Pakistan agreed a common form of words to use in future bilateral discussions with the Afghan government. These reemphasised the policy position the two had taken all along; specifically, that the Durand Line was the Frontier and Pakistan was Britain's successor, and that current Afghan policy would damage Afghan interests because it would make

Afghan–Pakistan collaboration impossible when it was actually in their joint interests to keep the tribes peaceful.[98] The message also included one concession, heavily edited by Pakistan, acknowledging Britain's long-standing advice that Pakistan should accept Afghan interest in the tribal areas. 'Pakistan has expressed her interest affecting the people of the two countries living on either side of the Durand Line, such as collaboration regarding the maintenance of peace on the Frontier and on economic, cultural and administrative matters.' On this basis, Pakistan 'are not only willing, but eager to resume discussions with the Afghan government'.[99]

Britain and Pakistan hoped these points would provide a framework to inform other countries' discussions with Afghan representatives too, either at their diplomatic missions abroad or in Kabul. Gardener was fairly confident they would be up for this. The United States were keen to protect their recent investments, which were dependent on regional stability, while Zahir Shah's tour of the Middle East had highlighted how little support Afghanistan currently enjoyed among other Muslim nations.[100] Indeed, the Saudi Ambassador had informed Gardener that King Ibn Saud himself had urged the King to find a solution, 'warning of the danger of [the] dispute weakening Pakistan with [the] result that Kashmir might fall into the hands of unbelievers and Afghanistan incurring opprobrium of Muslim world'.[101]

Over the following weeks, most of the countries approached used some or all of the text to make representations to the Afghans. The Turks backed the idea once it became clear that their offer to mediate – which had been put to the King by the Turkish Foreign Minister during a meeting in Tehran – was not going to be accepted.[102] The Iraqi government advised their Ambassador to speak to Gardener first and then communicate the message to the Minister of Foreign Affairs 'on the lines that dissention between Muslim states is contrary to Islam, that [the] Iraqi government understand that Pakistan have left the door open to discussion and that this is the right method for settlement of the dispute; the continuance of public dissensions cannot help Pakistan or Afghanistan, but could only be useful to a third party'.[103] The United States conveyed their support for this approach too in late April.[104]

The only serious contention came from Nehru. During a conversation with the British High Commissioner that May, he questioned whether the Durand Line really was the Frontier and challenged the proposition that the tribal areas were an integral part of Pakistan:

He said that whilst he would not suggest that Afghanistan had been faultless in the matter of Pasthunistan, nevertheless he could not subscribe to our view that Pakistan was in the right and Afghanistan wholly in the wrong. He rested his case primarily on the contention that there was considerable legal doubt as to whether [the] Durand Line was in fact an international frontier; that it was undeniable that the tribes were unadministered and had considerable freedom prior to our departure, ie a status something comparable in his view to that of an Indian State; and that it was therefore untenable for Pakistan to claim that tribal countries this side of the Durand Line should be an integral part of their territory.[105]

Although India refused to join the diplomatic demarche, the Afghans found that any support they had gained during the Moghulgai crisis was now lost, and they were increasingly isolated internationally. Muslim countries asked them to put solidarity among Muslims ahead of their dispute with Pakistan, and the United States, Europe and Turkey urged reconciliation. Afghanistan, they collectively argued, should accept the Durand Line as the border and Pakistan as the inheritor of Britain's rights and obligations in the tribal areas and NWFP.

As the British diplomatic effort gathered steam, there were tentative signs in Kabul that Daud himself was beginning to have some doubts about Afghanistan's position. The French Chargé d'Affaires, Monsieur Brasseur, told Gardener and the United States Ambassador, Louis G. Dreyfus, about the mood of a 'self-invited guest', Daud, at dinner on 1 March. Brasseur found him downbeat:

> The recital [on Pashtunistan] lacked its usual intensity and was interrupted by frequent long pauses … [He also] gained the impression that Prince Daud was becoming disillusioned over the Pashtunistan policy and was seeking a means of discarding it without damage to Afghan pride. Prince Daud then said that the Afghans would be quite happy if Pashtunistan were administered for a period of years under a mandate from the United Nations.[106]

When Gardener had dinner with the King on 25 March, he found him equally subdued. The King was convinced of the need for intimate friendship and economic cooperation with Pakistan. Former Prime Minister Hashim Khan was reflective too, telling Gardener that 'some way out of the deadlock needed to be found'.[107]

The Afghans nevertheless made one more serious attempt to get Britain to see their point of view that June by sending an aide-memoire to the Foreign Office. This stressed that they wanted to maintain good relations with Britain and proposed a conference in Karachi between Britain,

Pakistan and Afghanistan to resolve the matter. To help strengthen the Afghan argument, they also drew on lessons from the creation of Israel and Pakistan:

> In recent years, the world has witnessed many changes with regard [to] the sovereignty of a number of countries. Many have been granted independence. Some like Pakistan and Israel, which never existed before, were created to meet the needs of the present day. Yet an important and ancient race like the Pashtuns, who have known the meaning of freedom and who have all along asserted their will for freedom were completely overlooked. These Pashtuns, different from their Eastern neighbours from the point-of-view of language, race, culture, tradition and customs and who form a completely separate identity should have been one of the first to be granted their independence. It is not surprising therefore that they should feel that they were not treated fairly or in accordance with the Charter of the UN.[108]

The Afghan Ambassador in London reinforced these messages in a subsequent meeting with the head of South-East Asia Department, Robert Scott, in London on 22 June. His government knew the Afghans would lose in a war against Pakistan, but they 'preferred to die with honour rather than live with dishonour'.[109] If it did come to war, however, the Soviet Union could intervene, and he reminded Britain that his government had consistently tried to avoid this eventuality since the Russian Revolution because they were 'bitterly opposed to Communism'. Scott's response was not particularly encouraging or supportive. He informed the Ambassador that he 'had been unable to avoid forming the impression that the agitation was promoted by the Afghans and not by the Pashtuns', and he reaffirmed that Pakistan would not discuss the validity of the Durand Line.

Thereafter, Britain tried to encourage talks between Afghanistan and Pakistan, supported Pakistan's pre-condition for talks – namely recognition that Pakistan had inherited Britain's rights and obligations in the tribal areas – and refused to acknowledge that Afghanistan might just have a valid argument.

7

Maintaining the Buffer in the Shadow of the Cold War

I'm afraid I can't say much about my work because it is well tied up, as you will know. Everything is so secret that even the keys that eventually lead to my office and the safes have rubber soles and I creep to my desk, and when I want to talk to myself, I write it down on a slip of paper and hastily throw it in the fire.

Sam Simms, 10 February 1948

Introduction

As the date for Indian independence drew closer, Afghanistan was to find itself gradually drawn into a new superpower war – the fight by the West to preserve the 'free' world from the clutches of the Soviet Union. A Soviet bloc was being formed in eastern Europe and Germany, Soviet troops had occupied northern Persia, and communist movements were spreading in Italy and France, South-East Asia and China, seemingly influenced by Moscow. At the beginning, this seemed to have all the ingredients of the Great Game. Britain would continue to deploy its power and resources to maintain Afghanistan as a buffer state protecting South Asia and Persia from Soviet expansionism. A few new characters had been added to the mix – the United States and, after independence, India and Pakistan – but for the most part this new war looked remarkably similar to the previous clashes between the British and Russian empires over who controlled Afghan policy and territory.

British policy, as before, therefore aimed to build an effective Afghan army capable of securing Afghan territory against invasion, maintain stability in the Pashtun tribal areas on the North-West Frontier, and ensure that the Afghan regime had sufficient resources to protect itself against any internal threats to its hegemony but insufficient long-range capability to trigger a defensive reaction from the Soviet Union. To achieve these ends, Britain would continue to supply the Afghan military with arms, equipment and training, provide funds to help the government build and maintain this fighting force, and guarantee to protect the country if the Afghan military were unable to hold back a strong aggressor. This guarantee was to be met initially through the British Army in India and, after Indian independence, by India and Pakistan, the two countries most in the firing line if Soviet forces advanced south.

Except that nothing turned out quite as expected. At first glance, Afghanistan, with its long shared border with the Soviet Union, appeared to be on the emerging Cold War's frontline, and Britain, with its policy to protect Afghanistan from invasion and its historic economic and political ties with India and Pakistan, seemed to be ahead of the game. At the Pentagon talks in October 1947, the United States looked to Britain to leverage its influence to protect the eastern Mediterranean, East and North Africa and the Middle East from the Soviet Union. Over the next two years, however, Britain found it increasingly difficult to deliver its promises. Meanwhile, Afghanistan soon found itself caught in a new struggle between two global superpowers, the United States and the Soviet Union. It remained to be seen whether they would seek to exploit Afghanistan for their own ends, or whether this time round, Afghan leaders would be able to shape the country's future destiny themselves, free from the politics of the Great Game. By 1950, the key pieces were in place that would later define Afghanistan's role in the Cold War, while the Great Game was about to change irrevocably.

The Honeymoon Period

The condition of the Afghan army and air force had improved considerably through reforms to increase their efficiency and effectiveness, access to good-quality training opportunities and better equipment and armaments. By 1947, Afghan military leaders were confident they could handle two simultaneous threats to security, but told Lancaster they feared 'a third outbreak, especially one having secret or open backing from outside the country'.[1]

Lancaster himself thought there was a pretty good story to tell too. 'The army has played a notable part' in supporting Afghan development over the past fifteen years because it 'has been able to secure the comparatively stable conditions in the country which were essential for that progress.'[2] A key part of that success story had been the focus on developing and maintaining a small, well-equipped and trained army able to deal with one major or two smaller tribal disturbances in different areas at once, supported by air cover. The total strength of the army was now about 75,000 men, complemented by an armed police or gendarmerie of around 15,000 men, which relieved the army from patrolling frontiers and garrisoning small posts. In an emergency, the government could also call up tribal *lashkars*, amounting to around 35,000 additional fighters, but invariably tried to avoid doing so because if they handed out arms, it was difficult to get them back.[3] Alongside this, the Afghan Air Force was well on its way towards achieving its ambition to have forty-eight operational planes and twelve to sixteen training aircraft.

The military had also developed effective strategies to deal with tribal disturbances which played to their strengths. Senior officers avoided offensive action, preferring 'to use the army for supporting irregular forces, protecting communications or denying grazing grounds or fertile area to recalcitrant tribes'. The disturbance itself was often dealt with by playing one tribe off against another, 'by appealing to their loyalty, their religion, or their political differences, and then [they] utilise loyal elements backed by the army to suppress the disloyal tribe'.[4]

The way in which the Afghan military had been dealing with a revolt by the Safi tribe was a good illustration of this approach. In 1945, General Daud, the Minister of War, had tried to bring the rules governing army conscription among Pashtuns into line with the rest of the country. In non-Pashtun areas, one in eight young men were required to join up, while the Pashtuns provided conscripts through the *qaumi* system – they supplied the same proportion, but chose who was selected. The tribes unsurprisingly often retained their best men for inter-tribal warfare and sent recruits from poor families, meeting any shortfall with 'the halt and the lame'.[5] Daud decided to pilot the change with an eastern Pashtun tribe, the Safis, who lived in the Kunar Valley along the approach to the Khyber Pass. On paper, this seemed like a good choice. The Safis were considered less fractious than the tribes in the south. The plan, however, backfired badly when the supposedly compliant Safis rebelled and were not finally crushed until 1947/8.

At first, the government used another tribe, the Nuristanis, to counter them. This forced the Safis to back down and agree to enlist their men in the army, purchase grain at government prices, and give up their rifles. Fighting broke out again, however, in October 1947 when the Safis attacked the Nuristanis in retribution. This time, the government sent three infantry brigades to the eastern province to restore order.

Again, the army did not undertake offensive operations; rather they focussed on the gradual subdual of Safi tribesmen and the arrest of those involved in the rebellion. In a second settlement in 1947, the government not only insisted that the Safis accept the earlier terms, but also took hostages as a guarantee of future good behaviour and deported nearly a hundred Safi families to other parts of the country.[6] The government had held its own and shown who was boss.

During the Second World War, Britain had also recovered its pre-Afghan independence position in the Afghan arms market – over the two preceding decades, the Afghans had invited France, Italy, Czechoslovakia, Germany and the Soviet Union to supply military hardware, and Turkey had opened an army training mission.[7] Once Britain and the Soviet Union forced the Afghan government to remove all non-diplomatic Axis nationals during the war, Britain effectively recovered its position and only Turkey and the Soviet Union retained a significant foothold – the Turks training the army and the Soviets providing spare parts for guns they had supplied years earlier. This was highly advantageous for Britain. British industry was still geared to wartime production, there was a great deal of surplus wartime ordinance lying in stores across the empire available for the right customer, and Britain had a highly skilled army and air force with experience to sell.

By the late 1930s, Lancaster already had a number of major arms deals in play and could draw on an Afghan Fund of £30,000 – annually topped up by the British government in India – to pay for locally defined projects without first seeking approval from the Treasury. His most significant deal at the end of the war had been to secure a large contract with the Afghan Army to supply surplus military material from Indian government stocks to fill the main gaps in the Afghan military arsenal at an affordable price. Under the 'Lancaster Scheme', as it became known, arms and equipment worth 30 million rupees (or £2,250,000 at 1945 prices) would be supplied half-price, and paid for in ten annual instalments with interest foregone on the deferred payments.[8] By July 1947, 35 per cent of the order had been delivered and Afghanistan had paid the first instalment. Alongside this, Lancaster had arranged to train 110 Afghan officers and forty non-commissioned officers in India annually, and to supply three British Army sergeants for a year in Kabul to provide training on wheeled carriers, small-arms use and signalling. Most of the cost of this training was to be borne by the Afghan Fund.

Lancaster had also secured a dominant position with the Afghan Air Force too. Amir Amanullah had begun to build this up in 1922, initially purchasing planes from the Soviet Union and Italy and using Soviet and German pilots to fly them, followed in 1924 by six from Britain flown by British or Italian pilots. By the early 1930s the government had decided to maintain the air force itself, ordering eight Hawker Hinds from Britain and twenty-four different types of planes from Italy.[9] These arrived in 1938 accompanied by British and Italian pilot instructors, engineers and mechanics. A further twenty second-hand Hinds were ordered from Britain in 1939.

Once the Italians left Afghanistan in 1941, Lancaster was able to negotiate yet more deals. An RAF training mission was established in Kabul teaching air crews how to fly their planes and maintain them on the ground, and Afghan pilots were sent to India and Britain for intensive flying courses. In 1946, the Afghan government was back in the market for more planes. Since modern fighter planes, such as Spitfires and Hurricanes, were not suited to the altitude and climate, they ordered eight Tiger Moths as training planes and a year later, twelve Avro Ansons suitable for aerial reconnaissance. The Avros alone cost £338,000 and were delivered over the next two years, flown to Afghanistan from Britain by British pilots.[10]

The army and air force, however, still had a number of capacity gaps to resolve. By the time these planes started arriving, the Afghan Air Force was running close to empty. The existing fleet became unserviceable quickly because they were reluctant to cannibalise spare parts from crashed planes. As a result, by 1947, only seventeen of the twenty-eight Hinds and four of the twenty-four Italian planes were still serviceable.[11] The problems were compounded by the fact that Afghan pilots had limited flying experience – during the Second World War, for instance, they had only been allowed to fly for thirty minutes each week because petrol was in short supply. Preparations for the military parade for Afghan Independence Week in August 1949 underlined the challenge. The flypast was expected to have ten Avros and as many Hinds as were airworthy (probably seven or eight). During the practice runs, a couple of the Hinds crashed – although thankfully the pilots were unhurt – and the pilots privately complained to Prendergast that they often lacked the energy to do the preparations properly. They earned so little that they often came to work on an empty stomach so that their children could eat.[12]

The army had challenges too. Although conditions and morale among military officers had improved by the 1940s – with educational allowances, opportunities for training in India, and a pension scheme – there was still a long way to go. When Daud sought to remove illiterate and inefficient officers in December 1947, he was forced to back down because many of them had strong backing from the tribes and the ministry could not afford to incur a tribal backlash. Conditions for ordinary soldiers on the other hand remained poor. They were conscripted for two years, often unwillingly, and had to be financially supported by their families because their pay was so low. It was also difficult to raise their skill levels to take on more complex tasks, such as that of a wireless operator, because most had received little or no formal education. Of those who did, most chose to leave as soon as their two years were up because their pay and conditions of service were so poor.[13]

Lack of medical facilities also left the army vulnerable to almost every disease prevalent at the time. 'In a crisis,' Prendergast reported, 'many of the soldiers have only a few months' service and are unfit for active service.'[14] The poor physical state of the troops was in evidence during the Safi operation. When Daud visited the troops in 1948, he found that over 1,000 were sick in Jalalabad alone, and 160 cases of dysentery had been evacuated to Kabul. Many of the conscripts were Hazaras and Tajiks who had been brought from the hills, and now found themselves exposed to malaria for the first time. Daud learnt that their vulnerability to disease was exacerbated by their poor diet and atrocious billeting conditions, often being forced to sleep on stone or mud floors. He considered constructing better barracks but decided this was too costly. There was one change he was able to make, however. When he learnt the men saved their food ration allowance in order to supplement their meagre salaries, he cut their allowance in half and ordered good food to be issued from unit kitchens.[15] The troops became healthier, but this may have done little for morale.

Recalibrating the Rules of the Game in 1947

Although Afghan military leaders felt they could deal with internal threats to security, their capacity to deal with an invasion was a different matter altogether. They could hold back an invasion force for a short period until foreign assistance arrived, but a complex attack would leave them vulnerable. Indeed, an external force equipped with planes could quickly overcome any opposition, while for the 'army to come out into the plains against a well-equipped "modern" army would be suicide'.[16] According to Lancaster and Prendergast however, they were relatively confident that an external force would be deterred from aggressive action while the British army protected their backs in India. It was a mutually beneficial arrangement – the Afghan army acted as a buffer to protect India; and the British army in India protected Afghanistan.

For many in the Afghan government, this security shield had remained important, to a greater or lesser degree, since independence in 1919 in spite of appearances to the contrary. They had begun to diversify their trading relationships, including signing a trade treaty with the Soviet Union in 1921, but the bulk of trade had remained with the sub-continent.[17] The experiences of the rulers of Khiva and Bokhara in Central Asia served as a continual reminder that the Soviets were not to be trusted. Both had reasserted their independence after the Russian revolution, only to find themselves crushed by swift military action in the 1920s and their states absorbed into the Soviet Union. The last Emir of Bokhara spent the rest of his life in exile in Afghanistan. To shore up their security, the Afghans signed a non-aggression pact with the Soviets in 1931, but remained wary. They believed the Soviet Union used periodic boundary disputes whenever the Oxus River changed its course as an excuse to absorb Afghan territory.[18] They had also arrested a number of Soviet 'spies' during the Second World War along the border,[19] and believed the Soviets were deliberately increasing the standard of living of Uzbek and Turkmen people in the Soviet Union to create unrest among their kinsmen in northern Afghanistan.[20] Meanwhile, the Soviet Ambassador's proposal in 1945 to set up an air courier route between Kabul and the Soviet Union seemed yet another ruse to infiltrate Afghan territory.[21]

The continued need for British assurance was brought into stark relief in 1945 when Stalin refused to remove his troops from northern Persia in spite of an international agreement to do so. Stalin had then helped set up two breakaway republics in Persian territory – the People's Republic of Azerbaijan in September 1945 followed four months later by the Republic of Mahabad. In early 1946, the two breakaway republics, with Soviet military backing, had attacked Persian forces. Truman and Attlee took the issue to the newly formed United Nations Security Council for resolution, and Truman moved the American Sixth Fleet to the eastern Mediterranean. On 30 January 1946, the second-ever United Nations Resolution called for the immediate withdrawal of all foreign troops, and later that year, the United States helped the Persians reclaim these territories. If Stalin could do that in Persia, the Afghans speculated, and it took the combined weight of the international system to get him to retreat, what would prevent him doing the same in Afghanistan if Britain stood aside?

In December 1945, Hashim Khan therefore warned the legation that his country would not be able to hold back a Soviet invasion without British help. He put down a new marker too – that any change in the status of India and in Britain's priorities in the region would leave the door wide open to a Soviet invasion through Afghanistan:

> Afghanistan had always been and still was the outer bastion of India's defence system ... With the object lesson in Azerbaijan before them, the Afghans were afraid. Afghanistan was a poor country, sick and weak

from years of strife and poverty, an invalid. What could an invalid do against a powerful aggressor? In the past, it could at least take comfort from the thought that at its back was a powerful nation [India] ... but what of the future? ... If the grant of independence [to India] meant the removal of British power, Afghanistan would be between the devil and the deep blue sea. With no support at her back, she would fall an easy prey to Russia and then where would India be? She would have Russia on her doorstep.[22]

With these recent events still in mind, the question uppermost in the Afghan government's mind in 1947 was whether Britain would still commit to preserving their country's territorial integrity after Indian independence. The British were asking themselves the same question, but from a slightly different perspective. They wondered if Afghanistan would remain a British priority after independence, and if not, how quickly Britain's successor state in India would be able to take over responsibility for their own security.

The year started fairly well for Afghanistan. On 7 March 1947, President Truman announced the United States would not only help Greece and Turkey repel forces threatening their integrity, but also protect the 'free' world from oppression globally. Three weeks later, on 29 March, the British government reaffirmed that preserving the territorial integrity of Afghanistan was still an important foreign policy priority.[23] This reaffirmation addressed some of their concerns, but not all. Lancaster discovered that many Afghan military 'officers have shown some jealousy about the military and financial aid given by Great Britain and the United States of America to Greece, Turkey and Persia, and have on occasion stated that this help might well be extended to Afghanistan'.[24]

Daud made the same point to Lancaster on 12 June. He too had seen the support given to Greece, Turkey and Persia and wanted the same for Afghanistan. He was also concerned that the potential breakup of India could lead to a 'lack of control of the tribes on the Indo-Afghan Frontier and the creation of a vacuum which would lead to tribal lawlessness and unrest on both sides of the Frontier'. If necessary, he wanted to reorganise the Afghan army and air force to prepare for that eventuality, and sought more reassurance that Indian independence would not affect Afghanistan's relationship with Britain. From a practical perspective, he also wanted to avoid 'adding to their "magpie" collection of arms and equipment and wished to ensure that their future purchases of arms and equipment and ammunitions are of a standard type, and that replacements for the arms and equipment and ammunition, as well as spare parts already supplied to them by India and Great Britain, will be available as and when required'. As a parting shot, he warned that Afghanistan would turn to the United States and the United Nations for support against the Soviet Union if Britain did not deliver because they could not do it alone: 'Afghanistan had excellent material to draw on for her armed forces, [but] the lack of education, complete ignorance of organisation and administration, the laziness and conservatism, or even fanaticism inherent in the Afghan people, are tremendous barriers to progress.'[25]

Two weeks after Indian independence, however, and in spite of all the Afghan lobbying, the Joint Chiefs of Defence Staff concluded on 29 August that although Britain was still interested in preserving Afghanistan's territorial integrity, officials should explore whether India and Pakistan would help out too. If not, and only as a last resort, they recommended that the Treasury should be approached to fund a continued British commitment.[26] Given the domestic and international pressures on the British government and economy that year, it is difficult to see how they could have concluded otherwise. On 22 September, Bevin therefore told Squire to convey the following message to the Afghans:

> The transfer of power in India has, of course, radically altered the position of His Majesty's Government with regard to the wider question of the territorial integrity of Afghanistan, a problem, which is now essentially and in the first instance, a matter for the two new Dominion governments – and primarily for Pakistan ... although it remains of the greatest importance to us, as well as to India and Pakistan, to avoid a situation of Russian predominance in Afghanistan, which might bring with it the risk of Russian political, and possibly military, penetration further south east ... You are accordingly authorised, at your discretion, to convey to the Afghan government an assurance of the continued friendly interest of His Majesty's government in the welfare and prosperity of Afghanistan and of our determination to exert our influence [with India and Pakistan] with a view to ensuring that her sovereignty, independence, and peaceful development are neither menaced nor disturbed.[27]

To support this, Mountbatten was asked to consult the new governments of India and Pakistan in the Joint Defence Council about meeting Afghanistan's request for military supplies.[28] Alongside this, the Foreign Office and Ministry of Defence hoped to use their own channels to 'persuade Pakistan, as the government primarily interested – and perhaps to some extent India – to shoulder between them approximately the same burden of military assistance as the government of India has borne in the past', possibly supplemented by additional support from Britain.[29]

As Afghanistan upped the pace of its demands for Pashtunistan, however, the likelihood of an immediate deal with Pakistan did not look promising, especially after it was the only country to vote against Pakistan's membership of the United Nations that autumn. Given this broader context therefore, it was not at all surprising that the Afghans also started to cast around for new trading partners in 1947 to reduce their dependence on trade through Pakistan. The 1936 Afghan–Soviet trade treaty, which had gone into abeyance in 1941, was renewed that November, in spite of the considerable logistical difficulties involved. Goods had to be taken across the Oxus by ferry and then carried by camel to the nearest road head for transfer to motorised transport.[30] Transport of petrol was particularly difficult because there were no storage facilities at the border.

Most of this deal was in the form of a barter arrangement under which the Soviets undertook to provide Afghanistan with petrol, kerosene oil, cotton piece goods, window glass, sugar, iron girders, nails, sheep clippers and steel bars in exchange for a certain amount of wool of a specified quality and age. The balance was to be made up with a cash payment in dollars because the Afghans lacked sufficient goods to exchange for the petrol. Privately, Ali Mohammed admitted to Squire that the terms of the deal were not in Afghanistan's favour. The Soviets were charging a high price for their products, and were buying Afghan wool at a low rate. The government, however, had no choice: 'In view of the fact that there was no other market for their wool, and of the great difficulties that Afghanistan was experiencing over trade with India, the agreement with the Russians was of great importance.'[31]

From the outset, the British realised that the deal on petrol in particular was a potential game changer for the future. At 1.8 million gallons, it was equal to the amount the Afghans received from the Middle East through Pakistan, and the Afghans had already begun to address their lack of storage facilities by promptly placing orders for ninety tanks from India and eighty from Pakistan:

> The chief value of this agreement to the Afghan government is that it reduces the dependence of the country on the monthly allocation of petrol from Middle East sources, whose safe and regular delivery is contingent on the provision of transit facilities by Pakistan ... On the Russian side, the possible long-term advantage is that of assuming a much more important position in the Afghan economy than hitherto, while the short-term advantages are those of enabling the Afghans to

take a stronger line with Pakistan over the future of the North West Frontier Province.[32]

Pakistan clocked the significance of the deal too. Kizilbash, Jinnah's representative in Kabul, showed Squire a letter he had written to his Foreign Ministry underlining his disappointment 'that the Afghans found themselves forced to enter into an agreement with Russia for the supply of petrol as this development will prejudicially affect the commercial interests of Pakistan and will also deprive it of a useful sanction which could be applied against the Afghan government as an emergency'.[33] The Afghan–Pakistan dispute was clearly beginning to add a new dimension to regional politics, with cross-border trade seemingly a new weapon in the Soviet armoury.

The Cold War Starts to Reframe the Game

During 1947, these regional power plays were gradually overlaid by two new factors. First, there were growing fears that post-war Soviet expansionism in eastern Europe and Persia and the spread of communist ideology in France, Italy, China and South-East Asia posed a massive threat to freedom, world stability and peace. Second, the United States' decision to assume a global leadership role to repel these forces rather than retreat back into the isolationism of the inter-war years heralded a new era of superpower politics which were to put Asian affairs on a new global map. As far as Afghanistan was concerned, the key question was what place, if any, should it occupy in American and British calculations at the start of this new world war?

American interest in Afghanistan was relatively recent and fairly narrow. The first legation had opened in Kabul in 1942 as part of a wider strategy to ensure the supply routes to the Soviet Union and China through Afghanistan and India were secure.[34] After the war, an American company, Morrison Knudsen, had secured a multimillion-dollar contract from the Afghan government in 1946 to develop the Helmand river valley, and the legation was keen to protect the company's equities there. Beyond this, however, it was unclear in 1947 whether the United States planned to have a more substantive political presence in the region.

Relations between the United States and British legations had been fairly close during the war – the United States mission was described as the 'down-town office of the British legation' – but mutual suspicions simmered close beneath the surface. Squire questioned the staying power of the Americans in 1944 and wondered whether their lack of regional experience could pose serious risks to the status quo:

American interests are likely to be ephemeral whereas ours are permanent ... The effect of American intervention on Russia might be the reverse of our expectations and instead of being a source of security to Afghanistan, it might on the other hand increase Soviet suspicions and encourage them to more active intervention.[35]

The Americans for their part were wary of getting too close to a colonial power on its home turf.[36] Indeed, there were rumours that the first American Minister in Kabul, Cornelius Van H. Engert, had been fired precisely because he had become too close to the British.[37] The cool behaviour of Engert's successor, Ely Palmer, suggested these rumours were not far from the truth. Squire tried to meet him halfway on a number of occasions but made little headway. In April 1947, for instance, he had pointed out to him that once Britain's empire in India ended, 'our remaining interests in Afghanistan would then be almost identical with those of the United States ... [namely to] see a strong and independent Afghanistan ... to keep Russian influence away from India'.[38] Palmer, however, continued to go out of his way to avoid contact with his British counterpart. Even six months after Truman's announcement, Squire was still complaining in September that 'practically all the information we get about their activities is given to me by Ali Muhammed'.[39]

Relations in Kabul, however, did not mirror diplomacy in Washington and London. During negotiations to secure American assistance in Greece and Turkey in January and February 1947, Bevin had already indicated he was keen to sort out the security of the eastern Mediterranean, the Middle East, and East and North Africa.[40] In September, he sought more information on the United States' policy position and suggested to the Ambassador in London, Lewis Douglas, how they might work together. Douglas reported the conversation to Washington:

That we jointly review the whole position in the Middle East including Cyrenaica [in eastern Libya], Egypt, Palestine, Iraq and Persia for the purpose of arriving at a gentleman's understanding in regard to a common policy and joint responsibility throughout the area, with Britain acting as the front and ourselves [the United States] supplying the moral support.[41]

Bevin was already knocking on an open door. Historically, the United States' security shield had focussed on the Pacific and Atlantic Rim.[42] Now, Stalin's virtual occupation of eastern Europe and eastern Germany, recent events in Persia, the situation in Greece and Turkey, the conflict in

Palestine and nationalist movements in Egypt and Persia against Britain, suggested a rethink was called for. The Eastern Mediterranean and the Middle East were the gateways between East and West, and combined vast mineral wealth with rich agricultural resources – their loss would have a significant impact on Western security and the world economy. Something needed to be done, and fast. Foreign Office and War Office representatives were therefore invited to join secret meetings at the Pentagon in Washington that October to agree a bilateral strategy for the Near East and North Africa.

In background papers prepared for the meetings, United States officials advised their government that 'our ambition is therefore to prevent great power ambitions and rivalries and local discontents and jealousies from developing into open conflict which might eventually lead to a third world war'. When it came to deciding whether the United States should get more directly involved in the region, however, they supported Bevin's proposal that regional defence should be left to Britain: 'Given our heavy commitments elsewhere and Britain's already established position in the area, it is our strong feeling that the British should continue to maintain primary responsibility for military security in the area.'[43]

In the margins of the Pentagon meetings, Afghanistan did come up in discussion but was not considered a priority, at least not right now:

It was recognised by both groups that Afghanistan was of strategic importance because of its position on the flank of Iran and athwart the approach to India from the northwest. At the same time, it was noted that in view of the geographic situation of Afghanistan, the loss of Afghan political independence and territorial integrity, while fraught with serious consequences, would not in present world conditions be likely to menace the security of the Middle East to the extent of similar losses on the part of Iran [Persia], Greece or Turkey. A determined effort should be made in the framework of the United Nations to assist Afghanistan in resisting direct or indirect aggression.

This conclusion was consistent with United States views about South Asia too. In a report prepared by the Central Intelligence Agency for Truman, the region was ranked bottom in a list of American priorities, below western Europe, the Middle East and South-East Asia.[44] The participants at the Pentagon meetings did, however, put down a marker to review Afghanistan's position at a later date if necessary: 'It is possible that circumstances might so develop that the strategic importance of

Afghanistan might be considerably increased.' In the meantime, it was reaffirmed that Britain, India and Pakistan would meet Afghan needs for arms and military training while Britain signalled it would welcome American efforts to provide economic assistance in Afghanistan.

The decision was a great result for Lancaster. He had long argued against opening up the Afghan arms market to the Americans, and in the week before the Pentagon talks submitted an aide-memoire to the War Office in person reinforcing that message.[45] In his opinion, British military assistance had helped Afghanistan maintain its neutrality during the war, strengthened cooperation along the Frontier, and above all, helped ensure Afghanistan did not receive the kind of heavy weapons or armour which could be used against an external aggressor and thus provoke a reaction from the Soviet Union. American military assistance would also cause problems for Pakistan:

> It is to my mind dangerous for the new government of Pakistan should we permit the United States of America, inexperienced as they are in the North West Frontier affairs, to embark on the supply of military and air force equipment to the Afghan government since they may end by providing equipment and training superior to that of the Pakistan Dominion.

All in all, therefore, the British were satisfied with the outcome of the Pentagon discussions. In the immediate aftermath, there was a tangible outcome in Kabul too. The delegates acknowledged the 'apparent lack of cooperation' between the American and British legations and undertook to improve them.[46] A few weeks later when the Americans started to review how to bring the status of their legation in Kabul into line with their new embassies in Pakistan, India and Burma, they asked the Foreign Office if Britain planned to do the same. If so, they hoped to synchronise the timing of the public announcement.[47] The British received the idea favourably – the Soviets had already upgraded their legation, the French were considering it, and the Indians and Pakistanis were planning to open embassies from the outset.

Although they did not quite manage to synchronise the dates – in part because of delays in finalising the paperwork – Squire and Palmer made every effort to ensure everyone in Kabul knew the United States and British Embassies had a common cause henceforth. Squire presented his credentials to Zahir Shah in the Dilkusha Palace on Tuesday 25th March. Palmer followed suit on 5 June. The Foreign Minister normally hosted a reception for each incoming ambassador or minister, but Squire asked on this occasion if he would make an exception: 'I at once suggested that it would be a nice gesture if, instead of two functions, a single reception could be given for Mr Palmer and myself together. The suggestion was accepted and the party is to take place on Monday next, 14th June.'[48] The Afghan government announced in turn that Faiz Muhammed Zakria would be Afghanistan's first Ambassador to Britain, and Naim Khan, the King's cousin, would be the first Ambassador to the United States.

News of Squire's meeting with the King was reported widely in the Afghan press and it was overwhelmingly positive. London was immediately informed: 'It is indicative how little ill-will is now felt against Great Britain that a photo of the embassy staff leaving the Dilkusha Palace appeared on the same page as the leading article on Afghan independence and those who helped to achieve it, and immediately below, photos of the late King Nadir Shah and King Zahir Shah.'[49] Britain's star was still in the ascendancy in Afghanistan, and what was more, the new British and American embassies had proved they could work together. The ball was now firmly in Britain's court to fulfil its assigned strategic role, drawing on its historic knowledge of the country and experience in the region, its understanding of the military's strengths and weaknesses, and its close relationships with senior members of the Afghan army and air force.

Assessing the Soviet Threat

The overriding question that the British asked themselves repeatedly was whether the Soviets really did pose a new threat to Afghanistan in the late 1940s, or whether the Afghans were simply posturing to get a better deal for themselves after Indian independence. Was their recent trade deal with the Soviet Union, for instance, simply driven by a desire to diversify their trading routes – especially if trade through Pakistan turned sour – or to make a political point that they could just as easily ally with the Soviets as the West if it was in their interests to do so? Meanwhile, the British were wondering if anything had really changed. True, the Soviets and Soviet-style communism seemed to be making advances elsewhere, but did they really pose a greater threat to Afghanistan's territorial integrity and independence now than they had in the past? Squire, Lancaster and Prendergast assessed the situation from all angles and concluded they did not. In fact, quite the reverse.

In terms of practicalities, Squire, Lancaster and Prendergast agreed that Afghanistan could be invaded relatively easily, but it was quite another thing to hold onto any captured territory. The British had learnt this to their cost, twice, in the nineteenth century, and nothing had dramatically changed since. An invading Soviet army could reach the Pakistan border easily because Afghanistan would not be able to put up much opposition. Prendergast even mapped out an invasion route:

> A main thrust through Herat, Kandahar to Chaman, and since most of the territory along this route is tank-able, there would be nothing to stop them. Even an airborne landing with Herat as its limited objective, could hold its own even if ground follow-up troops were unforeseeably delayed. The Afghans might be able to hold up a subsidiary advance down the Mazar-i-Sharif – Darra Shikari route to Kabul by demolitions upon a route which is ideal for such methods, provided that they were not too much interfered with by airborne troops and air attack. This would seal off the Kabul valley for a short while.

Kabul would, however, still be vulnerable to an attack using the tank-able road from Kandahar to Kabul. Defensive 'operations would cause a delay of the final disintegration of the Afghan as a cohesive force for a period which could be best numbered in days rather than months'.[50] Prendergast's assessment of the speed with which the Soviets could overrun the country bears remarkable similarities with the pace of the Soviet invasion and occupation in December/January 1979/80.

Ultimately, though, as all Afghan and British military officers knew from their history books, the Soviets would get bogged down: 'Superior armament and military skill might lead to the capture of all-important towns within a few days, but the invader would then be faced, as the British have been in the past, with the troublesome business of subduing the country which would disintegrate into tribal areas with no central government' (Lancaster). 'The Afghan higher command admits their total inability to check the Russians. The Chief of the General Staff told me recently that he felt powerless but that once swallowed by the Russians, Afghanistan would prove an indigestible pill' (Lancaster).[51] If the Soviets advanced, the Afghan army would take to the hills and, with support from the tribes, conduct guerrilla warfare. Although there would be problems supplying the caves with ammunition and supplies, 'guerrilla tactics would produce good dividends as a large portion of the invading force would be tied up in keeping the vulnerable lines of communication open, as the British know full well'. Furthermore, concluded Prendergast, Afghanistan's part 'would be to deny the free and continuous use of her two main routes towards Pakistan. In doing so, the Afghans might neutralise three to eight more Russian divisions'.[52] If this was insufficient, the Afghan government could also, with help from the Mullahs, 'arouse a patriotic and religious fighting spirit'. Indeed, 'they might involve Russia in a wasteful and long war operating against formations and guerrilla bands in the mountainous masses which stretch throughout a country as large as Germany and infinitely less accessible'.[53]

Once the small matter of a successful Red Army campaign was out of the way, the British got down to considering whether the Soviet Union actually had any intention of threatening Afghan security, or were more focussed on protecting their own. In February 1946, during the Persian crisis, British military intelligence had reviewed whether Afghanistan was vulnerable too. They concluded that 'with the present scanty evidence at our disposal it not possible at this stage to do anything more than to sound a note of warning. However, Russia's present attitude to Persia may be a pointer to her subsequent approach to Afghan problems when she considers that the time is ripe for action.'[54] Squire came to a similar conclusion. The Soviets might appear benign, but things could change whenever it suited them: 'We always felt that though Russia might be taking no interest at the moment in Afghanistan, she had no intention of attempting any genuine rapprochement or of settling such long standing cases as the Oxus boundary dispute which was only being kept in cold storage for production as and when required.'[55]

Immediate concerns about the boundary were allayed in mid-1946 when the Afghans and Soviets agreed to set up a boundary commission to confirm the frontier, sort out who owned which island in the river, and put up boundary pillars.[56] If anything, the British were prepared to confess, it was just possible that Britain itself had provided the provocation. When reports starting circulating in March 1946 that the Afghans had moved two convoys of forty lorries to the north carrying troops and military equipment as a precaution against a Soviet invasion, Squire told London:

> The Russian embassy have on more than one occasion expressed interest in the amount of arms and equipment being supplied to the Afghan government from India. When questioned, I have always replied that the situation on the North West Frontier of India is naturally of the greatest concern to us, and that it is to our interest that the Afghan government should be strong enough to cope with it.

If, however, the equipment was transferred to the northern border, 'this would certainly not escape the notice of the Russian embassy, and would hardly help to strengthen their confidence in our good intentions'.[57]

Britain's interpretation of the Soviet position seemed to be reaffirmed a year later when the Soviet Ambassador in Kabul protested strongly against Afghan plans to construct an airport in Herat and reports that they planned to build one in the north too using American assistance.

Ali Mohammed told Squire exactly what the Ambassador had said during
a meeting in May 1947:

> Such a scheme was in Russian eyes, merely an extension of the Anglo-
> American policy of encirclement of Soviet Russia which was being
> followed throughout the Near and Middle East, and these aerodromes
> would be a threat to the security of Soviet Russia. The Russian
> government considered northern Afghanistan to be in their own sphere
> of influence and if the Afghan government wished to develop aerodromes
> and air services in this part of the country, the Russians were ready to
> give them assistance in so doing.[58]

On balance, therefore, Squire was not convinced in 1946 that the Soviet
Union posed a real threat to Afghan security:

> It may be doubted whether an upheaval in this country would really
> serve Soviet interests. The prospect of having to deal with the turbulent
> tribes of the North West Frontier cannot be particularly attractive to
> them, though the Ambassador is on occasions critical of the leniency
> with which they are treated by the Government of India and says that
> the Russians in our place would know much better how to keep them
> in order.[59]

Subsequently, he concluded that if the Soviets did have an invasion plan
up their sleeves between 1946 and 1948, it was clearly not dependent on
inputs from their embassy in Kabul. He had enjoyed a warm relationship
with Ivan Samylovsky, the Soviet Chargé d'Affaires during the war.
When Samylovsky returned as Ambassador in August 1947, 'Madame
Samylovsky during her four years' absence had acquired more poise
and a somewhat precious knowledge of English and seemed rather out
of place as the great lady she tried to be, but Samylovsky himself was
entirely unchanged and was determined to be friendly.' The real power in
the embassy in the intervening period had been a man called Kouznetsov,
'an unpleasant young man with the rank of Attaché'. When Ambassador
Samylovsky left only three months later in November, giving the
Afghan government just twenty-four hours' notice, Squire assumed it
was because he had tried to assert his authority over Kouznetsov. The
Ambassador's wife stayed on until March 1948 awaiting her husband's
return, but then she too left without being able to say if her husband
was returning or not.[60]

After that, the embassy had remained understaffed. Samylovsky's
successor died of a heart attack before arriving, and so the post remained

vacant until the end of 1948. The Military Attaché post was vacant too. The embassy seemed to be fairly inactive as far as Squire could ascertain, focussing more or less exclusively on pursuing commercial deals and promoting pro-Soviet propaganda as it had been doing for years. Two incidents reported to London in December 1945 and April 1949 illustrate how these efforts played out in Kabul. In December 1945, the Soviet embassy showed a film to Afghan ministers and members of the diplomatic community about the high quality of life enjoyed by Muslims in Soviet Central Asia. Afghan Ministers were indignant about this 'blatant propaganda' because it played into their fears that poor Uzbek and Turkmen villagers in northern Afghanistan would prefer to be part of the Soviet Union. In response, on 27 December 1945, the British legation invited the same group to see *The True Glory*, which graphically illustrated Britain's and others' contribution to the war effort. The show was a huge success, at least according to a despatch sent to London, and everyone, except the Soviets, enjoyed it. Later, the legation received a message from the palace that the King wanted to borrow the film.[61]

In the second example in 1949, Mahmud Khan and his brother, Shah Wali Khan, found themselves the only guests at the Soviet embassy watching a film about the invincibility of the Red Army, followed by one called *Meeting on the Elbe*. The latter contrasted Soviet courtesy to the Germans with American drunkenness and debauchery. A day later, the whole of the Indian embassy, as well as the French Minister and his First Secretary, were invited to the Soviet embassy to see the same films. While the Indians and the French wondered how the guest list had been compiled, the British and Americans speculated why the Soviets had turned down several dinner invitations to their respective establishments over the previous few weeks. On this occasion, however, they decided not to read too much into the issue – the Soviets could, they speculated, have had genuine previous engagements.[62]

Squire speculated that perhaps the Soviet embassy in Kabul was so inactive because the new embassies in Delhi and Karachi had become their primary focus. These were where 'they have much great interests and also greater freedom to operate and Kabul has therefore lost most of its former importance. I have for a long time felt that Russia had no particular interest in Afghanistan for itself, but only as a stepping stone to India.'[63]

That just left the thorny question whether the Soviets could use communism to influence Afghan policy. Lancaster concluded this was a non-starter:

I do not think the Afghans will ever play very far with Russia ... Afghanistan is a country with few rich men, many Mullahs, many tribes with conflicting interests and lots of poor people. The rich want to retain and increase their wealth, the mullahs and the tribes would not welcome any form of communism. The poor in certain areas might react against their leaders but history so far has shown no example of this. Russia to be successful in any aims she has in this country must first of all capture some leaders.[64]

Taking all these things into consideration, Squire told London in September 1948 that if there *had* been a threat to Afghanistan in 1945/6 when Russian troops were in Persia, that threat was no longer active.

British Policy Starts to Unravel

Squire and Lancaster's conclusions in 1947/8 were based on a number of assumptions. If any of these proved to be wrong, however, the tide could turn in the Soviet Union's favour. First, military intelligence in the War Office had warned in April 1946 that 'if we don't help Afghanistan and give her what she needs, we might in the end drive her into the arms of Russia. That, in my mind, is the real danger.'[65] Squire and Lancaster assumed that Afghanistan would continue to enjoy the same benefits after Indian Independence as it had when the British were still on the scene. Second, in a remarkably prescient assessment in June 1947, the legation's First Secretary, Major Redpath, pointed out that Afghanistan's biggest Achilles' heel was its dependence on overland trade routes, not its susceptibility to communism. If the new dominion in India blocked the free movement of goods and people through the North-West Frontier after independence, then Afghanistan would have to rely on improved relations with the Soviet Union as an alternative route.[66] In 1947/8, Squire and Lancaster in Kabul and officials in London thought the Pashtunistan dispute would blow over quickly. Once that was resolved, there would be no question of closing the Frontier to trade. Third, they assumed that Britain, Pakistan and India would continue to provide military support to Afghanistan since the alternative was not in any of their collective interests. Indeed, as Lancaster pointed out during his visit to London in October 1947:

We shall lose a great deal of prestige, create further difficulties for Pakistan, particularly in respect of cooperation in tribal affairs on the Indo-Afghan frontier, give the Union of Soviet Socialist Republics further scope for upsetting the political position in Central Asia, pave the way for a spread of communism to India, and risk losing many Afghan friends.[67]

Unfortunately, however, after 1948 none of these assumptions held true. Pakistan and India failed to replace Britain in guaranteeing Afghan security and supplying arms, bedevilled by their mutual suspicions; trade through Pakistan became increasingly compromised by the Pashtunistan dispute; and Britain found itself lacking the political leverage or financial means to reverse the tide. Moreover, if others entered the Afghan arms market now, Britain would be unable to stop Afghanistan purchasing longer range weapons, which would enable it to run an offensive operation in Pakistan or inadvertently trigger a hostile reaction from the Soviet Union – the 'perfect storm', a war on two fronts, which Britain had always aimed to prevent.

Squire had already anticipated in January 1947 that the Interim Government in India would be unlikely 'to appreciate the indirect value to India of subsidising the British experts in Afghanistan' from the Afghan Fund.[68] He was not therefore entirely surprised a month later when the government announced it would only commit to funding the training costs for the next batch of Afghan military officers arriving in April, and wanted to know if Britain would pick up the rest of the tab.[69]

Neither Squire nor Lancaster, however, anticipated that the Lancaster Scheme itself would soon collapse too. The onus for supplying the remainder of the contract fell on the Interim Government from 1 April 1947 when all military stores were handed over from British to Indian ownership.[70] Things went well initially. The contract was honoured and the first instalment was delivered to Afghanistan in the spring. The decision in June, however, to establish two dominions, not one, changed the political landscape completely. Within a matter of weeks, Jinnah and Nehru were at loggerheads over the future of Kashmir, and any plans to transport arms overland through Pakistan on route to Afghanistan took on a whole new meaning. Pakistan was initially short on armaments and dependent on India honouring the Joint Defence Council decision to divide existing military supplies between them on the ratio of 2 for India and 1 for Pakistan. As tensions escalated over Kashmir, however, it became highly unlikely that India would allow any arms destined for Afghanistan to be transported through Pakistan. On the one hand, the arms could be seized by Pakistan and then used against India's armed forces; on the other, they could come in handy for India too.

Initially, Whitehall believed this was simply a hiccup and assumed shipments would resume once the Kashmir dispute was settled. In March 1948, however, Bajpai, the Indian Foreign Minister, made it clear that India intended to keep the arms for itself because the country was short of military stores. Once they had a surplus, he reassured British officials,

India would renew the shipments to Afghanistan. In the meantime, he was happy for Britain or the United States to ship arms to Afghanistan, but just wanted to be kept informed.[71] As the months rolled by, however, the Joint Chiefs of Staff in London were advised that the likelihood of the stores being released within the next five years was remote.[72] On top of that, the actual condition of the stores themselves was now in doubt too. It was highly probable that the Indians had already taken those in best condition for their own use, while the rest would have passed their shelf life.[73]

Britain's training plans were getting stuck too. The RAF had anticipated they would be able to continue training Afghan pilots at the former RAF base in Mauripur just outside Karachi. In March 1948, however, Pakistan said the facilities were too limited and suggested the training should be done in Kabul. A visit by Squadron Leader Reid confirmed that Mauripur Air Base was being redeveloped and the Pakistan Air Force was undergoing a massive reorganisation. All available facilities were therefore already in full use.[74] The next problem with Lancaster's training plans came unexpectedly from the War Office in London. The problem was triggered when Afghan Chief of Staff Lt General Asadullah Khan asked Lancaster if he could send twelve Afghan officers to Britain for training:

[He] thought highly of British army discipline and methods of education and training and considered that the officers would obtain more benefit from training with British units than from the armies of either the Indian Dominion or the Pakistan Dominion where he feared that the officers would become politically minded.[75]

From Squire's perspective, 'the provision of help of this nature is one of the most important of the few means left at our disposal for the maintenance of our influence in this country and for this reason, I welcome the approach'.[76] In May, however, the War Office said the Afghan government would have to bear the full costs, and refused to make an exception. If they did so, other countries, including Egypt, Iraq and Turkey, would expect similar concessions which Britain simply could not afford. Lancaster and Squire in turn argued that the Afghans 'would interpret it as a sign that His Majesty's Government are losing interest in Afghanistan, and might even look out for somewhere cheaper to send them'.[77] In spite of their remonstrances, however, the War Office held firm.

It was not long before tensions between Pakistan and Afghanistan provoked Pakistan to question what military support the British were actually giving to their neighbour, especially the role of the RAF training mission in Kabul. When the government inadvertently found out that the Air Ministry in London had prepared a plan to expand the Afghan Air Force to five operational squadrons, they asked the High Commissioner to give them a copy because they 'consider Commonwealth membership entitles them to the supply of information direct from us on matters within our knowledge relating to military preparations in a neighbouring country'.[78]

The request was received with mixed reactions in London. The Foreign Office simply tried to avoid replying, while the Commonwealth Relations Office believed the request was reasonable since it was consistent with an agreement made in 1946 to share secret information essential for Pakistan's needs.[79] There was a bottom line, however. If Britain shared secret Afghan information with Pakistan and this became known, Britain's relationship with the Afghan government would be seriously undermined. Indeed, as one official wrote, 'as it must be to the advantage of Pakistan as well as ourselves that we should be in a position to organise and control the Afghan Air Force, the Pakistan authorities should be very careful not to endanger our position or our source of information by allowing any hint to get to the Afghans that we have been discussing the matter together'.[80] After much to-ing and fro-ing, weighing up the different arguments, they finally identified a solution to suit both parties, without actually having to compromise the integrity of either. The Pakistan government was asked if it would be happy for General Cawthorne, the Deputy Chief of Staff of the Pakistan Army, to read the files while he was visiting London. He would then, it was hoped, be in a position to tell them that the plan was already obsolete because it was overly ambitious – the Afghan Air Force was starting from a fairly low base with limited trained personnel and facilities, and lacked funds to turn this around in the immediate future. Privately, they also crossed their fingers that Pakistan would not then put two and two together and ask to see the updated plan.[81] The ploy, to their great delight, worked.

By the time he left Afghanistan in September 1948, Lancaster had already seen the way the wind was blowing. Just months earlier, he had opposed United States entry into the Afghan arms market. Now, when the Afghan War Ministry asked for twenty-four light tanks, six armoured cars and a further twenty-four wheeled carriers just days before his departure, he was happy for the United States to help out.[82] Months of raised hopes and dashed expectations had worn down his resolve. Ever the practical army man, he immediately told the Afghans that light tanks were unsuitable for Afghan terrain, and then set about exploring how to meet the other two requests.

Recalibrating British Policy

In less than a year after Indian independence and the Pentagon agreements, Britain's policy in Afghanistan was therefore in bad shape. It was now clear that Pakistan would not be assuming Britain's role guaranteeing Afghanistan's territorial integrity in the foreseeable future and that, in a competitive arms market, the Afghans would increasingly turn to others to supply them. The United States alone had already received several requests through the new Afghan Ambassador, Naim Khan. The Great Game policies of a previous era were well and truly redundant.

In the midst of this quagmire, the British government decided to reframe their policy entirely. It was henceforth to reflect British interests alone, with the hope that Afghanistan, Pakistan and India would eventually come to their senses and recognise that their common enemy was the Soviet Union, not each other.

The Joint Chiefs of the Defence Staff were asked to produce a steer in June 1948. To kick off the process, a top-secret paper entitled 'The Provision of War-Like Stores to Afghanistan, Pakistan and India' was circulated around Whitehall for comment on the 9th. It began with the challenge:

[The] only foreseeable external threat to the sub-continent of India at present comes from Russia. Such an attack would be launched through Afghanistan, and possibly Persia, and thence through Pakistan. From this brief analysis, it is clear that Afghanistan, Pakistan and India have one military problem in common, viz defence against external aggression from the north. Afghanistan and Pakistan also share a further common problem in the control of the Frontier tribes. Unhappily, the differences at present prevailing between India and Pakistan make it impossible to attempt to negotiate common action by them for the defence of the North West Frontier against external aggression. Pakistan and Afghan relations are also not good ... Failure on the part of either country to control its tribes might result in chaos in both countries. In that event, our strategic requirements from Pakistan would be unobtainable and a vacuum in the Muslim area might have far reaching results.[83]

In view of this, the paper recommended Britain should continue to use active diplomacy to help defuse regional tensions, and supply arms to maintain stability in the tribal areas to avoid a wider power vacuum which could leave the door open for the Soviets. There were some serious stumbling blocks, however. Britain had made commitments to supply arms to Pakistan and India in December 1947, and although the only long-term commitment to Afghanistan was the Lancaster Scheme, the

Chiefs of Staff had accepted in April 1947 that Britain would consider providing warlike stores if these were not forthcoming from any other source. Unfortunately, the requirements of all three vastly outstripped Britain's capacity to keep pace with demand. The ramifications were far-reaching:

> It seems likely possibly to increase the doubts of Pakistan and India as to the practical advantages of remaining in the Commonwealth and to cause them and Afghanistan to seek other sources of supply. Since most of the Western European powers seem to depend in some measure on British sources of supply, the field for large scale provision is narrowed down to the United States of America and the Union of Soviet Socialist Republics.

Lancaster may have been changed his mind about opening the Afghan arms market to the United States, but many in London were not so sure. A separate annex was devoted entirely to this issue. On the plus side, the United States shared Britain's views about the importance of keeping Afghanistan, Pakistan and India stable and free from communism, and was working closely with Britain to help resolve the Kashmir dispute in the United Nations Security Council. On the downside, however, the United States had a tendency to impose embargos 'somewhat lightly on the sale of arms to particular countries'. They had just imposed an embargo on sales to India and Pakistan because of Kashmir. If Britain now came to a joint regional arrangement with them, it might well find itself having to pick up the slack, or worse still, become tied to a policy British ministers did not support. Over the longer term, once Britain's own supply capability picked up, British arms sales would be held back until or unless it was possible to terminate the agreement.

Having set out the context, the paper concluded there were three issues for consideration. First, whether Britain should continue to allocate arms to India and Pakistan on a ratio of 2:1 as agreed at Partition in 1947. Second, what priority should be given to Afghanistan, Pakistan and India for arms and equipment over other countries' needs. And third, whether Britain should consider approaching other members of the Commonwealth, such as Canada or Australia, or the United States to meet their needs instead.

By the time the paper was circulated to ministers in August, the context within which these issues were being considered had changed dramatically. Just three months earlier, the Soviet Union had blocked all land routes to Berlin. Britain was now committed to an airlift providing essential food and supplies as part of a massive Allied effort to relieve the city through a narrow air corridor. When the Minister of Defence, Albert Alexander, saw the paper in August, he decided it was unnecessary to refer the matter to the Cabinet Defence Committee. He agreed the fixed 2:1 ratio between India and Pakistan should cease, supported the Joint Chiefs of Staff and Treasury position that the United States should not be approached to plug the gaps, and recommended that India and Pakistan's needs should be reviewed twice a year. As far as Afghanistan was concerned, he did not think 'it would be an advantage to give her any greater priority in supply than she has received hitherto'.[84] The papers were then shared with Bevin's office and he agreed in December with Alexander's conclusions. The Foreign Office decided to consult the embassy in Kabul before coming to a final view on Afghanistan.[85]

The read-out from London was considerably at odds with opinions in Kabul. Squire and Lancaster had already changed their minds about United States involvement. In their view, it was now more important for Afghanistan to receive sufficient arms for their own defence than to continue a petty squabble in London over who the supplier should be, especially if that supplier was Britain's close ally in the Cold War. They also believed the United States was already circling, albeit cautiously, around the Afghan arms market in any case. In May, rumours circulated that the United States planned to add an Air Attaché to the military team complete 'with bride and an entire air crew, though curiously enough, no aeroplane'.[86] Although this appointment was temporarily shelved because Pakistan refused to allow courier flights from Kabul to fly over the North-West Frontier, the idea nevertheless seemed to signal a shift in American intentions.[87] Squire and Lancaster were pretty confident now that the Americans saw the situation in Afghanistan in much the same light as they did. Indeed, Lancaster had been told by Palmer and the Military Attaché on 20 September that the United States would be happy to consider meeting any shortfall if the Lancaster Scheme fell through. They shared British concerns 'should the [Afghan] government prove incapable of maintaining internal security, chaos would result', and were happy to review the government's request for armoured cars and wheeled carriers.[88]

Squire and Lancaster's representations to London, however, met a brick wall, as did Palmer's to Washington. A State Department paper on American security interests in the Near East and South Asia, written on 11 October 1948, explains why:

> Unlike Iran, Afghanistan is not now being subjected to overt political pressure from the Union of Soviet Socialist Republics. The Soviet

position seems to spring from a not unjustifiable confidence that Afghanistan could be occupied by Soviet troops in two weeks, and the preliminary 'softening up' [through communist ideology] would be an unnecessary expense and provocation.[89]

Moreover, if the United States provided military assistance, this 'would proclaim Afghanistan's alliance with the West and its latent antagonism to the Union of Soviet Socialist Republics to a degree which might well provoke overt action by the latter'. The United States would have created the very situation that both they and Britain had been trying to avoid. Inaction was therefore the best policy. It also made sense from a practical point of view too – it was not worth training the Afghan military in the United States because of 'the considerable lag between the Afghan's general knowledge of motorised equipment and that of the average American trainee'.

A Painful Parting of the Ways

Squire was left to face the music in Kabul. When Prime Minister Mahmud Khan asked him outright in November 1948 if Britain would protect Afghanistan against the Soviets and a potential Third World War, Squire was forced to fall back on pleasantries, ducking and weaving his way out of giving a direct answer.[90] During the same humiliating meeting, Mahmud Khan also expressed disappointment that Afghanistan had to cover the bulk of the RAF Training Mission's costs, including salaries and housing, while the French provided teachers and doctors free of charge, and the Turks paid for their military instructors.[91] Squire spotted a potential reputation-saving lifeline. After the meeting, he swiftly asked the Treasury and the War Office if they would subsidise some of the training costs so that he could at least offer the Prime Minister the same deal as Afghanistan had enjoyed prior to Indian independence, when most costs had been covered by the Afghan Fund. For a small contribution, he argued, Britain earned great influence:

> These are only petty items; but if we really take a serious interest in the strategic situation in Afghanistan we should in my opinion be prepared to go a great deal further in the matter of additional expenditure, which even so would be infinitesimal in comparison say, with the cost of the air lift to Berlin.[92]

The despatch was met with a deafening silence.

In the meantime, the Afghan government, Squire, Lancaster, and then Lancaster's successor, Prendergast, continually asked the Indian embassy when they thought the Lancaster Scheme supplies would be released. It became a humiliating farce. The Indian Ambassador, Rup Chand, agreed to do some digging during his forthcoming visit to Delhi in December. When he returned, however, the news was far from encouraging. The Indian Defence Department had denied all knowledge of the scheme and had no information about any arms earmarked for Afghanistan. He had also visited the Ministry of Foreign Affairs and found the relevant papers were in a muddle and some were missing. A few months later, the Indian Military Attaché undertook his own search in Delhi and came back empty-handed too.[93]

There was a glimmer of hope in May 1949 when the Indian embassy asked Squire to show them details of the full financial arrangements and the actual legal agreement to prove India had a binding commitment to supply these arms. Once they had seen these, they promised to take the matter up again with their government.[94] Back in London, the Commonwealth Relations Office went through all their files from the former British government in India, including correspondence with the Treasury, and found a similarly muddled picture. They could not work out what the actual shortfall was between what the Afghans had received in 1947 and what they had actually paid for. It was also unclear whether all the different agreements about who should cover what cost between Britain and India had actually been sorted out.[95] Inevitably, Squire became the fall guy – in May 1949, the Afghan Foreign Minister asked him where liability for the failure to supply arms under the scheme actually lay and demanded an answer.[96]

Events in North Africa, Persia and South-East Asia were conspiring against British plans too. Less than a year after the Pentagon agreements, nationalist movements against British control began to make more headway in Egypt and Persia and a communist insurrection had broken out in British Malaya in 1948, followed closely by communist-inspired revolts in Indonesia, Burma and Indochina in 1948/9. As the regional situation deteriorated, it became distinctly possible that Britain would be unable to fulfil its part of the Pentagon deal and ultimately require American help.

Soon after, Mao Zedong's communist forces overran China and formed a Marxist-Leninist government in Beijing in September and October 1949. United States policy then shifted rapidly. Events in China signalled that the front line had moved from the Pacific to the heart of Asia itself, while the continued security of the Middle East and the Persian Gulf needed to be kept under constant review. Meanwhile, the gradual consolidation of a

Soviet bloc in eastern Europe underlined the need to stay engaged there too. By the end of 1949, the United States, Canada, Britain and other Western allies in Europe had signed the North Atlantic Treaty (NATO), committing its members to the defence of each other's territory.

Alongside this, the British and the Americans began to review their respective policies in South and South-East Asia.[97] The Foreign Office was concluding that the greatest threat to stability came from communist ideology, not the Soviet Red Army, and that this ideology had spread so fast because governments had not been able to address their populations' economic and social grievances.[98] In view of this, it made sense to place emphasis on a diplomatic offensive to encourage reform, backed by concerted efforts to provide economic support. This strategy was in Britain's gift. Britain could mobilise an economic strategy – provided it was not solely funded by the British – but not a military one. Over subsequent months, this thinking helped set the scene for negotiations in the run-up to the Commonwealth Foreign Ministers' Conference in Colombo, Ceylon, in January 1950.

The United States was happy to go along with Britain's Asia strategy. They were aware Britain lacked sufficient military and economic capacity to repel a concerted Soviet onslaught in Asia. A secret report by the State, Army, Navy and Air Force Coordinating Committee of 19 April 1949, however, concluded that Britain still had more influence than any other foreign power in the region to make a difference:

> The United Kingdom does not at present possess sufficient economic or military resources to supply South Asian countries with either substantial amounts of the capital goods and technical skills needed for their economic rehabilitation and development, or all the military equipment needed for the maintenance of their internal security. Despite this situation ... British commercial and financial interests still constitute the leading foreign element in most of the economies of South Asia and British advisers on military matters occupy important, though temporary, posts in former British possessions.[99]

Moreover, a regional rearmament programme could inadvertently precipitate conflict, the complete reverse of what the United States wanted to see happen: 'In light of the existing commitments of the United States and the United Kingdom, and the strained relations among Afghanistan, Pakistan and India, it would be unrealistic to propose the necessary strengthening of the armed forces of the three South Asian countries at present.'

Significantly, for the first time in over a century, Britain's new strategy did not accord Afghanistan a ringside seat – the tide of opinion in the face of competing regional and global priorities was slowly, and inexorably, moving in the opposite direction. There did not seem to be a pressing need to include Afghanistan in any case. Although the Soviet embassy had been beefed up at the end of 1948, there was still little evidence it was being used to foment trouble. A new Ambassador had arrived in December, General Artemi Fedorovich Federov, who was a former Commandant of the Russian army and had been an assistant Military Attaché in Japan throughout the war. Within a month, his team had been reinforced by a new Military Attaché and his two assistants, and a new Political Councillor.[100] The new team, however, gave little away. Prendergast noted in February 1949 that 'the Ambassador has expressed himself as likely to be bored in Kabul, sentiments that have been echoed by the Military Attaché ... The Military Attaché has also said that he has made no study of Afghanistan before coming there.' Prendergast, the War Office concluded, 'considers that the Russians appear to be making an effort to disarm suspicion and to convey the impression that they do not treat Afghanistan seriously'. Over subsequent months, Prendergast saw quite a lot of the Russian Military Attaché and his assistants, although 'I could never understand their marked advances. Perhaps they thought I was the Number One Commissar since I was heavy, stout and just like a bulky Russian general.'[101]

When the Joint Chiefs of Defence Staff looked at the Afghan case again in April 1949, they concluded that Britain could in principle meet Afghanistan's military needs once Afghanistan and Pakistan had patched up their differences, but only after Britain's other priorities and commitments had been met first. Significantly, they were no longer totally averse to United States support to Afghanistan, but 'this was only acceptable if it was the only way to prevent Afghanistan from applying to the Russians for the weapons which she needed'.[102] The Chiefs of Staff had not gone so far as to say that Afghanistan was not a foreign policy priority, but neither had they given much hope to those who still believed it should be.

As the months wore on, Britain's policy position became increasingly at odds with the political and economic situation in Afghanistan. The fallout from the Moghulgai incident provoked a Cabinet reshuffle in September 1949 which seriously eroded Mahmud Khan's power base and strengthened the influence of the pro-Pashtunistan lobby. Meanwhile, a series of trade skirmishes with Pakistan had encouraged the Afghans to strengthen their trading relationship with the Soviet Union still further. The 1947 deal was followed by more over the next two years. There were rumours that the quality of Afghan wool did not meet Soviet expectations – in part because some of it was diseased – and that the Afghans still lacked sufficient storage facilities to receive the petrol at the border. There were even reports of Russian tanker drivers pouring their petrol on the ground because they could not wait any longer for the Afghans to collect it.[103] This news did not, however, detract from the fact that regional relationships were being reconfigured, and rapidly. In the weeks running up to the imposition of Pakistan's petrol blockade on 1 January 1950, Ali Mohammed warned Gardener that the imminent blockade would force his government to open discussions with the Soviet Union to secure supplies and transit facilities.[104]

A Soviet trade delegation duly arrived in town and a new agreement was signed in July 1950. Irrespective of the terms of the deal, Gardener understood its political importance from the outset:

> As a result of her quarrel with Pakistan, Afghanistan has been made aware that she has gained the disfavour of both the Muslim and Western powers. Furthermore, Pakistan by exercising what the Afghans regard as an embargo on the export of petrol has been able to disturb the economy of this country and therewith internal stability.[105]

It took several weeks before the full import of the agreement leaked out. The diplomats learnt that the Afghans themselves were not overly happy with the terms – indeed the Soviets were not even offering to pay for Afghan wool at world market prices, and the government would therefore have to procure it from suppliers either by force or subsidies.[106] The Soviets had also offered to construct several petrol storage tanks, to take over oil exploration in northern Afghanistan from a Swedish company, and to permit Afghan goods free transit through Soviet territory.[107] The petrol deal, however, was not in sufficient quantities to remove Afghanistan's reliance on supplies from Pakistan.[108]

Although the Afghans did not seem overly happy, it marked another significant step towards the realignment of alliances in Asia. Meanwhile, at the Commonwealth Foreign Ministers' conference in Colombo in January 1950, and in the midst of Pakistan's petrol blockade, it was agreed that the first beneficiaries of the Colombo Plan for Cooperative Economic Development in South and South-East Asia would be South-East Asian countries vulnerable to communist infiltration. Afghanistan had been left out in the cold.

When Abdul Majid approached Gardener for another loan two months later, the Foreign Office and Commonwealth Relations Office agreed they should not press the Treasury this time round. Rather, if there was a reasonable commercial case, 'they would be anxious on political grounds to see it granted. They would not, however, consider that the political arguments were of overriding importance.'[109] In August 1950, soon after Britain had committed troops to Korea in the first conflict of the Cold War, Gardener was instructed to tell Abdul Majid that the world had changed dramatically since he had first mooted the idea of a loan. The Treasury had already committed an additional £1.1 million towards rearmament over three years in response to the crisis in Korea – the implication being that Britain had no money spare for Afghanistan.[110] By October, the position in London had hardened still further, as Murray in the South-East Asia Department explained to Gardener:

> After consultation with the interested departments, I am of the opinion that we should obtain no financial or commercial advantage by granting such a loan and that the political arguments in its favour are not of sufficient strength in these days of financial stringency to override these considerations.[111]

Gardener broke the news to Abdul Majid, now President of the Afghan National Bank, and Dr Abdur Rauf Khan, Director General of the Ministry of National Economy in December. Zabuli's parting shot now fell on deaf ears:

> In his opinion, it would be consonant with British interests and British policy to support the economy of Afghanistan to prevent existing dissatisfaction from reaching the stage when, under Soviet instigation, revolt against the present regime might result.[112]

Humiliation

As Britain's capacity and London's willingness to support Afghanistan diminished, it was left to Squire, Gardener, Prendergast and others in the legation to pick up the pieces in Kabul. Time was eventually called on the Lancaster Scheme, but only after more excruciating meetings with the Afghan government during which they explained that Britain wanted to help Afghanistan, but then had to provide excuses for Britain repeatedly failing to deliver. After several cables circulated between Whitehall, Kabul, Delhi and Karachi in late 1949 discussing whether to approach the Indian government again, the idea was shelved. Inaction, it seemed, was by far the best approach. Even if the Indian government now agreed to honour the contract, Britain realised this would only serve to fuel Afghan–Pakistan tensions:

> Whatever economic bait we may hold out to the Afghans in the hope of persuading them to drop their artificial quarrel with Pakistan, I take it that we do not intend to offer them arms until we have reasonable assurance that the Afghan government would use those arms to maintain peace on the Frontier and not to break it ... [Lets] treat the Lancaster Scheme as being for all practical purposes dead.[113]

That just left the future of Britain's RAF training mission and a proposal that had been floating around for British teachers to join a new military college. The prospect of the latter ever getting off the ground seemed doubtful when the Afghans shelved discussions in December 1949 until the following April.[114] The final crunch was the RAF mission.

In September 1949, this contained six men. A year later, it was down to just one officer and one other rank and both of their contracts were due to expire in April 1951. In what the British could only interpret as an insult, the Afghans had also hired a German Luftwaffe pilot, Willi Braun, as a flying instructor in 1950.[115] Gardener saw this as a punishment, concluding that 'their powers of rational thought in this matter have been warped and turned against us through our advocacy of Pakistan's case in the Pashtunistan crisis'. Gardener was a realist though. He understood why the Afghans had had enough. The British had refused to increase their financial contribution to the mission, so why should the Afghans bear the additional costs involved when they could get a better deal elsewhere? He made that point clear to London too: 'Economically, I think there is no doubt that they resent having to pay foreigners so much from their restricted supplies of foreign currencies.' He asked London once again to increase Britain's contribution.[116]

A month later, in September 1950, Daud made it very clear to him that Britain's cosy relationship with his ministry was over:

> The Royal Air Force was part of a defence plan which had failed ... The Afghan government were not pleased with the British approach to the problem of creating an Afghan Air Force, which smacked rather of commercial life than of a desire to help a small but friendly nation to protect itself. For instance, Prince Daud said the Avro Anson machines bought in the United Kingdom had originally been quoted at £12,000 but the actual delivered cost had been nearly £20,000.[117]

Furthermore, it was Britain's responsibility to honour the Lancaster Scheme, not India's. It had been a core part of the Afghan government's plans to build an army and air force on the British model, but Britain had seriously let them down. What was more, Afghanistan had committed to neutrality during the Second World War, which had not been an easy policy position, and received nothing in return.

After this bruising experience, Gardener reflected on just how far Britain's relationship with Afghanistan had changed since 1947:

> The Afghans must realise as well as ourselves that since our departure from the Indian peninsula we, as an individual nation, are no longer so interested in events in Afghanistan, nor prepared nor able to grant concessions to the Afghans to serve our needs. We are therefore, I submit, in no position to induce the realistic and materialistic Afghans to retain the RAF mission should they get a more attractive offer. Our strength here is that of a member of a team of nations interested in maintaining the independence and welfare of this country and one regarded by the Afghans as best able, in view of our experience (but not unfortunately by our material wealth) to contribute to those aims.[118]

He received little support or sympathy from London. The Air Ministry did not think there were any commercial or strategic reasons to pay more for the RAF mission and passed the matter back to the Foreign Office.[119] The Foreign Office had already concluded this was more or less a lost cause anyway and told Gardener: 'In present circumstances, with the urgent defence needs of North Atlantic Treaty countries [NATO] on the one side and the Pashtunistan dispute on the other, Afghanistan's priority for arms and equipment is very low indeed.'[120] In any case, irrespective of whether additional support was provided or not, London increasingly doubted whether British assistance in Afghanistan could really make a material difference either to the overall capability of its air force, or to resist a Soviet invasion:

> I cannot see that there is any particular advantage in trying to force a country like Afghanistan to accept, when those in power are clearly not keen on having it, an RAF mission that is in any case too small to have any real value, at a time when all RAF personnel are badly needed elsewhere, when we neither want nor are in a position to supply aircraft or equipment to Afghanistan, and when we do not think there is any chance of the country offering effective resistance to Russia in any event.[121]

Thereafter, the odd military contract was agreed – for instance, an order was placed with Armstrong-Siddeley's order for Cheetah aero-engines, spares, tools and workshop equipment worth £22,000 in 1950[122] – but these were nowhere near the scale of the Lancaster Scheme or the Avro Anson contract. The key question going forward was whether the Americans would now scale up their role in Afghanistan and pick up from where Britain had left off, or abandon the Great Game politics of the past altogether and move the frontier against Soviet imperialism further south, towards Pakistan and Persia.

31. Sir Giles Squire, his wife Irene, and two of their children, Gillian (left) and Kristen (right) in the embassy gardens. (Courtesy of Hazel Hastings)

32. A group photograph of the embassy team in 1948. Seated from left to right on the front row: Second Secretary Arthur Evans, Counsellor Derek Riches, Sir Giles Squire, Colonel Lancaster, Dr Macrae and Second Secretary Donald Jackson. Sam Simms's head is visible on the back row to the right of Lancaster's left shoulder. (Courtesy of Hazel Hastings)

33. The official photograph published in the Afghan press marking the occasion when the legation was upgraded to embassy status on 25 March 1948. Back row, left to right: Counsellor Derek Riches, Second Secretary Arthur Evans, Dr Ronnie Macrae, Colonel Lancaster, Second Secretary Donald Jackson; middle front, Sir Giles Squire. (Courtesy of Hazel Hastings)

34. Sir Giles Squire at the entrance to the Big House beside his official car, a Humber Snipe. (Courtesy of Hazel Hastings)

Right: 35. Kristen Squire riding her father's favourite stallion, Seistan, named after the area straddling the Persian–Afghan border where the Helmand River ends, and which was to become a point of contention during this period. (Courtesy of Hazel Hastings)

Below: 36. Colonel John Prendergast in Afghanistan. (Courtesy of Hugh Priestley)

37. Colonel Prendergast on a fishing holiday, which he often combined with intelligence-gathering. (Courtesy of Hugh Priestly)

38. John Prendergast fishing in Afghanistan. It was on one such excursion that he was trained to collect information using a fishing rod to calculate the length of a bridge. (Courtesy of John Prendergast)

Above: 39. Zahir Shah, the King of Afghanistan, celebrating Afghan Independence Day, August 1948. (Courtesy of Hazel Hastings)

Right: 40. Sardar Hashim Khan, Prime Minister 1929–46. (Courtesy of the Afghan embassy, London)

41. Sardar Mahmud Khan,
Prime Minister 1946–63.
(Courtesy of the Afghan
embassy, London)

42. Shah Wali Khan,
first Afghan Ambassador
to Pakistan, and later
Ambassador in London.
(Courtesy of the Afghan
embassy, London)

43. Sardar Daud Khan,
Minister of War/Defence and
Prime Minister after 1953.
(Courtesy of the Afghan
embassy, London)

44. Sardar Naim Khan,
Ambassador in Washington
and London, and brother of
Daud Khan. (Courtesy of the
Afghan embassy, London)

Left: 45. Ali Mohammed, Foreign Minister from 1938–53. (Courtesy of the Afghan embassy, London)

Below left: 46. Abdul Majid Zabili, Minister for National Economy. (Courtesy of the Afghan embassy, London)

Below right: 47. Faiz Mohammed Zakria, Afghan Ambassador in London. (Courtesy of the Afghan embassy in London)

48. The Avro-Ansons sold to Afghanistan as part of an arms deal arranged by Colonel Lancaster bringing the independent monitoring team to Khost and Moghulgai on 21 June 1949. (Patrick Keen, Courtesy of the National Archives FO371/75639)

49. The team transfer from jeeps to horses to ride to Moghulgai. (Patrick Keen, Courtesy of the National Archives FO371/75639)

50. Moghulgai: the four rocks with white labels in the foreground mark the spot where four men were killed; to the left of the labels is one of the bomb craters. (Patrick Keen, Courtesy of the National Archives FO371/75639)

51. Tribesmen at Moghulgai. (Patrick Keen, courtesy of the National Archives FO371/75639)

Above: 52. The man with the grey beard in the centre of the picture, Abdus Smad Khan, provided an eyewitness account to the international team. (Patrick Keen, Courtesy of National Archives FO371/75639)

Right: 53. Taken from a rough sketch by Squadron Leader Lee-Evans, showing the fitment from a rocket projectile that he found at Moghulgai. The letters and numbers on this and other fragments identified the rockets as originating from British manufacturers. (Reproduced from part of a National Archives image in FO371/75639 as a computer graphic by Tim Loughhead)

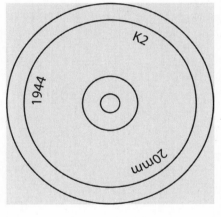

8

Britain's Symbolic Power Is Attacked from All Sides

As long as the war lasted, Great Britain was the only power that counted for anything in Afghanistan, and the British legation was the symbol of that power. Its continuance has, in the public eye, obscured the melancholy fact that other powers have now taken our place. Its lovely grounds, never more beautiful than in the present year, have continued to be the centre of attraction for many residents in Kabul. With its passing into other hands, there will inevitably pass also the last vestige of British influence in Afghanistan.

Sir Giles Squire, 1949[1]

Introduction

Between 1947 and 1950, the British embassy compound in Kabul found itself centre stage too, caught in a post-war austerity drive by Foreign Office officials who saw it as an anachronistic and expensive relic of empire, and a battle for control and ownership by India and Pakistan who claimed it was their property, not Britain's. Throughout my grandfather's time in Kabul, therefore, the legation residents frequently wondered if and when they would need to vacate their homes. At times, the diplomatic negotiations became every bit as tense as the Pashtunistan dispute as the issue became trapped in a two-way dance between Pakistan and India on the one hand and British ministers and officials on the other. The British Government wanted to keep hold of this one remaining symbol of Britain's former greatness in Asia, and were determined to keep this particular dispute away from the Afghan government before a suitable deal was struck.

The first stage of the ensuing drama began on 22 February 1947 when the Permanent Secretary at the Foreign Office, Sir Orme Sargent, issued a circular to all overseas posts requiring them to reduce their running costs, including staff, by 1 October.[2] The man tasked with overseeing this operation was John Gardener, the Head of Establishment and Organisation Department, who was to arrive in Kabul two years later, newly knighted, as Squire's replacement. Gardener's views were clear from the outset: 'We are being pressed to eliminate every possible item of expenditure, which although desirable in the old days, can nevertheless now be dispensed with without loss to the public interest.'[3] Everything he had heard of the premises in Kabul smacked of the waste and extravagance of a bygone age, and an unnecessary drain on the public purse. The transfer of the legation from British Government in India ownership to the Foreign Office seemed therefore to provide an ideal opportunity to cut waste and regularise the relationship between these former representations of empire and the diplomatic service of His Majesty's Government in London.

Soon, however, this issue was eclipsed by a new challenge. Within weeks of Independence, India claimed the legation for their own use on the grounds that it had been built and maintained by the former government of India, not Britain. Although this possibility had been floating around for some time, no-one in Kabul or London believed this would ever actually happen. The arrival of Indian and Pakistani diplomats in Kabul, however, in early 1948 brought things to a head. Britain now had to confront the very real possibility that their occupation of this prestigious address might actually come to an end. Within weeks, however, questions about who was entitled to what also became caught up in wider geo-political struggles – the India–Pakistan conflict over Kashmir, the Afghan–Pakistan dispute over Pashtunistan, and Britain's argument that the loss of the legation would benefit nobody except the Soviet Union.

Austerity

Some aspects of the austerity drive were fairly easy to implement. Once Pakistan opened an office in Kabul that autumn as a precursor to setting up an embassy, some of the legation's Muslim Government of India service officers simply shifted across to work there, including the Oriental and Commercial Secretaries and four of the office staff.[4] Although this was relatively painless, Squire remarked wryly in his journal that the Pakistanis 'have grabbed from us everyone they can get'.[5] By spring 1948, legation numbers had also been reduced through natural wastage, bringing the total number of diplomatic staff down from eight to five, office staff from nineteen to eleven, and messengers from thirteen to nine.

It was also relatively easy to transfer the legation's consulates in Jalalabad and Kandahar to Pakistan. Both were staffed by Indian Muslims and since their main role was issuing visas and motor passes to Afghans travelling to Peshawar and Chaman, it made complete sense for Pakistan to manage this service now, not Britain. The transition period was a little chaotic, but they muddled through: 'The unofficial Pakistan office here has started issuing visas for Pakistan and the two consulates on the Pakistan border issue them for India only. However, they all seem to be equally acceptable on the Frontier for the time-being and I do not propose to interfere until I have to do so.'[6] The confusion rumbled on while the Afghan government negotiated its own right to establish consulates in Peshawar and Quetta and, if possible, Lahore, throughout 1948. The consulates were officially handed over to Pakistan in 1949. Most of the staff opted to work for the new Pakistani consulates, some taking Pakistan citizenship, while the former Consul in Jalalabad moved to Kabul to work in the new embassy.[7]

As far as other costs were concerned, however, it was difficult to justify to London why the British taxpayer should cover the costs of six gardeners in the winter and fourteen in the summer months. Squire therefore offered to pay for some of them out of his own pocket, especially those working to maintain the extensive grounds around the Big House. The legation also paid for the stabling costs of two government horses, a legacy of the original mounted escort used by British ministers for ceremonial occasions. By 1947, their only official duties were to take messages to town. Squire therefore arranged for them to be kept privately at no further cost to the public purse.[8]

Some glitches appeared when the legation started to shift from Government of India to Foreign Office systems and terms and conditions. Initially things went well. The Foreign Office sent out a trained accounting officer to help with the shift to its financing and accounting practices.[9] Soon, however, the Establishment and Organisation Department began to question specific items in the legation's annual budget. One anomaly, it seemed, was why the legation paid a contribution towards the maintenance of the Christian cemetery in Kabul. True, it had begun as a burial ground for British soldiers during the Second Afghan War in 1879, but since 1937, Britain had made it available for use by other Christians irrespective of sect, and the costs were now shared by all the Christian Missions, including the Soviets.[10] After a tense exchange, Gardener accepted that the legation should continue to contribute its share of the costs.

Other expenditures, however, did not make sense to officials in London. Squire patiently explained that the legation had been built as a self-contained complex because Kabul in the 1920s had been 'nothing more than a large native town with no civilised amenities whatsoever'. Supplies had been brought from India because 'nothing at all was available in Kabul itself'. Although things had changed over the last twenty years – some shops now sold imported foodstuffs and other essential items – the prices were very high and generally exceeded people's allowances. He therefore argued that staff should be allowed to continue using the legation lorry, free of charge, to bring supplies from Peshawar. As far as maintaining the garage was concerned, he explained it was more cost-effective to keep the garage and run the lorry to Peshawar directly themselves at £15 a journey than to hire one for between £90 and £150.[11]

Squire and his management team placed great store on a visit by Foreign Office inspectors in early March 1948 to help resolve the impasse. They prepared 'memoranda on every conceivable subject', hoping 'to get some sort of guidance from them as to our future set-up and organisation'.[12] Staff also hoped to discuss pay, and their new terms and conditions of service as they shifted status from Government of India service officers to Foreign Office employees. They were less focussed on the existing benefits they might lose – free electricity, water and fuel in winter – than the fact that their pay and allowances had not kept up with local inflation rates and fallen way behind the levels paid in other Kabul missions. Squire's salary and allowances, for instance, were lower than that of the Second Secretary in the American embassy, and half that of the French Ambassador.[13] My grandfather set great store by their visit too:

> [The War Office] have not recognised my rates of pay and there is still a fight going on between them and the Military Attaché before I am recognised on an adequate scale ie about £55 a month. Even then, I'm not really affluent because everything is so dear around this way. I bought a tube of toothpaste, the very smallest size, cost me 3 shillings, and it's expected to get worse, but this War Office want to give me 5 shillings a day extra, while Foreign Office civilian clerks in inferior jobs are getting £6-700 a year.[14]

The inspection team headed by Gardener's boss, Harold Caccia, arrived expecting to find the legation was an extravagant drain on the public purse, but gradually appreciated the answer was not quite that straightforward, as Squire recorded privately:

> For the last two days, we have been almost completely absorbed with the visit of the Foreign Office inspectors, Caccia and Noble. The former was a delightful guest and we got on with him very well. Noble, who was more concerned with the details and with criticism of our existing set-up, was somewhat more difficult, being by nature silent ... They started off by thinking that we had an impossibly large set-up

with a lot of waste, but in the end seemed to come quite around, and not only to have supported almost all our proposals ... Of course, they recommended changes, chiefly in the way of decreasing our privileges ... and increasing our local allowances so as to bring us more into line with other Foreign Office posts. The upshot of the whole business seems to be that whereas under the allegedly extravagant Indian system, we did four times as much work as we do at present, we shall now be able to do with a net reduction of one officer and three or four clerks and their pay will be as much if not more than formerly.[15]

When the inspectors challenged why all staff, including the Afghans, received a free fuel allowance every winter up to the value of £5 a head, and free water and electricity, Squire dug his heels in. He was concerned that junior staff lacked sufficient pay and allowances to cover these costs, and later explained to London that although his administration office was keeping a record of junior officers' use of electricity, he did not intend to claim that money back from them until the matter of their allowances was resolved. He also sought advice about their fuel allowance for the coming winter.[16] His intervention worked. Nearly three months later, he received a response from the Foreign Office confirming that Simms and Brooks should continue to receive fuel and electricity free of charge.[17]

As far as medical services were concerned, Squire consistently made a strong case for retaining the services of a British doctor rather than employing an Afghan one. He pointed to the example of Ely Palmer, the Minister at the American legation, to underline his point. Palmer had preferred to use one of the King's Afghan physicians, a Dr Zahir, but this came at a high personal cost when the doctor failed to diagnose that Mrs Palmer had had a stroke.[18] Other than Palmer himself, most of the American community secretly visited the British doctor:

I may say frankly that though the American Minister may be prepared, in order to toady to the Afghans, to risk the lives of his wife and family, and of his staff, I am not ... The American legation staff seem to exist largely on a diet of sulpha drugs and penicillin; and still, perhaps for that very reason, most of them appear to be perpetually ill. Their Military Attaché and his subordinates have indeed refused to toe the line and insist on calling in [Dr] Macrae when they need attendance.[19]

Macrae separately informed London about the mysterious circumstances surrounding a robbery at Dr Zahir's house. After a safe containing 40,000 rupees was stolen, Dr Zahir's brother accused the maid's husband of the robbery. The man died during interrogation and a subsequent enquiry conducted by the Minister of Mines concluded that Dr Zahir's brother himself had in fact been the guilty party. He was arrested, Dr Zahir paid a fine, and his brother escaped.[20]

It was less easy, however, to defend why the legation still ran a hospital providing free medical treatment for local people, especially since the numbers had fallen significantly after 1941 when the Afghan government restricted access. Squire's predecessor in Kabul, Sir Francis Verner Wylie, had never been a fan. He felt that so long as the legation provided medical facilities, it undermined Afghan confidence in their own services, gave the impression that Afghanistan still came under British control, and fuelled a distorted view of the role of the legation.[21] He had a point. A number of alternative medical facilities had been established in Kabul over recent years, some employing foreign doctors and nurses from India, France, Russia and Turkey. Although Macrae argued that these medics were so overworked that all serious cases, including among the Soviets, still came to the British hospital, it was still difficult to make the case for such a large establishment, especially during an austerity drive at home.[22]

Squire and Macrae subsequently restructured the hospital and dispensary's finances and arranged to run it on a new cost-sharing basis with other missions in Kabul – India and China were among the first to join the scheme. Unofficially, the hospital and dispensary also continued to treat local Afghans for free, using an existing slush fund. Once Gardener himself arrived in late 1949, he actually changed his opinion about the hospital, so much so that when the Afghan government told him in 1950 to stop admitting Afghans, he told London he was sad to see the end of an era treating 'the inhabitants of "our" village free of charge as a good political investment'.[23] The hospital finally closed for good in 1963.

On some issues where Squire and his team were prepared to make additional cuts, London unexpectedly took a different point of view. The legation had published a daily news bulletin since the early days of the war, using information pulled together from the BBC World Service, material supplied from Delhi and as many news articles as possible from other sources.[24] It was the only European paper of any kind in Kabul and was circulated to all foreign missions and specific Afghan ministries with an interest in international affairs. With a print run of only 125 copies, however, the amount of time taken to produce it seemed to outweigh the benefits, especially as 'the Americans are going to begin their own bulletin shortly and perhaps here, as in so many other places in the world, the time has now come for us to yield our position to America with the best grace we can'.[25] London had already decided otherwise, however. In their view, the legation's information work was to be beefed up, not wound down. Instructions were duly sent to Kabul to recruit two or three more Morse code operators so that the whole of the daily London Press Service could be captured to make the bulletin more comprehensive. This decision drove up costs considerably, and far more than London had anticipated because there were no operators available in Afghanistan and so they had to be recruited from Pakistan. Over the longer term, however, London's judgement proved to be right. In the mid-1950s, demand was so high that the black market price for each copy was around 20 afghanis, nearly £4.[26]

The Campaign Begins

Alongside London's austerity drive, Squire and his team also found themselves receiving demands from the incoming Pakistani and Indian delegations to vacate the compound and hand it over to them. Questions had been circulating since 1942 about the potential impact of Indian independence on Britain's continued occupation of diplomatic and consular buildings in the Indian Empire and the Persian Gulf because the money used to purchase the land and build, furnish and maintain the houses and offices had been paid by the British Government of India, not the Treasury in London. Britain's continued right to retain any of these premises after independence was therefore potentially on questionable ground. Squire was quick to point out to London in 1946 that the legation was far more than a diplomatic compound. It represented Britain's status in Asia, while its loss would symbolise the ultimate collapse of Britain's influence in Afghanistan:

> It would be disastrous to hand over the buildings for the Indian legation. This legation has stood since its construction as a monument to Britain's position in this country and has been entirely associated with His Majesty's Government. It may be pretentious and unsuitable, as it is, certainly somewhat uncomfortable to live in, but it far outshines all other legations and embassies and stands in a class by itself. If we were to hand it over to the Indian government and move ourselves into an ordinary house in the town, we should suffer a tremendous loss of prestige and it would be considered a sure sign in Afghanistan that Britain's day was done.[27]

Whatever Squire may have thought, however, Clause 4 of the Indian Independence (Rights, Properties and Liabilities) Order, which was issued on the eve of independence on 14 August, changed the situation overnight. This stated that all properties, both moveable and immovable, of the former British Government in India should be transferred to the new governments in India and Pakistan.[28] Although Britain later argued that this had merely been a holding order drafted at short notice to prevent chaos in the interim period between independence and the joint India–Pakistan Partition Council in December where the details would be fleshed out, the die had been cast. Over subsequent months, the Order was to set the framework for all subsequent discussions.

Initially, Britain was fairly confident that the matter could be resolved relatively easily. On the same day as the Order was issued, the British sent an aide-memoire listing which diplomatic and consular properties they wanted to purchase from India and Pakistan. Kabul and Kathmandu were on the list. No one anticipated at that time, however, that the Pakistanis and the Indians would lay claim to the legation premises and furnishings more or less as soon as they set foot in Kabul.

The Pakistan team were the first to arrive in September 1947. Khan Bahadur Mumtaz Hasan Qizilbash came as Jinnah's personal representative and Saidullah Khan, a former Indian Civil Service officer, came as a special representative with the rank of minister and responsibility for negotiating the opening of a Pakistan embassy. Even before he arrived on the 25th, Saidullah had asked the British legation for furniture and office equipment.[29] As Squire tried to work out how best to meet his request, he was warned by the High Commission in Delhi that tensions between India and Pakistan over Kashmir and ongoing communal violence in Punjab and Bengal were likely to preclude negotiations to purchase the legation for the foreseeable future. He was also reassured that 'possession is nine-tenths of the law, and I should imagine that there is no fear that your occupation of the buildings, and use of their furniture, will be disturbed by either of the other two parties in the near future'.[30] Unfortunately, this conclusion soon proved to be wide of the mark.

To address the immediate issue, the legation supplied Saidullah with furniture from the former Government of India Trade Agency in Kabul, but on condition that this was not given outright since the new Indian government had a claim on it too. This seemingly innocuous act, however, sparked an immediate reaction in Delhi. The Ministry of External Affairs claimed they were unaware of an agreement that furniture in any diplomatic post in the region should be divided between Pakistan and India, and made clear that all furniture should remain with the buildings in which they were housed. Squire was then instructed by London to take no further action until an overall settlement about the division of premises was decided.[31]

He found himself caught between a rock and a hard place – dealing with fractious Indian and Pakistani demands on the one hand, and

Gardener's austerity drive on the other. He set out his frustrations in a memo to a colleague in the High Commission in Delhi on 17 October:

> [I] have no idea what His Majesty's Government's attitude will be if India and Pakistan insist that we should get out (as Pakistanis here say quite openly that we are going to be forced to do). As regards furniture and moveable property, I am completely in the dark. India and Pakistan seem to be fighting over it and I have been faced with very awkward but obviously premature demands to hand over at once to the new Pakistan mission anything that they want. That I have had to resist these demands does not make for good relations. And I do not know whether His Majesty's Government is even contemplating offering to purchase the furniture. If not, then obviously we should immediately set about buying furniture etc for our own needs though how that is going to be done, I do not quite know … But this is by no means the whole story. I am being urged by the Foreign Office to cut down expenditure; but how can I sell, for instance, a government horse unless I know whether it belongs to His Majesty's Government, India or Pakistan. Meanwhile I have to feed it at His Majesty's Government's expense.[32]

In the meantime, the Pakistan team in Kabul had asked for help. They had no guidelines about what rates of pay and allowances to offer staff, no copies of key regulations, and lacked detailed information about the political landscape in Afghanistan. To assist them, the British legation sent over 3,000 files to their office, as well as the Indian Sea Customs Manual, which had been specifically requested by Qizilbash 'to enable us to make a reference to the Pakistan government for refund of a customs duty charged for Major R.D. Macrae on a parcel received for him'.[33] Working out which files or parts of files could be shared was an extremely time-consuming business. Each file had to be screened to check it did not contain any secret papers that might compromise Britain's position or embarrass British officials. On at least one occasion, the system failed. An astute member of the Pakistan team spotted a reference to the legation's 'Black List' and Qizilbash then asked to see the file because 'we find ourselves in difficulties in regard to the records of blacklisted persons who are pestering us for visa facilities for Pakistan'. The legation agreed to share it after some hesitation, but made it clear that the 'list' related to Britain's policy to monitor 'highly placed persons' during the war, not to the present. Anxious to be even-handed, the legation asked for this file to be returned in due course because 'the Indian embassy, when set up, may also wish to refer to it in individual cases'.[34] By the end of 1947, Squire had asked for additional staff to help with this exercise.

On 3 January, Squire received more worrying news, this time from the British Ambassador in Persia. The Indian Ambassador had just informed him that India owned all former Government of India properties in Persia, including the present British embassy premises, and now planned to take over the ones they needed, leaving the remainder for Pakistan. If Pakistan was due any compensation after this division, payment would be handled by their respective governments. Understandably, the British Ambassador sought urgent advice from London.[35] A few days later, Sir Girla Bajpai, the Indian Foreign Minister, told the High Commission in Delhi that India wanted their Ambassador to Kabul housed in the British legation buildings as soon as possible after his arrival. He made no mention of Britain's request to purchase the premises, nor Pakistan's right to an equal share.[36]

Officials in London, Kabul, Delhi, Kathmandu and Karachi tried to work out what to do next. Their starting point was to consult the original papers in the archives to determine who had actually purchased the land and paid for the buildings in Kabul and Kathmandu – the British government or the British government in India. As far as Afghanistan was concerned, the answer had to lie in the terms of the 1921 Anglo-Afghan Treaty and how this was interpreted at the time. This included the exceptional right for a named foreign state to purchase land in Kabul on the understanding that it would use it for diplomatic premises.[37] A treaty with the Government of Nepal included similar provisions.[38] The clause suggested that the Afghan government's diplomatic relations were with the British government, not the British government in India, and that they had never envisaged the premises could be transferred to any future government of an independent India. If Britain now tried to pass the land and compound to another government, the Afghans could simply claim that this was contrary to the terms of the Treaty and claim it for themselves.[39] One of the papers in Kabul, a telegram sent in 1921 from Sir Henry Dobbs, the main British negotiator, seemed to confirm this:

> They [the Afghans] like to consider their present negotiations as being, not with Government of India, but with His Majesty's Government. For this reason, I believe they would regard it as a grave slight if the first British Minister under the new treaty were an Indian Muslim, as hitherto, and would interpret such an appointment as an attempt on our part to revert to [the] old state of affairs.[40]

Back in London, the Foreign Office's legal advisers concluded in March that the Indian Independence Order of 14 August did not have any bearing on Britain's existing rights to these properties.[41]

Given that the new India and Pakistan Ambassadors were scheduled to arrive imminently, it was deemed advisable to refer the matter to Bevin for a political steer. Harold Caccia, who had visited Kabul the previous month, was present at the meeting on 10 April and wrote up the note of the discussion. Bevin listened carefully to all the arguments, and concluded that 'it is highly undesirable in the present state of general political unrest that the efficient working of the two missions or the position they hold in the eyes of the Governments of Afghanistan or Nepal should be impaired by being removed from their present quarters'. Indeed, 'India's best interests would be served by allowing the United Kingdom government to remain in undisputed tenancy of the two missions'. He was, however, prepared to consider how best to meet India's demands. He agreed with an assessment that the Kathmandu site could be physically divided between Britain and India. Since Pakistan had not expressed a wish to establish an embassy there, this should, he felt, be relatively easy so long as India acknowledged its responsibility to compensate Pakistan.

Kabul, however, needed to be handled differently. The compound could not be divided because it worked as a homogenous physical unit with shared services. Bevin also accepted the argument that the Afghan government would be unlikely to allow any transfer to the Indian government since they had specifically given it to Britain for use by the British government. He was therefore 'firmly convinced that His Majesty's Government in the United Kingdom must continue permanently to occupy the present site and buildings'. He also acknowledged that Pakistan had a stake in Kabul too, even though the 'government has not yet formally claimed any share in the assets', and that Britain should therefore compensate the Indian government at an agreed valuation, but India in turn would need to accept responsibility for Pakistan's claims. As a last resort, Bevin concluded, Britain should 'be prepared to build residential and office accommodation for the account of the Indian government on any site which the latter may be able to acquire through the Afghan government'.[42]

The Indian Ambassador, Wing Commander Rup Chand, was scheduled to arrive in Kabul on 24 April, and Pakistan's Ambassador, Ismail Ibrahim Chundrigar, on 23 May. These two men's life stories epitomised the upheavals over the last year. Rup Chand had begun his life in what was now Pakistan, while Chundrigar had spent much of his personal and professional life in India. Rup Chand was born in Lahore and his father had been a general in the Indian Army. He had joined the British Royal Air Force, seeing action in the First World War, and then joined the Indian Air Force. After that, he had been elected by a non-Muslim constituency to the Indian National Assembly and later appointed to the Council of State. Chundrigar, in contrast, was a professional lawyer with a degree from Bombay, and been a member of Ahmedabad's Municipal Council from 1924 to 1927 and of the Working Committee of the All India Muslim League from 1943 to 1948. Most recently, he had been one of five Muslim League members of the Interim Government of India, acting as Commerce Minister from October 1946 to August 1947. After independence, he was appointed Pakistan's Minister of Commerce before being selected to head up the new mission in Kabul.[43]

Right up to the eleventh hour, Squire continued to receive instructions from London about what to say to Rup Chand on arrival, and what to offer by way of office space, equipment, accommodation and transport. On 22 April, he was told to inform him that the future of the embassy was still under discussion. 'You should of course, as you propose, soften this blow by extending courtesies and facilities to the Indian Ambassador. In particular you should do whatever you can informally to ensure that there is other suitable and adequate accommodation provided for him.' A day later, this despatch was qualified with another instruction. The term 'facilities' 'should *not* include offer of bungalow accommodation even on a temporary basis'.[44]

Meanwhile, the High Commission in Delhi arranged for a car to be sent from Srinagar in Kashmir to Kabul for the Ambassador's use, and informed the Ministry of External Affairs that the legation would provide assistance with transport and furniture until decisions about the future of the compound were finalised. Temporary accommodation was booked for him and his team at the Kabul Hotel in Dar-al-Aman, the site of ex-King Amanullah's proposed new capital five miles outside Kabul and now reserved for important visitors and state guests. Two offices were set aside for their use in the legation's chancery building. When the Ambassador and his team finally arrived, however, they decided that they preferred to use the former Indian Trade Agency. The immediate crisis was over. Clearly, all the efforts taken in the intervening weeks to find accommodation and office space had paid off. As Squire told London:

> It was as well that I did so as both Puri [Indian Cultural Attaché], and Kapur, the Military Attaché, have admitted that the reason why their government had taken no action to secure more permanent accommodation was that they had counted on taking over the present legation buildings immediately. They seem, however, to have accepted the present position with a reasonably good grace, and will now have to start looking around.[45]

The question of who owned which piece of furniture rumbled on, however, throughout 1948. The British assumed that the Pakistanis had already returned all the borrowed furniture and now sought to lend these pieces to the Indians. In November 1948, however, they found several pieces missing, but when Squire asked Chundrigar to return the chairs, he received a rather curt reply:

> Strictly speaking, neither you nor the Indian embassy at Kabul are ... justified in asking the Pakistan embassy for the return of the few articles of the Indian Trade Agency which are now with us. However, as Kizilbash had obtained these from you on the definite understanding that they will be returned when asked for, and as you find yourself in an embarrassing position because you have undertaken to deliver these to the Indian embassy when called upon, I have reluctantly come to the conclusion that I should return these to you without prejudice to the right of the Pakistan government to a share in the assets of the Indian Trade Agency.[46]

Searching for Ways out of the Impasse

Throughout the 'battle of the furniture', confusion about the legal status of the British compound rumbled on against the back-drop of worsening relations between Pakistan and India over Kashmir, and Pakistan and Afghanistan over Pashtunistan. British diplomats in Kabul found themselves in the increasingly bizarre situation of seeing the legation being upgraded to embassy status that April, but at the same time being under threat of imminent eviction. India continued to pile on the pressure. Rup Chand told anyone who would listen that he would be occupying the British embassy compound within six months.[47] In Delhi, Kumara Menon, the Permanent Secretary in the Foreign Ministry, not only asserted that the property indisputably belonged to India, but also that it was Britain's responsibility to help India raise her profile in Afghanistan by handing it over:

> The prestige of His Majesty's Government was both firmly established and high in Afghanistan, whereas India, a newcomer to international affairs, had yet to create hers; occupation of the embassy buildings would be a big step to that end, and the handing over of the premises to India would enhance, rather than diminish, the prestige of His Majesty's Government. It would, he thought, be a gesture much appreciated by the Afghans, and that His Majesty's Government were better able than the Government of India to build new premises in Kabul, since they could obtain materials from (or via) Pakistan the more easily.[48]

In spite of all the arguments presented by the Indian government, however, the British could not fathom out why India was making all the running, while the Pakistan government, except for a few complaints from Chundrigar, had said virtually nothing. Their silence over Kathmandu made sense since Pakistan had few interests to protect there, but Kabul was a different story. There, it should have been Pakistan, not India, calling the shots. As India increasingly piled on the pressure, the British therefore decided to find out what had happened at the Partition Council meeting in December 1947 where the finer details of the division of properties and assets had ostensibly been sorted out. Perhaps, they wondered, Pakistan had already agreed to sign the property over to India and Britain was therefore working from a false premise.

The Partition Council discussions had been held behind closed doors and so the High Commission in Delhi tried to find someone who had actually attended it and was willing to share his recollections. They eventually found a source at the Foreign Ministry, a Mr Ratnam. On 13 May, he unofficially showed them a letter purporting to be from the Pakistan Prime Minister to the Secretary of the Partition Council, dated 19 November, stating that Pakistan had contracted itself out of its rights to any of the properties at the council, and accepted a monetary settlement in lieu of any future claims.[49] Armed with this information, the British asked the Pakistan government if this was their understanding too. After a series of exchanges, the government finally told Grafftey-Smith on 6 July that Pakistan had definitely not contracted itself out of its rights to these properties in exchange for a financial settlement. Indeed, they had received a letter from the Indian Foreign Ministry on 21 February inviting them to indicate which properties they were interested in. They had not yet replied, however. Grafftey-Smith drew his own conclusions:

> The fact that it has taken nearly six weeks and several urgent reminders to obtain from [the] Pakistan government a final reply to our enquiry about [the] Government of India's latest contention suggests that they are not sure of their ground, and [the] first reactions of the Ministry of Foreign Affairs lead me to suspect that [the] Pakistan representatives at [the] Partition Council meeting may possibly have agreed to some form of compensation.[50]

It was becoming increasingly clear that Britain needed to tread very carefully. If Britain backed India's claims in Kabul, relations with Pakistan would be undermined. If they favoured Pakistan, the Afghans would object. At the same time, the Pakistan embassy themselves had given little indication that they wanted to move into the compound, even though the furniture dispute rumbled on. True it was patently too large for their needs, so perhaps, speculated London, their policy was driven more by a desire to stop it falling into Indian hands than wanting to obtain it for themselves.[51] The wisest course seemed to be to follow Bevin's advice and offer to buy the compound lock, stock and barrel. The Treasury had already agreed to release additional funds for this purpose so that just left the relatively minor problem of determining how much it was worth and which country should be paid what.

Over the next few months, officials explored whether compensation should be offered at the book value of the premises, the original purchase and building price, or the current value. Unsurprisingly, they opted for the lowest price and then stood ready to make an offer when the time was right. Alongside this, diplomatic efforts focussed on convincing the Indians that the purpose of the property in Kabul from the outset had been to represent the British government, not the British government in India, and that the Afghan government would not agree to a transfer of the site to a third party. The Acting High Commissioner in Delhi was instructed by London to convey these points to Bajpai, including talking through Bevin's offer to pay compensation to both the Indian and Pakistan governments, and recommending trilateral discussions to resolve the matter once and for all.

The meeting did not go well, at least initially:

> Bajpai, in a tone which was somewhat aggressive from the start, said that the Government of India did not recognise that His Majesty's Government had any rights in the properties whatever ... The fact that the Kabul embassy formerly pursued certain United Kingdom interests was no more relevant in regard to this question than the fact that a component of the Indian Army which had always been kept ready as an expeditionary force for United Kingdom purposes was relevant in connection with the division of the India Army. The United Kingdom government had been responsible during that period for the conduct of India's affairs in Kabul and, with the transfer of power, all rights in the Kabul property were similarly transferred.

Bajpai also thought the suggestion of tripartite talks was simply a ruse to delay a decision given the current standoff between India and Pakistan and rejected the idea that Bevin's viewpoint was even relevant: 'The position must be clearly understood that India was an independent country and any suggestion that the views of the British Foreign Secretary were mandatory as far as India was concerned was totally unacceptable.'

Given this inauspicious start, British diplomats were somewhat taken aback when the meeting took an unexpected turn. As Ratnam's communication with the British High Commission was brought into the conversation, Bajpai seemed unaware that Pakistan had agreed to compensation at the Partition Council, and 'was somewhat embarrassed by this reference from his own side to a case payment to Pakistan in respect of rights which he had been at pains to explain had never existed'.[52]

The next opportunity to move the issue forward was in the margins of the Commonwealth Prime Ministers' meeting in London in November. In preparation, British officials decided to change tack dramatically, moving away from legal arguments about who had the right to the premises, to an appeal based on the value to all three countries of Britain retaining its prestige and influence in Afghanistan. Caccia was charged with developing the argument:

> No amount of legal wrangling can solve this problem, and we do not think that it is to our interest to allow the argument to be restricted to legalities. Indeed, we should like Sir G. Bajpai to be brought to realise that this is precisely a question of policy and not merely a straightforward legal question of the interpretation of the Indian Independence Order. The fundamental reason why we do not want to give up the embassy is political … We consider it to be essential that our influence and prestige with the Afghans should be maintained, first for fear of increasing Russian influence, and, secondly, because the United Kingdom alone is in a position to act as a stabilising influence between Afghanistan and Pakistan (and for that matter, between Pakistan and India). If we were to give up the embassy, this would be regarded as a retreat on our part by everyone concerned, and to that extent, our influence would decline.[53]

His argument was very persuasive. The focus therefore shifted towards a plan to persuade Nehru that Britain had an important role to play in countering 'Russian domination,' their common threat, and that Britain's diplomatic presence in Kabul was a key pillar of that strategy. They decided not to mention, however, Britain's role in stabilising Afghan–Pakistan and India–Pakistan relations.

This new political approach hit home, in the short term at least. Sir Orme Sargent, the head of the diplomatic service, talked to Bajpai in London on 10 November:

> I asked Bajpai to consider what would be the effect of our clearing out of the embassy lock, stock and barrel, and being left without any house or home in Kabul. It would of course be regarded as an outward and

visible proof that we were finished in that part of the world ... The Governments of India and Pakistan could scarcely stand to gain by this. On the other hand, the Russian government would have every reason for rubbing in to the Afghans that our influence was at an end [and] that they had much better rely on their powerful neighbour who would not be here today and gone tomorrow.

As Caccia had hoped, Bajpai agreed this was an important consideration and, what was more, stated for the first time that one of the key factors influencing his government's view was actually practical, not political. The Indians, it seems, were having considerable difficulty finding a suitable site for their embassy. If they had to build one, many of the building materials would have to come from India, but it would probably be impossible to transport anything through Pakistan at present.[54]

Privately, the British had some sympathy with that argument. A British architect had visited Kabul earlier in the year and assessed the viability of building a new British embassy. He had concluded this was impractical from an engineering viewpoint and prohibitive financially. There were no British companies operating in Afghanistan with the capacity to undertake this work, and even the American company, Morrison Knudsen, would still need to transport engineers and equipment from Britain. He had also found out that smaller works undertaken by Afghans under European supervision were way behind schedule because of a lack of available materials. To cap it all, the actual cost of building an embassy similar to the current compound would now be 'astronomical and out of all proportion to the value of the existing buildings'.[55]

The Legal Advisers Change their Mind

Although there appeared to have been a meeting of minds in November, Indian demands did not let up over the following year. Nehru personally continued to raise the matter throughout 1949 with Bevin and Sir Archibald Nye, the High Commissioner, at every opportunity.[56] Britain's offer to buy the property was rejected outright. The Indian High Commissioner in London, Krishna Menon, told Bevin on 24 June 1949 that Britain should simply hand over the title deeds of the Kabul and Kathmandu properties to India, and leave India to sort out any compensation for Pakistan.[57] When Bevin was consulted, he decided it was time to get more legal advice.

This time around, the advisers revised their earlier view and now concluded that under the Government of India Act of 1935, 'the main purpose [of the legation] or at least a substantial purpose was [for] the

Government of India, even if there were also a further purpose which consisted in the protection of United Kingdom interests'. They had come to this conclusion because the 1935 Act used the expression 'vested in His Majesty for the purpose of the Government of India'. The site in Kathmandu was a slightly different case because it had been acquired for the British Resident in 1806 while India was governed by the East India Company, but nevertheless 'the United Kingdom could not successfully maintain title to either of these premises and that their ownership is a matter to be decided between the Governments of India and Pakistan'.[58]

Britain's legal and political grounds for retaining the Kabul and Kathmandu premises had been removed in one fell swoop. Attlee therefore agreed at a meeting of the China and South-East Asia Committee at the end of July that letters should be sent to Nehru and Liaquat Ali Khan informing them about the advice and asking for time to find alternative accommodation while the two governments agreed between themselves who should have what.[59]

The Indian reaction was unexpected. Krishna Menon told the Foreign Office they should have consulted Nehru about the revised legal opinion first before sending out the letters, and should not have informed Pakistan it had equal rights to the properties. He claimed this had been agreed between himself and Bevin during a meeting on 24 June. Although this assertion was vigorously refuted by the British both then and on subsequent occasions, the question of what Bevin had, or had not agreed, was to be raised several times by the Indians over the next two years.[60] In the short term, however, to keep the Indians on side, a hurried telegram was despatched to Grafftey-Smith on 3 August asking him to delay forwarding the letter to Liaquat Ali Khan, explaining 'we contemplate [a] delay of only a few days and not revision of our decision to tell Pakistan our views'.[61] It was too late. The letter had already been delivered three days earlier. Nye was then instructed to speak to Nehru, but he urged caution:

> It is more than probable that Pandit Nehru may be annoyed over this issue because India has consistently taken the line that these buildings belong to the Government of India and that Pakistan (and for that matter ourselves) have no rights to them. I am therefore disinclined to stir up a potential hornet's nest without really good reason for doing so … to discuss it on such a basis either with him, Bajpai or anyone else might, I fear, only make matters worse.[62]

A hornet's nest had already been stirred up, however. The Indian government sent an aide-memoire on 17 August stating that Britain's invitation to Pakistan to put forward a claim was 'an act wholly unjustified and amounted to an act of discourtesy to the Government of India'. To back up their argument, they referred to a note written by Sir Denys Bray on 27 August 1928, when he was Secretary in the Foreign Affairs Department in Delhi. In this, Bray stated that Afghanistan had not wanted to establish diplomatic relations with the British government in India in 1921, because 'her independence from India's tutelage is too recent'. The Afghans had therefore insisted 'as a wholly independent nation on having relations with His Majesty's Government'. However, since 'His Majesty's Government's interest in Afghanistan is almost wholly confined to India's interest,' this was merely a 'camouflage whereby India's relations with Afghanistan are conducted nominally through His Majesty's Government'.[63] The aide-memoire therefore asserted:

> On the contrary, the Government of India are of the view that the matter can only be discussed between His Majesty's Government and the Government of India and that the Government of Pakistan have no locus standi whatever ... The basic conception underlying the Partition of India was to ensure the continuity of the Government of India, particularly in foreign affairs. This position was accepted and finds confirmation in the fact that after Partition, India continued to be a Member of the United Nations, and it was the state of Pakistan which had to seek admission as a new state ... Pursuant to this basic conception, the broad policy adopted at the time of Partition was to vest in India all properties which were not specifically assigned to Pakistan.[64]

While officials in London were intrigued by the reference to Bray, they did not agree with the arguments about the relative status of the two countries at Partition, nor the potential implications for the division of properties and assets. The Foreign Office therefore sent a holding reply and then wondered whether to inform the Afghan and Nepalese governments about the situation since both had been kept completely in the dark up to that point. Squire was not at all encouraging. The Afghan government were still bruised by Secretary of State Noel-Baker's announcement in the House of Commons at the end of July backing Pakistan's claim to the tribal territories. Indeed, this had effectively removed his credibility as an honest broker in their dealings with Pakistan in one fell swoop. If Britain was to inform them now that the embassy itself was about to be handed over to India or Pakistan, 'the knowledge will I fear, destroy the last vestige of British influence in Afghanistan'.[65]

Privately, on the eve of his departure from Kabul for good, Squire was despondent. The last few days had been depressing on account of the legal opinion which has now been given after two years that these buildings do not after all belong to us and that India and Pakistan must decide among themselves what is to be done with the place. We have thus been living here under false pretences. I have seen the lawyers' opinion which seems pretty well convincing ... But the blow is a severe one. To think of all the love and labour that has been put into this place especially into the garden by successive Ministers. British influence too in the country will inevitably receive its final blow when the change is accomplished, and it all seems so unnecessary too. I am indeed glad that I am going but pity my successor ... It makes it even more depressing when I go round the garden in the morning to think that in another few months the place may not even be British, though of course there is many a slip – and certainly Pakistan and India will find it yet another bone of contention.[66]

He left Kabul for the last time two weeks later, believing that the embassy and its gardens were a lost cause, along with just about everything British power and influence had meant to him in Afghanistan. Sharing that last journey with him from Kabul was Chundrigar, one of his regular bridge partners, on his way to meetings in Karachi. This was unplanned, however – Chundrigar's car had broken down so he was cadging a lift to Jalalabad. One can only speculate whether Squire and Chundrigar shared their private thoughts as they whiled away the hours in the back of the embassy lorry.

The Confusion Continues

Back in London, officials in the Foreign Office had spotted an additional problem:

> If the dispute between India and Pakistan over these properties drags on for years, as it well may if we leave it to them, and if we move out of the Kabul embassy with its ownership still unsettled, the Afghans may well take over themselves as caretakers and never move out. They will probably be glad to find an excuse for denying to either India or Pakistan the prestige which occupation of these buildings would confer.

In that scenario, India and Pakistan would blame Britain. Indeed, 'we shall incur less odium in the long-run if we offer to help India and Pakistan to settle the question of ownership ... than if we attempt to wash our hands of the whole problem and to move out leaving our succession unsettled'.[67] They decided to delay responding to the Indian aide-memoire and writing to the Nepalese and Afghan governments until they had consulted the legal advisers once again.

This time round, the advisers concluded on 2 September that since Britain had never been informed officially about the outcome of the Partition Council meeting, and India and Pakistan appeared to have different interpretations of it, the two should resolve the issue bilaterally and not involve Britain at all. Irrespective of whether the legation in Kabul had represented the British government or the British government in India, 'the procedure at Kabul ... was that designed to preserve the facade of control of His Majesty's Government relations with Afghanistan by the Foreign Office'. All correspondence with the legation was always addressed to the Foreign Office, but copied to the Government of India in Delhi and the India Office in London, both of whom were primarily responsible for dealing with them, 'issuing through the Foreign Office in the name of the Secretary of State for Foreign Affairs'. Ultimate control was therefore never in the hands of India.[68]

Sir Hartley Shawcross, the Attorney General, was consulted too. He also focussed on whether the legations in Kabul and Kathmandu had represented the interests of India according to the evidence quoted from Bray's 1928 note, or of Britain. He concluded that Bray's points were a red herring and that nothing further could be produced to substantiate this argument one way or the other:

> It is difficult to conceive that the Indian government can produce further documents or information showing that the envoys at Kabul and Kathmandu were not the official representatives of His Majesty's Government in the United Kingdom, but on the contrary, the official representatives of the Indian government ... I cannot myself see that any very useful purpose is served by keeping the door open for further argument.[69]

Armed with this information, the Foreign Office felt ready to respond to the Indians on 23 September. The Attorney General himself was involved in crafting the final draft. The British made clear that the government 'would only be justified in handing the properties over unconditionally to the Government of India without ascertaining the view of the Government of Pakistan if it were abundantly clear that the latter government could have no possible right or claim to them'. Given the legal advice to date, however, 'the Government of the United Kingdom cannot consider that this is so'.[70] The Foreign Office expected a swift reply, but nothing arrived. More puzzling still, the Pakistan government had made no reference at all to the letter sent by Britain back in June to Prime Minister Liaquat

Ali Khan notifying him of Pakistan's rights to a share of the property in Kabul – the very same letter which had sparked Britain's dispute with India in the first place.

By now, the British had also concluded it made sense to treat the cases of Kathmandu and Kabul separately. Bevin therefore wrote a personal message to Menon on 25 November 1949, spelling out how difficult the whole issue had become, notwithstanding any of the political issues at stake:

> When Pandit Nehru was here recently, he mentioned this to me and said he thought we had made a mistake in bringing Pakistan into the problem. I replied that I had to be guided by the legal advice I had been given, according to which both governments had an interest in these embassy premises ... Our position is [now] a difficult one; we cannot proceed with building (or even with plans for building or with the necessary final appropriations) until we know what sites the buildings are going to occupy. We cannot, however, take steps to acquire sites without first notifying the Afghan and Nepalese governments of our intention to vacate the existing premises, and we do not wish to make this notification to the Afghan and Nepalese governments until we know that the Governments of India and Pakistan approve of our action. Thus we have got into a vicious circle.

To help get everyone out of the mess, he proposed a two-stage process. Britain and India should go ahead with their plans to divide the site in Kathmandu, seeking approval first from Pakistan before asking the Nepalese government to agree to the arrangement. As far as Kabul was concerned, he proposed that Britain should inform the Afghan government that a new site was needed for the British embassy.[71] In parallel, Grafftey-Smith in Karachi tried to get the long overdue response from the Pakistan government. He finally received one on 1 February 1950, more than six months after the original letter had been sent. The response unfortunately created more problems than it solved. Pakistan not only affirmed both properties were jointly owned with India, but also stated:

> The Governments of Afghanistan and Nepal are being formally notified of Pakistan's claim to a share in these buildings and are being informed that, while the Government of Pakistan will gladly concur in the continued occupation by the British Ambassadors pending a final settlement, they must make express reservations against any proposal for their transfer in present circumstances to the Government of India.[72]

Not surprisingly, officials in London concluded that this made the situation more confused, not less. It took them one step forward in that Pakistan agreed with the British position; one step backwards because Pakistan had now staked a claim in Nepal; and one step sideways because Pakistan had notified the governments of Nepal and Afghanistan of their interest![73]

A stalemate was reached over the following months. Menon finally replied to Bevin on behalf of his government on 17 June 1950, but this did not take matters any further. Although he did not agree with the legal advice that Pakistan had a claim to the properties, the result of this advice was that the Kathmandu compound could not be divided until Pakistan's position was taken into account. He asked Britain to write to the Afghan and Nepalese governments saying that Britain intended to leave the premises.[74] Pakistan was equally slow to act, but when they did, in September 1950, they adopted a new line of argument:

> The Government of Pakistan are unable to understand their [Britain's] eagerness to secure land on which to build new premises for themselves in Kabul and Kathmandu. The Government of Pakistan will have no objection to selling their share of the jointly owned properties to His Majesty's Government who may continue to occupy their present premises as they have done hitherto.

If, however, Britain wanted to leave the Kabul premises, then Pakistan would be interested in taking these over.[75]

Both governments had therefore now staked a claim to the premises in Kabul, but neither had accepted the rights of the other. The Foreign Office wrote in despair to Gardener in Kabul on 18 October that 'the chance of both agreeing to sell to us, rather than give to one another ... is extremely slight'.[76] Gardener agreed it was a no-win situation and reiterated Squire's view that if Britain moved out of the premises before an agreement was in the bag, the Afghans would in all likelihood take over the site in accordance with the terms of the 1921 Treaty, rather than 'making the invidious choice between India and Pakistan'. Moreover:

> As seen from here, while the Indians definitely want us to move out of the present compound, the Pakistanis just as definitely do not want us to move ... The local effect on the Pakistan embassy of our moving out would merely be regarded as another and a serious instance of His Majesty's Government's desire to appease India at all costs, including that of important interests of Pakistan. In this attitude, I must confess that I would have some sympathy with them since there is no

question but that Pakistan has greater and more important interests here than India, and if it is necessary to build up the prestige of one of the two countries, it should logically be Pakistan who should be favoured. In any event, our cooperation with the Pakistan embassy would be seriously undermined.[77]

The next opportunity to resolve the matter was at the Commonwealth Prime Ministers' meeting in London in January 1951. To help pave the way for a settlement, Gardener was asked to approach the Afghan government to find a new site for the British embassy, [78] while Bajpai was informed that Britain had got the ball rolling.[79] Meanwhile, Bevin asked Liaquat Ali Khan if Pakistan would be prepared to approve the division of the Kathmandu site between India and Britain in exchange for compensation. He agreed.[80]

As far as Kabul was concerned, however, timing was of the essence. The British calculated that if they moved out of the premises too quickly, this could add to India–Pakistan discord and damage relations between Britain and Pakistan irrevocably. As Gardener explained, 'India would in all probability immediately occupy the premises – with I feel, under present circumstances, Afghan approval – by force if necessary – and for this outcome Pakistan would with justice hold us responsible.' Whatever Britain did, it would lose its prestige and status as soon as it vacated the premises and so at the very least it should get the timing right:

In the eyes of Afghans who frankly will not understand our action, in the interests of Anglo-Pakistan relations, the longer the notice of leaving we give, the better. Therefore the timing must be a compromise between Indian requests to us to evacuate and Pakistan requests for us to stay.[81]

Finally, at the end of February 1951, Gardener was authorised by London to approach Ali Mohammed for a 5-acre site in Shari-i-Nau, a new development area in Kabul. A month later, in one of his first acts after taking over from a sick Bevin at the Foreign Office, Herbert Morrison wrote to Nehru and Liaquat Ali Khan informing them that Britain intended to build new embassies in Kabul and Kathmandu and would vacate the present properties when their new premises were ready.[82] He concluded by suggesting that, 'the best solution in each case might be for the Governments of India and Pakistan to agree that one should succeed to the occupation of the property, while the other is compensated by a financial payment'. A viable solution seemed close to hand, even though it meant Britain giving up Kabul entirely, as well as half of the Kathmandu site.

Herbert Morrison's letter to Delhi unfortunately crossed in the post with a new aide-memoire from India, which was delivered to the Foreign Office on 11 April 1951. This copiously listed all the meetings and correspondence between Britain and India on the subject since 1947 and, in frustration, pointed out that Britain had been shifting ground constantly:

> Originally, the British government were anxious to acquire the property in Kabul and divide the property in Kathmandu. Subsequently they sought to justify their retention of these properties on various legal grounds ... In the earlier stage of the discussions no more than a passing mention was made of Pakistan's possible interest in these properties ... Soon after, Pakistan's interest in these properties became, in the eyes of His Majesty's Government, the dominating consideration and the Government of India was forced to approach the Pakistan government. This they did in March 1950 and subsequently sent reminders. But the Pakistan government have not so far agreed even to meet and discuss the matter with the Government of India.[83]

A separate letter was sent by Liaquat Ali to Morrison on 14 May 1951 setting out Pakistan's frustrations too:

> We have been desirous not to embarrass the United Kingdom government in their occupation of their building and sites either at Kabul or Kathmandu, and I am glad you appreciate the attitude we have taken. In view of the difficulties we have experienced in negotiating with India for a settlement of this question, and your evident desire for an early conclusion, we suggest that the United Kingdom government should hand over the Kabul property to [the] Government of Pakistan and the property at Kathmandu to India.[84]

This solved one problem – Kathmandu could go to India – but it did not solve the problem in Kabul. By now, however, the British saw that Afghan–Pakistan relations were so bad over Pashtunistan that the Afghan government were 'unlikely to hand it over to Pakistan even if India agreed'.[85] The little matter of the British embassy in Kabul, London decided, should therefore be kept on hold for now. Morrison replied to Liaquat Ali Khan on 6 October:

> Although we are anxious to be as helpful as possible, we cannot ignore the fact that with a mission in Kabul, the Government of India are also closely interested in the question of obtaining physical possession of the embassy

property. In these circumstances and in view of the legal advice we have had, I am afraid that we could not justifiably hand over the Kabul embassy to your government as you have suggested, unless the Government of India are prepared to acquiesce in such an arrangement. We therefore feel that we must await the outcome of a settlement of this question between your government and the Indian government.[86]

A few days later, Liaquat Ali Khan, Pakistan's Prime Minister, was assassinated in Rawalpindi by an Afghan Pashtun called Saed Akbar, who was instantly shot dead by the police. In spite of suspicions at the time that the Afghan government had been involved, subsequent investigations established that Akbar had lived in Peshawar, had lots of money in large bills in his pockets, and belonged to one of Pakistan's extremist Islamic fundamentalist parties, whose leaders considered the Prime Minister a traitor to Islam.[87]

From then on, the British concluded that the best course of action was inaction. Rising tensions between India and Pakistan, and Afghanistan and Pakistan, precluded any tripartite discussions. It suited British foreign policy to maintain friendly relations with all parties by staying put, while at the same time sending out the occasional signal that they were still exploring other sites – including sending the Ministry of Works' representative from the High Commission in Delhi to look at options. It also suited the Foreign Office not to ask the Treasury for funds for a new embassy until and unless there was:

An overriding and immediate political argument for it. In practice, this means agreement between the Indian and Pakistan governments on ownership of the present property. This is most unlikely in the near future, so we have a sound reason for staying where we are in Kabul at least until we find money for a new building.[88]

There the matter rested until 1963 when a break in Indian–Pakistan hostilities led to a joint demarche to London to raise the matter of Kabul and other unresolved properties in the Persian Gulf once again. The story is picked up again in Chapter Ten.

9

Whither British–Afghan Relations?

More enlightened Afghans, who have come to realise what we have done for their country and to know how vital to their own existence has been British support and goodwill, will genuinely regret our decline. The general public, however, will remember rather the wars they have fought with us and the days when the British were their chief enemies, and will gloat over our discomfiture.

Sir Giles Squire, 30 August 1949[1]

Introduction

My grandfather left Kabul for good on 15 January 1950 after what was, by his reckoning, the longest stretch he had ever lived in one place continuously in the past twenty years. In the week running up to his departure, his time was taken up with farewell lunches, cocktail parties and dinners, ending with a dinner hosted by the Prendergasts on the 14th. Squadron Leader Jonnie Lee-Evans, the RAF pilot who had accompanied the international inspection team to Moghulgai the previous summer, had become one of my grandfather's closest friends and was among the guests. The next day, he left the same way as he had arrived, on the embassy lorry to Peshawar. This time, however, he took the forty-hour train journey to Karachi, rather than risking the plane, and then set sail on the *Caledonia* on the 23rd, which was scheduled to arrive in Liverpool on 11 or 12 February, a few days after his daughter's eighteenth birthday. Prendergast himself left Kabul eight months later.

My grandfather was home just in time to vote for the Conservative Party and Winston Churchill in the general election on 23 February. Labour won, increasing their share of the vote by 1.5 million in an 84 per cent turnout, but their majority was down to just five seats and it was fairly unlikely that they would manage a full five-year term if there was another crisis. When he weighed up whether his two years in Kabul had been personally worthwhile, his reflections were mixed. He had made some friends, had extraordinary adventures, and been at the heart of a fascinating period of British history. On the other hand, he was now forty-one and had not improved his financial position or career prospects at all. 'At the end, the assets are not very great – I have a suit or two of clothes from a tailor, quite a lot of shirts, ties and all that, some shoes – probably fitted out better than I've ever been, but I'll be lucky if I finish up with £100 in my hand.'[2] In the short term, though, he had a cushion because he was not discharged from the army until February 1952. As far as I am aware, he never went overseas again.

The Britain he returned to was far removed from the one he had left behind two years earlier. After the disastrous year of 1947, the economy had improved considerably. The arrival of Marshall Aid in 1948, followed by the devaluation of sterling in September 1949, which helped British exports become more affordable and replenished dollar reserves, had made a tremendous difference.[3] The prospects for the future were looking up. Within months of the February election, however, all eyes turned to the Far East after Stalin supported Kim Il Sung's invasion of South Korea across the United Nations' agreed border, the 38th parallel, in June 1950. Stalin had anticipated the invasion would enable him to expand his sphere of influence relatively easily and he assumed the United States would leave well alone, but he had miscalculated. Truman quickly sought and secured a United Nations mandate to protect the post-war peace settlement, and American troops were swiftly mobilised to defend South Korea. Britain was right behind him.

Military engagement in Korea had huge financial and political implications for Britain. It led to a massive rearmament programme, the mobilisation of 255,000 reservists, and engagement in the rapid construction of NATO bases and troop deployments across West Germany. It also saw Britain prioritise an alliance with the United States over the option of joining an emerging European customs union – the Franco-German European Coal and Steel Community.[4] Elsewhere, Britain's other international challenges were increasing, not abating. British troops were still based in Malaysia dealing with the communist-led insurgency, and although Britain had been relieved of its responsibilities in Greece, Turkey and Palestine, nationalist movements in Persia and Egypt were now threatening Britain's position in the Middle East and the Persian Gulf. Tensions reached boiling point in Persia in March 1951 when the Persian Parliament nationalised the Anglo-Iranian Oil Company amid widespread opposition to the unequal distribution of profits between Britain and

Persia. Meanwhile, in Egypt anti-British tensions were rising, especially after Britain had failed to protect Arab interests in Palestine. In October 1951, the Egyptian parliament unilaterally abrogated the Anglo-Egyptian Treaty of 1936 which had granted Britain rights to the Suez Canal for twenty years.

Attlee called another general election in autumn 1951. The common sense of purpose which had driven Labour's post-war socialist government had burnt itself out, while many of the big-name politicians associated with it had fallen by the wayside. Sir Stafford Cripps, Chancellor of the Exchequer, resigned due to poor health in October 1950. Ernest Bevin died in April 1951, one month after leaving the Foreign Office following years battling a weak heart. Aneurin Bevan, the architect of the National Health Service (NHS), and Harold Wilson, the President of the Board of Trade (and future Prime Minister), fell out with the party in April 1951 over the decision to prioritise funds for the war effort over including dental treatment and spectacles in the NHS. Turnout on election day, 25 October 1951, was high at 82.6 per cent. Labour won more votes than any other party, but lost to the Conservatives with 295 seats to 321. Winston Churchill was back in No. 10.

Policy Confusion

As for Afghanistan, Britain's status was at an all-time low. Britain no longer enjoyed privileged access to the Afghan military, while Afghan ministers were now just as likely to consult the American, Indian, Persian, Turkish or Soviet embassies as the British. On a personal level, Sir Giles Squire had borne the brunt of the Afghan backlash against Britain's twin assumptions in 1947 that Afghanistan, Pakistan and India would join in common purpose, and that the government's Pashtunistan policy was a storm in a teacup. Initially, he had dealt with all the practicalities involved in transferring responsibility for Indian and Pakistan affairs from the British legation to their new embassies, and ensuring legation staff transferred from Government of India to Foreign Office terms and conditions. He had enjoyed a high point in early 1948 when he had been upgraded from Minister to Ambassador, and the legation to embassy status. Quite unexpectedly, however, he had also been drawn into helping frame British policy over the Pashtunistan dispute, and trying to maintain the front that Britain was still a significant regional player and a global power in spite of growing evidence to the contrary. He had been placed in a more or less impossible position, and it came at a cost.

By the time he left Kabul in September 1949, he had found himself out of step with the Afghan government because Britain could not, and would not, deliver what they expected, and personally blamed for Britain's ultimate betrayal – Noel-Baker's speech in Parliament on 30 June proclaiming British support to Pakistan's rights in the tribal areas. They gave him a token present and a low-key farewell after six years of service. Up till then, as Squire pointed out in his August 1949 Valedictory Despatch to Bevin, the Afghans had thought Indian independence was 'only another British trick and that His Majesty's Government was in fact controlling the Governments of India and Pakistan. In this opinion, they were confirmed ... by the continuance of the British legation in Kabul and its elevation to the status of an embassy.' After the speech, however, the Afghans finally realised Britain would not solve the Frontier question and felt betrayed. He feared that once they also learnt Britain's prestigious Kabul address belonged to India and Pakistan, this would provide the 'final proof that our day indeed is done'.[5]

Richard Blackham and Robert Scott in the Foreign Office's South-East Asia Department reflected on the messages in the Valedictory before Scott met Squire in person on Tuesday 13 September. Blackham concluded:

> If Sir G. Squire is right in his assessment of the present situation – and it is difficult to see who could know better than he – it would seem almost pointless to continue to be represented in Afghanistan, at any rate at embassy level; we might just as well leave it to the Indians and Pakistanis to fight for succession to our position there, just as they will no doubt shortly be quarrelling over the division of the embassy spoils. It is clear that we will not be able to influence the course of events materially.[6]

During the meeting, Scott asked Squire if he agreed that 'the prestige and influence which he described as now passing away in Afghanistan were the prestige and influence of the British Raj in India, rather than that of Britain, and he agreed'.[7] Britain's 'golden age' in Afghanistan was now well and truly over. This was to be Squire's last meeting in the Foreign Office and the end of his career as a diplomat. Thereafter he explored opportunities to teach Persian at Oxford or volunteer with a war veterans organisation, before finally settling in British Rhodesia (now Zimbabwe).

Scott picked up the same themes again when he wrote to Squire's replacement, John Gardener, on 21 September:

> My impression is that in the past, the Afghan attitude to Britain was governed by the fact that power in India was in British hands – power in the shape of troops on the border, and power advertised and demonstrated in Kabul by magnificent mission premises built with Indian funds and staffed by officers from Indian Services. In the east at any rate, influence depends a good deal on fear and on the visible local signs of power and wealth,

and inasmuch as our armies no longer stand on the Frontier, and as our envoy may no longer be the 'best housed person in Asia', our influence in Afghanistan was bound to decline. Indeed, if we do lose the premises, can we not console ourselves that continued occupation of the symbols of power in India, when the reality had gone, put our relations with the Afghans on a false footing? Now a new period of Anglo-Afghan relations begins.[8]

When Gardener sent his initial reflections back to London on 10 November 1949, his tone was upbeat. Afghanistan, he reported, had become increasingly important to Pakistan, India and the United States, and Britain had a large role to play in making sure they worked 'together to resist communist pressure on Afghanistan'. True, Britain's prestige and influence was 'a diminishing asset', but in spite of that, 'the United Kingdom is probably better qualified than any other member of the team in view of her experience and moral prestige. The latter, despite setbacks, is still considerable and probably greater in the eyes of the Afghans than that of any other member of the very ill-assorted team.'

In fact, he argued, there was still a lot Britain could do. If Britain gave economic support, increased the supply of teachers and technicians, and provided military supplies, this would go some way to 'recreate for Britain a position of considerable influence here. But this position has yet to be created. In the meantime, the two thin threads connecting our past influence with the future are our moral prestige and experience ... and our occupancy of the present buildings, the latter strongly reinforcing the former.'[9]

In one fell swoop, Gardener had effectively put old wine back into a newly labelled bottle marked 'policy refresh'. Except it was not a refresh at all. He had beefed up Britain's importance in Afghanistan, challenged Blackham and Scott's assertion that the embassy premises were an anachronism, and then come up with a number of policy levers which looked remarkably similar to Squire – in fact, the very same ones he had been using, and battling to retain, over the previous two years. The real question going forward for anyone succeeding Squire was not how much residual power Britain still enjoyed in Afghanistan – either real or illusory – but whether it had a clear policy agenda at all.

Britain's goals were now mostly framed negatively in terms of what Britain would not do, rather than what it wanted to achieve. Over the past two years, ministers had decided that Britain would no longer act as guarantor of Afghan security, privilege Afghan arms deals over other priorities, or provide financial resources to support the economy even if this was important politically. At the same time, however, they still expected Afghanistan to provide a security buffer for Pakistan, India and the Middle East, and wanted to see the Afghan–Pakistan dispute resolved. These were noble ambitions but bore little relation to the present state of fractious Afghan–Pakistan and India–Pakistan relations, both of which needed to be resolved to meet these goals, or to Britain's capacity to influence the situation in the foreseeable future. In effect, Afghanistan had been placed in a holding position in which Britain would for the most part track events and then consider whether and how to act if and when the situation warranted it. In reality, any concerted action also meant relying heavily on others, especially the United States, to help deliver the desired result. For those working on Afghan issues in the Foreign Office and diplomatic missions in Kabul, Islamabad, Delhi and Washington therefore, the challenge was how to work towards meeting these increasingly unrealistic objectives with minimal outlay in time and resources, while preserving the veneer of Britain's continuing influence and power – now reinforced by superior 'experience and moral prestige', as Gardener had put it.

There were two bits of good news by early 1950. Afghan relations with Persia had improved after the independent commission had been established to sort out water rights in the Helmand river valley, and the United States had finally committed to providing a loan. In all other respects, however, things seemed to be going from bad to worse. Afghan–Soviet relations were becoming closer with a series of trade deals. The Afghan economy was in a parlous state, heavily in debt, and now reverberating from the impact of Pakistan's petrol blockade. Furthermore, even after the blockade was lifted, Afghanistan's Pashtunistan policy was likely to continue stirring up troubles along the Frontier, while Afghanistan's new Treaty of Friendship with India was likely to increase regional instability, not lessen it, because it left Pakistan encircled by hostile neighbours. At the same time, although Britain had done an about-face and now welcomed United States involvement in arming Afghanistan against Soviet ambitions in Asia, the new global superpower was still sitting on the fence, seemingly more interested in protecting its commercial interests in Helmand than preventing the Soviet Union from gaining ground.

The political situation in Afghanistan seemed to be deteriorating too. Although the Afghan democracy movement had been carefully nurtured within the palace, there were increasing signs that the newly elected members of the National Assembly had plans of their own, which did not entirely match those of the royal family and could potentially fuel unrest. There was a slight glimmer of hope that the arrival of new set of political actors might shake the royal family from their Pashtunistan policy and bring peace on the Frontier, but overall the omens did not look good. The combination of political reform alongside an economic crisis and a nationalist foreign policy had all the ingredients for provoking the instability that Britain had spent more than a century trying to avoid. When a regime had looked unstable, Britain had given money and weapons to help restore authority; when a leader was weak, Britain had helped source a new power broker to take command. Now, however, Britain found itself in new territory. On the one hand, there seemed to be a political imperative to support democracy since the Labour government championed civil liberties and social justice. Britain was also allied with the United States which was distinctly anti-colonialist, and had supported the democracy movements in India, Pakistan and Burma. On the other, Britain's historic knowledge of Afghanistan suggested the conditions for democracy to take hold – such as an educated and politically aware populace – did not exist. The British therefore feared recent events could trigger political chaos, perhaps even a civil war as Amanullah's reforms in 1927/8 had done. This eventuality had to be avoided at all costs otherwise the Soviets might step into the vacuum.

Continued support for the Yahya Khel-led government therefore made sense, but now perhaps in a reformed political system that gave voice and a modicum of power to a wider group of people outside the palace. To achieve this, Britain needed to chart a steady course between keeping a finger on the democracy pulse while backing the Yahya Khels, and remaining alert to any issues that might trigger a crisis – in which case they might have to do something, although it was not clear what. On a day-to-day basis, it was sensible to stay on the sidelines, support reasonable opportunities led by others, and then ponder in slower time what, if anything, Britain should do to recalibrate its future policy position to make it more fit for the 1950s.

Shifting Afghan Sands

Afghanistan's new foreign policy alliances were on show at the Independence Day celebrations in August 1950. India was the main guest once again, but this time the visiting Indian hockey and football teams were joined by a Persian football team too. 'In their honour, their national flags were flown alongside the Afghan flags in the sports stadium, making Pakistan's absence conspicuous.' Gardener noticed that 'on the third day of the six there also appeared (and remained until the end of the celebrations) the "Pashtunistan flag" ... So far as I am aware, this is the first time that this flag has been flown publicly and officially in this country.' Gardener, like Squire at the 1948 Independence Day games, also witnessed a dispute on the pitch, this time between the Indians and Afghans over who had won a particular match. He recorded how Afghanistan's new allies reacted when pushed:

On one occasion, level with the Indians, they [the Afghans] were denied a goal which they went on to score a few seconds after the Persian referee had whistled a penalty against them. The Afghan sports director appealed from the pitch to the Prime Minister, near whom I was sitting. Mahmud Khan, literally livid with rage, gave encouragement to the director that if the latter thought it was a goal, then it was a goal. Nevertheless, the referee was adamant and the goal was disallowed, leaving the Indians winners. The Indian embassy, however, presumably fearful of spoiling the present Indo-Afghan honeymoon, went over the referee's head, declared the result a draw and so it was announced by All India Radio the next morning.[10]

Meanwhile, there were positive signs that Afghanistan was about to get economic assistance from the United Nations' nascent development programme. A four person United Nations Technical Assistance Mission (UNTAM) arrived in Kabul in March 1950, headed by an American expert on China and Central Asia, Owen Lattimore, with the objective of identifying opportunities for support to add value to existing national enterprises. At the end of their preliminary visit, they concluded that Afghanistan did not need any more surveys – as the British had known all along – but rather advice to support them to do better at what they did already, such as improving the breeding of karakul sheep and marketing the skins. They also recommended establishing an economic intelligence and statistics unit to investigate new projects, modernising export procedures and providing advice on importing petroleum.

The team also recommended support to the Helmand Scheme, to the dismay of the British. Although the United Nations in New York questioned the economic viability of this proposal, this continued to be an option for consideration and was picked up again when the next UNTAM mission arrived in mid-June to spend four months digging deeper into the country's development needs.[11] This time round, the team had a new leader because Lattimore had fallen foul of United States Senator Joseph McCarthy's witch-hunt against communists.[12] At the end of the visit, the mission proposed that the United Nations should provide twenty-four experts, ten of whom would work on the Boghra canal, one of the key irrigation arteries of the Helmand scheme. Squire and Gardener's nemesis, the Helmand Scheme, was clearly not going to go away, at least not in the immediate future. Meanwhile, the Afghan government's request that a United Nations permanent representative be based in Kabul was readily accepted.[13]

Progress on the political front was more mixed, however. The government reintroduced restrictions on Afghan contacts with foreigners in the summer – a sure sign, Gardener explained to London, that they were concerned:

We have, as you know, always been watched and no-one is allowed to see us except with police permission. This has recently been tightened. We are now watched when we go around the town etc; we are forbidden to correspond even with Afghan officials or to send invitations to Afghans except through Protocol Department, who show signs of wishing to prevent junior Afghans from coming to our houses ... The basic reason, as I see it, is that the Afghans are in one of their xenophobe phases, brought on by 'Pakistanitis' and aggravated by their economic plight. They want to keep all foreigners and particularly Pakistanis in ignorance of what is happening in the country.[14]

In addition, Afghans working for foreigners now required a police certificate confirming their 'honesty', which cost, when bribes were included, between £1 and £5 each, an exorbitant sum. It proved impossible, however, to put a complete clampdown on information, especially as the diplomatic community were continually resourceful in finding sources of their own, including tit-bits from the King's personal physician, the French Dr Boulanger.

As Gardener and others started to piece together a picture, they concluded that although talk of democracy was 'now rapidly becoming a catchword in Afghanistan', it seemed to be more about form than substance. Indeed, it would have been 'strange if the feeling of political consciousness now thoroughly awakened in mid-Asia should not be spread even to isolated Afghanistan'.[15] On the other hand, 'the real meaning of democracy is not at all clear to those who use the word, but because it is used, the leaders of the country pay lip-service to it'.[16] Gardener was also increasingly convinced that the driving force among the democrats was more a desire to 'escape from the oligarchic rule of the Yahya Khel family (known here as the Rule of the Uncles) rather than to create a democratic state – a political concept not yet understood in the country'.[17] Indeed, until 'the educational and social standards of the three racial groups inhabiting Afghanistan have been considerably raised, the nation cannot be deemed fit to adopt a democratic form of government'.[18]

In the first few months after the National Assembly elections in 1949, the embassy thought the movement might actually burn itself out, and wondered whether 'the government should "capture" the movement and prevent it perishing from its own rashness'.[19] The government was apparently thinking along the same lines. They established the National Democratic Club in 1950 as a meeting place, explained Ali Mohammed, 'for the exchange of democratic ideas and the education of leaders who could be incorporated in the administration'.[20] Daud was the club's founding president. The King started to become more visible and out-going too. On 11 May for instance, he ploughed over muddy roads in a torrential rainstorm to meet the Mullah of Shor Bazaar, who had opposed the government for not intervening in Kashmir.[21]

Over the following months, it was difficult for the British to assess whether the movement might fail through inexperience and 'rashness', or trigger a wave of new ideas that the government would find hard to control. In October 1950, *Wesh Zalmian*, the Movement of Awakened Youth, set itself up as a political party, the first to call itself such in Afghan history. It had a populist platform appealing to young and more radical Pashtuns alike advocating for Pashtunistan and the spread of the Pashtun language. By 1951, it had 816 members in nine cities. It was soon joined by two other parties: *Hezb-e-Watan*, meaning Fatherland, led by Mir Ghulam Mohammed; and *Hezb-e-Khalq*, People's Party, led by Dr Abdul Rahman. The Pakistan Chargé d'Affaires told Gardener that *Wesh Zalmian* sought to eliminate the influence of the royal family and to establish a democratic government.[22]

The new National Assembly soon became became increasingly assertive, demanding greater political reform and accountability. Since the government was not retaliating, Assembly members became increasingly emboldened in their demands. They criticised the government's handling of the Helmand scheme, and then took nearly nine months to approve the $21 million American loan.[23] Mahmudi and Ghobar also tabled a 'no confidence' motion against Abdul Majid, the first of several over the coming months.[24] The two government-controlled papers, *Isis* and *Islah*, now under new editors, began to print concerns about corruption and inefficiency, and published verbatim accounts of discussions in the National Assembly about the American loan and the work of the Morrison Knudsen Company.[25] Throughout, they took care to criticise only the government, not the King, but since the government and the royal family were more or less one and the same, this was a fine line to tread.

By late 1950, a number of independent newspapers had been set up as well, aided by new legislation at the end of the year which sanctioned the creation of privately owned newspapers and abolished preliminary censorship. Some of them, such as *Angar* (*Burning Embers*), *Watan* (*Fatherland*) and *Nida-i-Khalq* (*Voice of the People*), were closely associated with the new members of the National Assembly and their party followers. *Watan* was the organ of the *Hezb-e-Watan* party and edited by Ghobar, and *Nida-i-Khalq* was associated with *Hezb-e-Khalq* and edited by Mahmudi. Each had circulations of around 1,500.[26]

With this growth of political activity, albeit mostly confined to Kabul, it was hardly surprising that tensions between the old world and the new were simmering not far beneath the surface. In late March 1950, news leaked out that the government had arrested between 80 and 100 people, although the diplomatic community were unclear why. Some heard rumours that they were criminals who had been kidnapping children for ransom and robbing women; others that they were senior army officers and tribesmen who had planned to kill Mahmud Khan at a public ceremony on 21 March.[27] In the midst of this, 'it was rumoured that Prince Daud had fabricated the whole affair in order to advance his claim to be Prime Minister by showing the King ... how capable he was of controlling such disorder'.[28]

A month later, former Prime Minister Hashim Khan returned to Kabul after a long period abroad for medical treatment. As chief architect of the Yahya Khel's autocratic style of rule, the international community were fairly certain that he would now do everything in his power to ensure that the royal family, through his protégés Daud and Naim Khan, were keeping tight control over the movement's activities, even if that meant undermining his brother's policies. Mahmud Khan's position was not helped by the sudden departure of Abdul Majid from the Cabinet in May 1950, prompted apparently by a personal and very public disagreement between the two men. According to Gardener's sources, soon after the National Assembly had criticised the way Abdul Majid was running the economy, he had been questioned by the Prime Minister during a Cabinet meeting over his approach to exchange controls. It seems he had refused to permit the issuance of $1,500 to an Afghan visiting the United States, despite a personal request from Mahmud Khan himself. In response, the Prime Minister had queried why he sent money overseas to his wife and son every month. Apparently, 'this aroused Abdul Majid to the full. He had, it is stated, to be manhandled out of the room, and I am told on good authority that he thereupon resigned.'[29]

Gardener thought there was more to this dispute than a mere clash over currency controls and concluded it stemmed from a fundamental disagreement about the best course for the country, and for the regime. Abdul Majid was an easy target to scapegoat because he was not a member of the royal family. Mahmud's strategy, however, soon backfired – although 'no one of us here can get hold of the facts' – because Abdul Majid then received support from Daud and Ali Mohammed, the latter perhaps because he feared a similar fate as a palace outsider. 'Thus the battle is on. How and when it will end I cannot say.'[30] Abdul Majid later told a member of the UNTAM mission that Mahmud Khan had subsequently invited him to resume office, but he had declined because he did not wish to cooperate with members of the ruling clan who were currently in the government.[31]

Whatever the real facts surrounding Abdul Majid's departure, it prompted a Cabinet crisis, which had been simmering since the onset of the petrol blockade and paralysed the workings of government for months. In October 1950, Mahmud reshuffled his Cabinet once again. This time round, Abdul Majid and the Minister of Education were replaced 'with lightweights' and Daud was asked to cover the post of Minister of Interior until the Governor of the Eastern Provinces was ready to take over.[32] Daud's power therefore increased immeasurably overnight. Now he was in full control of the three institutions – the army, the police and the tribes – with the capacity to make, and unseat, the government, and for the time being at least was no longer required to take account of the views of another powerful minister. His brother, Naim Khan, became Minister of Mines.[33] Three months later, in January 1951, Mahmud Khan left Afghanistan for medical treatment overseas and was out of the country for the next eight months, leaving Ali Mohammed in charge as Prime Minister.

Thereafter, things seemed finely balanced between the government and the democrats. The royal family started to reintroduce some controls, while at the same time continuing to pull strings behind the scenes, using instruments like the National Democratic Club to mould opinion and keep a close eye on what was being said by whom. The British embassy reported extensively on the introduction of new rules governing the press, which received the royal assent on 31 December 1950. Although news articles proclaimed they 'represent a great advance towards freedom of information and general democracy', the British were not wholly convinced.[34] Publishers and editors were required to deposit substantial sureties with the Press Department before being licensed, while the department was mandated to review all publications and impose penalties, including imprisonment, if it judged the material prejudicial to the interests of an individual or class, Islam, the constitution or national unity. The rules did give more freedom to editors to publish articles that would never have seen the light of day before. On the other hand, *Angar*'s premises were raided within four months and 'the issue of 22 April was confiscated under article fourteen of chapter five of the Press Regulations, ie on a charge of prejudicing national unity ... The publication of the next issue, namely that of the 25th April, has also been prohibited.'[35]

There was evidence of give and take in other spheres too, albeit limited. The British speculated that the royal family was actually examining practical options to respond to some of the anti-government rhetoric when the Permanent Secretary in the Ministry of Foreign Affairs approached Gardener in April for information. He wanted to know 'what members of the British royal family receive annuities from public funds and particularly the most distant degree of relationship which would be regarded as the qualification for that purpose'.[36] Was this a sign, wondered the British, that the palace was thinking about pensioning some of the Yahya Khels off?

Furthermore, although the influential Kabul University Student Union had been disbanded in November 1950 when it refused to open a meeting 'in the name of the King',[37] the democrats remained on a roll, using their newspapers to push the right to free speech to its limits. Gone were the sycophantic articles in government-owned papers which had simply described the activities of the Prime Minister and his ministers. In their place, reported the British embassy to London, were articles challenging the regime and the Yahya Khel's stranglehold on the economy:

> In general, the line taken by these papers is that the present administration is corrupt and inefficient and that the only cure for the present political and economic bankruptcy of the country is to establish, by elections, parliamentary control of the administration. This tacitly implies the disappearance from power of the Yahya Khels except in the person of the King.[38]

The British also sent regular updates to London when one paper printed material challenging religious opinion. On 9 April, *Nida-i-Khalq* published an article by Gholam Hasan Khan Safi called 'An invitation to nonsensical worship', which condemned the assumption that a particular tomb in Jalalabad contained a hair of the Prophet's head. Not surprisingly, leading mullahs, including the Mullah of Shor Bazaar, proclaimed Safi an 'unbeliever'. The government was placed in a difficult position. Safi was not only the director of the sugar monopoly and a prominent friend of Abdul Majid, but also a member of the Safi tribe, which had recently rebelled against the regime. Clearly a man, observed the British, 'who should be handled with care'. The diplomatic community watched closely as events unfolded.

Safi was placed in jail and a Royal Proclamation on 23 May decreed that he would appear immediately before the Supreme Court of Appeal. Their judgement would be final. On 20 June, the Court concluded that although he had not insulted the Prophet, he had created dissension among the Afghan public, which was a punishable offence under sharia law. He was therefore to be kept in prison for his own protection and to strengthen his faith until 'signs of reform were seen in him'. As more information leaked out, it became increasingly apparent that the government had pulled off a skilful compromise. Safi was taken to prison each day in his car at 7 a.m. and then released just before sunset in order to reach his house before the 'gun proclaims sunset at the end of another day's fast [for Ramadan] which he is now obliged to keep'. The strategy seemed to work. The Safis led some demonstrations in Kabul demanding his instant release, but these were fairly low-key, while the Mullah of Shor Bazaar seemed to have discouraged his supporters from pushing for a stiffer sentence because, suspected the British embassy, he wanted to avoid bloodshed.[39] The incident provided an interesting litmus test of how far the government was still prepared to go to tolerate a degree of free speech.

When the embassy looked back on the first four months of 1951, however, the overall picture looked pretty unstable:

> Parliamentarians, newspapers and the general public have discovered that they can severely criticise the government without losing their heads. And all are now vocal ... Instead of dismissing Parliament and energetically pursuing its enemies while seeking to remedy such a popular grievance as the increased cost of living, this present cabinet appears to have given up the struggle and to have entrusted policy making to Parliament ... This power vacuum cannot last indefinitely for in time, the absence of authority may lead the Pashtun tribes to try and loot Kabul, as they have done before, or the Russians might profit. Democratic processes are definitely not sufficiently developed to fill the gap.[40]

They now concluded that the democracy movement was more likely to act as a catalyst for a wider uprising against the Yahya Khels, fuelled by the food shortages and price hikes, rather than the establishment of a broad coalition to change the structure of Afghan politics. That was the real challenge to the government and to stability, not democratic ideology per se:

> Whatever the details of the growth of the democratic movement may be, it seems clear that there is opposition probably growing to the continued oligarchy of the Yahya Khel. The ending of this oligarchy would certainly seem to be the first objective of the democratic movement, rather than the establishment of a fully democratic government.[41]

If it actually came to a showdown between the Yahya Khels and the democrats, however, Gardener and his team were convinced the democrats would be on the losing side. The democrats lacked grassroots support and had little, if any, connection with the rest of the country where the vast majority of the population lived.[42] Meanwhile, the army, the machinery of government, revenue, and access to information were still controlled by the existing regime. True, Amir Amanullah had been toppled by an anti-government coalition only twenty-three years earlier, but this was because the powerful conservative elements in Afghan society – the tribes, the mullahs, the landowners – had jointly opposed his liberal reforms and wanted a return to the status quo ante. They had certainly not fought for a new constitution permitting democratic politics, and had been content to see another autocratic dynasty, the Yahya Khels, replace Amanullah on the throne just one year later. If anyone was going to be replaced this time round, it would be Mahmud Khan himself and the democrats, not the conservative establishment in the palace. This meant that so long as the Yahya Khels retained their power base, it was more than likely they would have the capacity to crush the democratic movement if it stepped too far out of line. The two alternatives – abdication and exile, or real power-sharing with the democrats – were highly improbable. The real risk to Afghan stability was potentially during the period when the Yahya Khels fought to reassert their power over the democrats, and not from the democrats themselves, especially if this occurred in the midst of another economic crisis.

Meanwhile, in July, rumours circulated that Daud was planning a coup, and the embassy heard there had been an attempt to kill Mahmudi on the 4th. 'He had been told late at night that a patient needed him, and was then taken in a car which stopped, the pretext being engine trouble, by a pond on some waste land. There some men appeared, fell on Dr Mahmudi and tried to strangle him with his tie.' He was saved by the shouts of nearby children, which caused his attackers to run away. In a report of the incident in the *Nida-i-Khalq* the following day, the author implied the attack had been an attempt to stop Mahmudi's democratic work.[43]

Ali Mohammed, the acting Prime Minister, confessed to Gardener in July that the government was now very concerned but did not know what to do.[44] He was still confident that the democracy movement could be good for Afghanistan, but he also realised the government had been naive in believing its development could be manipulated. The idea that a government-sponsored institution like the National Democratic Club could be used to educate democratic leaders and absorb them into the existing polity 'was destined ... from the start, as being alien to the spirit of democracy'. At the same time though, he and others in the palace were disappointed by the 'democrats' themselves:

> So far the government had been seriously disappointed with the progress made by the democratic movement despite the freedom granted to it. The chief weakness had been the failure of the parties and of individual

leaders to show a sense of responsibility. The general tone of criticism had been very partisan and irresponsible showing no regard for the country as a whole. The secondary weakness was the tendency for the movement to split up into a number of parties under different leaders, none of whom produced a coherent programme of political reform but rather worked for personal interests.

The government had started watching Ghobar, Mahmudi and four or five other well-known democrats to see if they were secret communists, and he warned Gardener that the government's policies were now being challenged by various reactionary elements in society:

> The liberal attitude thus adopted by the present regime had, however, been seriously criticised by important sections of the nation, especially those in the provinces. Delegations from different parts of the country had expressed the opinion that the criticism voiced by the democrats should be suppressed as disloyal to the King and disruptive of national unity. The regime had, however, decided to persist in its policy of encouraging democratic movements, suppressing only those activities which may seem to the government ... to be communist inspired. It was on account of this suspicion that the newspaper *Angar* had been suppressed in April.

In view of all these challenges, he told Gardener, the Cabinet had decided to stop guiding the democracy movement until after the next National Assembly elections in 1952 when its three-year term expired.

Crystal-Gazing

Meanwhile, back in the Foreign Office, few gave much thought to Britain's policy in Afghanistan until June 1951, when Scott, now newly knighted and promoted to Under-Secretary of State for Asia, initiated a 'little crystal-gazing'.[45] He was not concerned about analysing whether Britain actually had the capacity to deliver a new policy. Rather, he simply wanted to see if there was one to be had. To do that, he had decided to throw out some wild ideas to stimulate discussion, which should be viewed in the spirit they had been made, and not because they necessarily had any practical merit.

He started by wondering what Britain's basic interest in Afghanistan now was. In the past it had provided a crucial buffer protecting the Indian empire, but was that still the case? He concluded that a buffer was still valuable, especially given the vulnerability of Persia's north-eastern border, but questioned if this goal was actually attainable any more. Then he turned to Britain's two main policy approaches – keeping the present regime in power and improving Afghan–Pakistan relations – and wondered if these were incompatible. Relations with Pakistan would only get better if Afghanistan ended its agitation for Pashtunistan, and this in turn would improve the Afghan economy. Unfortunately, if the Afghan government ever did concede defeat, this might in turn fuel instability at home since the Yahya Khel dynasty relied on support from the Pashtun tribal belt. Given this, he wondered idly if Britain should ditch its long-standing allegiance to the Yahya Khels and switch to supporting the democrats:

> I wonder whether we should not, while accepting there is no immediate alternative to the Yahya Khel, start thinking about the possibility that some more democratic form of government might eventually emerge in Kabul ... Admittedly, the so-called democratic movements so far are feeble and suspect. Nevertheless, it would, I believe, be foolish to suppose that Afghanistan can escape the movements towards popular representation now flowing so strongly in Asia, particularly since she is surrounded by more advanced neighbours, and commerce between herself and the outer world has so greatly increased since the war. It seems to me important that we should be on the lookout for any opportunity to assist any reasonable democratic institutions which may show signs of emerging – in so far as we can do this without disloyalty to the Afghan government; and there might of course come a point where it would even be to our advantage to try and get in on the ground floor of Afghan democracy, thus possibly beating the Russians to it, rather than hitch our chariot to a waning Yahya Khel star. It is, I suppose just conceivable that a movement towards liberalisation might come from within the Yahya Khel, perhaps from the King downwards. I do not know what support he could expect from other members of the family.

Having dealt with the Yahya Khels, he then launched into his most provocative and controversial idea yet – that perhaps Afghanistan as a separate independent state should cease to exist. He compared the situation in Afghanistan with Nepal. Both had autocratic governments, a nascent democracy movement (although that was more advanced in Nepal), and 'a powerful neighbour with religious, political, and racial ties with the country. In each case, there is a temptation for this powerful neighbour [Pakistan or India respectively] to interfere, and it is arguable that in each case, a logical – and from our point of view not undesirable – ultimate

solution might be for the larger country (Pakistan) to absorb the smaller.'
This might cause bloodshed, at least up as far as the Hindu Kush:

> However, if there is to be an upheaval sometime, as looks not unlikely,
> the ultimate disappearance of Afghanistan (as we know it) might be no
> tragedy. In modern conditions, Afghan viability may in the long-run
> be doubtful. It may interest you to know that Leon Brasseur [a visiting
> regional expert], talking last week to a member of the South East Asia
> Department here, went even further. He suggested that the obvious
> solution was for us to engineer the removal of the Yahya Khel, and
> partition Afghanistan between Pakistan and Russia.[46]

In just one short letter, Scott had presented a range of ideas to breathe
new life into Britain's floundering policy rethink. Gardener, perhaps
unsurprisingly, took two months to reply. When he did, on 9 August, he
was able to draw on the wealth of material he had been assembling since
his arrival in Kabul nearly two years earlier.[47]

He was not at all convinced that Britain either could or should do
more to support the democracy movement. He had already provided
the democrats with information about the British system, but the new
political parties on the whole were actively holding foreigners at bay
to avoid upsetting the government. It also needed to be borne in mind
that 'the influence of the parties (even if they were to pull together!) is
small and their allegiances and political platforms are still undefined'.
In addition, 'the government is now adopting a more aggressive attitude
towards the parties'. It was cracking down on 'irresponsible democratic
movements', writing its own press articles to respond to criticism in the
independent newspapers, and putting its own people into the National
Assembly to defend government actions. Given this, he told Scott that
the democrats did not provide a viable alternative to the Yahya Khels and
British policy should stay firmly where it was.

He then turned his attention to Scott's more radical suggestion that
perhaps Afghanistan should cease as a separate nation state and be
divided among its neighbours to strengthen the buffer. He fully agreed
that Afghanistan still had 'strategic importance as part of the as yet
unorganised guard of two vital areas, the Middle East and South Asia',
but also, like Scott, questioned whether Afghanistan could still perform
that strategic role since the conditions which had enabled it to do so in
the past were long gone:

> For just over a century when (a) the Indian Peninsula was united
> under British rule and had a strong army, (b) political warfare

scarcely existed and (c) armies depended on wheeled transport, Afghanistan fulfilled more or less satisfactorily the role of buffer state. Now that the three above named conditions have disappeared, it is useful to re-examine the case for retaining Afghanistan as a buffer state. Militarily, the courageous but untrained Afghans armed only with rifles are no longer any match for modern European armies ... Economically always poor, Afghanistan is now, by modern enhanced standards, nearly unviable. Unless much capital is now invested here, it seems possible that increasing economic discontent may predispose the Afghans to accept communist propaganda favouring the creation of a pro-Soviet state. Politically, Afghanistan is dangerously unstable in reason of (a) the effects of the Pashtunistan dispute, (b) the waning power of the Yahya Khel oligarchy, and (c) the growth of a democratic movement without any accompanying education of leaders or masses to assume responsibility.

In effect, the conclusion was clear. If Britain and others did not inject that necessary capital, Afghanistan could not be relied on as a security shield for South Asia, the Persian Gulf or the Middle East. Furthermore, the longer term viability of the Afghan state was in question too.

Given this, he agreed with Scott that it was indeed possible to carve up Afghanistan between the Soviet Union and Pakistan and outlined the advantages. It would ensure '(i) the speedy solution to the Pashtunistan dispute, (ii) the efficient defence of the Hindu Kush (the strongest available natural line), and (iii) the non-establishment of a pro-communist government in Kabul able to create trouble for Pakistan among the Pashtuns both sides of the Durand Line'. This would, for all those reasons, be potentially attractive to Pakistan, while the Soviets would be able to unite the Uzbeks, Tajiks and Turkmens both sides of the Oxus River and thus absorb the most fertile part of Afghanistan. He was at pains to point out, however, that although this looked good on paper, the idea was not at all straightforward in practice. The Persians and Soviets would squabble over who took Herat, and the Pashtun tribes east of the line from Kabul to Kandahar, who had helped put the Yahya Khels on the throne, were unlikely to submit to a foreign occupying force – unless, perhaps, they were paid an awful lot of money. He concluded, in fact, that force would have little to gain, and everything to lose:

If that occupying force were Pakistan, it would be difficult to avoid bringing the standard of living in occupied Afghanistan, urban and tribal (subsidies) to the same much higher level as that of Pakistan proper ... The forceful occupation of south and east Afghanistan would create considerable political and economic problems. These could easily be exploited by the enemies of the occupying forces, eg Russia and India ... Furthermore, could the new state of Pakistan, itself lacking in civil servants and administrative experience, undertake such a task? ... In view of the regionalism prevalent in Pakistan, could it be that occupied Afghanistan would join with the tribal areas of the North-West Frontier Province to form, after all, an independent Pashtunistan – a scourge and a menace to the settled areas of Pakistan?

As for the Soviets, he had long concluded that Afghanistan ranked fairly low in their expansion priorities. Their strategy was to bring about the establishment of a pro-Soviet regime in Kabul, not to capture territory. Overall therefore, it was best to leave things pretty much as they were.

This just left the small matter of the Pashtunistan dispute – resolving that thorny issue would unlock the key to a secure Afghan future. He had increasingly come to the view that Pakistan's tough anti-Afghan policy and Britain's loyalty to Pakistan's juridical position had not only produced 'nil results' but had also led to 'some danger that the original point of dispute, ie Pashtunistan, may become submerged in a feeling of hatred for Pakistan'. This in turn was unlikely to 'produce anything conducive to building up an effective buffer'. Unfortunately, however, he could see 'no alternatives but to keep plugging away at our present rather ineffective policy'. The best that could be achieved was a deal that enabled the Afghans to save face and the Yahya Khels to stay in power but also offered something for Pakistan too. He admitted, however, that he had absolutely no idea what that might be, or indeed how to get to a point where a roadmap might become evident. In the meantime, the only thing to do was keep 'the temperature of the disputants as low as possible so that no grave incidents occur'.

So there it was. Once Gardener concluded there was no alternative to Britain's existing policy position and offered up few new ideas, Scott's attempt to revamp Britain's policy to make it fit for the 1950s fell flat. There were no further attempts at a radical shake-up and Britain quietly de-prioritised Afghanistan thereafter. There was one bit of unexpected good news, however. Indian and Pakistani negotiations over the division of the embassy spoils broke down in 1951 as relations between the two countries deteriorated. The British were therefore able to continue using their prestigious address in the hope this would disguise at least some of Britain's fading glory – until that is, the next joint India–Pakistan initiative.

Meanwhile, the Foreign Office and British diplomats kept alive the vague notion that Afghanistan was still a useful buffer state and that Britain in turn was still a regional force to be reckoned with, but it was not difficult for either the Afghans or others to realise that Britain's days in Afghanistan were over. Thereafter, those working on the Afghan desk in London or based in Kabul quietly represented British interests as best they could, sent political and economic information regularly to London, monitored Soviet activity, sought the odd commercial or military contract here or there (often unsuccessfully), and continued to encourage others to take on Britain's role, until or unless another rethink was called for. As for Pashtunistan, Gardener's successors were advised that if they could not avoid discussions about Pashtunistan, 'the point should be made that the matters at issue are of a nature that can best be discussed directly between the Governments of Afghanistan and Pakistan'. Sir Daniel Lascelles agreed to adopt this official line, but commented back to London in 1953 that this was a 'most frustrating policy of "shamming deaf" in the hope that the Afghans will scream themselves out'.[48]

An incident in 1952 when Abdul Majid asked Britain for a £2 million loan to purchase industrial equipment from a British company, Platt Brothers, illustrates just how disconnected British policy had become by then. Whereas in 1950, the Foreign Office had concluded there was neither a financial nor political rationale to invest more money in Afghanistan, two years on they changed their minds. This time round, the Foreign Office believed a loan could be used as a sweetener to encourage a settlement of the Pashtunistan dispute, and they asked the Treasury to support the application.[49] By the end of the year, however, it looked as though the contract would go to Germany instead and the deal was off.[50] Afghanistan no longer needed to rely on British largesse – it now had plenty of other friends only too ready to oblige.

As for Gardener's thoughts on the viability of partitioning Afghanistan, these were carefully filed away in the Foreign Office, just in case. One official studiously commented that 'they will be a valuable guide when the time comes to consider seriously whether partition is to be recommended as part of our policy'.[51]

The files in the National Archives today tell their own story. When Gardener started the annual update of the Foreign Office's Afghan personalities file in 1950, he was asked by Scott to reduce the list considerably from the eighty-six names that featured in the previous year's edition:

I consider that this record might in future be reduced in size. The report in its present form includes many names which although of interest to the British Government of India in the days when Afghan matters concerned them closely, are no longer 'personalities' from the point-of-view of His Majesty's Government in the United Kingdom.[51]

The files after 1951 are more or less empty. When I spoke to Sir Nicholas Barrington, who had been based in the British embassy between 1959 and 1961, he recalled that only three or four urgent cables were sent from Kabul to London each year. For the rest, the much slower diplomatic bag was perfectly suitable.

The Curtain Falls on Afghan Democracy

Meanwhile, a veil was finally drawn across Afghanistan's democracy movement in 1953, just as Gardener had predicted. In the end, the collapse of Mahmud Khan's liberal reforms had bizarre parallels with the last months of the Labour government in Britain in 1951. Members of the Afghan government, like Attlee's Cabinet, were plagued with ill-health – indeed there was one period when both Attlee and Bevin were in hospital at the same time. The palace was also awash with internal intrigue, just as Attlee's Cabinet had become, as the consensus about their respective policy agendas gradually broke down. At the end, Mahmud Khan, like Attlee, was removed from office in a peaceful transition of power – a fairly rare occurrence in Afghan history – but with one slight difference. Whereas Attlee's government was defeated at the ballot box, Mahmud's downfall was masterminded within the palace itself, a reactionary backlash against a democratic experiment which had become too much like a political opposition and too unpredictable for the ruling elite to continue supporting.

When Mahmud Khan had first returned to Kabul on 11 September 1951 after eight months abroad, it looked as though he might regain the upper hand – Daud resigned from his ministerial portfolios amid rumours that his uncle had refused to continue as Prime Minister until he was removed from power.[52] In October 1951, Mahmud himself assumed charge of the Ministry of Interior, while the Commander of the Kabul Central Forces was appointed Minister of War until suitable permanent appointees could be found. Daud's brother, Naim Khan, was moved out of harm's way too – back to Washington as Afghanistan's Ambassador, but this time with additional responsibilities as the country's United Nations Representative too. The British embassy, however, was not convinced that the situation was recoverable. Indeed, 'with Daud remaining in the country, the Prime Minister has been unable to reconstitute his government, which remains with divided direction and loyalty and generally in a mess'.[53] Meanwhile, many wondered when, not if, Daud would make a bid for power.

Writing in February 1952, the new British Ambassador, Eric Lingman, agreed with his predecessor, Gardener, that 'the fundamental political problem facing Afghanistan is how to pass from a feudal, autocratic form of government to a democratic, constitutional monarchy, without stumbling into revolution or near chaos in the process'.[54] Once the screws began to tighten on the democracy movement over the following months, he worried that Britain's silence gave the appearance of propping up a weak, corrupt and reactionary regime.[55] There was little appetite in the Foreign Office, however, to change course. By May, the leading independent paper, *Watan*, had been suppressed and seventeen liberal intellectuals arrested including Ghobar and Mahmudi. Ghobar was first sent to do hard time in a tiny town in the south-western desert, and then spent the next ten years in exile.[56] Speaking soon after the end of the Liberal Parliament, Ghobar reflected that even if they had not been

> completely successful ... the National Front ... has honestly and courageously fulfilled its mandate until the last minute ... in a spirit of reformism and reconciliation between the nation and the state ... The ability of the nation to achieve a democratic government ... has become obvious.[57]

It came as no surprise that the elections for the eighth National Assembly that year were tightly controlled by the government. A year later, in 1953, Afghanistan's experiment with democracy was over. A severe famine in 1952, coupled with the violent suppression of popular protest against government corruption in 1953, undermined Mahmud's grip on power still further.[58] Daud's attendance at Queen Elizabeth's coronation in June at Westminster Abbey underlined his ascendancy. Less than three months later, Mahmud Khan resigned on 20 September and the 'Rule of the Uncles' was replaced by the 'Rule of the Cousins' with Daud as Prime Minister and Naim as Foreign Minister. Their greatest supporter and mentor, Hashim Khan, lived just long enough to see his nephews take power.

There is a small postscript to this story – a testament to the strength of the personal relationships forged by Lancaster and Prendergast and the impact of the country on their years in Kabul. Lancaster wrote to Mahmud Khan to express his sadness about the death of his brother, and received a handwritten reply on 28 March 1954: 'I was pleased to hear from you and to know that you are keeping well and are still keen on shooting and fishing. Since I have retired, I spend most of my time touring the country.'[59] Lancaster kept this letter among his treasured possessions, and on his death in 1967, bequeathed it to the National Army Museum. Meanwhile Prendergast, once renowned for his skills in mountain warfare, continued to visit Afghanistan regularly and began a new career as a travel writer. In his 1977 book *The Road to India*, he recounted the lessons learnt from his regular overland trips by motor caravan from Britain, via Persia and Afghanistan. During his frequent visits to Kabul, however, he only visited the embassy once, in 1970, specifically to view the almond trees he had planted along the driveway to the Military Attaché's house. He was anxious not to bother the present incumbents.[60]

10

Superpower Politics, the Cold War and the Final Scramble for the Embassy

Afghanistan is of little or no strategic importance to the United States ... Its geographic location, coupled with the realisation by Afghan leaders of Soviet capabilities presages Soviet control of the country whenever the situation so dictates. Further, Afghanistan is an avenue of approach to the sub-continent and might be overrun by the Union of Soviet Socialist Republics in the initial stages of a war between East and West. These factors would dictate the desirability of its remaining neutral in any East-West war. Such neutrality will remain a stronger possibility if there is no overt Western sponsored opposition to communism [in Afghanistan] which opposition in itself might precipitate Soviet moves to take control of the country. [Original underlined.]

United States Joint Chiefs of Staff, 1953[1]

Introduction

After 1950, Afghanistan's story was very much intertwined with the development of new regional and international alliances under the aegis of the superpower politics of the Cold War. Afghanistan's relations with its South Asian neighbours, India and Pakistan, became caught up in this binary struggle between East and West, while its dependence on funds, technical support, arms and military training left it vulnerable once again to the games played by others.

How and why Afghanistan was ultimately shaped by the Cold War is not straightforward, but it is relatively easy to see a thread running between the legacies of the late 1940s and subsequent events in Afghanistan's history decades later – the collapse of a second democracy experiment in

1973, the Soviet invasion in 1979, the civil war and rise of the Taliban in the 1990s, and the post-9/11 American-led invasion to the present day. Britain's Great Game in Afghanistan may have been well and truly over, but now it was the turn of the superpowers, the United States and the Soviet Union, to call the shots instead, while Afghanistan, as before, tried to play ball with the highest bidder. Sadly, many of the events since the early 1950s would not have come as a complete surprise to Squire and Gardener or Lancaster and Prendergast. They fully understood the vulnerability of the Afghan state to capture by an outside power or internal forces. Over subsequent decades, these twin threats to Afghan stability exploited the historic fissures in the country's complex social relations, geography, weak economy and fragile institutions for their own ends. No one, however, could have foreseen quite how cataclysmic these would become for today's Afghan story, or how their legacy would have such a profound impact on efforts to rebuild Afghanistan after 9/11.

Treading Water

Between 1950 and 1953, the United States and the Soviet Union circled around each other in Afghanistan and South Asia, but neither side took decisive action one way or the other. Until 1949, the United States had focussed on strengthening their security shield in the Pacific and the Atlantic, and had pretty much left Britain to shape Cold War policy in the Middle East, the Persian Gulf, and South and South-East Asia, using the resources and authority of empire to influence the direction of change. The growing nationalist movements in Persia and Egypt, and the Jewish-led insurgency in Palestine had, however, gradually exposed the potential limitations of Britain's influence. If Britain could not protect the Middle East's oil resources and essential transport routes through the Middle East, Persian Gulf and Eastern Mediterranean from falling into Soviet hands, then perhaps the division of labour agreed at the Pentagon two years earlier needed a rethink.

American attention also focussed on South and South-East Asia after Mao Zedong's forces overwhelmed China and established a communist government on 1 October 1949. Prior to that, India had been of little strategic importance, and although the Americans had kept a close eye on the communist insurgencies in Malaya, Burma, Indochina and Indonesia, they had felt relatively confident that these would not breach the security shield in the Pacific. Their assessments changed more or less overnight, however, when Mao effectively brought the communist front line within reach of the United States. The Indian Ocean and South Asia now became potential barriers to protect the Middle East and Persian Gulf from a communist threat from the east.

It was not straightforward, however. India and Pakistan were locked in a dispute over Kashmir, and Afghanistan and Pakistan over Pashtunistan. Of the three, India had by far the greatest resources but Nehru was talking increasingly about non-alignment and not about building a solid alliance with the West. Meanwhile, Pakistan had consistently shown its support for the West and requested arms from Britain to build a bulwark against Soviet communism, but had been repeatedly turned down – in part because Britain feared any deal could destabilise India–Pakistan relations still further, and upset relations with India. In any case, they argued, Egypt was the key to Middle East security, not Pakistan, especially while its resources were being continually drained by the Pashtunistan dispute.[2]

After Indian independence, the United States had stayed true to its word at the Pentagon talks and consistently turned down repeated requests for military aid from Afghanistan, Pakistan and India. Two years on, however, in April 1949, the British Joint Chiefs of Staff had reluctantly concluded the United States should provide military assistance to Afghanistan if this was the only way stop them turning to the Soviets for help.[3] The United States Ambassador in Kabul, Louis Dreyfus, was keen to get things moving and asked the State Department if Afghanistan could be included in the new Mutual Defence Assistance Act, alongside Turkey, Greece and Persia, to protect it from the Soviets:

> Afghan requirements seem reasonable for the internal security needs of Afghanistan and are consistent with United States policy to support the stability and independence of friendly governments in this area. The Department may also wish to consider the opportunity for influencing the settlement of the Afghanistan-Pakistan dispute by a conditioned offer of assistance. Would the United States consider including Afghanistan in a regional pact qualifying it to participate in military aid under present legislation?

He was sent a point blank refusal on 20 December and instructed not to discuss Afghan participation in the Act.[4]

After that, there was a hiatus while the United States tried to find a diplomatic solution to the Pashtunistan dispute now it was clear Britain had just about used up all its cards. Perhaps, they speculated, a third party with little previous experience in the region and no stated allegiances might just be able to shift the dispute and find that missing negotiating space which had eluded the British for so long. The Americans were motivated less by Afghan arguments than by the fear that the dispute could only benefit the communists, coupled with an increasing awareness that Pakistan was fast emerging as a willing, and potentially valuable, regional partner. According to George McGhee, the United States Assistant Secretary of State for North-Eastern and South Asian Affairs, who visited the region in December 1949, his government was therefore:

> Making a major strategic effort to resolve [the dispute] in order to prevent the communists from using it to their advantage. Moreover, an independent Pashtunistan would not, in our view, have been a viable state, and there was no-one to pay for it except us. United States' relations with Pakistan were at that time on the upswing ... In seeking aid, particularly arms aid, Pakistan took pains to disassociate itself from Indian neutralism and promised that its forces would be at our side in the event of communist incursions in South Asia.[5]

Initially, the United States suggested the establishment of an international commission on Pashtunistan, but this was rejected by both parties. Then in November 1950, the Americans offered to act as a go-between, encouraging them to cease their respective propaganda attacks against the other, prevent tribal incidents as far as possible, exchange ambassadors, and designate named representatives to meet within three months to restart negotiations. The Afghans agreed to the terms, but Pakistan wanted a prior assurance from the United States that they recognised the validity of the Durand Line as the Frontier, which was of course a non-starter – it would have completely compromised the United States' neutral role. The negotiations dragged on for a year. In their midst, McGhee himself visited Afghanistan in March 1951, the most senior American to visit the country up to that point. In the end, however, the United States, like the British before them, had nothing to show for their efforts and finally gave up in October 1951.[6]

McGee's discussions in Kabul also covered Afghan requests for arms. In the weeks and months after the visit, establishing what had, and had not, been agreed left a rather unpleasant after taste in Afghan mouths. The Afghans thought he had given them the green light to send a shopping list to Washington. After much to-ing and fro-ing between Kabul and Washington, the embassy was instructed on 27 November 1951 to give the Afghans a long list of excuses why it was impossible to meet their request – American arms were in high demand so they could not give an assurance that all the items were available; could the Afghans confirm they had correctly written down the right sort of ammunition against the weapon specifications; and did they actually realise how much the bill would come to? They would have to pay the full amount, $25 million, up front, because credit was not on offer. Not surprisingly, when this response was presented to Mahmud Khan on 8 December, he described it as a 'political refusal' and an insult both to Afghanistan and to him personally.[7]

When it came down to it, however, the Americans were still not convinced that providing arms and military equipment to Afghanistan was a particularly good idea. From a practical perspective, they realised, like Lancaster and Prendergast, that the Afghan military could not repel a well-armed and equipped Soviet invasion force. Instead, the key to the Afghan problem was to prevent the Soviets from wanting to invade the country in the first place, and this could best be achieved by avoiding a provocation. American objectives, echoing Britain's Great Game, were therefore far more likely to be met by building up Afghanistan as a pro-Western buffer state, than by supplying arms which would upset the Soviets. They also appreciated that if the Soviets ever did decide to invade, the tribes would in all probability give them a hard time. This approach therefore killed two birds with one stone. The United States could avoid providing the Soviets with an excuse to invade, while any invading army would struggle, with or without American assistance to the Afghan government. Equipped with this analysis, the United States National Security Council concluded in 1953:

> The Kremlin apparently does not consider Afghanistan's relatively meagre assets to be worthy of serious attention and probably believes that it can take Afghanistan easily whenever its broader objectives would be served. There is little doubt that Afghanistan could be conquered regardless of its will to resist. In the event of an invasion, it is possible that certain elements, particularly the Afghan tribesmen, would continue to resist.[8]

Afghanistan, the Americans concluded, should therefore be left well alone.

Changing Gear: Aid and Trade

Economic assistance, however, was an altogether different matter, and in this, the Afghans proved very adept at playing the United States and Soviet Union off against each other. In the early 1950s, American financial, cultural and economic interests in Afghanistan grew rapidly, spearheaded by the new Technical Cooperation Administration in the State Department. By the end of 1951, the United States had the largest embassy in Kabul bar the Soviets, an Air Attaché had arrived complete with a plane which enabled staff to fly around the country at will, and President Truman's Point Four Programme, providing economic assistance to underdeveloped countries, had been extended to Afghanistan. Initially, Point Four funds provided scholarships for Afghan students to study in the United States, and paid for two mining engineers to support the Ministry of Mines on the extraction, use and marketing of mineral resources and how to improve coal production.[9] These initiatives were soon followed by the establishment of an American technical training school in Kabul, an Archaeological Mission the arrival of an Archaeological Mission examining the ancient civilisations along the Helmand river valley and in and around Mazar-i-Sharif, and the employment of American geologists to investigate oil exploration opportunities in the north close to the Soviet border, and the feasibility of modernising a coal mine near Kabul.

The fact that the United Nations Technical Assistance Mission (UNTAM) was primarily staffed by Americans too seemed to add to the 'proprietorial air' of the United States embassy according to Gardener in March 1951. Indeed 'the Americans unconsciously do their best to lend colour to the Soviet accusation that [the] United Nations is a creation of United States national policy'.[10] He also feared that American interest in oil exploration in northern Afghanistan and their encouragement to the United Nations to include this among their project priorities was 'needlessly arousing Russian suspicions about Western intentions in Afghanistan'. He reminded London that all this went counter to the Soviet-Afghan Treaties of 1921 and 1926 which stated that Afghanistan should not be used as a base for propaganda and/or military activities hostile to the Soviet Union.

The Soviets undoubtedly were concerned. In August 1952, they delivered an aide-memoire to the Afghan government objecting to specialists from NATO operating near the border and hinting this could aggravate relations between the two countries. The Afghans swiftly assured them that all westerners would be removed from border zones and that Afghan territory would not be used for anti-Soviet purposes. When Shah Mahmud raised concerns about this intervention with the Americans, the Secretary of State refused to be drawn.[11] In the end, the Soviet Union had little cause for concern since the main focus for much American development assistance in the 1950s and 1960s, and indeed much of UNTAM's work initially, became the Helmand Scheme, well away from the Soviet border.

In 1952, UNTAM and the United States' Technical Cooperation Administration agreed Helmand would be the priority. UNTAM would focus on policy and strategy support to the Afghan government, while the United States would provide, according to American publicity, 'help in overcoming the effects of ravages during the twelfth and fourteenth centuries by Genghis Khan and Tamerlane on vital irrigation works in the Helmand river valley'.[12] Point Four funds amounting to $348,740 were allocated, of which $93,446 were to be used to supply American technicians and equipment to support farmers on the newly irrigated and arable lands. The remaining funds were to be used for education programmes, including training sixteen Afghans in specialised areas such as agriculture, coal mining, irrigation and locust control.

The Afghans needed more money than this, however, to complete the Helmand scheme and sought another loan from the Export Import Bank in late 1952. A year later, an Afghan delegation went to Washington requesting $36 million. According to rumours circulating in Kabul, the money was needed to complete and maintain the expanding canal network and additional work recommended by Morrison Knudsen to construct a power plant at Arghandab and 200 kilometres of asphalt roads in and around Kabul.[13] The challenges were compounded by a failure to undertake extensive studies of soils and drainage before construction work commenced.[14] As early as 1949, a small diversion dam at the mouth of the Boghra canal raised the water table to within a few inches of the surface, and a snowy crust of salt had become visible around the reservoir.[15] Over subsequent years, the problem of salinity would increase.

Soon, the scheme also became a symbolic battleground in the Cold War, as the British Ambassador, Eric Lingeman, reported to London in 1953:

> The project is at present a formidable liability to the Afghan economy, and that the Afghan government must surmount formidable obstacles before they can hope to achieve even a limited measure of success ... At the same time, it is obvious that it would be even more dangerous for them to abandon the scheme than to press forward with it, because, as I have already pointed out, both their own prestige and that of the United States in this country – and in fact that of the West at large – is irrevocably committed to an at least partially successful conclusion of this venture. It is clear moreover that the immediate question is not so much one of achieving positive success as of averting disastrous failure.

He lay much of the blame at the door of the Morrison Knudsen company. 'The two chief causes of the current difficulties are, in my opinion, the abysmal technical ignorance of the Afghans and the exploitation of that ignorance by the American construction company, Morrison Knudsen ... [They] have in fact withheld a great deal of useful information and advice from the Afghan government in order to make a large profit more easily.'[16] While Lingeman was relieved that the United States was getting more involved, his successor, Daniel Lascelles, was not. He believed a further loan would be an extravagant waste of money and simply increase the tendency of the Afghan regime 'to regard themselves as an institution which the western powers cannot afford *not* to keep alive regardless of how it behaves'.[17] A further $18.5 million loan was agreed in late 1953.[18]

Meanwhile, the Afghan government had a grand political and social plan for the scheme too. In addition to irrigation and power, they hoped it would buttress support among the Pashtun tribes and propel Afghanistan into the twentieth century with western-style towns, education for girls, a health service and a formal justice system, based on written law not tribal customs. One new town, Lashkar Gah (meaning army barracks), was built with wide boulevards and western-style houses close to Qala Bost, the ancient Ghaznavid arch, which enabled the royal family to assert an imagined line of succession from the Ghaznavid dynasty.[19] When Arnold Toynbee, the British travel writer, visited in May 1960, he aptly described it as 'a piece of America inserted into the Afghan landscape'.[20] Nearly fifty years later, Lashkar Gah became the headquarters for the joint British, Danish and Estonian Provincial Reconstruction Team (PRT), a hub for military operations and development activities across Helmand from 2006 to 2013.

To meet labour needs, families were relocated from other parts of the country, enticed by offers of food rations, a house and ploughed land. Many became tenants of Pashtun landowners, who did not pay tax on their increasingly profitable lands.[21] The first areas to be settled in 1954 were Nad-e-Ali and Marjah, two districts which later became significant battlefields for British and American troops over the past decade. The United States funded a complementary dam project on the other side of the Line too, in the Indus Valley in Pakistan, to help reduce migration in the other direction.[22] By the mid-1950s, considerable progress had been made. The Arghandab dam – now the Dahla dam – was completed in 1952, and thereafter supplied electricity to serve the whole of south-west Afghanistan, including the city of Kandahar. The Kajaki dam, high up in the Helmand valley, was completed in 1953.[23] The Afghan government also created the Helmand river valley Authority (HVA) modelled on the Tennessee Valley Authority in 1952, and the president of the HVA was given a seat in the Cabinet.

Over the same period, the Soviet Union was also slowly but surely continuing to expand its own economic and trading relationship with Afghanistan, taking advantage of the ongoing Afghan–Pakistan dispute to offer an alternative overland supply route. By 1952, they had established their first trade office in Kabul, cotton cloth from Tashkent was becoming cheaper than imports from India and Japan, and Soviet cement had replaced supplies from India and Pakistan.[24] Financial and economic inducements significantly increased after Stalin's death in 1953. Stalin had studiously avoided giving loans on concessional terms to neutral developing countries, but his successors thought otherwise. Within a year, they had loaned Afghanistan $3.5 million to construct grain silos in Kabul and Pul-i-Kumri, and a flour mill and bakery in Kabul.

Arms and Aid

Up to 1954, the United States had focussed on providing economic aid to both Afghanistan and Pakistan, and had resisted their calls for military assistance. Now, however, they did an about face and decided to throw in their lot with Pakistan. Henceforth, it was to be Pakistan, not Afghanistan, that would partner with Turkey in a 'Northern Tier' line of defence to protect the Middle East and Persian Gulf from the Soviet Union. Accordingly, on 25 February 1954, the United States announced it would give military aid to Pakistan; on 2 April, Pakistan and Turkey signed a treaty of mutual cooperation, on 19 May, the United States and Pakistan signed a Mutual Defence Assistance Agreement;[25] and in September, Pakistan became a founder member of the South-East Asian Treaty Organisation (SEATO), a United States-sponsored collective security organisation. A few months later, Pakistan also joined the Middle East Treaty Organisation, or Baghdad Pact, binding the United States, Britain, Persia, Iraq, Turkey and Pakistan into a mutual security agreement to deter Soviet expansion in the Persian Gulf. The Afghans refused to join the Baghdad Pact, preferring, so they said, to preserve their neutrality.[26] In return, Pakistan received military and economic aid worth $105 million a year, as well as covert support to equip four infantry divisions, six fighter squadrons and twelve naval ships. By 1957, covert American military assistance had risen to $500 million a year.[27]

Meanwhile, the Afghan government continued to ask the United States for military support, but received short shrift. Naim Khan visited Washington in October 1954 and asked once again for assistance. Secretary of State John Foster Dulles' reply three months later left no room for doubt: 'After careful consideration, extending military aid to Afghanistan would create problems not offset by the strength it would generate. Instead of asking for arms, Afghanistan should settle the Pashtunistan dispute with Pakistan.' He also sent a copy of his reply to the Pakistan government.[28]

Given these repeated refusals, it was not surprising that the Afghans had a Plan B up their sleeves. By mid-1955, they had accepted a supply of $3 million worth of arms from Czechoslovakia and were now actively considering assistance from the Soviet Union.[29] Afghan disenchantment with the West escalated further that year over the so-called 'Flag Incident' when the Pakistan government announced it was merging all provinces in West Pakistan into 'One Unit'. Although the tribal areas were excluded, the Afghans interpreted this policy as a move to prevent the emergence of Pashtunistan. A mob attacked the Pakistan embassy in Kabul and the consulates in Kandahar and Jalalabad, and burnt the Pakistan flag. In retaliation, a Pakistani mob attacked the Afghan consulates in Quetta and Peshawar. The crisis led to a new trade blockade, a break in diplomatic relations, and the possibility of fighting along the Frontier. The stand-off was eventually resolved by Egypt, Persia, Iraq, Turkey and Saudi Arabia.

For the Afghans, the Flag Incident represented a huge defeat and an assault on their honour. It underlined their need for strong regional allies, and the best offer on the table came from the Soviet Union, which had negotiated another transit agreement for petrol and cement during the recent blockade. In December 1955, the Afghans therefore welcomed a visit by Stalin's successor, Nikita Khrushchev, and the Premier of the Soviet Union, Nikolai Bulganin, on their way back from India. They offered a $100 million loan at 2 per cent interest and backed Afghanistan's Pashtunistan policy. The loan enabled the Afghans to undertake a large number of infrastructure projects, including new hydro-electric plants and fertiliser factories, an airport at Bagram just outside Kabul, and the world's highest tunnel, the 3-mile-long Salang Pass under the Hindu Kush linking Kabul with the Soviet Union. Both the Salang tunnel and Bagram air base would be invaluable during the Soviet invasion and occupation in the 1980s. A year later, the Soviets provided $21 million worth of tanks and jets and other military equipment and weaponry, and began providing military support to India.[30]

After that watershed year, Afghanistan became awash with development and military assistance and joined the World Bank and the International Monetary Fund. While the Soviets invested in the base at Bagram, the United States improved Kabul airport, built a new international airport at Kandahar, and supported the development of the country's national airline, Ariana, which became partly owned by Pan American. A 1,500-mile paved ring road was constructed around the country, linking up the major cities and connecting Afghanistan to the outside world. The Americans constructed most of the eastern and western sections, the Soviets the north and the south. The Soviets also prospected for oil and gas and built pipelines to transport it to power stations servicing northern Afghan cities and the factories they had built. The pipelines also carried the gas to Soviet Central Asia.[31] Investment in education rapidly expanded too. By 1979, a million children were in primary school, 136,000 were in secondary school and 23,000 in higher education.[32]

The imbalance between Soviet and American military assistance remained, however. Between 1956 and 1978, Afghanistan received $1.24 billion in military aid from the Soviet Union, mostly in the form of credits, while a third of the entire Afghan officer corps, 3,725 men, received training in the Soviet Union. Over the same period, only 487 officers were trained in the United States.[33] The army effectively became a Trojan horse, steeped in Soviet communist ideology and trained in the Soviet way of doing business and conducting warfare, all of which came in useful when there was a coup against Daud's rule in 1978. The Soviet Union also provided around $1.27 billion in economic aid – in the form of grants and soft loans – whereas the United States provided only $533 million.[34] Daud became adept at playing the superpowers off each other. One CIA report in 1975 described him as a man at his 'happiest when he could light his American cigarettes with Soviet matches'.[35] By the early 1970s, Afghanistan was also receiving significant development assistance from West Germany, the United Nations and China, complemented by smaller amounts from others, including Britain.

Impact on Afghanistan

In spite of all the foreign investment and the initiatives to develop industry, the Afghan economy remained primarily based on agriculture and pastoralism. Meanwhile, its fiscal base increasingly relied on the tax on overseas trade, and foreign aid and military assistance now replaced British subsidies and technical know-how to help run government services and pay for the army and air force. The amount collected from land and agriculture declined from around 18 per cent of domestic revenue in March 1953 to around 1 per cent in 1973, while the proportion raised from foreign trade reached around 60 per cent in the mid-1960s, falling slightly to around 43 per cent in the early 1970s.[36] By then, only Nepal had a lower ratio of tax revenue to estimated tax capacity. At the same time, between 1956 and 1973, foreign grants and loans accounted for 80 per cent of Afghan investment and development expenditure.[37] The massive flow of new money into Afghanistan came at a cost, however. On the one hand, the government was able to keep domestic taxation low, and thus keep a potentially hostile combination of peasant farmers and rich landowners at bay, but over the longer term, the state became increasingly accountable to its international financial backers, and not to the Afghan people. Afghanistan therefore remained a rentier state, just as it had in the British period, drawing on foreign money to run the country and the use of patronage to reward supporters and secure compliance from would-be opponents. The only significant difference now was that the source of money had changed.

These trends contributed to a sense of malaise in Afghan politics. Although successive governments tried to introduce economic, social and political reforms, the deep fissures embedded within the country's historic make-up continually came to the fore. They found expression in competing views about the future – between autocracy and democracy, Islamic fundamentalism and Marxism, urban chic versus rural conservatism, and Western freedoms versus Soviet-style control and militarism. Afghanistan became the victim of its location between the superpowers, between different cultural and religious values, and between local tribal-based systems and state institutions that had never become sufficiently resilient to internal or external pressures.

Meanwhile, throughout the 1950s, Daud ruled Afghanistan by combining repressive measures with progressive reforms which opened up new opportunities in the civil service and state-controlled industrial sector for the educated elite. By the late 1950s, he felt sufficiently confident to lift purdah from women and in August 1959, his wife, along with the wives of other top officials, appeared bare-faced for the first time on the viewing stand during the Afghan Independence Day celebrations. The tide began to turn against him in the early 1960s, however, when he closed the Afghan–Pakistan border in yet another attempt to put pressure on Pakistan to come to a settlement over Pashtunistan. The gesture backfired badly, and the only ones to suffer were the Afghans themselves. As goods emptied from market shelves, prices increased, and ministry budgets were cut by 20 per cent, he gradually faced a groundswell of unrest against his repressive policies.

The person who came to the rescue was none other than King Zahir Shah. He had mostly continued to take a back seat in politics right up to that point, but when Daud submitted his resignation on 3 March 1963, he decided it was time to form a government himself. He released political prisoners, invited political exiles like Ghobar to return, and commissioned a new constitution, which included an elected lower and upper house for the National Assembly. Article 24 stated that no member of the royal family could be in the Cabinet, serve as a member of the Assembly or belong to a political party.

The so-called New Democracy seemed to an older generation to have picked up from where Mahmud Khan had left off. Mahmud himself had died in 1959, but his last surviving brother, Shah Wali Khan, was to live long enough to see the continued ups and downs of the Yahya Khel dynasty until his own death in 1977. Interestingly, Zahir Shah's reforming zeal would not have come as a complete surprise to Gardener either. When he had his farewell interview with the King in October 1952, soon after the end of the Liberal Parliament, the King described himself as the 'local apostle of democracy'.[38]

During the New Democracy period, urban Afghanistan was transformed. Many young Afghan women removed their burqas and started to wear western clothes, at least twenty-five new newspapers were launched, cinemas flourished, live music was performed, and Western hippies started to hang out in Kabul en route to India. Beneath the surface, however, all was not well. Two distinct Afghanistans were emerging. The first was a new, but incredibly small, westernised urban elite, which mostly lived in Kabul. The second, the traditional Afghanistan, began within a mile or two of the bright lights of the capital, and little had changed significantly therefore for generations. Afghanistan's new infrastructure, funded by foreign money, had not consistently delivered progress either. The Salang Tunnel was a success, but Kandahar international airport was soon obsolete because it was not designed for jet aircraft and lacked sufficient petrol supplies to refuel them – just as the British had realised decades earlier when they had explored alternative options for evacuating embassy staff instead of through Pakistan.[39]

Meanwhile the Helmand scheme continued to be a mixed blessing. The government had cancelled the Morrison Knudsen contract in 1959. By the early 1960s, the HVA controlled 1,800 square miles of the river valley, and Helmand became a new province in 1964 with its capital in Lashkar Gah.[40] Although some parts of Helmand had now become lush agricultural areas, the scheme remained costly for the United States and Afghan governments alike. Between 1960 and 1970, three-quarters of all American aid was spent in the Helmand river valley alone, and a third of Afghanistan's total expenditure went into the HVA in the 1950s and 1960s.[41] Success was patchy. By 1960, only 30 per cent of the first settlers were still living in Nad-e-Ali, and in some areas agricultural productivity had not returned to 50 per cent of its pre-1950 levels even by 1969.[42]

Elsewhere, land disputes festered as those temporarily dispossessed of their ancestral lands while the canals were being built clashed with incomers. At the same time, multiple layers of patronage developed as landowners rented out their newly irrigated lands to ever more diverse labour groups farming smaller and smaller plots. By 1965, according to one recent commentator, 'it was clear the project was failing ... but Helmand was an economic Vietnam, a quagmire that consumed money and resources without the possibility of success, all to avoid making failure obvious'.[43]

On the political stage, the first signs emerged in the 1960s that Afghanistan's finely honed balancing act between the two superpowers might come back to haunt it. The results of the first elections to the National Assembly in 1965 gave a taste of what was to come. Six informal groupings emerged in the new Assembly: ultra-conservatives led by Islamic religious leaders; a Pashtun group fearing the erosion of Pashtun dominance; a pro-entrepreneurs group seeking the relaxation of state controls on the economy; a pro-monarchy group; some liberals who wanted rapid public sector-led development; and a small far-left Marxist clique.[44] Kabul University became a hotbed of radical thinking. Some were drawn to ideas about what a true Islamic state might look like based on principles of equality, brotherhood and social justice. Others debated Marxist ideology, caught up by ever closer links with the Soviet Union as it opened its doors to Afghan students. The People's Democratic Party of Afghanistan (PDPA) was launched in 1965, a communist party in all but name. Thereafter, young Afghan urbanites mobilised strikes and 'sit-ins' at the university, and spread their ideas through the new media outlets. Not surprisingly, this provoked a backlash from the conservatives.

The end, when it came, was from an unexpected source. A three-year drought from 1969 to 1972 killed between 50,000 and 500,000 people, caused thousands of farmers to lose their livestock and their land to moneylenders, and ruined the economy.[45] In the midst of this crisis, there was good news that one legacy from the 1940s was finally dealt with – Afghanistan resolved its water dispute with Persia – but in all other respects, the New Democracy period was drawing to a close. While the King was in Italy in July 1973, Daud deposed him, declared a republic and made himself President.

Daud initially proved adept at marginalising the communists and the Islamists, many of whom fled to Pakistan. After an attempt to support an opposition movement in Pakistan's North-West Frontier Province, he switched sides and formally recognised the Durand Line in 1976. He also became increasingly pro-Western, which in turn angered the Soviet Union.

He had a disagreement with Leonid Brezhnev, Khrushchev's successor, in Moscow in April 1977, when Brezhnev told him to stop looking west and to remove western advisers from the country. Six months later, during a meeting with Secretary of State Cyrus Vance in Vienna, he accepted an invitation to visit Washington and an increase in American development assistance and military training.[46]

Back at home, however, the underlying conditions which had enabled factious politics to bloom in the 1960s proved less easy to put back in a bottle than they had in 1953. Radicalism of the left and right continued to flourish. Even Lashkar Gah was not immune to unrest and became the centre of violent clashes between educated students, who had become interested in communism, and conservative tribal elements opposed to change.[47] The end came swiftly. On 27 April 1978, a communist faction in the army – many of whom had been trained in the Soviet Union – attacked the palace and Daud, his brother Naim Khan, his wife, and sixteen other members of their families were assassinated.

The Soviet Union was the first to recognise the new left-wing regime amid rumours that they had supported the coup. Within weeks, however, the new regime hit problems. Different communist factions within the ruling group started to vie for power amid the increasingly violent oppression of anyone who opposed the new regime. Thousands of Afghans fled to Pakistan, Europe and the United States. Meanwhile, the new government set about introducing a range of reforms, which, as in Amanullah's day, swiftly alienated different groups across Afghan society. An upper limit on land ownership alienated rural power holders, a new decree setting an age limit for marriage alienated conservative tribesmen, and a literacy campaign aimed at men and women alike upset patriarchal values.

Soviet civilian and technical advisers began to flood the country because Moscow feared Afghanistan could spiral out of control and fall into the hands of the Islamists. A Treaty of Friendship and Cooperation was signed in December 1978 empowering Kabul to call on the Soviet Union for military assistance. In March 1979, a major revolt against the regime broke out in Herat during which nine Soviet advisers were killed. In response, Soviet planes bombed the city, reducing a third to rubble and killing as many as 25,000 people.[48] Unrest soon spread to other cities and towns. In each case, the rank and file of the army turned their backs on their officers and joined the opposition. Meanwhile, the Soviets feared that the United States was about to re-position itself in the region following the fall of its ally the Shah of Persia in 1978 and the establishment of an ultra-orthodox regime in his place, led by Ayatollah Khomeini.

The Soviet leadership however had no desire to absorb the country within Soviet territory – like the British before them, had long realised that Afghanistan lacked the pre-conditions for a socialist revolution. Instead, the top members of the Politburo – Gromyko, Andropov, Ustinov and Ponomarev – concluded on 1 April 1979 that the Afghan leadership needed to stop falling out among themselves, broaden their political base (including by tolerating a degree of religious freedom), strengthen the army, and develop a more viable economy.[49] These recommendations were not far removed from the British embassy's thinking in the late 1940s. Unfortunately, however, the Soviets were also being swept up in a renewed arms race as the Americans developed new weapons. It began to look as though the principle of 'strategic parity', which had maintained a relatively stable balance of power for many years, no longer held good, and it was the Soviet Union, not America, that was falling behind. In the midst of these events, the Soviets could not afford to let Afghanistan fall into American hands too as it stumbled towards civil war. The Soviets, using the excuse provided by the 1978 treaty, invaded Afghanistan in late December 1979, overthrew the government and put their own man in power.[50]

Just as Squire, Gardener, Lancaster and Prendergast had predicted nearly three decades earlier, the Soviets had invaded Afghanistan because they needed a stable neighbour on their southern border, and because they feared American interest in the region would threaten their interests. And as they had anticipated, the Soviets were also to find it far easier to invade and overwhelm the country than to keep control of it, just as the British had found out to their cost in the nineteenth century. This time round, however, the Soviet Union's problem was compounded by international involvement too. The December 1979 invasion had finally propelled Afghanistan centre stage once again, thirty years after the British and Americans had first wondered what role it should have in the Cold War. Now, the West decided to provide funds and military equipment to anyone fighting against the occupying force.

A Spiral of Violence and Chaos

After 1979, Afghanistan descended into a spiral of destruction and violence which has continued for more than thirty-five years.[51] The Soviet invasion suddenly brought them about 500 miles closer to the Strait of Hormuz and the oil reserves of the Persian Gulf. Persia and Pakistan were now outflanked, and the whole balance of power across the region seemed to have shifted in the Soviet Union's favour. As a consequence, Afghanistan finally became a top United States priority.[52] America withdrew from the Moscow Olympics in 1980, organised a massive military aid programme for Pakistan, and then pumped a huge amount of covert money and military resources into Afghanistan to support a cross-ethnic and tribal insurgency consisting of nearly eighty groups – the Mujahedin or 'Defenders of Faith'. Two of the prominent Pashtun leaders were Burhanuddin Rabbani and Gulbuddin Hekmatyar, while two prominent leaders in the north were the Uzbek Rashid Dostum and the Tajik Ahmed Shah Massoud, all of whom were to play significant roles in the country's subsequent history. By 1987, the Mujahedin was receiving a billion dollars a year from the United States and as much again from Saudi Arabia.

The Soviet Union finally withdrew their last troops from Afghanistan in 1989 after ten years trying to build a more robust Afghan regime and suppress a violent insurgency. Thousands of lives were lost on both sides. Their failure in Afghanistan in turn helped trigger the ultimate collapse of the Soviet Union and the end of the Cold War. Meanwhile, just three years after the Soviets left, leaving their man, Mohammed Najibullah, in charge in Kabul, violence broke out once again when lucrative Soviet subsidies ran out. Najibullah first hid in a United Nations building and was then assassinated in 1996 in the midst of a bloody civil war as the anti-Soviet Mujahedin alliance broke down. Nearly half of Kabul was reduced to rubble as Massoud's forces battled others for control. During this period, Rabbani served as President from 1992 and Hekmatyar as Prime Minister for periods after 1993 until the Taliban conquered Kabul in 1996. This radical Islamic group, whose name means 'student' in Pashtu, had gradually emerged from within the Pashtun heartlands in and around Kandahar, and then swept across most of the south, west and east of the country. They were backed by Pakistan, who saw them as the means to remove Indian influence from Afghanistan and secure a pro-Pakistan state across the border. By the late 1990s, Osama Bin Laden had established a base for al-Qaeda in the country.

After 9/11, American-led NATO forces allied with the so-called Northern Alliance (predominantly Tajiks, Turkmens and Uzbeks) of former Mujahedin leaders, including Rabbani and Dostum, to clear out al-Qaeda and topple the Taliban-led government. Massoud had been assassinated just two days before 9/11 and is now billed as an Afghan hero, although not by all, while Hekmatyar opposed foreign engagement and has since been denounced as a global terrorist. Once the first phase of the NATO-led coalition was over, Britain focussed its efforts in Helmand; within three years, the Americans had increased their presence in Helmand too.

It turned out the Helmand scheme had stored up yet more opportunities and challenges. The arrival of new settlers in the 1950s and '60s had upset existing power structures and historic tribal dynamics, and thus contributed to the rise of a number of new power brokers who used the province's resources for their own ends. They found that opium poppy grows well in dry climates and in alkaline and saline soils, could be stored for up to two years and what was more, was extremely profitable.[53]

Ironically, the Taliban themselves completed one aspect of the Helmand programme – linking the Kajaki Dam's hydroelectric power to Kandahar.[54] Foreign occupation, however, unleashed dormant, often localised, social, political and economic conflicts, so that when British NATO forces, and later American soldiers and aid workers, invested men and money bringing another turbine to Kajaki in 2006 to increase its electricity generation, this was the midst of an ever-increasing cycle of violence. There was at least one helpful legacy from the Helmand project, however – the mixed communities in Nad-e-Ali and other areas were more amenable to efforts to rebuild and strengthen Afghan local government systems than the traditional tribal areas elsewhere in the province.[55] Since 9/11, Britain, the United States and other members of the international community have been rehabilitating the irrigation systems and training Helmand river valley Authority staff.

Meanwhile, Afghanistan's post-9/11 constitution reintroduced democratic processes and institutions designed to build a democratic consensus and bind Afghanistan's diverse populations to a new politically inclusive state. Since then, elections for the President, National Assembly and Provincial Councils have been based on universal suffrage. At some point in the future, elections will also be held for municipal, district and village councils. Each election has been highly politicised, with Afghanistan's political elite competing for political preferment, amid claims and counter-claims of corruption, stuffed ballot boxes and bought votes. After the 2014 presidential election, the United States helped broker a deal between the two election winners – Ashraf Ghani, a Pashtun and former World Bank technocrat, became President; Abdullah Abdullah, his Tajik opponent and a former Mujahedin commander, became Chief Executive Officer; and General Dostum became one of the Vice-Presidents. Their fellow ex-Mujahedin leader, Rabbani, however, was no longer around to join the government. He was assassinated in 2011, just one year after becoming head of the High Peace Council to negotiate with the Taliban.

Alongside this, Afghanistan has once again been the recipient of vast sums of foreign money to run the government and deliver basic services such as health and education, maintain infrastructure such as roads and dams, and pay for the Afghan police and army. Between 2002 and 2012, the country received $45.6 billion (or £29.09 billion) in development assistance alone from the Organisation of Economic Cooperation and Development (OECD) group of rich countries, the bulk of which, at around $6 billion a year, came after 2005 when there was a steep rise in support. This amounts to 40 per cent of GDP, reflecting a level of aid dependency more typically found in smaller economies such as Liberia and the West Bank and Gaza.[56] Over the same period, there has been a corresponding increase in domestic revenues, from 3 per cent of GDP in 2002/3 to 11 per cent in 2010/11. This is still extremely low, but a significant improvement over previous decades.

There are multiple challenges going forward, however. Afghan institutions have become extremely fragile after decades of warfare, with huge capacity gaps which cannot be turned around overnight. This challenge is compounded, according to a World Bank study in 2012, by the fact that total government spending could reach 43 per cent of GDP within a decade to cover expenditure on the security forces, the civil service, operation and maintenance, and essential services. Internal revenue generation will only cover a fraction of that. Meanwhile, Afghanistan's per capita GDP was only $528 in 2010/11, and poverty and deprivation are pervasive – a third of the population lives below the poverty line, more than half are vulnerable and at serious risk of falling into poverty, and three-quarters are still illiterate. This leaves the country with a fiscal gap of nearly $8 billion a year, heavily dependent on foreign assistance for many years to come, but hopeful that mining contracts with China, India and others will eventually provide a fiscal escape route.[57] Unfortunately, these foreign companies, like their forebears in the 1940s, still face logistical challenges in transporting the minerals out of the country, notwithstanding the challenges of travelling through insecure regions. India, Persia and Afghanistan are finalising a new transit agreement, which will use a new route connecting Afghanistan with a deep-water port at Chabahar in Persia on the Indian Ocean, just 45 kilometres from Pakistan's deep-water port at Gwador, which is funded by the Chinese. India is investing heavily in the port's expansion, and has already funded the construction of a road linking the port with Kandahar.

As for the idea of Pashtunistan, the renaming of the North-West Frontier Province by the Pakistan government as Khyber Pakhtunkhwa in 2010 has reassured some Afghans that their historic cause has finally been recognised.[58] For the Pakistan government, however, the new name was driven more by a desire to shake off a legacy of colonialism and bring NWFP into line with the names of other provinces – Sindh for the Sindhis, Punjab for the Punjabis – than any irredentist idea of Pashtunistan. Indeed, the concept of Pashtun nationalism is more or less a non-issue in Pakistan now, replaced since the mid-late 1970s by an active Islamisation policy designed to cement a nationalist Pakistan identity above and beyond the politics of ethnicity and tribe. If there ever was a unified Pashtun story, it has been transformed multiple times since then by Pakistan's control over the distribution of international funds to different anti-Soviet Mujahedin groups in the 1980s and their subsequent support for the Taliban in the 1990s – both of which were designed to weaken Pashtun nationalism and reduce Indian influence in Afghanistan. Over the last twenty years, these groups have expanded and fragmented, mostly outside the influence of the Pakistan government.[59] As a result, parts of the Frontier, both sides of the Durand Line, are now controlled by different factions which use the border region for their own ends, vying for control over each other and for the imposition of their particular versions of an Islamic state in Afghanistan and Pakistan. More recently, Uzbek militants have moved into the area too, using it as a safe haven from which to run their operations in Uzbekistan in Central Asia. The Pakistani army, like the British before them, are repeatedly engaged in operations to reclaim territories from those who would seek to topple the Pakistani state.

Meanwhile, Pakistan and Afghanistan still accuse the other of military incursions across the Durand Line, and the terms of the 1965 Afghan–Pakistan Transit Agreement are continually renegotiated. The Afghans remain sensitive about any comments that imply recognition of the border, while intelligence-sharing between Afghanistan and Pakistan about smuggling, drug and arms trafficking, and the movement of armed groups, is fraught with difficulties. At the same time, Pakistan continues to view the tribal areas and a pro-Pakistan government in Kabul as critical to 'strategic depth' in their security shield against India to the east.

Time Is Called on the British Embassy in Kabul

Given its chequered history so far, it was not surprising that the scramble to own the British embassy compound was to mirror events in Afghanistan and the region more widely. All was quiet for over a decade while India and Pakistan were unable to resolve their differences, and Afghan–Pakistan relations deteriorated after another border dispute in 1961. During this hiatus, the condition of the embassy compound had changed considerably.

Kabul had expanded and the embassy was now part of a new urban development, the 'West End', which included an international hotel and was soon to be connected by a ring road to the airport. The access roads had been improved too, with tarmac and street lighting. On the main compound, there were now ten houses for British members of staff alongside the Big House, office, servants' quarters, motor transport yards and a Gurkha compound. Meanwhile the former hospital buildings had been divided into six residences for British staff and four for Afghans, derelict buildings had been demolished and a central lawn with flowerbeds created. The electricity and water supply were still part of a single system, but a new sewage disposal plant was under construction. Throughout, the garden paths had been gravelled or paved with stone. Although more work was still needed to replace the chancery office, which was both inconvenient and insecure, as well as to improve the 'more pokey junior staff houses', the Ambassador, Sir John Whitteridge, concluded in 1967 that overall 'the compound is now in very good shape'.[60]

On 30 September 1963, the pace picked up again when India and Pakistan sent a joint aide-memoire seeking a decision on the former British India properties in Kabul, Kuwait, Muscat and Bahrain which were still occupied by the British government.[61] India was now happy to propose that Kabul 'should be handed over to the Government of Pakistan for their occupation against monetary adjustment on the agreed basis with the Government of India'. It all looked pretty straightforward – Kathmandu was in India's possession so it now seemed fair that Kabul should go to Pakistan. The British, however, thought otherwise. It took another five years before they replied.

They were still not keen to leave the property and again explored whether the site could be divided as in Kathmandu. As before, however, plans got stuck because the services could not be separated. Furthermore, the Ambassador thought the Afghans would not tolerate the division of the property or allow Pakistan to occupy either the whole or a part of the site. In the meantime, the Ministry of Public Works in London tried to calculate how much it would cost to buy it from Pakistan. This time round, opinion was framed in terms of cost, not arguments about the compound's symbolic value. An internal note from the Foreign and Commonwealth Office (FCO) explains why:

We are rather doubtful whether there are political considerations of overriding importance and are inclined to feel that the decision on whether to give it up to the Pakistanis or to try and retain it should be taken on basically economic grounds i.e. the comparative cost of buying out the Pakistanis and continuing to maintain the present site as against handing over and setting ourselves up somewhere in the town. It is, of course, possible to make out a political case that to leave the existing embassy would be a blow to our prestige and that, since any substitute would be infinitely less grand in scale, we should lose face. But it can equally be argued that the existing embassy is really much too imperial and Curzonian for our present circumstances and that it is out of tune with the limited role we now play in Afghanistan.[62]

The matter was shelved until 1967 when the new team in the FCO's Accommodation Department picked it up again, determined not to repeat the errors of the earlier 'most ill-considered' Kathmandu financial settlement. Indeed, 'however illogical our position, we must not agree to accept the Kathmandu case as a precedent, either for the payment of compensation at current market value for any properties we retain or for the payment of an economic rent for our use of any or all of the properties since 1947'.[63] They concluded the starting offer should be the 1947 book value, and then they referred the matter to the Treasury for approval.

British diplomats in Kabul, however, saw things rather differently. Ambassador Whitteridge still believed the Big House 'far outshines that of any other embassy in Kabul and gives us a prestige in local eyes which still to a considerable extent masks our relative decline as a great power. Appearance counts for a very great deal on the Afghan scene.'[64] On the other hand, however, he was painfully aware of its value to Pakistan. 'The Pakistan Ambassador himself never loses an opportunity to remind us of the claim, and both he and his Counsellor and Military Attaché go about openly saying that the compound is theirs. In response, we have sought to drop a little poison in their ears with references to the considerable expenditure needed to maintain it.'[65]

He also had some bad news for London. Although Britain's negotiating position had partly rested on the assumption that Afghanistan would always oppose a deal with Pakistan, this, he felt, was no longer the case. In fact, Afghan–Pakistan relations had been improving and the Afghans would probably see any negotiations as an opportunity to secure their own concessions from Pakistan. Top of the list was ending disruptions to trade with India, which was costing them $5 million worth of exports a year. In view of this, he explained, if Britain really wanted to stay put, they would need to move fast before Pakistan realised the Afghans had changed their minds:

As soon as the penny drops, the Pakistanis will bend all their efforts to 'fix' the Afghans perhaps by means of an inducement ... and we will find the ground cut from under us. We ought therefore to consider making sure that we get our own word in first. If we had the Afghans 'in the bag' before the negotiation began, we could, apart from anything else, afford to be much tougher on the question of the amount of compensation.[66]

The High Commission in Karachi added their perspective too – Pakistan was now ready and willing to negotiate just about any deal with the Afghans because they wanted to open a trade route to the Soviet Union.[67] Speed may have been of the essence, but that was not quite how the wheels within Whitehall worked. It took until October 1968 before the Treasury agreed that Britain could offer a settlement based on 1947 values plus compound interest at 3 per cent.[68]

Britain's response to the aide-memoire on 9 November therefore offered a financial settlement and reminded India and Pakistan that the Afghan government would never agree to the transfer of the site to Pakistan.[69] It met with another silence. Two years later, Pakistan rejected the proposal, and then it all went quiet again as Pakistan and India went to war during East Pakistan's bid for independence to form the new state of Bangladesh. Once the crisis was over, Pakistan submitted a new aide-memoire on 6 March 1975 insisting on the transfer of the property or payment of compensation at current market values, plus payment for the expenses incurred by Pakistan while it had rented alternative accommodation for eighteen years. By then, according to the British Ambassador, the Afghans had no interest in striking a deal with Pakistan:

We should be under no illusion about Afghan determination not, repeat not, to let the Pakistanis take over the compound. For the Afghans, an important point of principle is involved. They are determined not to recognise the Pakistan government as the successor government to the British government of India, primarily because they do not wish to recognise the Durand Line agreement. If they agree to our transferring the compound to the Pakistanis, they would in their view be breaching this important principle. In other words, this question is for the Afghans more than a haggle about a piece of real estate.[70]

By this point, however, the struggle over who owned the compound was increasingly out of step with opinion in the FCO about its continued value to Britain and its suitability for British diplomats. Whereas in the mid-1960s the 'West End' of Kabul had been an up-and-coming area, it was now considered 'distinctly unfashionable'. Moreover, FCO inspectors had concluded in 1977 that most of the houses were seriously sub-standard and the chancery office accommodation, which had been built in the 1950s, deeply unsatisfactory. The Big House came in for criticism too. The inspectors agreed it was stunning, but considered it far too grand for an ambassador in a grade-three post and far too costly to run. Indeed, 'it is just a pity that it is not situated in another capital where the scale of our representation was more compatible with it'. Lord Curzon's vision was now a complete anachronism:

> The exceptionally fine Residence is far too large for the present scale of our representation in Afghanistan. The government of Pakistan may well not want to adopt the albatross at present around our necks because the house is equally unsuitable for their purposes too. Indeed, it seems to us that the only body which could make proper use of it is the Afghan government, for whom it would make an excellent official residence or guest house.

In view of this, they concluded that Britain should pay rent to Pakistan for the period from 1947 to the present day but should show no interest in acquiring the title deeds. In fact, they should now explore whether the Afghan government itself was interested in acquiring the site.[71]

Then the matter was shelved for another fifteen years as Afghanistan lurched from one crisis to another. After the Soviet invasion in December 1979, Britain's interests were represented by a Chargé d'Affaires and a small team of British staff. When the Soviets left Kabul in 1989, the British, like many others, closed the embassy and withdrew their staff because it was too unsafe to stay. Thereafter, Britain's interests were looked after by the High Commission in Pakistan and the compound was guarded by a team of Gurkhas, led by retired Captain Ranhaj Rai, who had been based there since 1978. The buildings were maintained by a handful of Afghan staff. Between 1992 and 1994, at least sixty projectiles hit the compound. Most landed in the grounds, but in January 1994, a 'large 100mm tank shell careered through the front veranda of the main residence and ricocheted upstairs, crashing through a chest of drawers and into the Ambassador's bedroom where it destroyed a television before coming to rest without exploding'.[72]

Pakistan began to sound out the British once again during this period, especially since they still maintained a diplomatic team in Kabul. This time around, they struck lucky. Sir Nicolas Barrington, the British High Commissioner in Pakistan, who also represented Britain's interests in Afghanistan, felt the time was right to sort the issue out once and for all. He understood that India had acquired the former British embassy in Kathmandu after independence, and that therefore Britain's embassy in Kabul was rightfully Pakistan's as part of the same deal. The Afghan Foreign Minister, His Excellency Hedayat Amin Arsala, was not wholly convinced. He tried to persuade the Pakistani government not to pursue their claim because, in his view, he had always associated it with the British presence in Afghanistan and expected the British to reoccupy the embassy when they returned to Afghanistan. He was overruled by the Mujahedin government, however, because they were keen to support Pakistan. In 1994, he therefore came to an agreement with Barrington that the main embassy compound, including the Big House, should be transferred to Pakistan, while Britain would retain the hospital compound.[73] A journalist's description of the old British embassy just before the handover ceremony in April 1994 provides a picture of what it looked like at that time:

> It consists of a two winged ambassadorial residence, complete with lavish reception rooms, a large ballroom and oak panelled library, surrounded by a cluster of English style country houses in whitewash and green trim, and reached along roads fringed by hedges. The walled compound covers twenty-six acres of terraced gardens and includes three tennis courts, a swimming pool, a hockey pitch and squash courts ... In the Ambassador's oak panelled study, an old framed map of Kabul still hangs on the wall. Next door, the drinks trolley is still stocked with bottles, some of which have been untouched for five years. In the ballroom, large portraits of George V and Queen Mary await their turn for removal.[74]

Most of the furniture from the Big House, including the grand piano and the library of antiquarian books, was transferred to the hospital compound before the Pakistanis moved in.

They were not to enjoy their new home for very long, however. On 6 September 1995, a 5,000-strong pro-Mujahedin government mob attacked the embassy in retribution for the fall of Herat to the Taliban the previous day. They believed Pakistan had provided the Taliban with financial and military support. One person was killed, several were injured, including the Ambassador, and the Big House and other buildings were set on fire and looted. Thereafter, the premises remained empty.

Once Kabul calmed down under Taliban rule, Britain considered reopening a joint embassy and development office in the hospital compound in 1998, but in the end this came to nothing, and an aid office was opened in another part of town. The head of the office, Dr Ann Freckleton, recalls jogging round the grounds regularly and seeing some buildings here and there, but they were in a very poor condition.[75]

The events of 9/11, however, put the spotlight back on Afghanistan and with it on the former British embassy compound. When British troops arrived at the gates in November 2001 with instructions to secure the building, two Afghan staff, Zahoor Shah and Afzal Syed, resolutely refused to allow them entry until they were completely satisfied that the troops were British. These two men had begun their careers at the embassy at the ages of eight and nine as tennis ball boys, and had worked there solidly for thirty-four and forty-five years respectively.[76] They had braved years of uncertainty and violence, and hidden everything of value, including the portraits of Queen Mary and King George V, the Wilton china service, the Foreign Office embossed silver teapots, the English crystal glasses and several ancient blunderbusses. At night, they had slept in the gatehouse with five other local staff, ready to repel any intruders. In 1996 a rocket had come into the compound and killed a carpenter, and they regularly convinced the Taliban that there was nothing inside worth taking. In August 2002, they were awarded MBEs during a ceremony in the gardens hosted by the new British Ambassador, followed by tea, sandwiches and cake, a poignant reminder of times past. The British embassy opened for business in the hospital compound in late 2001, and then tried to formalise ownership of that part of the site with the Pakistan government, but they hit an unexpected brick wall – no one could find a formal record confirming that Britain had retained rights to it under the 1994 agreement. The British finally vacated the premises for good in 2003.[77] The Pakistan embassy opened for business on its new site in 2012.

Since then, the British embassy has been located less than a quarter of a mile from the site of the first British cantonment in the 1830s. Over the years, this site had become the Afghan army officers' social club, and most recently the headquarters of the NATO-led International Security Assistance Force (ISAF). In a piece of dramatic irony, the diplomatic enclave is called Wazir Akbar Khan, named after the Afghan hero of the First Afghan War. This was the man who killed Sir William Macnaghten, the first British Envoy, in cold blood, and then oversaw one of the most humiliating defeats in the British army's entire history – the retreat from the British cantonment to the Khyber Pass in the winter of 1841–2 and the slaughter at Gandamak. His painting hangs in many Afghan government offices to this day.

When Squire first arrived in Afghanistan in 1943, he had asked Prime Minister Hashim Khan why the frontispiece of every school history book showed a picture of Dr Brydon, the sole survivor from Gandamak, riding towards the British Fort at Jalalabad to tell the tale of Britain's crushing defeat.[78] He was concerned that this reading of history simply served to fuel anti-British sentiment. Hashim Khan replied: 'I quite understand your point, but I know my people better than you do. You must leave the timing to me. The timing is not yet right.' Some weeks later, Ali Mohammed told him that the picture had been removed. For Squire, it had been a poignant reminder that Britain's Great Game in Afghanistan still lived on in people's memories and was an integral part of how the Afghans defined themselves and their history in relation to others. Hashim Khan's response serves as a gentle reminder that the Afghans, throughout their history, have invariably found their own solutions to uniquely Afghan challenges in their own time.

Glossary

Afghani	Afghan currency.
Ayah	Nanny.
Bearer	Servant.
Chowkidar	Guard.
Dari	Persian or Farsi language.
Jirga	Tribal assembly, associated with Pashtuns, used to settle disputes and make decisions.
Lakh	A hundred thousand.
Lashkar	Tribal army.
Legation	A diplomatic mission with lower status than an embassy, and headed by a minister, not an ambassador.
Loya Jirga	Meeting of tribal leaders from across the country, convened by the king.
Malik	Tribal elder or leader.
Mullah	Islamic religious leader.
Plebiscite	Another name for a referendum.
Quami System	Process for tribal conscription into the army.
Rupees	Indian currency.
Sardar	Honorific term given to male members of the royal family, derived from military commander.
Shamiana	A large tent with open sides.
Shirkat	Monopoly.

Notes

Abbreviations

IOR   India Office Records in the British Library, London
NA   National Archives, London
FO   Foreign Office, London
CRO   Commonwealth Relations Office, London
WO   War Office, London

Foreword
1. S. Simms to R. Simms, 7 January 1948.
2. Gardener to Scott, FO, 10 July 1951, NA: FO371/92084.
3. Thomas Ruttig, Amin Saikal, Vartan Gregorian, Maxwell Fry, Ludwig Adamec and Robert Crews are notable exceptions covering Afghan history, finance and politics, although none of these examines the impact of Indian independence on Afghan politics and foreign policy in detail. Leon and Leila Poullada cover the period from the United States' perspective.
4. Squire to Bevin, FO, 8 July 1948, NA: FO983/35.
5. British embassy circular, 16 March 1949, NA: FO983/36.
6. A key strand in Ahmed Rashid's book, *Descent into Chaos*.
7. Himsworth, p. 15.
8. Especially Mir Ghulam Mohammed Ghobar's 1967 history book, *Afghanistan dar Masir-i-Tarikh*, which is not available in translation in the Britain; and Abdul Majid Zabuli's account of the Afghan economy, *Iad-Dasht-Ehai*, published in Peshawar in 1982.
9. Gardener to Murray, FO, 2 June 1950, DO35/2951.
10. Information from Alan Whaites, who was based at the British embassy from 2008–10.

1 All Change

1. Squire's journal, 15 June 1947.
2. Von Tunzelmann, p. 3.
3. Squire's journal, 11 June 1947.
4. Gaddis, p. 11.
5. Report from Lancaster to Squire, 12 June 1947, forwarded to London 20 June 1947, in IOR: R/12/170.
6. Squire to the Foreign Office, 17 November 1948, in IOR: L/WS/1/1168.
7. Eg During informal discussions on Frontier policy, held at the Ministry of Foreign Affairs with Afghan Foreign Minister Ali Muhammad Khan, Kabul, 20 Nov 1944, in IOR: R/12/177.
8. Squire's journal, 11 June 1947.
9. Squire's journal, 15 June 1947.
10. Squire's journal, 23 July 1947.
11. Squire's journal, 5 August 1947.
12. Squire's journal, 11 August 1947.
13. Squire's journal, 18 August 1947.
14. Squire's journal, 15 August 1948.
15. Squire's journal, 18 August 1948.
16. Referred to in a memo from the Secretary to the Joint Chiefs of Defence Staff on 29 August 1947, IOR: R/12/170.
17. Squire to FO, January 1947, NA: CAB122/722.
18. Secretary to the Joint Chiefs of Defence Staff, note to the FO, 29 August 1947, IOR: R/12/170.
19. Bevin to Squire, 22 September 1947, IOR: R/12/170.
20. The current conflict in Afghanistan has also been described by some as the 'New Great Game' – e.g. Klass 21. Hennessy, p. 76.
22. Gaddis, p. 8.
23. Hennessy, p. 91.
24. Kynaston, p. 20.
25. Hennessy, p. 174.
26. Hennessy, p. 99.
27. Pelling, p. 56.
28. Pelling, p. 165–6.
29. Hyam, p. 94, Darwin, p. 171.
30. Aung Sang did not live to see the formal transfer of power later in the year because he and his Cabinet were assassinated in July 1947.
31. Smith, pp. 37–8.
32. George F. Kennan's February 1946 telegram from the US embassy in Moscow is now seen as a defining moment in shaping US post war

policy. This was later published in 1947, expanding on the theme of 'containment', a key aspect of Cold War strategy. Gaddis, p. 29.

33. Foreign Relations of the United States (FRUS), The Pentagon Talks, 1947, The Near East and Africa, Wisconsin Digital Archive, p. 2.
34. Hennessy, p. 290.
35. Pelling, pp. 169–70.
36. Hennessy, p. 339.
37. S. Simms to R. Simms, 4 March 1946.
38. S. Simms to R. Simms, 18 October 1946.
39. S. Simms to R. Simms, 6 October 1947.
40. S. Simms to R. Simms, 29 January 1948.
41. Talbot, 1998, p. 104.
42. This was the same hotel where Nadir Shah had stayed twenty years earlier on his way to capture the Afghan throne in 1929.
43. S. Simms to R. Simms, 18 January 1948.
44. S. Simms to R. Simms, 29 January 1948.
45. Carse's visit report, 25 August 1949, in NA FO371/75643.

2 British–Afghan Relations

1. Quoted in Foreign Office Research Department, 'A Survey of Anglo-Afghan Relations 1747–1947', 11 August 1949, in NA: FO371/75642. This was a comment on the 1905 Anglo-Afghan Treaty signed by Amir Habibullah, which effectively confirmed the conditions which had been agreed by his father after the Second Afghan War.
2. Bastion military base, which has supported ISAF operations across the South, including Helmand and Kandahar, is located there.
3. Foreign Office Research Department, 11 August 1949, in NA: FO371/75642.
4. Barfield, pp. 47–8.
5. Arney, p. 4.
6. Hopkirk's book, *The Great Game*, provides one of the best overviews of Britain and Russia's exploits in Central Asia and Afghanistan in the nineteenth century.
7. Rubin, p. 32.
8. There has been no Afghan census since 1974 so it is still impossible to get accurate data on the size and ethnic make-up of the country. The 1974 census found that Afghanistan had the same number of people, twelve million, as the British had estimated in 1912.
9. Foreign Office Research Department, 11 August 1949, in NA: FO371/75642.
10. A useful explanation of this process is provided in Bates, p. 31.

11. Rubin, p. 45.
12. Rubin, p. 5.
13. Bates, p. 50.
14. Dalrymple, p. 8.
15. Elphinstone, p. 173.
16. Elphinstone, pp. 516–7.
17. Elphinstone, pp. 174–8.
18. Quoted in Dalrymple, p. 53.
19. Hopkirk, p. 123.
20. Dalrymple, p. 53.
21. Hopkirk, p. 5.
22. Dalrymple, p. 57.
23. After 9/11, the site of this cantonment became the headquarters for the International Security Assistance Force (ISAF), the centre for coalition military operations against Al Qaeda and the Taliban.
24. Barfield p. 4–5.
25. Dalrymple, p 501.
26. Hopkirk, p. 278.
27. The Treaty of Gandamak of 1879 ceded the politically important districts of Pishin and Sibi in Balochistan, and the Kurran Agency in the north west Frontier Province to the British, as well as control of the Khyber and Michni Passes.
28. Barfield p. 154.
29. Quoted in Arney, p. 11.
30. Barfield p. 153.
31. Rubin p. 49.
32. Quoted in Arney, p. 12.
33. Quoted in Arney, p. 12.
34. Although they are more commonly referred to today as the Musahibans, the rest of this book refers to them as the Yahya Khels since that is how they were referred to by the British in the 1940s.
35. Wolpert 1982, pp. 71–2.
36. Squire, Royal Geographical Society, 1951.
37. Foreign Office Research Department, 11 August 1949, in NA: FO371/75642.
38. Foreign Office Research Department, 11 August 1949, in NA: FO371/75642.
39. Barfield p. 206.
40. Adamec, 1974, p. 98; Crews, p. 164.
41. Adamec, 1974, p. 186.
42. This period is described in detail in Stewart.
43. Told to the author by HE Hedayat Amin Arsala.

44. Arney, p. 23. The Afghan Ambassador in Moscow, for instance, Ghulam Nabi Charkhi, collected a mercenary force and marched south towards the border, allegedly with Soviet help.
45. This was during a period in Lawrence's life when he had reinvented himself as an ordinary aircraftsman working under the pseudonym Shaw and was writing a translation of the *Odyssey* in his spare time. There is no evidence that he was involved. Wolpert, 1982, p. 98; Wilson, p. 843.
46. Ewans, p. 102.
47. William Kerr Fraser-Tytler was based at the legation in Kabul at different times in the 1920s and 30s, becoming Head of the legation between 1935 and 1941. This quote comes from his book on Afghanistan, written on his return to Britain, p. 243.
48. Dupree, p. 471.
49. Fry, pp. 82–4.
50. Barfield, p. 203.
51. Fry, pp. 37 and 152.
52. Gregorian pp. 316–7.
53. Fry, pp. 37, 152, 181–89. International data for the period 1995 and 2000 show average internal tax revenues, as a proportion of GDP, were 13 per cent in low income countries, 19 per cent in middle income countries, and 36 per cent in high income countries, Moore, p. 7.
54. Quoted in Giuistozzi, from an Afghan press article in 1970, p. 17.
55. Ansary, p. 136.
56. Information from the British legation's Leading Afghan Personalities file, IOR: L/PS/12/1562.
57. Information from conversation with HE Hedayat Amin Arsala, who knew all three as a child and teenager in Kabul.
58. Squire to CRO, 6 February 1948, IOR: FO371/69451.
59. Saikal, p. 122.
60. Afghan Personalities file, IOR: L/PS/12/1562.
61. Dupree, p. 471.
62. Foreign Office Research Department, 11 August 1949, in NA: FO371/75642.
63. Rasanayagam, p. 25.
64. Foreign Office Research Department, 11 August 1949, in NA: FO371/75642.
65. Saikal, p. 133.
66. K De B Codrington's Report on British Afghan Relations, in NA: WO208/4710.

67. Report by Major H. A. Legard, Surgeon of the legation on state of medicine in Afghanistan, 15 February 1943, IOR: L/PS/12/1733.
68. Foreign Office Research Department, 11 August 1949, in NA: FO371/75642.
69. Squire, Royal Geographical Society, 1951.
70. Squire, Royal Geographical Society, 1951.
71. Squire, Royal Geographical Society, 1951.
72. Wallace Murray, State Department, to Under-Secretary of State, Sumner Welles, 8 April 1940, quoted in Poullada and Poullada, 1995, p. 71.
73. Conversations with Engert reported in Poullada and Poullada, 1995, p. 71.
74. For at least a century, and right up to the Soviet invasion in December 1978, agriculture and pastoralism accounted for nearly 60 per cent of domestic production and employed two-thirds of the population. Once rural handicrafts and trade were included, 85 per cent of the population depended on the rural economy for their livelihood. Rubin, pp. 32–33.
75. Fry, pp. 11–12. By 1972, there were 3972 schools teaching 760,469 pupils.
76. Data from the UNESCO Statistical Year Book, quoted in Rubin p. 70.
77. The Medicine Faculty and the Law and Political Science Faculty were supported by the French, the Agriculture, Engineering and Education Faculties by the United States, the Faculties of Science and Economics and the Department of Anthropology by the Germans, and the Faculty of Sharia by Al-Azhar University in Eqypt. The Polytechnic Institute was sponsored by the Soviet Union. Dupree, p. 598.
78. Gregorian, p. 356.
79. Fry, p. 28.
80. Gregorian pp. 368–9.
81. Gregorian, p. 390.
82. Gregorian, p. 390.
83. Stated by Abdul Majid Zabuli at a conference in Kabul on 26 April 1947, and reported to London 7 May 1947, IOR: L/PS/12/1801.
84. Squire to FO, 7 May 1947, IOR: L/PS/12/1801.
85. Squire to FO, 7 May 1947, IOR: L/PS/12/1801.
86. Reported by Squire in the 1946 Annual Political Review, in NA: L/PS/12/1572.
87. Dr Macrae's 1947 medical report, IOR: L/PS/23/1733.

3 *The British Embassy in Kabul*

1. Byron, p. 326.
2. See Woodburn for a good description of the Bala Hissar.
3. Byron, p. 327.
4. Adamec, 1985, p. 324.
5. Andrew Roth, 'The State of Afghanistan today: Mass of the people live in poverty', 11 April 1950, *The Scotsman*.
6. Gardener to Scott, FO, 3 March 1950, NA: FO371/83093.
7. This point is mentioned several times in the archives as well as in a booklet written by the then Oriental Secretary, Katherine Himsworth in 1976. I am grateful to Sir Nicholas Barrington for sharing his copy with me.
8. The question of who actually owned this land became important forty years later when Britain had to sort out whether they had the right to hand the premises and land over to Pakistan or India – see Chapter 8.
9. Himsworth, p. 2.
10. Information provided by Dr Ann Freckleton, the former head of the Department for International Development's programme in Afghanistan, who regularly visited the compound in the late 1990s.
11. Information from Squire's daughters, Hazel and Gillian, who lived in the 'Big House' in the late 1940s, and from Luke Harding, *The Guardian*, 28 August 2002.
12. Sir Nicholas Barrington, Oriental Secretary at the embassy from 1959–61, was responsible for the library and providing access to it for scholars. He remembers the significance of this collection, and the effort taken after the Soviet invasion in December 1979 to get the books out of the country. They are now housed with the India Office Records in the British Library.
13. An inventory prepared in 1947 of the carpets in the Residence provides some sense of the size of the rooms – in the Minister's bedroom alone, the three carpets measured 19 by 15 feet, 4 foot 5 inches by 3 foot 4 inches, and 7 foot 6 inches by 4 foot 11 inches.
14. Himsworth, p. 15.
15. Byron, p. 321.
16. S. Simms to R. Simms, 12 May 1948.
17. S. Simms to R. Simms, 18 October 1948.
18. S. Simms to R. Simms, 1 November 1948.
19. Report by Major H. A. Legard, Surgeon, on the state of medicine in Afghanistan, 15 February 1943, IOR: L/PS/12/1733.
20. Squire and internal legation note, 31 May 1947, in IOR: R/12/169.
21. Wylie to FO, 2 March 1943, in IOR: L/PS/12/1733.

22. Squire, Valedictory Despatch, Anglo Afghan Relations, 30 August 1949, NA: FO371/75627.
23. S. Simms to R. Simms, 10 February 1948.
24. S. Simms to R. Simms, 22 November 1948.
25. Himsworth, p. 8.
26. FCO Inspection Report, March 1977, NA: FCO37/1854.
27. S. Simms to R. Simms, 22 April 1948.
28. Michener, p. 58.
29. Himsworth, p. 8.
30. Details of the Bacha Saqua period and the airlift are described in Stewart, 1973.
31. Lady Humphrys' diary, and the rest of the papers relating to the incident, are in IOR: L/PO/5/30. The diary was read with interest by Prime Minister Stanley Baldwin.
32. Report by Mr Best to Sir Francis Humphrys, 31 December 1929. IOR: L/PO/5/30.
33. Over the following two months, the RAF managed the first ever full-scale air evacuation in history, eventually flying 586 foreigners as well as the King's younger brother out of the country in eighty-two plane journeys. Humphrys and his remaining staff were on the last plane out.
34. After the attack, Nazir Rahmat Khan gave an account of what happened to a British investigation. IOR: R/12/189.
35. There's an interesting post-script to this story. Humphrys' gratitude to Rahmat was somewhat tempered when he learnt that the latter had found the keys to the store room and cellars in the Big House. Not only that, but Rahmat admitted in a statement to the investigating officer, Mr Parsons, on 5 June 1930: 'I used stores and wines for entertainment when members of other legations and Afghans came. I also had to feed about twenty-four Indian motor lorry drivers who took refuge in the legation for about six weeks during the time of Bacha Saqao ... I was given no proper charge of anything, but Sir Francis Humphrys merely informed me the evening before the evacuation that I should remain.' Humphrys felt Rahmat's behaviour had been a 'monstrous' abuse of position. Parsons, however, thought differently. He was impressed by Rahmat's honesty and concluded: 'In general, he has rendered valuable services to the government. He has delivered valuable property practically intact after a disturbed period of more than a year. He volunteered to remain behind, and single-handed fulfilled his trust, no small achievement for a man of his status and antecedents'. It was eventually decided that although it would not be appropriate for him to continue working for the

legation, he should receive four months' pay, and be offered a post in the North-West Frontier Province in India. See IOR: R/12/189.

36. I am grateful to Maximillian Drephel for sharing this piece of information with me, based on his trawl through the former India Office Records in London and Delhi.
37. The challenges are set out in full in NA: FO371/83093.
38. Gardener to Scott, FO, 3 March 1950, NA: FO371/83093.
39. This description comes from a discussion between the author and Squire's daughters, Hazel and Gillian.
40. Sir Olaf Caroe, Obituary of Sir Giles Squire, *Journal of the Royal Central Asian Society*, October–December 1959.
41. S. Simms to R. Simms, 10 February 1948.
42. Caroe, ibid.
43. Keen's Memoirs, IOR: Mss Eur F226/16.
44. Although Gardener's first name was Albert, he preferred to be known by his middle name, John.
45. Lancaster's papers in the National Army Museum in London are an invaluable resource for any anthropologist keen to understand Afghan tribal and ethnic structures in the 1940s, or military historian interested in learning about the early development of the Afghan army and air force.
46. This Ministry was called Defence or War inter-changeably in the telegrams and despatches to London during this period.
47. These descriptions come from Lancaster's military record in IOR: L/MIL/14/61186.
48. Squire to FO, 12 April 1948, in NA: FO371/69451.
49. Lancaster's papers in the National Army Museum.
50. S. Simms to R. Simms, 12 May 1948.
51. S. Simms to R. Simms, 12 May 1948.
52. S. Simms to R. Simms, 5 July 1948.
53. Told to the author by Major (Retd) John Prendergast.
54. Within hours of his arrival to lead a force of British troops and Norwegian reservists, his troops had come under attack. In the ensuing battle, fifty Germans were killed with the loss of only one Allied soldier.
55. Prendergast's obituary, *The Daily Telegraph*, 3 March 2008.
56. Prendergast, 1979, p. 246.
57. Prendergast, 1979, p. 248; 1993, pp. 4–7.
58. S. Simms to R. Simms, 20 September 1948.

59. Squire to Barclay, War Office Personnel Department, 15 May 1948, IOR: L/WS/1/1168; Conversations between the author, Hazel Hastings and John Prendergast.
60. Prendergast, 1993, p. 13.
61. Prendergast, 1993, p. 11.
62. Himsworth, p. 15.
63. Reported in IOR: L/PS/12/1827.
64. King Zahir Shah was buried in the same mausoleum in 2007, after his return to Afghanistan from exile in Italy in 2002.
65. S. Simms to R. Simms, 25 May 1948.
66. Told to the author by Major (Retd) John Prendergast.
67. Keen, IOR: MSS Eur F226/16.
68. The report of their tour can be found in NA: WO208/4709.
69. Quoted from the Military Intelligence Files in NA: WO208/4972.
70. S. Simms to R. Simms, 22 April 1948.
71. S. Simms to R. Simms, 29 July 1948.
72. S. Simms to R. Simms, 8 April 1948.
73. S. Simms to R. Simms, 12 August 1948.
74. S. Simms to R. Simms, 22 April 1948.
75. S. Simms to R. Simms, 19 April 1948.
76. S. Simms to R. Simms, 18 August 1948.
77. S. Simms to R. Simms, 1 November 1948.
78. Information shared with the author by Major (Rtd) John Prendergast, Colonel Prendergast's son.
79. Squire's journal, 28 December 1948.
80. Squire's journal, 1 February 1949. Harrington continued to live in Kabul for several months thereafter, and partially redeemed himself in Squire's and others' eyes: 'In many ways, he has done well and has already made quite an impression on the Afghans. (In fact, he operated on one today in our hospital), though the death last week of M. Shah Khan, the Chief of the CID, is being attributed by some Afghan doctors to a drug prescribed by him and administered by Armine. I hope that his incident will not have any repercussions. But his relations with the embassy have made it impossible for him to stay.' Thereafter, Squire concluded 'he has not been quite such an embarrassment as he might have been, [and] several of our own colony in the town and some foreign missions, as well as Afghans, continue to employ him. He even called on Armine to help in the case of a dying girl the other day.' (Squire's Journal, 29 June 1949).

4 Afghanistan in Transition

1. Briefing note prepared by the British embassy, Kabul, for the visit of Sir Esler Dening, British High Commissioner in Karachi in March 1951. The visit was called off when Dening got sick and was too ill to travel. 13 March 1951, NA: FO371/92084.
2. Information shared with the author by HE Hedayat Amin Arsala.
3. Ruttig, 2006, p. 5.
4. Afghan Personalities file, IOR: L/PS/12/1562.
5. Gardener to FO, 14 April 1950, NA: DO35/2951.
6. Report of conversation between Ali Mohammed and Gardener, sent to FO, 24 July 1951, in NA: FO371/92084.
7. Military Intelligence Summary, 1 September 1949, NA: FO371/75623.
8. Leading Afghan personalities, IOR: L/PS/12/1562.
9. Arney, p. 32; Saikal, p. 114; Ruttig, 2011, p. 3–8. There are many different spellings for the Movement of Awakened Youth in English. I've used Ruttig's, *Wesh Zalmian*.
10. Dupree, p. 483.
11. Mentioned in Squire to FO, 22 January 1947, IOR: L/PS/12/1572 and Military Intelligence Summary number 7, 3 April 1948, in NA: FO371/9457.
12. Squire to FO, 26 June 1948, in NA: FO371/69451.
13. Intelligence Summary number 10, NA: FO371/69458.
14. Reported in Squire to FO, 6 May 1949, NA: DO35/2951.
15. Ansari, p. 43. Ruttig, 2011, p. 6–9.
16. Dupree, p. 496. Ruttig, 2013, p. 6.
17. Squire to FO, 14 January 1948, NA: FO953/273.
18. Ruttig, 2013, p. 6.
19. Fry, p. 28.
20. Squire to FO, 20 March 1948, NA: FO371/69448.
21. Squire to FO, 20 May 1948, NA: FO371/69449.
22. Economic Report, September to December 1948, British embassy, NA: FO371/75646.
23. Dupree, p. 483.
24. Squire to FO, 7 and 24 May 1947, IOR: L/PS/12/1801.
25. Report of Squire's meeting with the Afghan Foreign Minister, 27 March 1948, NA: FO371/69448.
26. Squire to FO, 7 and 24 May 1947, IOR: L/PS/12/1801.
27. Squire to FO, 7 May 1947, IOR: L/PS/12/1801.
28. Squire to FO, 24 July 1948, NA: FO983/13.
29. Squire to FO, 19 June 1948, NA: FO983/13.
30. Letter from Afghan Ambassador to FO, 17 January 1949, NA: FO371/75647.

31. This background material comes from two reports produced by the Foreign Office Research Department and one from the United States State Department's equivalent research branch, which was shared with the FO in 1948, 'The Perso-Afghan Dispute over the River Helmand', 31 March 1948, in NA: FO371/69463, and 'The Helmand River Dispute between Persia and Afghanistan', 5 December 1949, in NA: FO983/50. US State Department: 'Controversy between Iran and Afghanistan over the Helmand river Waters', 24 October 1947, in NA: FO371/69464.

32. Mentioned in a FO file note in February 1948, referring to a letter from the Afghan Chargé D'Affaires dated 10 February 1948, NA: FO371/69462.

33. Letter from FO to United States embassy, 9 July 1948, NA: FO371/69463.

34. FO file note by T. S. Tull, 29 June 1948 settling out the pros and cons concerning what Britain's involvement should be, and his conclusion, NA: FO371/69463.

35. Papers between Kabul, London and Washington, NA: FO371/69462 and 69464.

36. Report of meeting between Squire and Ali Mohammed, 9 September 1948, in NA: FO983/8.

37. The Indian government agreed to release this document, so long as it was made clear that although the documents were published in India, the Indian government had not in any way been involved with the original agreements.

38. FO file note by T. S. Tull, 29 June 1948, NA: FO371/69463.

39. Squire to FO, 24 June 1948, in IOR: L/PS/12/1591.

40. When Malcolm Jones prepared for his preliminary visit to Kabul in early 1950, the State Department showed him the original papers, but then returned these to the British embassy on 15 August 1950, saying that 'no copy or extract has been retained in our files'. The embassy recorded: 'We gather that the State Department are not sure whether there might not perhaps be unfavourable reactions on the part of either the Afghan or Persian government if it became known that Mr Jones had referred to these earlier studies on the Helmand river question, hence their desire that the document should be returned to you, and not kept in their records'. British embassy Washington to FO, 25 August 1950, NA: FO371/83041. To the relief of the British, however, Jones did visit the embassy in Kabul and read the original papers thoroughly.

41. Lingeman to FO, 21 April 1953, NA: FO371/106669.

42. Annual Political Review 1948, NA: FO371/75621.

43. Military Intelligence Summary, 3 February 1949, NA FO371/83037.
44. Military Intelligence Summary, 3 February 1949, NA: FO371/83037.
45. Military Intelligence Summary, 17 February 1949, NA: FO371/83037.
46. Military Intelligence Summary, 3 February 1949, NA: FO371/83037.
47. Military Intelligence Summary, 26 May 1949, NA: FO371/83037.
48. Military Intelligence Summary, 26 May 1949, NA: FO371/83037.
49. Adamec, 1987, p. 50.
50. Afghanistan, Annual Review for 1949, NA: FO371/83035.
51. The cluster system was revived by President Karzai in 2010. HE Hedayat Amin Arsala headed the governance cluster of Ministries and Departments.
52. Described in Gardener to FO, 28 October, 2, 4, 5 November 1949, NA: FO371/75624.
53. Gardener to FO, 5 November 1949, NA: FO371/75624.
54. FO File Note by Macham, November 1949, NA: FO371/75624.
55. Squire to FO, 7 May 1947, IOR: L/PS/12/1801.
56. Correspondence between Marconi, the Treasury and the Foreign Office, January and February 1948, in NA: FO371/69448.
57. Squire to Hector McNeil, MP, FO, NA: DO142/118.
58. Squire to FO, 25 April 1947, IOR: R/12/165.
59. Squire to FO, 9 March 1948, IOR: L/PS/12/1554.
60. Squire to FO, 9 March 1948, IOR: L/PS/12/1554.
61. Squire to Grey, FO, 10 November 1948, NA: FO983/12.
62. Record of meeting, November 1946, IOR: L/PS/12/1801.
63. Chancellor of the Exchequer, Hugh Dalton, to Major C. P. Mayhew, MP, 17 December 1947, IOR: L/PS/12/1801, and quoted in minute from the Treasury to the CRO on 3 February 1949, NA: FO371/75647
64. Ledwidge, FO, to Chapman, Board of Trade, 19 January 1949; CRO to Treasury, 8 February 1949, NA: FO371/75647.
65. Minutes of the meeting, in IOR L/PS/12/1829.
66. Correspondence between Kabul and London on import opportunities is in NA: FO371/75647.
67. Board of Trade to CRO, 20 July 1949, NA: FO371/75648.
68. Treasury to the FO, 31 August 1949, in FO371/75648, and 23 July 1949, NA: FO371/75647.
69. Gardener to Bevin, 10 March 1950, NA: FO371/83093.
70. Squire to FO, 27 March 1948, NA: FO371/69448.
71. Squire to FO, 27 March 1948, NA: FO371/69448.
72. Squire to FO, 22 June 1948, in NA: WO208/4934.
73. Squire to FO, 7 May 1947, IOR: L/PS/12/1801.
74. Squire to FO, 26 June 1948, NA: FO983/13.
75. Squire to FO, 21 September 1948, NA: FO371/69449.

76. Squire to FO, 21 September 1948, NA: FO371/69449.
77. Squire to FO, 21 September 1948, NA: FO371/69449.
78. File note by Ledwidge, 11 October 1948, NA: FO371/69449.
79. Drefus to Washington, 19 September 1949, in Foreign Relations of the United States, Near East, South Asia and Africa, University of Wisconsin digital library.
80. US Press Release, 23 November 1949, NA: FO371/75648.
81. Poullada, 1987, p. 41.
82. Gardener to FO, 10 December 1949, NA: FO371/75648.
83. Kabul to FO, 10 December 1949, NA: FO371/75648.
84. Gardener to FO, 29 November 1949, NA: FO371/75648.
85. British embassy Washington to Foreign Office, 6 December 1949, NA: FO371/75648.
86. Kabul to FO 22 October 1949, NA: FO371/75648.
87. Minutes of a meeting held in the Treasury, 18 November 1949, NA: DO142/118.

5 Afghan Demands on the Frontier

1. Squire, Lecture to the Royal Geographic Society, March 1951.
2. Squire, 1951 Ibid.
3. Talbot, 1998, p. 97.
4. Talbot, 1998, pp. 98–100; French, p. 363.
5. Quotes are taken direct from the 1893 agreement, and are quoted in 'A Survey of Anglo-Afghan Relations, 1947–1947, Part 3', produced by the Foreign Office Research Department (FORD), p. 26, final version, 11 August 1949, NA: FO371/75642.
6. Quoted in Wolpert, 1982, p 67 from Amir Abdur Rahman's Autobiography.
7. Foreign Office Research Department, 'A Survey of Anglo-Afghan Relations 1747–1947, Part 3, The Indo-Afghan Frontier', 11 August 1949, p. 27, in NA: FO371/75642.
8. Taken direct from the 1921 Anglo-Afghan Treaty. A copy is in NA: FCO78/1.
9. The details of this rebellion are covered in Chapter 7. It concerned a shift in the way men were conscripted into the army – from a system through which the tribes themselves chose who would be called up, to making all young fit men liable for conscription. Hashim Khan's points are recorded in Major Crichton, Political Counsellor, Kabul, to Lt Col R. R. Burnett, Secretary, External Affairs Department, Delhi, on 30 December 1945, IOR: R/12/177.

10. Note on informal discussions on Frontier policy held at Ministry of Foreign Affairs with Ali Muhammed Khan, Kabul, 20 Nov 1944, in IOR: R/12/177.
11. Squire's meeting with Ali Mohammed Khan and Najibullah Khan, DG Political Department, Ministry of Foreign Affairs, Kabul, 7 February 1946, IOR: R/12/177.
12. Squire to H. Weightman, Secretary, External Affairs Department, Delhi, 15 March 1946, IOR: R/12/177.
13. Report of a conversation between Ali Mohammed Khan, Najibullah Khan (the Director General of the Political Department of the Foreign Minister), Squire and Crichton, 7 February 1946. Squire to the Secretary, External Affairs Department, Delhi, 15 March 1946. IOR: R/12/177.
14. Undated FO note on Afghan interest in the Indian Constitutional problem prepared for a Cabinet meeting in March 1946, 'The Tribes of the North-West and North East Frontiers in a Future Constitution,' IOR: R/12/177.
15. Aide Memoire from the Afghan to the British government, 3 June 1947, IOR: R/12/17.
16. Note of meeting between Squire and Hashim Khan, 30 June 1947, IOR: R/12/17.
17. These arguments are spelt out in full in Chapter 7 and are taken from a discussion within the legation in June 1947, in IOR: R/12/17.
18. Foreign Office Research Department, A Survey of Anglo-Afghan Relations, p. 31.
19. Note Verbale from HMG to the Government of Afghanistan 4 July 1947, in IOR: R/12/17.
20. See IOR: L/PS/12/1812.
21. 'Afghan' was an alternative label to 'Pashtun', but meant the same thing, as explained in Chapter 2.
22. The British called them the 'Red Shirts' because their members wore uniforms dyed with red brick dust.
23. Janssen, p. 47.
24. Schofield, p. 221.
25. Moore, 1988, p. 152.
26. For example, Allah Nawaz Khan, Speaker of the Frontier Provincial Assembly, stated 'Pashtuns and Punjabis are two major nations by any definition or test of a nation, and the very thought of grouping the NWFP with the Punjabis is revolting to the Pashtun mind. We are a nation of three million, and what is more, we, the Frontier Pashtuns, are a body of people with our own distinctive culture, civilisation, language, art and architecture, names and nomenclature

and sense of values and proportion ... In short, we have our own distinctive outlook on life and by all canons of international law, a Pashtun is quite separate from a Punjabi,' quoted in Talbot, 1998, p. 14.

27. Janssen, p. 210.
28. Arney, p. 35.
29. Talbot, 1988, p. 26.
30. Talbot, 1988, p. 27.
31. Squire's journal, 23 July 1947.
32. Secretary of State for Foreign Affairs, India Office, to Squire, 17 July 1947, IOR: L/PS/12/1812.
33. Note from Mountbatten, 25 July 1947, IOR: L/PS/12/1812.
34. It took until 15 September to get to the bottom of what had really happened. The papers relating to this incident can be found in IOR: L/PS/12/1812.
35. Squire's journal, 5 August 1947.
36. Released as a press statement, Jinnah, 31 July 1947, IOR: R/12/177.
37. Squire's journal, 15 August 1947.
38. Translated copies in IOR: R/12/17.
39. FO to Karachi, 6 December 1947, IOR: R/12/17.
40. Relevant papers are in IOR: R/12/17, IOR: L/PS/12/1812, and IOR: L/WS/1/1168.
41. Quoted from the background paper prepared for the Commonwealth Relations Committee in IOR: L/WS/1/1168.
42. General Scoones was Principal Staff Officer at the Commonwealth Relations Office (CRO) in 1947.
43. Scoones, 8 December 1947, in IOR: L/WS/1/1168.
44. Minutes of Cabinet meeting, 9 December 1947, IOR: L/PS/12/1812.
45. Note of meeting sent 23 December 1947, IOR: L/PS/12/1812.
46. Told to the author by HE Hedayat Amin Arsala.
47. Ambassador Alling had been at the State Department the previous autumn and had discovered this information there, he told the Foreign Office, after much digging. In IOR: L/PS/12/1812.
48. The other two were Hyderabad and Junagadh.
49. Von Tunzelmann, pp. 244–256.
50. War Office Note on Military Aspects of Affairs between the Pakistan Government and the North-West Frontier Tribes, 4 December 1947, IOR: L/WS/1/1168.
51. One condition of the ceasefire was that a referendum of the Kashmiri people should take place to determine Kashmir's status. To date, this referendum has not happened and fighting between India and Pakistan over Kashmir continues to this day.

52. Squire to the FO, 8 December 1947, in IOR: R/12/17, and 8 January 1948, in IOR: L/PS/12/1812.
53. War Office Note, 4 December 1947, IOR: L/PS/12/1814.
54. Included in a report from Mountbatten to Lord Listowel, the last Secretary of State for India and Burma, 8 August 1947, in IOR: L/PS 12/1812. The Pakistanis also planned to follow the British policy of replacing regular troops in the tribal areas with civil armed forces, but it was too early for the British to calculate in late 1947 whether they had the capacity to do that then.
55. Despatch from C. B. Duke, Office of the Deputy High Commissioner, Peshawar, to R. R. Burnett, Deputy High Commissioner, Karachi, 18 December 1947. This was forwarded on to senior Foreign Office officials, and to the Permanent Under-Secretary of State, CRO, Sir Archibald Carter, because it provided information it was felt important they should be aware of. IOR: R/12/17.
56. Military intelligence estimated that the Pakistan army comprised about 186,000 highly trained men, sixteen fighter jets, and eight transport and eighteen communications aircraft, with a further twenty-two fighters and two bombers in reserve. In contrast, the Afghan army had about 70,000 soldiers, plus 15,000 armed police, twenty-nine obsolete fighting planes and thirteen training aircraft. Data from briefing paper prepared for a meeting of the Joint Intelligence Committee, 28 July 1949, in IOR: L/PS/12/1814.
57. Despatch of 5 December 1947 to Kabul in IOR:L/WS/1/1168. Squire's reply, 8 December 1947, IOR: R/12/17.
58. Squire to Grey, FO, 20 February 1948, IOR: L/WS/1/1168.
59. Instructions sent from the FO, 24 January 1948, IOR: L/PS/R/12/1822.
60. Squire's journal, 26 October 1947.
61. Grafftey-Smith, Karachi to Sir Archibald Carter, CRO, 2 January 1948, IOR: L/PS/12/1812.
62. Squire to FO, 19 December 1947, IOR: L/PS/12/1812.
63. This wide-ranging correspondence is in IOR: L/PS/12/1812.
64. FO to New York Office, 17 April 1948, in NA: FO371/69460.
65. Pakistan Intelligence Report, 21 May 1948, in NA: FO371/69458.
66. These papers were found so useful that they were also shared with the Secretary of State for Commonwealth Relations. NA: FO371/75630.
67. Squire's journal, 14 December 1947.
68. Quoted in Grafftey-Smith to CRO, Kabul and India, 12 December 1947, IOR: L/PS/12/1812.
69. Note of the meeting between Grafftey-Smith and Najibullah Khan, sent to CRO, 12 December 1947, in IOR L/PS/12/1812.
70. Grafftey-Smith to CRO, 2 January 1948, IOR: L/PS/12/1812.

71. Grafftey-Smith to CRO, 7 January 1948, IOR: L/PS/12/1812.
72. BHC Karachi to CRO, 7 January 1948, in IOR: L/PS/12/1812.
73. BHC Karachi to CRO, 21 and 29 January 1948, IOR: L/PS/12/1812.
74. Broadcast by Najibullah Khan, 3 February 1948, IOR: L/PS/12/1825.
75. Squire to FO, 25 April 1948, IOR: L/PS/12/1825.
76. Squire to FO, 1 September 1948, in IOR: L/PS/12/1669.
77. Squire's journal, 30 August 1948.
78. Grafftey-Smith to CRO, 7 December 1948, NA: FO371/75631.
79. FO to Kabul, 4 March 1949, NA: FO371/75631.
80. Squire's journal, 1 February 1949.
81. Communication from the Afghan Ambassador in London, Faiz Mohammed, to Bevin, FO, 2 January 1949, NA: FO371/75631.
82. Karachi to Kabul and CRO, 31 March and 1 April 1949, IOR: L/WS/1/1168.
83. Squire to FO, 16 April 1949, IOR: L/PS/12/1814.
84. Broadcast on Kabul Radio, 17 March 1949, NA: FO371/75631.
85. Squire to FO, 17 March 1949, NA: FO371/75631.
86. Squire to FO, 16 April 1949, IOR: L/PS/12/1814.
87. Grafftey-Smith to London, Kabul and Delhi, 14 April 1949, in IOR: L/PS/12/1829.
88. Squire to FO, 16 April 1949, in IOR: L/PS/12/1814.
89. Scott to Squire, 20 April 1949, in IOR: L/WS/1/1168.
90. Squire's report to London, 24 May 1949, in NA: FO371/75654.
91. Scott to Squire, 2 June 1949, NA: FO371/75654.
92. Ikramullah to Rumbold, 3 May 1949, IOR: L/PS/12/1825.
93. Ali Mohammed Khan to Pakistan embassy, Kabul, 24 April 1949, IOR: L/PS/12/1814.
94. Record of a meeting between Faiz Mohammed, Makins and Scott (FO) in London, 20 June 1949, IOR: L/PS/12/1814.
95. Internal FO note following meeting of June 1949, in L/PS/12/1814. The legal status of the Durand Line has been analysed in detail in many subsequent books, such as Poullada, 1977, pp. 134–144.
96. CRO despatch to the BHC, Karachi on 6 April, IOR: L/PS/12/1829.
97. Legal Advisers' report, 5 November 1947, IOR: R/12/17. According to a proviso in Section 7(1) of the Treaty, the tribal areas remained in treaty relations with Pakistan after 15 August 1947, in spite of the Independence of India Act.
98. Karachi to CRO, 3 April 1949, IOR: L/PS/12/1829.
99. Squire's journal, 27 April 1948.
100. Cunningham to CRO, 12 April 1949, in IOR: L/PS/12/1829.

101. Comment by Dundas after a speech by Squire at the Royal Geographical Society, 1951.
102. Cunningham, *The Statesman*, 4 June 1949, in IOR: L/PS/12/1829.
103. This was based on the fact that the term 'tribal areas' had been defined in Section 31 of the Government of India Act of 1935 as 'the areas along the frontiers of India or in Balochistan which are not part of British India or of Burma or of any Indian State of or any foreign state'. Under Sections 11(1), 108(1)c and 108(2)c, neither the central Indian Legislature or the Legislature of NWFP had any authority over them. Only the Governor General of India, and his representatives, had some rights and jurisdiction over them. It was these rights that Britain assumed had been passed to Pakistan. 6 April 1949, IOR: L/PS/12/1814.
104. Scott to Rumbold, CRO, 28 April 1949, IOR: L/PS/12/1814. The argument about Afghan interest in the tribal areas stemmed from Article 11 of 1921 Treaty and letter number four appended to the Treaty.
105. Meeting between Liaquat Ali Khan and Grafftey-Smith, 3 April 1949, in IOR: L/PS/12/1829.
106. Foreign Office Research Department Report, 'The Background of Pashtunistan', 28 February 1950, NA: FO371/83051.
107. Squire to FO, 18 April 1949, IOR: L/PS/12/1829.
108. Note to Commonwealth countries, 17 April 1949, IOR: L/PS/12/1169.
109. The London Declaration at the end of the conference on 28 April 1949 acceded to Indian wishes and so India remained a member.
110. Rumbold to Scoones, CRO, 7 April 1949, In IOR: L/PS/12/1829.
111. Nye, BHC Delhi, to CRO, 18 April 1949, IOR: L/PS/12/1829.
112. Details of military needs were set out in a despatch from Karachi on 19 April 1949, IOR: L/PS/12/1829.
113. Major General K. W. D. Strong, covering brief for the Defence Committee meeting, 19 April 1949, NA: FO371/75630.
114. The full list of those present at the Defence Committee meeting were: the Minister for Defence, A. V. Alexander, the Foreign Secretary, Ernest Bevin, the Chancellor of the Exchequer, Sir Stafford Cripps, the Secretary of State for War, Emanuel (Manny) Shinwell, the Secretary of State for Commonwealth Relations, P. J. Noel Barker, the Chief of the Imperial General Staff, Field Marshal Slim and the heads of the army and naval armed forces.
115. Minutes of the meeting recorded in IOR: L/PS/12/1829.

116. The minutes of this meeting are reported verbatim so it is possible to get the full flavour of the conversation. They can be found in IOR: L/PS/12/1829.

6 *Pashtunistan: Positions Harden*

1. Foreign Office Research Department, 'The Background of Pashunistan' 28 February 1950, in NA: FO371/83051.
2. The Persian offer was mentioned in a meeting between Ikramullah and Roger Makins, 21 May 1949, in IOR: L/PS/1814.
3. *The Times*, 29 May 1949, in NA: FO371/75636.
4. File Note by Rumbold, FO, 30 May referring to *Times* article of 29 May 1949, in NA: FO371/75636.
5. Squire to FO, 16 June 1949, IOR: L/PS/12/1830.
6. *The Hindustan Times*, 17 June 1949, not only blamed Pakistan for the bombing, but also argued Pakistan was using the 'tribal hordes' to secure Kashmir. The 'horde' had, however, failed and the 'tribal invaders had got a beating from the Indian Army.' IOR: L/WS/1/1169.
7. Conversation between Dundas and Ikramullah, which was reported to Grafftey-Smith by Ikramullah a day later, and then sent by despatch to London on 7 December 1948, in NA: FO371/75631.
8. Reported in Squire to Dening, FO, 14 December 1948, in NA: FO371/75631.
9. Squire to Dening in the FO, 14 December 1948, in NA: FO371/75631.
10. Note of meeting between Ikrammullah and FO officials, following the meeting with Bevin, 29 April 1949, in IOR L/PS/12/1814. Personal letter from R. H. Scott to Squire on 6 May 1949, in NA: FO371/75635.
11. Internal correspondence within the FO between 26 and 29 April 1949, in NA: FO371/75634.
12. FO file note, 9 June 1949, IOR: L/PS/12/1830.
13. Karachi to CRO, reporting meeting in Pakistan Ministry of Foreign Affairs, 8 June 1949, IOR: L/PS/12/1830.
14. Reported in telegrams from Karachi to CRO, 8 and 15 June 1949, IOR: L/PS/12/1830.
15. Karachi to CRO, 9 June 1949, IOR: L/PS/12/1830.
16. Squire to FO, 13 June 1949, IOR: L/PS/12/1830.
17. Karachi to CRO, 13 June 1949, IOR: L/PS/1830.
18. Squire to FO, 16 June 1949, IOR: L/PS/12/1830.
19. Afghan Note to British government, 16 June 1949, IOR: L/PS/12/1830.
20. Squire to FO, 18 June 1949, IOR: L/PS/12/1830.

21. Despatch from Karachi, 21 June 1949 in L/WS/1/1168.
22. Reported in a despatch from Karachi, 22 June 1949, in L/WS/1169.
23. Keen's report and photos can be found in NA: FO371/75639, and the report only in IOR: L/PS/12/1830.
24. This point was ultimately reflected in the Military Attaché's report to Washington. The British found out because Rumbold in the FO was shown a copy by the United States embassy in London. Rumbold, FO, 25 June 1949, IOR: L/PS/12/1830.
25. Squire to FO, 23 June 1949, IOR: L/PS/12/1830.
26. Squire's letter to Bevin, enclosing Keen's report, 25 June 1949, IOR: L/PS/12/1830.
27. Squire's journal, 29 June 1949.
28. Squire to FO, 27 July 1949, in NA: FO983/44.
29. The briefing material and records of the meetings are in IOR: L/PS/12/1814.
30. Minutes of meeting, 28 June 1949, IOR: L/PS/12/1814.
31. Minutes of meeting, 29 June 1949, IOR: L/PS/12/1814.
32. *Hansard*, 30 June 1949, and in IOR: L/PS/12/1814.
33. Squire to FO, 6 July 1949, IOR: L/PS/12/1814.
34. FO to Kabul, 15 July 1949, IOR: L/PS/12/1814.
35. The High Commissioner met Bajpai on 1 July 1949, but the Foreign Minister merely commented he had seen the press reports and made no further reference to them. Delhi to CRO, 4 July 1949, NA: FO371/875641. Meeting with Bajpai reported in Delhi to CRO, 18 July 1949, NA: FO371/75641.
36. Military Intelligence Summary, 21 July 1949, NA: FO371/75623.
37. Squire's journal, 27 July 1949.
38. Karachi to CRO, 4 July 1949, NA: FO371/75641.
39. Press Release from Afghan embassy in Washington, 25 July 1949, NA: FO371/75641.
40. State Department request to British embassy in Washington, 27 July 1949, NA: FO371/75642.
41. Zafrullah Khan's note of 26 July was passed by BHC Karachi to Attlee on the same day, NA: FO371/75641.
42. This reflection by R. H. Scott, FO, followed meetings between the Afghan Ambassador and FO staff, 28 July 1949, NA: FO371/75641.
43. Delhi to CRO, 26 July 1949, NA: FO371/75641.
44. Reported from a meeting between Bajpai and FK Roberts in the High Commission, Delhi to CRO, 27 July 1949, NA: FO371/75642.
45. Crook to Ledwidge, FO, 2 August 1949 in NA: FO371/75641.
46. Squire to FO, 26 July 1949, NA: FO371/75642.
47. Grafftey-Smith to CRO, 30 July 1949, NA: FO371/75641.

48. Afghan Press statement issued in Karachi, Karachi to CRO, 5 August 1949, NA: FO371/75641.
49. Squire's journal, 21 August 1949.
50. Squire to FO, in NA: FO371/75643.
51. Squire from Karachi to FO and CRO, 8 September 1949, NA: FO371/75643.
52. Kabul to FO, 1 July 1949, NA: FO371/75641.
53. The debris was a saddle from a rocket projectile – specifically the fitment which went around the rocket projectile and formed the attachment to the projectile on the aircraft. The figure 10/45 on them denoted the month and year of manufacture. The figures 'K' and '1944' on the cartridge drawing denoted this too was made in Britain. Air Ministry to Ledwidge, SE Asia Department, FO, 7 September 1949, NA: FO371/75643.
54. FO to Kabul, 21 September 1949, NA: FO/371/75643.
55. Squire to FO, 15 August 1949, NA: FO371/75642.
56. Squire to FO, 15 August 1949, NA: FO371/75642.
57. Squire to FO, 16 August 1949, NA: FO371/75642.
58. Squire to FO, 20 August 1949, NA: FO371/75643.
59. Squire to FO, 15 August 1949, in NA: FO371/75642.
60. Squire's Journal, 16 September 1949.
61. File note by R. C. Blackham, South Asia Department, FO, 2 September 1949, NA: FO371/75642.
62. Karachi to CRO, 18 November 1949, NA: FO371/75645.
63. Squire to FO, 19 August 1948, NA: FO371/69449.
64. Kabul to FO, 1 September 1949, NA: FO371/75643.
65. BHC Karachi to CRO, 26 September 1949, NA: FO371/75643.
66. Press notice, 30 September 1949, Karachi to CRO, NA: FO371/75644, and additional information provided by the Pakistan Ambassador in Kabul to Gardener, 28 October 1949, NA: FO371/75644.
67. Karachi to CRO, 16 November 1949, in NA: FO371/75644.
68. For example, Gardener to FO, 12 December 1949, NA: FO371/75645.
69. Gardener to FO, 15 December 1949, in NA: FO371/75645.
70. Correspondence between Derek Riches and Patrick Keen in the British embassy, Kabul, 19 December 1949, NA: FO983/45.
71. Referenced in Karachi to FO, 17 May 1950, NA: FO371/83074.
72. The petrol crisis is covered in NA FO371/75645 and 83050. *Anis* is quoted in NA: FO983/45.
73. Gardener to FO, 6 May 1950, NA: FO371/83097.
74. R. R. Burnett to I. M. R. Maclennan, CRO, 10 Feburary 1950, NA: FO983/60.
75. Gardener to Scott, 21 January 1950, NA: FO983/60.

76. Grafftey-Smith to Gardener, 3 March 1950, NA: FO983/60.
77. Letter from Grafftey-Smith to Ikramullah, 8 March 1950, NA: FO983/60.
78. Gardener to FO, 15 March 1950, NA: FO983/60.
79. Quoted in Grafftey-Smith to CRO, 22 March 1950, NA: FO983/60.
80. File note written by Keen, British embassy Kabul, 26 May 1950, NA: FO983/60.
81. Afghan Note, 19 March, Pakistan Note, 3 May, forwarded to London under cover of a despatch form Karachi to FO and CRO, 17 May 1950, NA: FO371/83074.
82. Gardener to FO, 17 June 1950, NA: FO983/60.
83. Gardener to FO, 17 June 1950, NA: FO983/60.
84. Karachi to FO, 8 July 1950, NA: FO983/60.
85. Deputy High Commissioner in Peshawar, Mitchell Carse, to Gardener, 9 October 1950; note from Pakistan embassy in Kabul to Gardener, 6 December 1950, NA: FO983/60.
86. Gardener to FO, 9 January 1950, in NA: FO371/83060.
87. Gardener to FO, 3 February 1950, NA: FO371/83051.
88. Gardener to FO, 6 January 1950, NA: FO371/83048.
89. Foreign Office Research Department Report, 28 February 1950, p. 10–11, in FO371/83051.
90. Karachi to CRO, 1 February 1950, enclosing a report from Mitchell Carse on the effect of Afghan propaganda on the tribes dated 11 January 1950, NA: FO371/83050.
91. Carse's report ibid.
92. FO comments on Carse's report, NA: FO371/83050.
93. The Parliamentary Question is in NA: FO371/83050.
94. Karachi to FO, 8 January 1950, NA: FO371/83050.
95. FO Research Department Report, Final version, 28 February 1950, p. 13, in FO371/83051.
96. Research Report, 1950, Ibid, p. 9.
97. Minutes of the meeting, 16 January 1950, NA FO371/83048.
98. FO and CRO to Karachi, 9 March 1950, in NA: FO371/83051.
99. Karachi to CRO, 21 March 1950, NA: FO371/83051.
100. Analysis provided for London by the British embassy, Kabul, 1 February 1950, in NA: FO371/83050.
101. Kabul to FO, 7 May 1950, NA: FO371/83053.
102. Ankara to FO, 26 April 1950, NA: FO371/83052.
103. Baghdad to FO, 9 May 1950, NA: FO371/83053.
104. Washington to FO, 28 April 1950, NA: FO371/83052.
105. Gardener to FO, 3 June 1950, NA: FO371/83053.
106. Gardener to FO, 3 April 1950, NA: FO371/83051.

107. Gardener to FO, 28 April 1950, NA: FO371/80352.
108. The Aide Memoire, 20 June 1950, NA: FO371/83054.
109. Meeting between Scott and Afghan Ambassador, 22 June 1950, NA: FO371/83054.

7 Maintaining the Buffer in the Shadow of the Cold War

1. Annual Report on the Afghan Army for 1947, NA: WO208/4709.
2. Report by the Military Attaché on the military review held at the Kabul Garrison by the King on 24 August 1948, IOR: L/PS/12/1668.
3. Prendergast put the figure at 62,000 in 1950, but both he and Lancaster acknowledged it was difficult to get accurate figures. Lancaster's higher figure was probably because he anticipated, as happened in the Third Afghan War, the numbers would swell in an emergency – from the recruitment of untrained men and use of tribal lashkars, who could, felt Prendergast, easily add another 35,000 riflemen. Army Annual Military Report, 1950, in NA: DO35/2951.
4. Annual Report on the Afghan Army for 1947, in NA: WO208/4709.
5. Annual Military Attaché's Report, 1948, in IOR: L/PS/12/1668.
6. The fortnightly intelligence report for 20 March 1948 reported that 30 Safi families had been sent to the north of the country, and 60 to the West, NA: FO371/69457. See also Annual Report on the Afghan Army for 1947, NA: WO208/4709.
7. Adamac, p. 107.
8. The original arms sale deal was agreed with the Afghan government in 1945, but the financing arrangements between Britain and India, and with Afghanistan, were not finalised until 1946, when they became known as the Lancaster Scheme. CRO Report in FO371/5649.
9. Sixteen Romeo R.O., thirty-seven light bomber reconnaissance planes, and eight Breda trainers.
10. There were a number of logistical challenges in meeting this contract. Initially, the runway in Kabul had to be lengthened because of the heat and high altitude, and then the first Avro scheduled for delivery in June 1948 crash landed in a swamp in Persia. To begin with, there were hopes that the crashed plane could be salvaged and flown on to Afghanistan. An Avro was flown to the site to help coordinate the operation, but then found itself temporarily detained by the Persian authorities. Once this misunderstanding was resolved, the salvage operation began in earnest. The plane was dug out of the swamp, put on raft and slowly moved to a place where it could reach dry land – but then the raft sank and the whole operation had to be called off. Britain subsequently delivered a new plane to Afghanistan. All 12

Avro Ansons were delivered by January 1949. Details in Military
Intelligence Summaries in NA: FO371/69459 and 83037.

11. Lancaster's note to Squire, 12 June 1947, in IOR: R/12/170.

12. Military Attaché Fortnightly report, 18 August 1949, in NA:
FO371/75623.

13. This was a consistent story in all the Annual Military Attaché
Reports sent to the War Office, 1947–50.

14. Annual Report on the Afghan Army for 1948, in IOR: L/PS/12/1668.

15. Military Intelligence Report, 30 November 1948, NA: FO371/69459.

16. Annual Report on the Afghan Army for 1948 and 1950, NA:
WO208/4909 and NA: DO35/2951.

17. The 1921 Treaty allowed the free and untaxed transit of goods and
an annual subsidy of 1 million gold or silver roubles. Adamec, pp.
60–61.

18. Details in IOR: R/12/129 and IOR: L/PS/12/1672 and 1673.

19. Squire to Bevin, 1 March 1946, in IOR: R/12/166.

20. Squire to Bevin, 1 March 1946, IOR: R/12/166.

21. G. C. L. Crichton, Chargé d'Affaires Kabul to FO, 15 September
1945, IOR: R/12/166.

22. From a note of a meeting between Major Crichton, Counsellor of
the British legation, and Prime Minister Hashim Khan during the
former's round of farewell meetings, sent by Crichton to Lt Col R.
R. Burnett, Secretary of the External Affairs Department in Delhi, on
30 December 1945, in IOR: R/12/177.

23. Referred to by the Secretary to the Chiefs of Staff, in correspondence
with the Foreign Office on 29 August 1947, in IOR: R/12/170.

24. Annual Report of the Afghan Army, 1947, IOR: L/PS/12/1668 and
NA: WO208/4709.

25. Report from Lancaster to Squire, 12 June 1947, forwarded to
London 20 June 1947, in IOR: R/12/170.

26. Secretary to the Chiefs of Staff, note to the FO, 29 August 1947,
IOR: R/12/170.

27. Bevin to Squire, 22 September 1947, IOR: R/12/170.

28. Bevin to Squire, 22 September 1947, IOR: R/12/170.

29. R. H. S. Allen, FO, to Stapleton, MOD, 25 August 1947, IOR:
R/12/170.

30. Kabul to Karachi, 10 October 1950, NA: FO371/83091.

31. Squire to Foreign Office, 5 November 1947, in NA: L/PS/12/1823.

32. Foreign Office comments on the agreement, March 1948, NA:
FO371/69448.

33. Despatch from the Office of the Personal Representative of the Qaid
i Azam in Kabul, Khan Bahadur Mumtaz Hassan Kizilbash to the

Deputy Secretary, Ministry of Foreign Affairs and Commonwealth Relations, Karachi, 31 December 1947, NA: FO371/69448.

34. Poullada and Poullada, p. 71.
35. Squire to Sir Olaf Caroe, External Affairs Department, government of India, April 1944, in IOR: R/12/165.
36. Poullada Poullada, p. 72.
37. Sir Giles Squire to C. M. G. Baxter, FO, 28 June 1947, in IOR: R/12/165.
38. Squire to FO, 25 April 1947, IOR: R/12/165.
39. Squire to FO, 3 September 1947, in IOR: R/12/165.
40. Kent
41. Papers relating to 'The Pentagon Talks 1947', Foreign Relations of the United States (FRUS), 1947, The Near East and Africa, Wisconsin Digital Archive, p. 2.
42. Inder Singh, p. 7.
43. Background US papers in preparation for 'The Pentagon Talks 1947', FRUS, p. 29.
44. McGarr, p. 39.
45. He was in London on extended leave and had timed it to receive his Companion of the Indian Empire (CIE) medal from King George VI on Tuesday 28 October 1947. Lancaster's Aide Memoire for Richard Allen in the Foreign Office, 7 October 1947, IOR: L/WS/1/1168.
46. FRUS, p. 122.
47. This issue is covered in correspondence between London, Washington and Kabul in NA: FO371/69464.
48. Squire to FO, 8 June 1948, NA: FO371/69464.
49. In Military Intelligence Summary no 11 for 28 May 1948, in FO371/69458.
50. Annual Military Attaché Report, 1950, in NA: DO35/2951.
51. Annual Military Attaché Report, 1948, in IOR: L/PS/12/1668.
52. Annual Military Attaché Report, 1950 in NA: DO35/2951.
53. Military Attaché Report, January 1951, in NA: DO35/2951.
54. Military intelligence assessment of the Soviet threat, 15 February 1946, in NA: WO208/4935.
55. Squire to FO, 1 March 1946, IOR: R/12/166.
56. Details in IOR: L/PS/12/1672 and 1673.
57. Squire to FO, 1 March 1946, IOR: R/12/166.
58. Squire to FO, 29 May 1947, in IOR: R/12/166.
59. Squire to FO, 2 April 1946, in IOR: R/12/166.
60. Squire to FO, 21 September 1948, in response for a request from London on 12 August 1948 to update the FO about the activities of the Soviet embassy. IOR: L/PS/12/1597.

61. Sd G. C. L. Crichton, Chargé d'Affaires, Kabul, to Secretary of State for Foreign Affairs, Ernest Bevin, 29 December 1945, in IOR: R/12/166.

62. In April 1949, Soviet embassy staff refused an invitation to a party given by the American Chargé d'Affaires, and the Russian Ambassador and his wife, and the Soviet senior Military Attaché and his wife refused an invitation to dinner by Derek Riches, First Secretary at the British embassy, prior to a screening of *Hamlet* by Squire to the diplomatic corps and senior Afghan officials. In Military Attaché Fortnightly Intelligence Report for 28 April 1949, in NA: FO371/83037.

63. Squire to FO, 21 September 1948, IOR: L/PS/12/1597.

64. Discussion in the British legation, Kabul, June 1947, IOR: R/12/17.

65. War Office File Note, 5 April 1946, in IOR: L/PS/12/1957.

66. These points come from a discussion in the legation in June 1947. Major Redpath, the legation's departing First Secretary, made the point about trade routes, IOR: R/12/17.

67. Lancaster's Aide Memoire for Richard Allen in the Foreign Office, 7 October 1947, IOR: L/WS/1/1168.

68. Squire to FO, 11 January 1947, IOR: CAB122/722.

69. Kabul to London, 27 February 1947, in IOR: R/12/170.

70. File Note General Scoones, CRO, undated 1948, in IOR: L/WS/1/1168.

71. Sir Paul Patrick, Head of the British Delegation to the UN, reporting on a conversation with Bajpai, the Indian Foreign Minister, in New York, 26 March 1948, NA: DO35/2952.

72. Background paper for the Joint Chiefs of Staff, 9 June 1948, IOR: L/WS/1/1197.

73. Mr Grey, CRO to Brigadier Page, War Office, 3 April 1948 in NA: DO35/2952.

74. Squire to Grey in the Foreign Office, 2 April 1948, in NA: DO35/2952.

75. Lancaster to the War Office, 26 March 1948, in NA: FO371/89457.

76. Squire to Foreign Office, 2 April 1948, in NA: FO371/89457.

77. Squire to WO, 28 July 1948, NA: FO371/89457; Brigadier Scott-Elliot, WO, to Lloyd, FO, 21 September 1948, NA: FO371/69459.

78. The Pakistan government found out that a plan existed because it had been mentioned in the papers sent to the Ministry by the British requesting permission for a special flight for Wing Commander Griffiths to visit Kabul from Karachi. BHC Karachi to Kabul and FO, 27 July 1948, in NA: FO371/69451.

79. The CRO believed Pakistan should see the plan – 'If we are anxious to preserve the confidence of the Afghans, we must surely be still

more concerned to preserve the confidence of a Commonwealth country. As we understand it, our policy regarding the passing of top secret and military information to Pakistan was laid down in DCOS (46) 193 (final) of 2 October 1946, as being that only such information in these categories as was necessary for Pakistan's immediate military needs should be sent; and that in accordance with DO (48), 11th meeting of 15th July 1940, the question of what secret information should be communicated to any particular dominion is to be dealt with ad hoc pending the discussions with Commonwealth Prime Ministers in October. It seems to us that the information asked for can hardly be regarded as other than secret, or top secret, information essential to Pakistan's needs.' 20 September 1948, NA: FO371/69451.

80. FO File Note, October 1948, NA: FO371/69451.
81. Correspondence between the FO, CRO and Air Ministry, August to September 1948, NA: FO371/69451.
82. Lancaster's note of discussion, 27 September 1948, NA: IOR: L/WS/1/1197.
83. Paper is in IOR: L/WS/1/1197.
84. Minister of Defence to the Secretary of State, CRO, Noel-Baker, 31 August 1948, IOR: L/WS/1/1197.
85. Foreign Office note, 7 December 1948, IOR: L/WS/1/1197.
86. Squire to Grey, FO, 22 May 1948, NA: FO371/69451.
87. News about the suspension of US Air Attaché plan was reported in a despatch from Squire, 23 September 1948, in NA: FO371/69451.
88. Lancaster's note of discussion, 27 September 1948, IOR: L/WS/1/1197.
89. Memo by Chief of Division of Greek, Turkish and Iranian Affairs (Jernegan) to Assistant Chief of the Division of South Asia Affairs, on 'The Near East: Consideration of Basic US Security interests in the Near East and South Asia', 11 October 1948, FRUS 1949, volume 6, p. 7.
90. Squire to the FO, 17 November 1948, IOR: L/WS/1/1168.
91. Squire to the FO, 17 November 1948, IOR: L/WS/1/1168. By 1950, there were more than 70 French nationals in Afghanistan working in the medical and cultural fields, reported in Gardener to Bevin, 12 August 1950, in NA: DO35/2952.
92. Squire to FO, 17 November 1948, in NA: FO371/89457, and Squire to FO, 1 December 1948, in NA: FO983/12.
93. Squire to FO on 12 May 1949, NA: FO371/5649.
94. Squire to FO on 12 May 1949, NA: FO371/5649.
95. Memorandum by CRO, 15 June 1949, NA: FO371/5649.

96. Squire to FO, 12 May 1949 in FO371/5649; 14 May 1949, NA: L/PS/12/1814.

97. Inder Singh, 1990, p. 220.

98. These points are taken from Paul McGarr and Anita Inder Singh, who are two of the few authors to examine Britain's post-war approach to the Cold War in South Asia.

99. Report by the State, Army, Navy and Air Force Coordinating Committee appraising US National Interests in South Asia, 19 April 1949. Foreign Relations of the United States (FRUS), Near East, South Asia and Africa, 1949, Volume 6, University of Wisconsin Digital Library, pp. 16–27.

100. Details about the new line up in the Soviet embassy in Kabul are recorded in NA FO983/44 and in Squire to FO, 6 January 1949, IOR: L/PS/12/1597.

101. Reported in a note produced by Military Intelligence 2, of 18 February 1949, in IOR: L/WS/1/1168; Prendergast, 1993, p. 18.

102. 'The requirements of Afghanistan would, however, have to be considered in relation to our many other commitments for the supply of warlike stores to foreign nations and it would not be possible to accord high priority to Afghanistan.' Summary of the Chief of Staff meeting provided in note from Cresswell, MoD to Scott, FO, 14 April 1949, NA: FO371/5649.

103. Reported in Intelligence Summary of 6 January 1949, NA: FO371/75622.

104. Gardener to FO, 12 December 1949, NA: FO371/75645.

105. Gardener to FO, 3 August 1950, NA: FO371/83071.

106. Gardener to FO, 16 August 1950, NA: FO371/83091.

107. Dupree, pp. 493–4.

108. Gardener to FO, 18 November 1950, FO371/83071. The Persian Ambassador found out from the Prime Minister that the deal also included the supply of 13 tonnes of Afghan opium to Russia, even though Afghanistan was banned from cultivating opium except in small quantities under licence. When he queried this, Mahmud Khan had hurriedly replied that the opium was being supplied from existing stores. Reported in Gardener, 16 August 1950, NA: FO371/83091.

109. Minutes of a meeting in the Treasury, 9 March 1950, in NA: FO371/83075.

110. Gardener to FO, 25 August 1950, NA: FO371/83075.

111. Murray FO to Gardener, 25 October 1950, NA: FO371/83094.

112. Gardener to FO, 1 December 1950, in NA: FO371/83094.

113. MacLellan in the CRO to Fry in the FO, 16 January 1950, NA: FO371/83078.

114. File Note, 23 December 1949, NA: FO371/75627.

115. Gardener to FO, 12 August 1950, NA: DO35/2952.

116. Gardener to Bevin 12 August 1950, in NA: DO35/2952.

117. Reported by Gardener in Despatch of 15 September 1950 to London, in NA: DO35/2952.

118. Gardener to FO, 15 September 1950, NA: DO35/2952.

119. Murray FO to Gardener, 9 October 1950 in DO35/2952. The Air Ministry confirmed their position in a minute to Scott in the FO on 13 October 1950, in NA: FO371/83081.

120. J. D. Murray, FO to Gardener, Kabul, 18 January 1951, NA: FO371/83081.

121. FO file note, written by J. D. Murray on receipt of Gardener's news on 5 January 1951 that the contracts would not be renewed, NA FO971/92116.

122. Other contracts in 1950 included an order for Hind aircraft spares from Hawkers, and for vulcanising equipment from Dunlops.

8 Britain's Symbolic Power Is Attacked from All Sides

1. Squire, Valedictory Despatch, Anglo Afghan Relations, 30 August 1949, NA: FO371/75627.

2. Foreign Office Circular from Sir Orme Sargent to diplomatic missions, 22 February 1947, in IOR: R/12/175.

3. Letter dated 1 September 1947, in IOR: R/12/175.

4. The Oriental Secretary was Khan Sahib Muhammad Aslam Khan Alizai, and the Commercial Secretary was Khan Bahadur M. M. Hasan Kizilbash.

5. Squire's journal, 26 October 1947.

6. Squire to FO, 18 October 1947, NA: DO133/9.

7. Papers concerning the arrangements for the transfer are in IOR: R/12/176. The agreement to transfer the Consul in Jalalabad to the Pakistan embassy was made in September 1948, NA: FO371/69464.

8. Squire to FO, 1 November 1947, IOR: R/12/175.

9. FO to Kabul and Kathmandu, 8 August 1947, IOR: R/12/175.

10. Squire to Gardener, FO, 1 November 1947, IOR: R/12/175. The British and other Christian embassies in Kabul still share use of this cemetery to this day. The inside walls now bears the names of all the ISAF soldiers who have lost their lives in the present conflict.

11. Squire to Gardener, FO, 1 November 1947, IOR: R/12/175.

12. Squire's journal, 1 March 1948.

13. Squire, 1 November 1947.
14. Simms, 11 March 1948.
15. Squire's journal, 13 March 1948.
16. Squire to FO, 8 July 1948, NA: FO983/35.
17. FO to Squire, 25 September 1948, NA: FO983/35.
18. Squire to FO, 28 June 1947, in IOR: R/12/165.
19. Squire to John Gardener, 1 November 1947, IOR: R/12/175.
20. Information provided in the Mission Medical Report, 13 December 1948, in IOR L/PS/12/1733.
21. F. W. Wylie to FO, 2 March 1943, IOR: L/PS/12/1773.
22. Dr Macrae's 1947 medical report, IOR: L/PS/23/1773.
23. Gardener to Scott, FO, 6 May 1950, NA: FO983/36.
24. Squire to FO, 4 October 1947, NA: FO953/273.
25. Internal correspondence between Riches and Squire, Kabul, August and September 1948, NA: FO983/56.
26. Himsworth, p. 11.
27. Squire to Donaldson, India Office, London, 27 September 1946, in IOR: R/12/169.
28. Clause 4: 'All land which immediately before the appointed day is vested in His Majesty for the purposes of the Governor-General in Council shall on this day:

    (a) In the case of land situated in India or in the tribal areas on the borders of India, be under the control of the Dominion of India;
    (b) In the case of land situated in Pakistan or in the tribal areas on the borders of Pakistan, be under the control of the Dominion of Pakistan;
    (c) In the case of land which immediately before the appointed day is used for the purposes of any official representative of the government of India in any other part of His Majesty's Dominions or in a foreign country, be under the control of the Dominion of India;
    (d) In any other case, be under the joint control of the Dominions of India and Pakistan:
    Provided that any land which, by virtue of the preceding provisions of this Article, is to be under the control of the two Dominions, and which is situated in an India State, shall, if within one month from the appointed day the State accedes to either of the two Dominions, be under the control of that Dominion as from the date on which

the accession of the State becomes effective,' In NA: FO366/2651.

29. Squire to FO, 22 September 1947, NA: DO133/9.
30. Gault, High Commission, Delhi to Squire, 26 October 1947, in IOR: R/12/175.
31. This correspondence is in NA: DO133/9.
32. Squire to Gault in Delhi, 17 October 1947, in IOR: R/12/175.
33. Qizilbash to Major Redpath, British embassy, 18 February 1948, IOR: R/12/154.
34. Qizilbash to Redpath, 9 February, and Redpath to Qizilbash, 27 February 1948, IOR: R/12/154.
35. Sir J. Le Rougetel, Teheran to FO, 3 January 1948, NA: FO366/2651.
36. First Secretary, BHC Delhi to Teheran and FO, 20 January 1948, NA: FO366/2651.
37. Schedule II, paragraph (e) of the 1921 Treaty stated: 'The Ministers, Consul-General and Consuls of the two governments in either country shall be permitted to purchase or hire on behalf of their governments residences for themselves and their staff and servants, or sites sufficient and suitable for the erection of such residence and grounds of a convenient size attached, and the respective governments shall give all possible assistance towards such purchase or hire: provided that the government of the country to which the Ministers or Consuls are accredited shall, in the event of an embassy or consulate being permanently withdrawn, have the right to acquire such residences or lands at a price to be mutually agreed on; and provided that the site purchased or hired shall not exceed 20 jaribs in area'. [a jarib=3600 square yards]. Subsequently, Amir Amanullah allowed the mission to have a larger plot, sufficient to house all the staff in a self-contained compound three miles outside Kabul. Full details about how Britain acquired this land are recorded in the *Precis on Afghan Affairs*, Volumes one and two, published by the government of India Press in 1928 and 1938. The key points in the Precis related to the sale are summarised in a paper prepared by the legation for the Foreign Office, under cover of a despatch from Squire on 8 March 1948, NA: FO366/2652.
38. O. K. Caroe, Delhi External Affairs Department to D. M. Cleary, India Office, London, 10 July 1945, IOR: R/12/169.
39. Squire to FO, 8 March 1948, in NA: FO366/2652.
40. Quoted in Squire to FO, 8 March 1948, referring to relevant pages from the Precis on Afghan Affairs, which were published in the Government of India Press in 1928 and 1938, NA: FO366/2652.
41. Legal position, 6 March 1948, NA: FO366/2651.

42. Bevin's views were recorded in a note of the meeting by Caccia, on 10 April 1948 in NA: FO366/2652.
43. Rup Chand's background was published in the *Islah* newspaper in Kabul 4 May 48, and quoted in full in Intelligence summary NA: FO371/69458. Chundrigar's background is in the same file.
44. London to Kabul, 22 and 23 April 1948, NA: FO366/2652.
45. Squire to Grey, FO, 1 May 1948, in NA: FO366/2652.
46. Squire to FO, 4 December 1948, NA: FO983/35.
47. Squire to FO, 9 July 1948, NA: FO366/2652.
48. British High Commission, Delhi, to Sir Archibald Carter in the CRO, in London, 1 July 1948, concerning a meeting between Mr Fry from the BHC and K. P. S. Menon, Indian External Affairs Department, NA: FO366/2652.
49. The BHC reported on 13 May 1948 that Selby was unofficially shown a letter by Ratnam from the Indian External Affairs Department, purporting to be from the Pakistan Prime Minister to the Secretary of the Partition Council dated 19 November, which, in reference to the proceedings of Expert Committee II of the Ministry of External Affairs, contained a sentence indicating that Pakistan agreed to accept Rs 700,000 for the foreign mission buildings which 'India disposed of'. 'Ratnam indicated that the fact that it was then agreed that there were no further disputes between the two Dominion governments to be referred to the Arbitration Tribunal by the Partition Council and that the former's functions would henceforth be limited to adjudicating on disputes between the two Punjab and Bengal governments were evidence that this question of buildings must be considered as settled ... Ratnam seems sincerely convinced that the Government of Pakistan have in fact contracted out of their rights in these properties, but Selby gained the impression that he may possibly find it difficult to prove unless the Pakistan government are themselves prepared to confirm his understanding of the position'. In NA: FO366/2652.
50. Karachi to FO, 6 July 1948, NA: FO366/2652.
51. CRO to Delhi, 15 July 1948, NA: FO366/2652.
52. Delhi to FO, 6 October 1948, NA: FP. 366/2652.
53. Caccia, FO, to Sir Archibald Carter, CRO, 27 October 1948, NA: FO366/2652.
54. Record of meeting, 11 November 1948, NA: FP. 366/2652.
55. File Note by E. H. Brown, 1 September 1948, NA: DO133/10.
56. For example when he met Bevin on 2 May, recorded in NA: DO35/3069.
57. Meeting between Menon, Bevin and Noel Baker, 24 June 1949, NA: DO35/3060.

58. Law Officers' opinion, 20 July 1949, NA: DO35/3069.
59. Foreign Office note, 22 July 1949, NA: DO35/3069.
60. Menon's meeting of 2 August 1949, NA: DO35/3069. What was and was not agreed at the meeting on 24 July was a matter of dispute between Britain and India over the next two years, with the Indians claiming once again in their Aide Memoire of 11 April 1951 that Bevin had promised to confer with Prime Minister Nehru about the results of the revised legal opinion before informing the Government of Pakistan. Bevin himself wrote to the Indian High Commissioner on 30 August 1949 saying had no recollection of this promise. Britain's reply to the Aide Memoire on 26 June 1951 also stated that they had no record that Bevin made any such undertaking. In NA: DO35/3069.
61. CRO to BHC, Karachi, 3 August 1949, NA: DO35/3069.
62. Nye to FO and CRO, 10 August 1949, NA: DO35/3069.
63. Details of Sir Denys Bray's note as quoted in the Aide Memoire in NA: DO35/3069: 'Modern Afghanistan declines to have any relations with India direct because her independence from India's tutelage is too recent. She insists as a wholly independent national on having relations with His Majesty's Government. His Majesty's Government's interest in Afghanistan is almost wholly confined to India's interest ... The Government of India is willing to play up to the camouflage whereby India's relations with Afghanistan are conducted nominally through His Majesty's Government. But the Government of India is not willing to relinquish effective control to His Majesty's Government because relations with Afghanistan are of supreme importance to India, and that it is only by retaining full financial liability that India can prevent effective control passing to His Majesty's Government, hence, though His Majesty's Government have from time to time contemplated sharing the liability, the Government of India have consistently set their face against any change.'
64. Aide Memoire in NA: DO35/3069.
65. Squire to FO, 15 August 1049, NA: FO371/75642.
66. Squire's Journal, 21 August 1949.
67. File Note, South-East Asia Department, FO, August 1949, NA: DO35/3069.
68. E. J. Emery to Blackham, 2 September 1949, commenting on the Indian Aide Memoire and Bray's 1928 note, NA: DO35/3069.
69. Shawcross' legal opinion, 14 September 1949, NA: DO35/3069.
70. British response to Indian Aide Memoire, 23 July 1949, NA: DO35/3069.
71. Bevin to Menon, 25 November 1949, NA: DO35/3069.
72. Letter from the Pakistan Deputy Minister of Foreign Affairs and Commonwealth Relations, Mahmud Husain, 1 February 1950, NA: DO35/3069.
73. Maclennan, CRO, to Scott, FO, 6 March 1950, NA: DO35/3069.

74. Indian High Commissioner, Menon, to Kenneth Gilmour Younger, Minister of State, FO, 17 June 1949, NA: DO35/3069.
75. Grafftey-Smith to FO, 15 September 1950, NA: DO35/3069.
76. Murray to Gardener, 18 October 1950, in NA: DO35/3069.
77. Gardener to FO, 9 November 1950, NA: DO35/2955.
78. Murray to Gardener, 16 January 1951, NA: DO35/2955.
79. Record of meeting between Scott and Bajpai, 18 January 1951, NA: DO133/12.
80. Record of meeting between Liaquat Ali Khan and Bevin, 18 January 1951, and BHC Karachi to FO, 9 February 1951, NA: DO133/12.
81. Gardener to Murray, FO, 31 January 1951, NA: DO35/3069.
82. Morrison to Nehru, 28 March 1951, NA: D0133/12. Britain had already acquired a new site in Kathmandu, adjoining the existing embassy compound and had asked to buy one plot in the existing site so that their new embassy was on one contiguous site, and not divided either side of the Indian compound. Once this sale was agreed by India and Pakistan, they hoped to finalise the agreement. Nehru wrote to Morrison on 13 April 1951 asking that Britain vacate the Kathmandu premises, save for one site which India was happy for HMG to hold to ensure their new adjoining premises were on a contiguous site. By the end of 1951, Britain, India and Pakistan had agreed that the embassy site in Kathmandu would be handed over to India, with adequate compensation to be given to Pakistan by India. Correspondence in NA: DO35/3070.
83. Aide Memoire, 11 April 1951, NA: DO35/3069.
84. Liaquat Ali Khan to Morrison, 14 May 1951, NA: DO35/3069.
85. CRO to BHC Karachi, 6 June 1951, NA: DO35/3069.
86. Morrison to Liaquat Ali, 6 October 1951, NA: DO35/3070.
87. Wolpert, 1982, p. 121.
88. FO to British Ambassador E. R. Lingeman in Kabul, 16 April 1952, NA: DO35/3070.

9 *Whither British–Afghan Relations?*

1. Squire's Valedictory Despatch to the FO, 30 August 1949, NA: FO371/75627.
2. Simms, 4 January 1950.
3. Hennessy, p. 339.
4. Hennessy, p. 404.
5. Squire's Valedictory despatch, 30 August 1949, NA: FO371/75627.
6. File Note, R. C. Blackham FO, 7 September 1949, NA: FO371/75627.
7. Scott to Gardener, 21 September 1949, NA: FO371/75627.
8. Scott to Gardener, 21 September 1949, NA: FO371/75627.
9. Gardener to Scott, 10 November 1949, NA: FO371/75627.

10. Gardener to FO, 1 September 1950, NA: DO35/2951.
11. Reported in a despatch by Gardener to FO, 24 March 1950, NA: FO371/83069, and in Fry p. 200, quoting from P. J. Franck, "Technical Assistance through the United Nations: The United Nations Mission in Afghanistan, 1950–53", in *Hands Across Frontiers: Case Studies in Technical Cooperation*, ed. by H. M. Teaf and P. J. Franck, for the Netherlands Foundation for International Cooperation.
12. Lattimore was taken in for questioning and although he was later cleared of all the charges, the United Nations decided not to take any risks and replaced him with another American, Edwin Henson, from the Department of Economic Affairs. The British embassy became briefly embroiled in clearing Lattimore too. Gardener was asked by the United States embassy if he knew what dates the new Soviet Ambassador to Pakistan had passed through Kabul and whether those coincided with Lattimore's visit. The Americans 'apparently considered it just as well to check up on every point which might indicate that Lattimore had contact with Russians or held views on the "freedom of the masses" etc which might in fact make him an unwitting tool of the communists'. Gardener to the FO, 1 July 1950, in NA: FO371/83054.
13. Gardener to FO, 2 and 18 August 1950, NA: FO371/83069.
14. Gardener to Scott, FO, 6 May 1950, NA: FO371/83097.
15. Gardener to FO, 29 April 1950, NA: DO35/2951.
16. Gardener, referring to a speech given by the President of the National Assembly welcoming the King's return from eye treatment in France, 14 April 1950, NA: DO35/2951.
17. Gardener to FO, 29 April 1950, NA: DO35/2951.
18. Gardener to FO, 29 April 1950, NA: DO35/2951.
19. Gardener to FO, 29 April 1950, NA: DO35/2951.
20. Gardener to FO, 24 July 1951, NA: FO371/92084.
21. Gardener to FO, 18 May 1950, NA: DO35/2951.
22. Ruttig, 2011, p. 6–9; Gardener to FO, 15 February 1951, NA: FO 371/92084.
23. Afghanistan Annual Review 1950, FO371/92080.
24. Gardener to FO, 29 May 1950, NA: DO35/2951.
25. Gardener to FO, 29 April 1950, NA: DO35/2951.
26. Ruttig, 2011, pp. 6–9; Saikal, p. 115; Gardener to FO, 27 April 1951, NA: FO371/92084.
27. Gardener to FO, 28 and 30 March 1950, NA: DO35/2951.
28. Afghanistan Annual Review 1950, NA: FO371/92080.
29. Gardener to FO, 27 May 1950, NA: DO35/2951.
30. Gardener to Murray, FO, 2 June 1950, NA: DO35/2951.

31. Abdul Majid became President of the National Bank and its largest shareholder. Evidence of reconciliation with the PM is recorded in a letter from D. M. H. Riches, Kabul to Attlee, 24 September 1950, NA: FO371/83054.
32. Gardener to FO, 18 October 1950, NA: FO371/83054. Abdul Majid was to find himself dropped by Daud too when he took over from Mahmud Khan in 1953. Giuistozzi p. 18.
33. Afghanistan, Annual Review 1950, NA: FO371/92080.
34. Gardener to FO, 2 February 1951, NA: FO371/92084.
35. Gardener to FO, 27 April 1951, NA: FO371/92084.
36. Gardener to FO, 25 April 1951, NA: DO35/2951.
37. Ruttig, 2013, p. 6.
38. Gardener to FO, 25 April 1951, NA: 35/2951.
39. Gardener to FO, 6 July 1951, FO371/92084.
40. Gardener to Scott, FO, 10 July 1951, NA: FO371/92084.
41. Gardener to FO, 15 February 1951, NA: FO 371/92084.
42. Gardener to FO, 25 April 1951, NA: DO35/2951.
43. Gardener to Scott, 10 July 1951, NA: FO371/92084.
44. Gardener to FO, 24 July 1951, NA: FO371/92084.
45. Scott to Gardener, 22 June 1951, NA: DO35/2951.
46. In the original document in the National Archives, it is difficult to tell whether Scott wrote Russia or Persia. One word was written and then typed over by another. I think on balance, Scott meant Russia, based on Gardener's subsequent reply.
47. Gardener to Scott, 9 August 1951, NA: FO971/92084.
48. Foreign Office despatch to Kabul, 11 July 1953; Despatch from Kabul to FO, 30 October 1953, NA: FO371/106652.
49. FO to Treasury, 12 September 1952, T236/3825.
50. FO to Export Credit Guarantee Department, 1 January 1953, NA: T236/3825.
51. File note, H. H. Phillips, 30 August 1951, NA: FO371/92084.
52. Note from FO (Scott, on behalf of Mr McNeil) to Gardener 30 January 1950 in IOR: L/PS/12/1562.
53. Gardener to Dalton Murray, South-East Asia Department, FO, 21 September 1951, NA: FO371/92084.
54. Afghanistan: Annual Political Review for 1951, NA: FO371/100960.
55. Lingeman to FO, 23 February 1952, NA: FO371/92084.
56. Lingeman to FO, 17 May 1952, NA: FO371/100978.
57. Ansary, p. 145.
58. Ruttig, 2011, p. 7.
59. Giuistozzi, p. 13.

60. Letter from Shah Mahmud Khan to Lancaster, 28 March 1954, Lancaster's papers, National Army Museum, London.
61. Prendergast, 1977, p. 138.

10 Superpower Politics, the Cold War and the Final Scramble for the Embassy

1. Poullada and Poullada, p. 146.
2. Inder Singh, pp. 31–2.
3. Summary of Meeting, 14 April 1949, NA: FO371/5649. Details in Chapter 7.
4. Poullada and Poullada, pp. 136–7.
5. Quoted in Poullada and Poullada, pp. 101–2.
6. Annual Political Review, 1951, NA: FO371/100960; Poullada and Poullada, pp. 102–3.
7. Poullada and Poullada, pp. 139–40.
8. Poullada and Poullada, pp. 146–7.
9. US Press Release, 8 February 1951, NA: FO371/92110.
10. Gardener to FO, 28 March 1951, in NA: FO371/92089.
11. Saikal, p. 119.
12. US State Department Press Release, 30 June 1952, NA: FO371/100978.
13. Lingeman to FO, 18 October 1952, NA: FO371/100978.
14. These studies had considered unnecessary because even a margin of error of 20 per cent would not detract from the overall value of the project. Cullather, p. 522.
15. Cullather, p. 523.
16. Lingeman to FO, 31 January and 16 May 1953, in NA: FO371/106661 and 106669.
17. Kabul to FO, 13 November 1953, NA: FO371/106661.
18. Dupree p. 485.
19. Cullather, p. 515.
20. Quoted in Cullather, p. 512.
21. Barnett Rubin (1992, p. 66) also argues that by investing in the Pashtun heartlands in the south and south-east, the government was effectively using tax earned from non-Pashtun traders – the pastoralists – to subsidize wheat production and transportation and thereby strengthen its patronage to favoured groups: 'The Musahiban rulers used the resources obtained from their international connections to create a patronage network calculated to strengthen Pashtun nationalism, which they hoped would in turn prove an ideological buttress for their rule.' This point is also picked up by Chandrasekaran, p. 18.
22. Cullather, p. 529.

23. Afghanistan Annual Reviews, 1952 and 1953, NA: FO371/106647 and 111932.
24. Dupree, p. 493–4.
25. Inder Singh, p. 111.
26. Saikal, pp. 119–120.
27. Rashid, p. 36.
28. Rasanayagam, p. 28.
29. Ewers, p. 112.
30. Barfield, p. 209.
31. Ansary, p. 153.
32. Barfield, p. 210.
33. Rasanayagam, p. 34.
34. Newell, pp. 143–4; Arney p. 39.
35. Quoted in Arney, p. 39.
36. Fry, pp. 170–1.
37. Rubin, p. 65.
38. Annual Political Review, 1952, NA: FO371/106647.
39. Ansary, pp. 166–170.
40. Martin, p. 31.
41. Cullather, p. 525.
42. Martin, p. 30.
43. Cullather, p. 532.
44. Dupree, pp. 590–1.
45. Ansary, p. 66.
46. Braithwaite, p. 33.
47. Martin, pp. 31–6.
48. Ansary, p. 187.
49. Braithwaite, p. 52.
50. Braithwaite, pp. 80–81.
51. Taken from Ahmed Rashid's book, *Descent into Chaos*, which so aptly describes Afghanistan's subsequent story.
52. Poullada and Poullada, p. 4.
53. Chandrasekaran, p. 41.
54. Cullather, p. 532.
55. Told to the author by Jon Moss, who led governance work in Helmand from 2008–13.
56. Hogg et al, p. 2.
57. Hogg et al, p. 11.
58. Conversation HE Hedayat Amin Arsala, 2013. President Karzai himself gave nationalist speeches to Pashtun audiences and celebrated Pashtunistan Day, but this has had few ripples across the border. Meanwhile Karzai had to balance any rhetoric about Pashtunistan with parallel efforts to embrace

Afghanistan's other groups within a unified, multi-ethnic, pan-tribal Afghan state.

59. Abubakar Siddique, pp. 35, 58–60.
60. This description of the embassy in 1967 comes from the Briefing Paper in the FCO Accommodation file NA: FCO78/1, and from Whitteridge's despatches to Accommodation Department, 19 July and 8 August 1967, NA: FCO78/2.
61. Pakistan and Indian Aide Memoire, 30 September 1963, NA: FCO78/1.
62. Cradock, FCO, file note, 3 Sept 1964, NA: FCO78/3.
63. J. C. Cloake, Accommodation Department, FCO, 23 February 1967, NA: FCO78/1.
64. Whitteridge to Accommodation Department, FCO, 19 July 1967, NA: FCO78/2.
65. Whitteridge to FCO, 14 June 1967, NA: FCO78/2.
66. FCO briefing paper, 1967, NA: FCO78/1.
67. BHC in Rawalpindi, Pakistan, to CRO, 6 October 1967, NA: FCO78/2.
68. Treasury to Administration Office, FCO, 9 October 1968, NA: FCO78/3.
69. HMG Aide Memoire to Pakistan and India, 11 November 1968, NA FCO78/3.
70. Drinkall to FCO, 19 March 1975, NA: FCO37/1545.
71. FCO Inspection Report, Kabul, March 1977, NA: FCO37/1854.
72. Edward Gorman, 30 April 1994, 'Union Jack comes down over Kabul', Times Newspapers.
73. Told to the author by Sir Nicholas Barrington and HE Hedayat Amin Arsala.
74. Gorman, Ibid.
75. Information provided by Dr Ann Freckleton, who was head of the UK government Department for International Development (DFID) office in Kabul from 1997 to 2003.
76. Reported in Luke Harding, 'Tea and MBEs for the Two Kabul Heroes who kept the Flag flying for Britain', 27 August 2002, *The Guardian*.
77. Told by Sir Nicholas Barrington to the author, and reported by the UK Ambassador to Kabul, Ronald Nash, in 2003 to the *Daily Telegraph*: Lucy Morgan Edwards, 22 January 2003, 'Britain's outpost in Kabul under Threat', *Daily Telegraph*.
78. Squire, Royal Geographical Society, 1951.

Bibliography

Manuscript Sources
Oriental and India Office Collection, British Library (formerly India Office Library) London, India Office Records (IOR).
National Archives (NA), Kew, London.
National Army Museum.
Foreign Relations of the United States (FRUS), University of Wisconsin (online).

Unpublished Documents
Himsworth, Katherine, *A History of the British Embassy in Kabul, Afghanistan.* (Kabul: British Embassy Booklet, 1976).
Simms, Sam, *Letters to Rene Simms, 1947–50.*
Squire, Giles, *Journal, 1947–50.*

Secondary Sources
Adamec, Ludwig W., *Afghanistan's Foreign Affairs to the Mid-Twentieth Century: Relations with the USSR, Germany and Britain* (Tucson Arizona: University of Arizona Press, 1974).
Adamec, Ludwig W., *A Biographical Dictionary of Contemporary Afghanistan* (Akademische Druck-u. Verlagsanstalt, Graz, Austria, 1987).
Ansary, Tamim, *Games without Rules: The Often Interrupted History of Afghanistan* (New York: Public Affairs, 2012).
Arney, George, *Afghanistan: The Definitive Account of a Country at Crossroads* (London: Mandarin Paperbacks, 1990).
Barfield, Thomas, *Afghanistan: A Cultural and Political History* (Princeton: Princeton University Press, 2010).
Bates, Robert E., *Prosperity and Violence: The Political Economy of Development* (London: W.W. Norton and Company, 2001).

Braithwaite, Rodric, *Afghantsy: The Russians in Afghanistan 1979–89* (London: Profile Books 2011).

Byron, Robert, *The Road to Oxiana* (London: Penguin Classic, 1937).

Chandrasekaran, Rajiv, *Little America: The War within the War for Afghanistan* (London: Bloomsbury, 2012).

Charmley, John, 'Splendid Isolation to Finest Hour: Britain as a Global Power 1900–1950, in Johnson, Gaynor ed., *The Foreign Office and British Diplomacy in the Twentieth Century* (London: Routledge, 2005).

Crews, Robert D., *Afghan Modern: The History of a Global Nation* (Cambridge Massachusetts: Harvard University Press, 2015).

Cullather, Nick, 'Damming Afghanistan: Modernisation in a Buffer State,' *The Journal of American History* 89, 2, (2002) pp. 512–37.

Dalrymple, William, *The Return of a King: The Battle for Afghanistan* (London: Bloomsbury, 2013).

Darwin, John, *Britain and Decolonialisation: The Retreat from Empire in the Post War World* (Basingstoke: Macmillan, 1988).

Dupree, Louis, *Afghanistan* (Princeton: Princeton University Press, 1980).

Elphinstone, Montstuart, *An Account of the Kingdom of Caubul and its Dependencies in Persia, Tartary and India* (Austria: Akademische Druck u Verlagsanstalt, Graz, 1969 edition).

Ewans, Martin, *Afghanistan: A New History* (Richmond, Surrey: Curzon Press, 2001).

French, Patrick, *Liberty or Death: India's Journey to Independence and Division* (India: Harper Collins, 1997).

Fraser-Tytler, W. K., *Afghanistan: A Study of Political Developments in Central and Southern Asia* (London: Oxford University Press, 1967).

Freedman, Lawrence, 'Introduction' in Dockrill, Michael and Young, John W. (ed.), *British Foreign Policy, 1945–56* (Basingstoke: Macmillan, 1989).

Fry, Maxwell J., *The Afghan Economy: Money, Finance and the Critical Constraints to Economic Development* (Leiden: EJ Brill, 1994).

Gaddis, John Lewis, *The Cold War* (London: Penguin, 2005).

Giuistozzi, Antonio, *Afghanistan: Transition without End: An Analytical Narrative on State Making* (London: LSE: Crisis States Research Centre, Working paper no. 40, Series 2, 2008).

Gregorian, Vartan, *The Emergence of Modern Afghanistan: Politics of Reform and Modernisation 1880–1946* (United States: Stanford University Press, 1969).

Hennessy, Peter, *Never Again: Britain 1945–51* (London: Penguin, 2006).

Bibliography

Hogg, Richard; Nassif, Claudia; Gomez Osorio, Camilo; Byrd, William and Beath, Andrew, *Afghanistan in Transition: Looking beyond 2014* (Washington: World Bank, 2013).

Hopkirk, Peter, *The Great Game: On Secret Service in High Asia* (Oxford: Oxford University Press, 1990).

Jansson, Erland, 'India, Pakistan or Pakhtunistan? The Nationalist Movements in the North-West Frontier Province 1937–47', *Studia Historica Upsaliensia*, volume 119 (1981).

Kent, John, 'The Empire and the Origins of the Cold War', in Deighton, Anne (ed.), *Britain and the First Cold War* (London: Macmillan, 1990).

Hyam, Ronald, *Britain's Declining Empire: The Road to Decolonisation* (Cambridge University Press: 2006).

Inder Singh, Anita, *The Limits of British Influence: South Asia and the Anglo-American Relationship, 1947–56* (London: Pinter Publishers, 1993).

Klass, Rosanne, 'The Great Game Revisited' in Klass, Rosanne (ed.), *Afghanistan: The Great Game Revisited* (United States: Freedom House, 1987).

Louis, William Roger, 'The Dissolution of the British Empire' in Brown, Judith M. and Louis, William Roger, *The Oxford History of the British Empire, Volume IV: The Twentieth Century.* (Oxford: Oxford University Press, 1999).

Martin, Mike, *An Intimate War: An Oral Account of the Helmand Conflict, 1978–2012* (London: Hurst, 2014).

McGarr, Paul M., *The Cold War in South Asia: Britain, the United States and the Indian Subcontinent 1945–1965* (Cambridge University Press, 2013).

Michener, James A., *Caravans* (London: Random House, 1963).

Moore, Mick, *How does Taxation Affect the Quality of Governance* (Institute for Development Studies Working Paper 280, University of Sussex, Brighton, 2007).

Moore, R. J., *Endgames of Empire: Studies of Britain's Indian Problem* (Oxford University Press, 1988).

Moore, R. J., *Escape from Empire: The Attlee Government and the Indian Problem* (Oxford: Clarenden Press, 1983).

Newell, Richard S., *The Politics of Afghanistan* (Ithaca: Cornell University Press, 1972).

Pelling, Henry, *The Labour Governments, 1945–51* (London: Macmillan Press, 1984).

Prendergast, John Hume, *The Road to India: A Guide to the Overland Routes to the East* (London: J. Murray, 1977).

Prendergast, John Hume, *Prender's Progress; A Soldier in India, 1931–47* (London: Cassell, 1979).

Prendergast, John Hume, *A Plume of Dust* (Edinburgh: Pentland, 1993).

Poullada, Leon B., 'Pushtunistan: Afghan Domestic Politics and Relations with Pakistan', in Embree, Ainslie T. (ed.), *Pakistan's Western Borderlands: The Transformation of a Political Order.* (Delhi: Vikas Publishing, 1977).

Poullada, Leon B., 'The Road to Crisis 1919–1980: American Failures, Afghan Errors and Soviet Successes', in Klass, Rosanne (ed.), *Afghanistan: The Great Game revisited* (United States: Freedom House, 1987).

Poullada, Leon B., and Poullada, Leila D. J., *The Kingdom of Afghanistan and the United States 1828–1973* (Centre for Afghan Studies at University of Nebraska, Omaha, and Dageford Publishing, Lincoln Nebraska, 1995).

Rasanayagam, Angelo, *Afghanistan: A Modern History* (London: I.B. Tauris, 2005).

Rashid, Ahmed, *Descent into Chaos* (London: Penguin Books, 2008).

Rubin, Barnett, *The Fragmentation of Afghanistan* (Yale University Press, 2002).

Ruttig, Thomas, 'Afghanistan's Early Reformists: Mahmud Tarzai's ideas and their influence on the Wesh Zalmian Movement', in *Afghan Analysts Network*, Occassional Paper, (Kabul, April 2011).

Ruttig, Thomas, 'How it all Began: A Short Look at the pre-1979 Origins of Afghanistan's Conflicts' in *Afghan Analysts Network* (Kabul: January 2013).

Ruttig, Thomas, *Islamists, Leftists – and a Void in the Centre; Afghanistan's Political Parties and Where They Come From 1902–2006* (Kabul: Kondrad-Adenauer – Stiftung, 2006).

Saikal, Amin with assistance from Farhadi, Ravan and Nourzhanov, Kirill, *Modern Afghanistan: A History of Struggle and Survival* London: I.B. Tauris, 2004).

Schofield, Victoria, *Afghan Frontier: Feuding and Fighting in Central Asia* (London: Tauris Parke Paperbacks, 2003).

Siddique, Abubakar, The Pashtuns: The Unsolved Key to the Future of Pakistan and Afghanistan (India: Random House, 2014)

Smith, Raymond, 'Ernest Bevin, British Officials and British Foreign Policy, 1947–47', in Deighton, Anne (ed.), *Britain and the First Cold War* (London: Macmillan, 1990).

Squire, Giles, 'Afghanistan and her Neighbours', *Royal Geographical Society* (London: February 1951, pp. 68–71).

Stewart, Thea Tally, *Fire in Afghanistan* (New York: Doubleday, 1973).

Talbot, Ian, *Provincial Politics and the Pakistan Movement: The Growth of the Muslim League in North-West and North East India 1937–47* (Karachi: Oxford University Press, 1988).

Talbot, Ian, *Pakistan: A Modern History* New York: St Martin's Press, 1988.

Von Tunzelmann, Alex, *Indian Summer: The Secret History of the End of Empire (*New York: Henry Holt and Company, 2007).

Wilson, Jeremy, *Lawrence of Arabia: The Authorised Biography of TE Lawrence* (London: Heinemann, 1989).

Wolpert, Stanley, *Roots of Confrontation in South Asia: Afghanistan, Pakistan, India and the Superpowers* (Oxford: Oxford University Press, 1982).

Wolpert, Stanley, *Jinnah of Pakistan* (Oxford: Oxford University Press, 1984).

Woodburn, C. W., *The Bala Hissar of Kabul: Revealing a Fortress-Palace in Afghanistan* (Chatham, Kent: The Institute of Royal Engineers, Professional Paper no. 1, 2009).

Newspaper Articles

Cunningham, Sir George, *The Statesman*, 4 June 1949.

Gorman, Edward, 'Union Jack comes down over Kabul', *Times Newspapers*, 30 April 1994.

Harding, Luke, 'Tea and MBEs for the two Kabul heroes who kept the flag flying for Britain', *The Guardian*, 27 August 2002.

Morgan Edwards, Lucy, 'Britain's Outpost in Kabul under Threat', *Daily Telegraph*, 22 January 2003.

Roth, Andrew, 'The State of Afghanistan Today: Mass of the People live in Poverty', *The Scotsman*, 11 April 1950.